INTERNATIONAL SERIES OF MONOGRAPHS IN THE SCIENCE OF THE SOLID STATE

GENERAL EDITOR: B.R. PAMPLIN

VOLUME 4

OXIDE SEMICONDUCTORS

OXIDE

SEMICONDUCTORS

By

Z. M. JARZĘBSKI

Translated from the Polish by
Dr. B. Grzybowska-Świerkosz

Translation edited by
DR. BRIAN RANDALL PAMPLIN, Bath University

PERGAMON PRESS
Oxford · New York · Toronto
Sydney · Braunschweig
WYDAWNICTWA NAUKOWO-TECHNICZNE
Warsaw

Pergamon Press Ltd., Headington Hill Hall, Oxford
Pergamon Press Inc., Maxwell House, Fairview Park, Elmsford,
New York 10523
Pergamon of Canada Ltd., 207 Queen's Quay West, Toronto 1
Pergamon Press (Aust.) Pty. Ltd., 19a Boundary Street,
Rushcutters Bay, N.S.W. 2011, Australia
Vieweg & Sohn GmbH, Burgplatz 1, Braunschweig

First English edition 1973

This is a translation of the Polish

Półprzewodniki tlenkowe

published by Wydawnictwa Naukowo-Techniczne

Library of Congress Cataloging in Publication Data

Jarzębski, Zdzisław.
    Oxide semiconductors.

    (International series of monographs in the science
of the solid state, v. 4.)
    Translation of Półprzewodniki tlenkowe.
    1. Metallic oxide semiconductors. 2. Crystals--
Defects. I. Title.
TK7871.85.J313 1973   621.3815'2   73-6971
ISBN 0-08-016968-6

CONTENTS

PART THREE

**DEFECT STRUCTURE, ELECTRICAL AND ATOMIC TRANSPORT PHENOMENA IN
SELECTED OXIDES**   137

INTRODUCTION

THE rapid development of semiconductor techniques is requiring an ever greater application of materials of varying physical and physico-chemical properties. This demand cannot be fully met by a handful of elements having semiconducting properties, nor by the few relevant chemical compounds, which are already understood. Therefore increasing attention is being paid to studies on less known chemical compounds able to act as semiconductors.

Among them, compounds of metals or semiconducting elements with oxygen may be considered as most promising. Oxide materials claim particular attention owing to their interesting properties for both physicists and chemists, as well as to their more and more extensive application in technology, especially in electronics and microelectronics, e.g. in the production of transistors, rectifiers, thin-layer capacitors, resistors, thermistors, etc. Oxides are also used as thermoelectric materials. Some of them are successfully employed in quantum electronics in the production of lasers and masers, and in physical chemistry—as catalysts and electrodes. Advantage is also being taken of their other properties such as optical, magnetic, ferroelectric, piezo-electric, electroluminescence thermoemission, etc.

It should be noted that the application of some oxide semiconductors is abreast of the use of germanium and silicon in technology. In spite of this fact, current knowledge of oxide materials is, with the few exceptions, e.g. NiO, ZnO, TiO_2, rather limited. This is due to many reasons, among which the principal are: (a) technological difficulties in the preparation of single oxide crystals of high perfection and purity, and (b) the considerably more complex structure of oxides in comparison to that of elemental semiconductors and of some other chemical compounds.

The difficulties encountered in preparing single oxide crystals account for the fact that the early studies on oxides were performed mainly on sintered materials, or on single crystals of not too high purity, and thus the data available at present are not always reliable and in some cases difficult to interpret.

Another reason why oxide properties are not well understood is the occurrence of ionic bonds in the oxide molecules; the mechanism of transport of current carriers in these materials is hence more complex than in elemental semiconductors or in the compounds with covalent bonds. In addition to acoustic interactions, characteristic of covalent bonds, in the case of oxides one must also consider optical interactions characteristic of ionic bonds.

The chemical properties of oxides are also more complex, since they show a tendency to form native point defects (departures from stoichiometry), the concentration of which depends on temperature and partial pressures of components of the gas phase surrounding the crystal.

By virtue of their ionic character, the forbidden energy gap in oxides assumes large values, and hence at moderate temperatures these compounds behave as insulators, provided that their chemical composition is close to stoichiometry.

The relevant semiconducting properties of oxides originate from the presence of the lattice defects already mentioned, and of foreign atoms (impurities or admixtures), as both the former and the latter defects may be regarded either as donors or acceptors.

It follows from the above considerations that in the case of oxides the semiconducting properties are dependent on temperature and composition of the surrounding atmosphere. Therefore it is necessary to prepare the samples under strictly defined conditions. Moreover, the temperature at which the sample is prepared must be suitably high to allow rapid establishment of the state of thermodynamic equilibrium between the bulk of the crystal and its surroundings.

It should be noted that the tendency to deviate from stoichiometry is a general property of the majority of chemical compounds, resulting from the laws of statistical thermodynamics.

In recent years, owing to the wider application of oxides in technology, rapid progress is observed in the techniques of both measuring and preparing oxide materials.

In the first place, a great advance has been made in the technology of single crystal preparation. Parallel to the development of methods in oxide crystal growth, the technique of preparing oxide films has also made a large step forward. Results of research into the technology of oxide materials will be reviewed in parts one and three of this book.

The mastering of single crystal growth techniques for numerous oxides has made possible a better understanding of their basic properties, in particular of their defect structure and transport properties (including both atomic and electronic transport). Especially experimental and theoretical studies on the structure of point defects in oxide materials have drawn much attention. This may be explained by the need for knowing the defect structure, in order to understand electronic processes occurring in crystals which show deviations from stoichiometry, and also to be able to control the properties of these compounds. Foundations of the theory of defects in oxide materials are the subject of part two.

In order to explain the principal semiconducting properties of oxide materials, and in particular the phenomenon of transport of current carriers, the concepts developed in studies on germanium and silicon are employed and supplemented by new ideas relating to ionic bonds. This, however, concerns only oxides having broad energy bands and hence a comparatively high mobility of current carriers. For materials, e.g. transition metal oxides of low mobility in the region of about 1 cm^2/Vs and lower, a special theory has been developed, known as the *small-polaron theory*. The theory has not, however, yet been verified owing to experimental difficulties encountered in the studies on non-stoichiometric ionic crystals.

The results of recent studies on the structure of defects, and on the transport of current carriers of some selected oxides, both those with broad energy bands and also of transition metal oxides, are discussed in part three. Part three is concerned also with the results of studies on the self-diffusion in selected oxides which provide valuable information about the structure of native point defects. In the case of non-stoichiometric compounds the phenomena of electronic and atomic transport are interrelated, and as such should be considered together.

PART ONE

PREPARATION, CRYSTAL GROWTH AND THIN FILM DEPOSITION OF OXIDE MATERIALS

CHAPTER 1

THE PREPARATION OF OXIDE MATERIALS

1.1. Methods of Preparing Oxides

Oxides may be obtained by high-temperature oxidation of metals in an oxygen-containing atmosphere, and also from other chemical compounds of metals or semiconductor elements.

A typical example of the first method is provided by the preparation of Cu_2O. A high-purity copper plate is first heated to about 1070 K in an atmosphere of dry, purified nitrogen, and then kept for a suitably long time at 1270 K in nitrogen containing up to 1% of oxygen. The reaction between copper and oxygen occurring under these conditions leads to the formation of cuprous oxide.

The preparation of iron oxides, e.g. magnetite, may be given as another example of this method. This compound can be prepared by heating an iron plate to about 1600 K in an atmosphere of carbon dioxide.[1] Other oxides, e.g. NiO, may be prepared in a similar manner. The temperature at which the oxidation is carried out should be suitably high, so as to ensure a sufficiently high rate of the process. The partial pressure of oxygen should also be selected individually for each oxide, so as to obtain materials of the desired chemical composition. The purity of the oxide material thus obtained depends on the purity of the metal and gases used in the process.

Most frequently oxides are prepared from other chemical compounds by methods described in textbooks of inorganic chemistry. In this book we will confine ourselves to the description of only few of these methods for some selected oxides.

Cuprous oxide can be prepared by both wet and dry methods. In the wet method, Cu_2O is obtained from solution of Cu^{++} salts by reduction to Cu^+ followed by the precipitation of CuOH with NaOH. The CuOH thus formed decomposes according to the reaction:

$$2\,CuOH = Cu_2O + H_2O \tag{1.1}$$

Sugar, glucose, or hydroxylamine are used as reducing agents. The dry method for preparing Cu_2O is based on the following reaction:

$$2\,CuCl + Na_2CO_3 = 2\,NaCl + Cu_2O + CO_2 \tag{1.2}$$

To prepare Cu_2O by this method, 5 parts by weight of cuprous chloride are heated in

3

a closed crucible with 3 parts by weight of soda. After cooling, the mixture obtained is washed with water, and Cu_2O is dried under vacuum at 310–340 K.

The most promising dry method for preparing Cu_2O consists in reducing cupric oxide with powdered metallic copper:

$$CuO + Cu = Cu_2O \tag{1.3}$$

An adequate amount of the copper powder is heated in air, and the cupric oxide formed is subsequently reduced at 1270 K in evacuated quartz reactors. The purity of the final product depends mainly on the purity of the copper powder used.

The most frequently used method of preparing zinc oxide is based on the following sequence of reactions:

$$Zn \rightarrow Zn(NO_3)_2 \rightarrow Zn(OH)_2 \rightarrow ZnO \tag{1.4}$$

Purified metallic zinc is dissolved in diluted (1:1) nitric acid, and the solution is evaporated to the density of 1·61 g/cm^3 and cooled. Crystals of $Zn(NO_3)_2 \cdot 6H_2O$ are filtered, dissolved in water and aqueous NH_3 is added while stirring. The precipitated $Zn(OH)_2$ is filtered, washed with hot water and dried. The zinc hydroxide obtained is dried in a porcelain crucible at 370–390 K, and calcined for 3–4 hr at 770 K.

Zinc oxide may also be obtained through thermal decomposition of zinc carbonate. The carbonate is prepared from $ZnSO_4$ by precipitation with $KHCO_3$ saturated with carbon dioxide. Thermal decomposition of zinc carbonate to ZnO and CO_2 begins already at 410 K, and at 569 K the vapour pressure is equal to the atmospheric one. However, the carbonate should be heated until it is red hot.

Another method of preparing zinc oxide consists in the precipitation of $Zn(OH)_2$ from zinc chloride distilled under vacuum, followed by the calcination of the precipitate.

Finally, zinc oxide may be obtained by thermal decomposition of zinc nitrate at 630 K; the resulting product contains, however, traces of the nitrate.

Pure aluminium oxide is obtained by decomposition of alums:

$$2NH_4Al(SO_4)_2 = Al_2O_3 + 2NH_3 + 4SO_3 + H_2O \tag{1.5}$$

The alums are initially dehydrated by heating in a porcelain crucible at 370–470 K and then calcined at 1520–1570 K. Al_2O_3 may also be prepared by the calcination of aluminium hydroxide at temperatures higher than 1220 K. In the latter case α-Al_2O_3 is obtained which is practically stable up to 1770 K.

Titanium dioxide is prepared by calcination of freshly-precipitated titanic acid. The latter may be obtained in the reaction of aqueous NH_3 with $TiCl_4$ or $Ti(SO_4)_2$. Very pure TiO_2 is obtained by the hydrolysis of $TiCl_4$ in an excess of hot water:

$$TiCl_4 + 2H_2O = TiO_2 + 4HCl \tag{1.6}$$

The advantage of this method consists in that $TiCl_4$ is a liquid (m.p. 409 K), which can be readily purified by distillation.

Pure nickel oxide is obtained by thermal decomposition of nickel nitrate $Ni(NO_3)_2 \cdot 6H_2O$, which has been repeatedly recrystallized. The nitrate is heated for 6 hr at 1270–1370 K in a platinum crucible, and cooled in a stream of pure argon.

1.2. Purification of Oxide Materials

The semiconducting properties of oxides, as is the case with all semiconductors, depend to a considerable extent on the concentration of impurities they include. Hence, the purification of oxide materials becomes an important problem from the point of view of their properties. To obtain oxide materials of controlled properties the concentration of impurities should be reduced to a minimum. This can be achieved by purification in each stage of the preparation, and in particular by purifying both the initial materials and the products obtained.

Methods of purifying oxide materials are analogous to those commonly used in semiconductor chemistry. They all make use of the fact that the distribution coefficient of impurities between the two phases of a given semiconductor is, in the state of equilibrium between the two phases, different from unity.

It follows from thermodynamics that at equilibrium the chemical potentials of the same impurity, present in different coexisting phases of a given semiconductor, are equal.

The chemical potentials of the same component in phase 1 and 2 of a given system may be written as follows:

$$\mu_1 = \mu_1^\circ + kT \ln a_1; \qquad \mu_2 = \mu_2^\circ + kT \ln a_2 \qquad (1.7)$$

where μ_1° and μ_2° are standard chemical potentials of a given component in phase 1 and 2, respectively, a_1 and a_2 are activities of this component in phase 1 and 2, k is the Boltzmann constant and T is the absolute temperature.

By comparing these two equations we get

$$\frac{a_1}{a_2} = \exp\left[\frac{\mu_2^\circ - \mu_1^\circ}{kT}\right] \qquad (1.8)$$

For small concentrations of impurities, the ratio a_1/a_2 may be replaced by the ratio C_1/C_2, where C_1 and C_2 are concentrations of an impurity in phase 1 and 2, respectively. The ratio C_1/C_2 is called the *equilibrium distribution coefficient*. As follows from eq. (1.8), the equilibrium distribution coefficient depends on the difference of the standard potentials in phases 1 and 2, and on temperature.

This problem will be considered briefly for a system composed of two coexisting phases—liquid and solid. The equilibrium distribution coefficient k_0 in this case is given by the formula:

$$k_0 = \frac{C_0^s}{C_0^l} \qquad (1.9)$$

where C_0^s and C_0^l are concentrations of a given impurity in the solid and liquid phases of a semiconductor, respectively.

The equilibrium distribution coefficient can be larger or smaller than unity, depending on whether the substance dissolved in an oxide increases or decreases its melting point. Obviously the purification of an oxide material is the more efficient, the more the coefficient k_0 differs from unity. By repeating the process of purification, the concentration of impurities can be considerably reduced, even in cases when the coefficient k_0 is close to unity.

Figure 1.1a shows liquidus–solidus diagrams of an ideal system composed of an oxide and one admixture (impurity), for the case when the substance dissolved in the oxide lowers its melting point, i.e. when $k_0 < 1$. In the region above the liquidus curve we have only liquid oxide, containing an admixture of one type. It is assumed that the admixture is distributed uniformly throughout the oxide, and that its concentration is C_0^l.

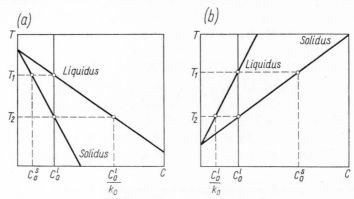

FIG. 1.1. Liquidus–solidus diagrams for a semiconductor containing only one admixture: (a) for $k_0 < 1$, (b) for $k_0 > 1$.

Crystallization starts when the oxide under discussion is cooled to the temperature T_1. When the temperature gradients in the system approach zero, the rate of crystallization is so small that the concentrations of the admixture in the bulk of the solid and liquid phases are equalized by diffusion. It may be thus assumed that the system is always in the state of equilibrium. At the beginning of crystallization, the concentration of the admixture in the solid phase is $C_0^s = k_0 C_0^l$. As the amount of the solid phase increases, the concentration of the admixture in the liquid phase rises (the liquidus curve), and according to eq. (1.9) the concentration of the admixture in the solid phase is also increased (the solidus curve), the temperature of crystallization being lowered at the same time. At the end of crystallization, at the temperature T_2, the concentration of the admixture in the bulk of the solid phase approaches the value of the initial concentration in the liquid phase, while the concentration of the admixture in the last drop of the liquid is equal to C_0^l/k_0.

Figure 1.1b shows the liquidus–solidus phase diagrams for a similar system, the only difference being that the substance dissolved in the oxide raises its melting point, i.e. $k_0 > 1$. By lowering the temperature of the solution very slowly, we reach the point T_1 at which crystallization begins. In the first, infinitely small portion of the solid phase the concentration of the admixture is $C_0^s = k_0 C_0^l$, where C_0^l denotes the initial concentration of the admixture in the liquid phase. As the amount of the solid phase is increased, the concentrations of the admixture decrease, both in the solid and liquid phases (see solidus and liquidus curves). The latter process is accompanied by the lowering of the crystallization temperature. At the temperature T_2, when the crystallization is completed, the concentration of the admixture in the bulk of the solid phase approaches the value of C_0^l, whereby the concentration in the last drop of the liquid is approximately equal to C_0^l/k_0.

The two cases considered above are very seldom encountered in practice, since the rate of diffusion of the admixture in the solid and liquid phases is usually very small, and therefore the concentrations of the admixture in these two phases cannot be equalized. Moreover, it has been assumed in the discussion that the equilibrium distribution coefficient is independent of the concentration of the admixture. Practice shows, however, that such a situation may occur only when the concentration of the admixture and the temperature gradient are very low.

In the case of larger temperature gradients in the system, the concentrations of the admixture in the bulk of the two phases cannot be equalized, since the crystallization is considerably faster than the diffusion of the admixture. When $k_0 < 1$, the diffusion of the admixture from the solid to the liquid phase takes place only in the layer of the liquid near the solid–liquid interface. Hence, in the vicinity of this interface a layer of liquid rich in the admixture is formed, as shown in Fig. 1.2, and it is this layer that

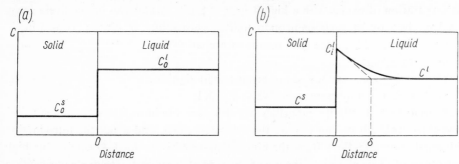

FIG. 1.2. Concentrations of an admixture in the vicinity of the solid–liquid interface in various conditions of crystal growth: (a) for an infinitesimally small rate of crystallization, (b) for a finite value of the crystallization rate.

determines the concentration of the admixture in the newly formed portion of the solid phase. The thickness of the diffusion layer discussed here is denoted in Fig. 1.2 by δ. Its value is contained between 10^{-3} and 10^{-1} cm, depending on the rate of crystallization. Outside this layer, the admixture is transferred by the motion of the liquid, and hence it may be assumed that the concentration of the admixture in the remaining part of the liquid is constant.

The distribution coefficient at the solid–liquid interface

$$k_i = \frac{C^s}{C_i^l} \tag{1.10}$$

differs from the effective distribution coefficient

$$k_{eff} = \frac{C^s}{C^l} \tag{1.11}$$

where C^l is the concentration of the admixture outside the diffusion layer, C_i^l is the concentration of the admixture in the liquid at the interface, and C^s denotes the concentration of the admixture in the solid phase.

Burton et al.[2] have shown that when the liquid is immobile and the admixture is transported solely by diffusion, the effective distribution coefficient is equal to unity.

In practice, however, certain movements of liquid due to convection or mechanical stirring always take place, and hence the effective distribution coefficient k_{eff} is contained within the range from k_0 to unity. These authors derived the following relationship between the effective distribution coefficient k_{eff} and the interface distribution coefficient k_i:

$$k_{eff} = \frac{k_i}{k_i + (1-k_i) \exp{[-v\,\delta/D]}} \tag{1.12}$$

where v is the rate of advance of the interface, δ is the thickness of the diffusion layer, and D is the diffusion coefficient of the admixture in the diluted solution. In the case when the diffusion coefficient D is large as compared with the rate of crystallization, the interface distribution coefficient is equal to the equilibrium distribution coefficient.

The purification of oxide materials presents a complex and difficult problem, owing to their high melting points and decomposition at high temperatures.

The preparation of oxides with a high degree of purity, which can be relatively easily achieved in the case of such semiconductors as germanium or silicon, constitutes a difficult technical problem. The best results in preparing oxide materials of high purity are achieved by using:

(1) The floating zone method (equilibrium: solid–liquid),
(2) Sublimation (equilibrium: solid–vapour), and
(3) Evaporation of volatile impurities (equilibrium: liquid–vapour).

These three methods do not require the use of crucibles, and hence the introduction of additional contaminations from the crucible material is avoided. Owing to the high melting points of oxide materials, the use of any type of crucible during oxide purification is not advisable.

The floating zone method is the most effective technique of purifying semiconductor materials. Essentially it consists in purification by repeated crystallization from the molten phase. Using a suitable source of heat, a small section of a rod, made of the material to be purified, is melted. The narrow molten zone thus obtained is supported between the two solid sections of the rod by virtue of the surface tension of the molten oxide. The movement of the rod relative to the heat source causes the passage of the molten zone along the entire length of the rod. By repeated passage of the molten zone along the rod, always in the same direction, zone refining may be achieved. A detailed description of this method may be found in the monograph by Pfann,[3] and in many other books pertaining to the technology of semiconductor materials.

The following heat sources appear to be most suitable for oxide melting in the floating zone method: a focused beam of carbon arc radiation, laser radiation, plasma torch, and in the case of oxides of low resistivity, an induction coil coupled to a high-frequency generator of suitable power.

In order to obtain the desired composition of the oxide, the purification should be performed in the atmosphere of an inert gas containing a predetermined amount of oxygen of suitable partial pressure.

Purification of oxides by the floating zone technique requires complex and expensive equipment. So far this method has been successfully applied to the purification of a few oxides such as rutile and uranium dioxide (cf. section 2.3).

If the vapour pressure of an oxide is considerably higher than the vapour pressure of the impurities, the oxide can be purified by manifold sublimation and recrystallization. Sublimation is usually carried out in a stream of inert gas, containing a definite amount of oxygen (cf. section 2.4). This method may be applied in the purification of such oxides as MgO, BaO and others.

In cases when the vapour pressure of impurities is much higher than that of the oxide, the latter may be purified by evaporation of the volatile impurities. Usually any single method is suitable for the removal of some of the impurities only. To remove all contaminations, various methods of purification should be employed in succession.

Owing to technical difficulties involved, the methods described above are not frequently used in the preparation of oxide materials. The common chemical methods still prevail, though they do not yield high purity oxide materials, and so they are better suited for the initial stages of purification. Descriptions of the chemical methods of purification are to be found in textbooks of analytical chemistry, and in the monograph by Lawson and Nielsen.[4]

Taking account of the fact that impurities may be introduced in every stage of the process, not only the original substances (the substrates in the process of oxide formation), but also, if possible, the final material should be subjected to purification. Care should also be taken to avoid the introduction of impurities to the finished product. At room temperature and in the case of relatively large crystals, impurities can be incorporated only into the surface layer of the crystal. On heating, however, the foreign atoms present in the surface layer may move towards the bulk of the crystal, changing its physical properties. Hence it is recommended to subject the crystals to etching prior to their heating. The selection of suitable etching agents poses another serious problem, as the contamination of a crystal in the course of etching must be prevented. The same reasons require that the crystal be heated in an atmosphere of suitable purity. Eventually, to obtain a material of controlled composition, the final thermal treatment should be carried out in conditions ensuring thermodynamic equilibrium between the crystal and the surrounding gas phase. This problem will be considered individually in part two of this book.

1.3. Analysis of Oxide Materials

Methods for determining impurities in semiconductor materials have been described in great detail in many monographs and reviews on analytical chemistry. In the present book we shall confine ourselves to presenting only a brief survey of these methods.

In the case of oxides, the determination of the deviations from stoichiometry presents an important problem, and will be considered more extensively.

Spectral analysis is the most commonly used conventional method for determining impurities in chemical compounds. The number of elements which may be determined by this method amounts to about 70. It is, however, inadequate for determining elements of high ionization potential, such as halogens, sulphur, selenium and noble gases. The sensitivity of this method lies within the limits of 10^{-2} to 1 ppm, depending on the element analysed and the matrix substance in which it is contained.

Another method, similar to spectral analysis, is X-ray fluorescence analysis.[5] It advantage lies in that it does not destroy the substance under examination, however its sensitivity is lower and amounts to 1–10 ppm.

All elements can be determined by mass spectrometry, the sensitivity of which i contained between 10^{-2} and 1 ppm.[6,7] The methods mentioned above enable th simultaneous analysis of many elements.

In the recent years polarography[8] has been gaining ever wider application in th determination of impurities in semiconductor materials. The sensitivity of this metho is 10^{-1} to 1 ppm. This latter method is suitable for the fast determination of man impurities, several elements being determinable simultaneously.

Among conventional methods, colorimetry and fluorometry may be mentioned a being frequently employed for determining impurities in semiconductor materials Their sensitivity ranges from 10^{-1} to 10 ppm. They are suitable for analysing all element but each one has to be determined in a separate analysis.

A greater sensitivity can be obtained by the labelled atoms method,[9] and by neutro activation.[10] The sensitivity of the former ranges from 10^{-7} to 10^{-2}, and that of th latter from 10^{-5} to 10^{-2} ppm.

In cases when a given oxide contains only one type of impurity incorporated into it crystal lattice, all foreign atoms being completely ionized, their concentration may b determined by measurement of the Hall effect. This method is very sensitive, althoug its applicability is somewhat limited. It is suitable for evaluating the degree of purit of semiconductor materials, provided that the given material contains completely ionize donors or acceptors.

As compared with the determination of impurities, the measurement of deviation from stoichiometry presents a much more complex problem, particularly in cases whe this deviation is small, since conventional methods of chemical analysis can be use only when this deviation is higher than 10^{-3}.

For smaller deviations special methods are applied, in which a non-stoichiometri oxide is regarded as a solid solution, the components of which have different valencies For example, CdO which shows an excess of the metal is considered as a mixture o cadmium oxide in which Cd atoms are divalent with an excess of Cd atoms having th valency zero. Similarly, iron oxide which shows an excess of oxygen may be regarde as a solid solution composed of molecules of FeO, in which the ions of the metal are divalent, and of molecules of Fe_2O_3, containing trivalent metal ions. When the majority of ions (of normal valency) are stable, the concentration of the minority ions (of differen valency), responsible for departures from stoichiometry, may be determined in two ways

If the minority ions are also stable, their concentration can be determined by dissolving the oxide in an acid in conditions preventing the exchange of oxygen with the surround ings, and by measuring the amount of the excess component colorimetrically or b titration with a redox agent. In the case of the colorimetric method, an accuracy o 1 ppm may be attained.

If the minority ions are unstable, e.g. BaO + Ba in water, or ZnO + Zn in hydro chloric acid, hydrogen is evolved. Its amount, which can be determined accurately, i a measure of the deviation from stoichiometry.[11] An oxidizing agent which oxidize the excess metal can also be added to the solution. The amount of this agent which has undergone reduction is then determined by titration.[12-14]

Deviations from stoichiometry in oxides may be also determined by electrochemical methods.[15-17] In the method proposed by Engell,[15] the oxide, e.g. CdO + Cd, is used as an electrode placed in the acid solution with platinum as a counter-electrode. Evolution of hydrogen is prevented by making the CdO electrode positive. Under these conditions the cadmium oxide dissolves slowly, the Cd giving rise to an electric current in the circuit which can be measured. From the amounts of electric charge passing through the circuit we can find the number of excess cadmium atoms.

ALSO FOR CdS ?? [handwritten annotation in right margin]

Sockel and Schmalzried,[16] and Tretyakov and Rapp[17] have established a deviation from the stoichiometric composition y in oxide materials, e.g. $Ni_{1-y}O$, by high-temperature electrochemical measurements in a stabilized-zirconia electrolyte cell. The oxygen activity in oxides was measured by means of coulometric titration.

When the majority of ions are unstable, or when the oxide contains ions of various valencies even at stoichiometric composition, the methods given above cannot be used. In such cases the deviations from stoichiometry in oxides may be found thermogravimetrically.[18-20] In the thermogravimetric method, variations of the composition of an oxide with regard to some initial state can be determined by weighing the sample suspended in the furnace on platinum wire. Usually, such measurements have been carried out at various partial pressures of oxygen and at several temperatures in equilibrium conditions.

The design of accurate thermobalances requires taking the following precautions: (1) insulation of the microbalance from furnace heat, (2) accurate control of the reaction temperature, (3) effective earthing of the glass components to avoid electrostatic charging, (4) correction of weight readings for buoyancy forces, and (5) use of a narrow reaction tube to minimize turbulence.[20]

The sensitivity of methods for determining departures from stoichiometry is low: even determinations of deviations of 10^{-4} are burdened with a considerable error. In special cases, when the deviation is due to the presence of only one type of atomic defects, which are completely ionized, their concentration can be determined by Hall effect measurements.[21]

CHAPTER 2

THE PREPARATION OF SINGLE CRYSTALS OF PURE
AND DOPED OXIDES

2.1. General

The growing of single oxide crystals presents a difficult problem. Experimental difficulties arise first of all from the relatively high melting points of these materials. At such high temperatures many oxides decompose. In addition, they show a tendency to deviate from stoichiometry, particularly at high temperatures, which necessitates a strict control of the conditions of crystal growth. Despite these difficulties, a rapid development in the techniques for oxide crystals growth has been observed in the recent years.[22-24] This is undoubtedly due to the more and more extensive application of oxide materials in technology and to the promising prospects of their further practical use. Many well-known methods of crystal growth are being adopted and improved, to meet the various specifications of crystal growth for particular oxides.

In order to prepare single oxide crystals of high purity and perfect structure, as well as of a strictly controlled impurity content, special attention is paid to the purity of the initial materials, and also to the stability and control of temperature and its gradient, while at the same time such methods of crystal growth are selected which do not allow for the contamination of the crystal during its formation. Rapid progress in experimental studies in this field is accompanied, though to a lesser extent, by development of the relevant theory, which in turn gives us a better understanding of the mechanism governing the growth of oxide crystals, and makes possible further improvements in the methods of their preparation.

In this chapter some selected methods of oxide crystals growth are reviewed, which seem most promising for the future development.

As the problem of doping semiconductor materials is closely related to crystal growth, both these processes will be considered together.

Generally speaking, doped crystals may be obtained in two ways: either by introducing foreign elements into pure single crystals grown previously, or by incorporating foreign atoms into the crystal lattice during the crystal growth.

In the first method three possible ways of doping are distinguished:

(1) The procedure most commonly used consists in contacting a given single crystal with another phase, solid, liquid or gaseous, containing the element to be incorporated

12

into the crystal lattice. This process proceeds by diffusion. However, to obtain a homogeneous solid solution by this method a long period of time is required. This limits the applicability of this method to the cases when the diffusion coefficient of foreign atoms in a given crystal is relatively large, or when the crystal is small (powders or thin plates). On the other hand non-uniform distribution of admixtures is frequently desirable in the technology of semiconductors (production of transistors, diodes, or photo-diodes). In these cases the diffusion method may be successfully employed. Besides, it may be also employed for the preparation of non-stoichiometric crystals, if the foreign phase contains one of the basic crystal components.

(2) The second method of doping consists in bombarding the crystal with ions of the element to be incorporated. In this instance admixtures are introduced only into the thin surface layer of the crystal.

(3) In the third method a doped crystal is obtained by nuclear transformations, induced by the bombardment of a crystal with α-particles or neutrons. It should be noted, however, that the bombardment may give rise to the displacement of some native atoms or ions from their normal sites (e.g. to the interstitial positions).

As may be seen here, the methods described above cannot be employed for doping of large single crystals. Uniform distribution of admixtures in larger single crystals may be achieved in another way, consisting in the incorporation of foreign atoms into a crystal during its growth. This method has been successfully applied in the preparation of doped single crystals of many oxide semiconductors.

The methods of growing pure and doped single oxide crystals can be divided into three basic groups:

(1) Methods in which the single crystals are obtained from molten oxide materials

$$\text{liquid} \rightarrow \text{crystal}$$

(2) Methods consisting in dissolving a given oxide in a suitable solvent and supersaturating the solution by cooling or evaporation

$$\text{solution} \rightarrow \text{crystal}$$

(3) Methods of crystal growth from the gas phase. These are subdivided into three groups:
(a) vapour $\rightarrow$ crystal (sublimation),
(b) chemical reaction $\rightarrow$ crystal,
(c) solid phase $\rightarrow$ chemical transport $\rightarrow$ crystal.

2.2. The Preparation of Single Crystals from Molten Oxide Materials

The techniques of growing single crystals from the liquid phase are undoubtedly best suited for preparing oxide crystals. The contamination of crystals by foreign substances is then minimal, the rate of crystal growth being at the same time relatively high.

To obtain single oxide crystals from the pure liquid phase the following conditions should be fulfilled:

(1) The oxide should not decompose at temperature below or equal to the melting point.

(2) The oxide should not undergo any polymorphic transitions in the range between room temperature and the melting point.

(3) The vapour pressure of the oxide at the melting point should not be high.

(4) In view of the high melting point of oxide materials, the apparatus for crystal growth should be equipped with an appropriate heating system, ensuring good control of the temperature gradient.

There are many methods of growing crystals from the melt. Some of them require the use of an appropriate crucible for carrying out crystallization. This brings the risk of the crystals getting contaminated with the crucible material. In the case of oxides, uncontrolled contaminations of this type may be significant, as high temperatures are involved. Another disadvantage of using crucibles is the possibility of formation of dislocations in crystals during cooling due to dilatation changes in the crucible material. Therefore better prospects for further extensive use may be expected from methods which ensure the free growth of a crystal, without it coming into contact with the walls of the crucible. These methods include: the Verneuil method, the pulling technique, and the floating zone method.

2.2.1. THE VERNEUIL METHOD

A diagram of the apparatus for growing crystals by the Verneuil method is shown in Fig. 2.1. The powdered material is fed in small quantities by an appropriate mechanism into the inner tube of the burner, wherefrom it is removed by a stream of oxygen. The oxygen, containing the powder, combines with hydrogen and is ignited at the nozzle of the torch. The powdered material is melted in the resulting flame and is deposited on the top of a rod made of the same material. The flame is directed in such a way that only the top of the rod is heated. The single crystal grows at the solid–liquid phase boundary. As the crystal grows, it is gradually shifted downwards. The Verneuil method has been successfully employed for preparing single crystals of Al_2O_3, NiO, Ga_2O_3, MnO, Y_2O_3, and other oxides.

The original Verneuil method described above has, however, many disadvantages. These lie mainly in the difficulty of achieving precise control over the temperature and its gradient, and also in the problem of controlling the gas atmosphere surrounding the crystal; these drawbacks do not allow us to obtain a single crystal of strictly determined chemical composition. In recent years many essential improvements of this method have been developed, by applying other sources of heat, such as high-frequency induction heating,[26, 27] heating by focusing carbon arc radiation,[24, 28, 29] and the plasma torch.[24, 27, 30, 31, 32]

The application of new sources of heat have made possible the control of the atmosphere surrounding the crystal.[27] The control of the temperature and its gradient still remains, however, a difficult and as yet unsolved problem. Some advance in this respect has been observed thanks to the use of the optical pyrometer[33] and thermoelements.[25, 34]

Figure 2.2 shows a diagram of the Verneuil apparatus, in which the melting of the oxide material is carried out by induction heating with a high-frequency current (*ca.* 25 MHz).[27] The appropriate temperature gradient is obtained by applying a conical induction coil with an inclination of 120°. In order to reduce the temperature gradient in the crystal, an additional coil is placed around the crystal. The appropriately sealed casing ensures the crystal growth in the controlled atmosphere. This design includes a vibrational feeder of the powdered material.

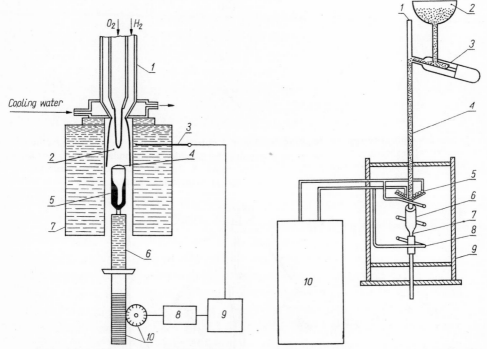

FIG. 2.1. Diagram of the Verneuil apparatus:[25] 1—oxygen–hydrogen torch, 2—flame, 3—thermoelement, 4—molten tip, 5—the growing crystal, 6—rod of refractory material, 7—casing of a cylindrical furnace, 8—motor, 9—automatic control system, 10—mechanism for moving the single crystal.

FIG. 2.2. Diagram of the Verneuil apparatus with induction heating:[27] 1—gas inlet, 2—powder, 3—vibrational feeder, 4—admitting tubing, 5—conical induction coil, 6—single crystal, 7—crystal seed, 8—additional induction coil, 9—sealed casing, 10—high frequency generator.

An interesting modification of the Verneuil apparatus consists in heating with a focused beam of thermal radiation. Figure 2.3 shows the optical system applied for focusing the radiation, described by De la Rue and Halden,[28] and Fig. 2.4 presents the crystal growth chamber.[29] This design permits rotation of the crystal during its growth. This apparatus makes it possible to melt materials with melting points up to 3270 K. It has been successfully applied for preparation of single crystals of corundum, sapphire, ruby, TiO_2, ZrO_2, Er_2O_3 and Nd_2O_3. Heating with a focused thermal radiation beam offers many advantages. Primarily it does not introduce any contaminations and makes possible the growth of crystals in a controlled atmosphere. This method can be also applied in the floating zone technique.

Another promising technique of material melting in the Verneuil method makes use of plasma heating. The Verneuil apparatus with a plasma torch has been described

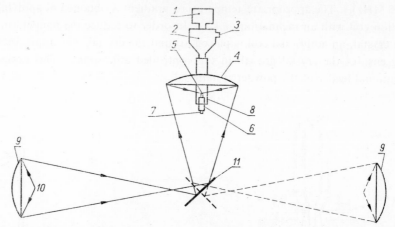

FIG. 2.3. Optical system for focusing the thermal radiation beam in the Verneuil method:[28] 1—vibrational feeder, 2—container with a funnel, 3—gas inlet, 4—secondary mirror, 5—mirror focus, 6—pedestal for single crystal, 7—gas outlet, 8—furnace chamber, 9—main mirror, 10—position of carbon arc, 11—regulating mirror.

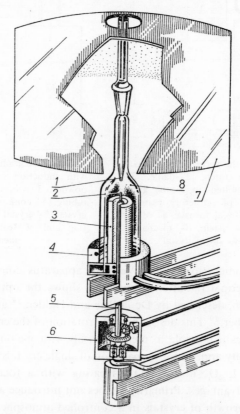

FIG. 2.4. Verneuil apparatus with focused radiation beam for melting powdered material:[29] 1—nozzle for feeding the powder, 2—crystal seed, 3—radiation shield, 4—frame of vacuum chamber, 5—rod on top of which the single crystal is grown, 6—gear box, 7—ellipsoidal mirror, 8—furnace chamber.

by Reed,[30] Gambino,[31] and Williams and Smith.[32] The scheme of the apparatus reported by Gambino is presented in Fig. 2.5. To obtain the desired temperature gradient,
the axis of the plasma torch forms an angle of 60° with the axis of crystal growth.
A mixture of argon and oxygen is used as the working gas. The powdered material,
10–75 μ grain diameter, is fed by a vertical quartz tube with a stream of argon. The
growing single crystal rotates with a frequency of 50 cycles per minute. This apparatus
has been used for the preparation of single crystals of refractory oxides like BaO (m.p.
2191 K) and SrO (m.p. 2693 K).

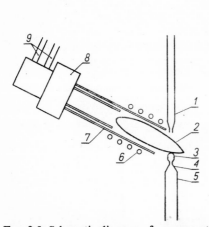

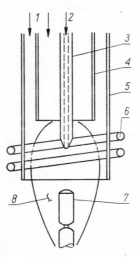

FIG. 2.5. Schematic diagram of an apparatus
with a plasma torch used in the Verneuil
method:[31] 1—feeding tubing, 2—plasma, 3—
growing single crystal, 4—cone made of a
sintered material, 5—ZrO₂ pedestal, 6—high-
frequency coil, 7—quartz tubing, 8—brass
holder, 9—gas inlets.

FIG. 2.6. Geometry of the plasma torch
assembly in the Verneuil technique:[32] 1—
plasma gas, 2—powder and powder gas, 3—
powder probe, 4—inner quartz tube, 5—outer
quartz tube, 6—water-cooled copper r.f. work
coils, 7—boule, 8—plasma fireball.

The apparatus with a plasma torch, as used by Williams and Smith,[32] is shown in
Fig. 2.6. The powder enters through the water cooled powder probe 3, aided by a small
gas flow. The powder impinges on the molten tip of a boule 7, which is withdrawn at
a rate equal to its axial growth rate so that the tip is maintained at one position in the
plasma 8. Plasma gas is introduced tangentially into both the inner 4 and the outer 5
quartz tubes. The dual tubes and the manner of entry have an effect of stabilizing the
plasma within the coils 6 of an r.f. generator. The flow rates of the gas to both quartz
tubes are controlled separately, and are adjusted to give optimum spatial stabilization
of the plasma. The internal diameters of the outer and inner quartz tubes are 4·7 and
2·6 cm, respectively. The maximum power rating of the r.f. generator is 15 kW, and the
generator is operated at a frequency of approximately 3·7 MHz.

　　As can be seen from the above account, the modified Verneuil method can be successfully applied in growing single crystals of metal oxides.

2.2.2. The Method of Crystal Pulling

The pulling technique is one of the best known methods for preparing single crystals of semiconductor materials. It has been described in detail by Tanenbaum,[35] also by Lawson and Nielsen.[4] In this book only some aspects of this method, related to the growth of oxide crystals, will be considered. The crystal pulling method, developed in 1918 by Czochralski, has during the last two decades been improved and adapted to the growth of various semiconductor materials, becoming a standard industrial method. Recently this method has been used in preparing large crystals of some oxides like sapphire, ruby and magnetite.

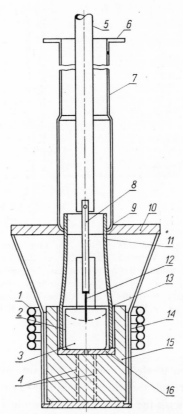

Fig. 2.7. Diagram of an apparatus for the growth of magnetite single crystals by the Czochralski method:[36] 1—high-frequency coil, 2—iridium crucible, 3—molten Fe_3O_4, 4—orifices for thermoelements, 5—rod of stainless steel, 6—flange, 7—quartz cylinder, 8—sapphire rod, 9—joint, 10—quartz plate, 11—Al_2O_3 shield, 12—iridium seed, 13—cylinder of Al_2O_3, 14—quartz cylinder, 15—Al_2O_3, 16—Al_2O_3-plate.

In Fig. 2.7 a diagram of the apparatus for preparing single crystals by the Czochralski method is given after Horn.[36] This variant has been employed for the preparation of large, single crystals of magnetite. The oxide was melted in an iridium crucible by induction heating. It was shown that the iridium content in single crystals of Fe_3O_4 was less than 0·01%, whereas when melted in platinum crucibles the crystals of Fe_3O_4

ontained several hundredths of a per cent of Pt. The crystals were grown in an atmo-
phere of CO_2.

Paladino and Roiter,[37] using the Czochralski method, obtained large sapphire and
uby crystals of a high degree of perfection. Aluminium oxide was melted in a tungsten
rucible by induction heating from an r.f. generator with a power rating of 20 kW at
. frequency of 450 kHz. The crystal was rotated during its growth with a frequency of
0 cycles per minute. A nitrogen atmosphere was maintained throughout the growth.
t has been found that the single crystals obtained by this method are more pure than
he polycrystalline material, owing to the segregation of impurities at the solid–liquid
nterface, and that they contain less than 0·01% W.

Despite many advantages, the Czochralski method has an essential limitation resulting
rom difficulties in selecting an appropriate crucible material.

This problem is avoided in the crucible-free method, proposed by Horn.[38] The Horn
method consists in crystal pulling from liquids, located at the top of a polycrystalline

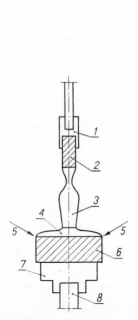
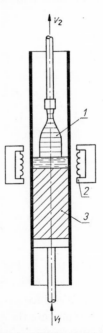

FIG. 2.8. Crucible-free growth of magnetite
single crystals:[40] 1—crystal rotating holder,
2—seed, 3—single crystal, 4—molten zone,
5—focused beam of thermal radiation,
6—polycrystalline magnetite, 7—pedestal,
8—rotating cylinder.

FIG. 2.9. Growth of single crystals of controlled
diameter:[42] 1—single crystal, 2—high-frequency coil, 3—polycrystalline rod.

od fixed vertically in the pulling chamber (pedestal pulling). Using this method Poplaw-
ky and Thomas[39, 40] prepared single crystals of magnetite (Fig. 2.8). A focused beam
f carbon arc radiation was used as the heat source, and the crystals grew in the atmo-
phere of CO_2. Recently this method was used by Trivich and Pollack[41] for the prepara-
ion of single crystals of ZnO.

A modification of the Horn method is the technique reported by Barlic[42] which enables the growth of crystals of equal diameter (Fig. 2.9). The principle of this technique is as follows: A polycrystalline rod is moved upwards with a velocity v_1, and the single crystal with a velocity v_2; $v_1 d_1 = v_2 d_2$, where d_1 and d_2 are the densities of the poly-crystalline material and of the single crystal, respectively. If the diameter of the single crystal slightly increases as a result of lowering of the heater temperature, the thickness of the liquid zone is reduced, which in turn causes a lowering of the liquid level and thus an increase in the liquid temperature. The effect is opposite when the temperature of the heater rises. A relatively simple method of melting refractory materials is that of melting a very thin layer of the given material, by passing current through a perforated iridium band.[43] The molten polycrystalline material can leak through the small holes producing a single crystal (Fig. 2.10).

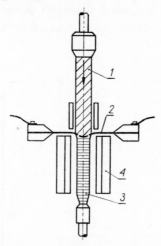

FIG. 2.10. Melting of materials with aid of iridium band:[43] 1—polycrystalline rod, 2—iridium band, 3—single crystal, 4—furnace.

It should be noted that in the initial stage of crystal growth numerous nuclei of crystallization are formed, which may give a polycrystalline material. To avoid this, it is recommended to introduce crystalline seeds. The growth of one crystal only may also be induced by removing the growing polycrystallite from the melt and bringing it into contact with the liquid so that only one little crystal touches the liquid surface. Finally, the third method consists in considerably reducing the diameter of the growing crystal (formation of a neck). More recent developments on the method of crystal pulling can be found in refs. 199 and 200.

2.2.3. THE FLOATING ZONE METHOD

Beside the Czochralski method, the floating zone method has found wide application in the growing of semiconductor crystals.[4, 35] This method consists in melting a narrow zone in a polycrystalline rod; the zone is maintained between two solid sections of the rod by virtue of the surface tension of the liquid. The rod is moved relative to the heat source, thus producing the wandering of the molten zone and formation of a single crystal from the liquid phase. The principal advantage of this method is that the liquid phase and the growing crystal do not come into contact with any foreign substances. In this respect the floating zone method is superior to the Czochralski method. Moreover, this method is suitable for the purification of semiconductor materials (cf. section 1.2). The floating zone technique yields large crystals of high quality. The material may be melted by induction heating, focused thermal radiation, or laser radiation.[†]

Figure 2.11 gives a schematic diagram of the apparatus, in which Chapman and Clark[44] grew single crystals of UO_2. A polycrystalline rod of UO_2 was fixed on a molybdenum pedestal, which could be rotated and moved vertically. The oxide material

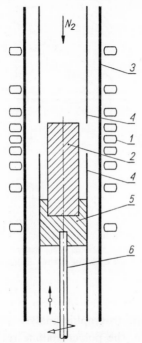

FIG. 2.11. Preparation of UO_2 single crystals by the floating zone method:[44] 1—induction coil, 2—UO_2 rod, 3—quartz tubing, 4—molybdenum heater, 5—molybdenum pedestal, 6—ceramic rod (the arrows indicate the direction of movement).

together with the pedestal was contained in a quartz tube. Owing to the relatively high resistivity of UO_2, the oxide was preliminary heated to ca. 1770 K by means of a molybdenum induction heater, which was coupled directly to the generator coil. The molybdenum heater served also for reducing the temperature difference in the growing crystal. The crystal growth took place in an atmosphere of flowing nitrogen.

Holt[45] employed the floating zone method for preparing crystals of rutile. He found that sintered rods are not suitable as an initial material for single crystal growth, owing

---

† A narrow molten zone may also be produced by electron bombardment; this method, however, is not applicable to oxides as it requires vacuum conditions.

to their porosity, deformations, and also to the contraction of the material during melting, but that good quality rods could be obtained by melting the powdered material. For this purpose powdered titanium dioxide was placed in a water-cooled copper container (Fig. 2.12). A small piece of pure titanium was added to the powder and melted by means of an induction coil, coupled to a generator (power rating 15 kW, frequency 4 MHz).

The powdered rutile was melted by contact with liquid titanium. The TiO_2 rod was obtained by pouring the molten material into a suitable copper matrix cooled by water. By introducing the defined amount of titanium into the powdered TiO_2, a material

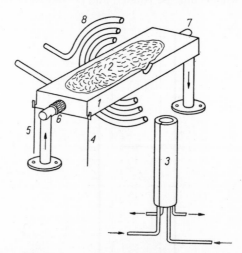

FIG. 2.12. Melting of materials by induction heating:[45] 1—water-cooled copper container, 2—molten rutile, 3—water-cooled copper mould, 4, 5—wires for tilting the container, 6, 7—bearings, 8—high-frequency coil (the arrows indicate flow of water).

was obtained with a low resistivity of 0·1 ohm cm. Such a rod could then be directly coupled to an induction coil. Spectrographic analysis proved it to be copper-free. To prepare a single crystal of rutile, the polycrystalline rod of TiO_2 was fixed in a steel holder and introduced into a vertical, air-cooled quartz tube. The narrow molten zone was achieved by induction heating (the surface tension of TiO_2 is approximately equal to 400 dynes/cm). The zone was moved along the rod by moving it downwards at a rate of 0·5–2 cm/hr.

As already mentioned, direct induction coupling may be applied only to materials of low resistivity. This requires the crystal growth to be carried out in a reducing atmosphere (in this case argon was used). Too great a departure from stoichiometry can cause deformations of the crystal lattice. Because of this Holt had to add some oxygen to argon (ca. 0·1% O_2). In cases when many cycles were involved, smaller quantities of oxygen were added, and only the final displacement of the zone was conducted in an atmosphere containing 0·1% O_2. High-resistivity single crystals were obtained by heating non-stoichiometric TiO_2 at 1073 K for several hours in an atmosphere of oxygen. The material thus obtained showed the resistivity of 10^8 ohm cm.

Recently Gasson and Cockayne[46] employed a gas laser (CO_2–N_2–He) as the heat source in the floating zone method, preparing in this way crystals of Al_2O_3, Y_2O_3 and other oxides (Fig. 2.13).

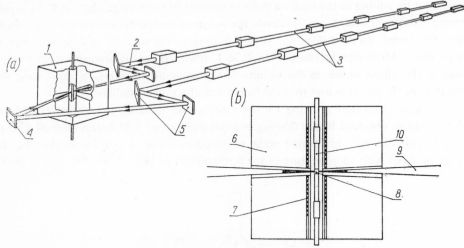

FIG. 2.13. Schematic representation of the combined laser, optical and crystal-growth system:[46] (a) laser and optical system, (b) furnace cross-section; 1—auxiliary furnace, 2—laser beam, 3— CO_2 gas lasers, 4—concave mirror, 5—plane mirrors, 6—thermal insulation, 7—iridium furnace winding, 8—molten zone, 9—laser beam, 10—oxide charge rod.

2.2.4. SOME PROBLEMS INVOLVED IN CRYSTAL GROWTH AND THE DOPING OF OXIDE MATERIALS

The discussion has shown so far that the growth of single oxide crystals must be carried out in a strictly controlled atmosphere, as metal oxides reveal a tendency to deviate from stoichiometry, the extent of these deviations being dependent on the composition of the gas phase surrounding the oxide crystals (cf. Part Two). Many oxides sublimate or decompose at high temperatures. The rate of sublimation may be reduced by applying a high pressure of an inert gas. The decomposition of oxides can be hindered, when the pressure of a volatile component of the crystal is equal or higher than the dissociation pressure of the latter. A controlled composition of the atmosphere is obtained by sealing the space of growth.[47] This creates additional difficulties, e.g. in crystal pulling and rotation. In cases when a given oxide shows a tendency to deviate from stoichiometry towards developing an excess of the metal, decomposition of the oxide may be alleviated by introducing pure oxygen under a determined pressure to the closed system. In the opposite case when an oxide tends to have a deficit of metal, a small amount of pure metal should be introduced into the system. Obviously, in the latter case the whole system must be kept at a temperature higher than the condensation temperature of the metal. Additional heating must then be applied. In some cases, the required pressure of the volatile component is obtained by decomposition of a certain amount of the oxide material itself.

The decomposition of a liquid oxide may also be prevented by covering the liquid surface with a layer of another substance. Such a substance should have a low vapour pressure and a low reactivity towards the oxide material. It has been found that B_2O_3 is most suitable for this purpose.[48]

The doping of oxide crystals, grown from liquids by the pulling method, can be carried out by adding to the liquid a definite amount of the foreign element to be incorporated into the crystal. Since, however, the distribution coefficient usually differs from unity, this simple method does not yield a homogeneous solution of foreign atoms in the crystal.[35] Moreover, in cases when $k_i < 1$, the increased concentration of foreign atoms in the liquid phase, in the vicinity of the solid–liquid interface, may cause the saturation of the solution and thus the formation of a polycrystalline material.

In the case of crystal growing by the Czochralski method, a homogeneous solid solution can be obtained by the floating crucible technique.[23, 49] In this method a small movable crucible with perforated walls is introduced into a crucible containing the molten material with an admixture of the foreign element (Fig. 2.14). The crystal grows

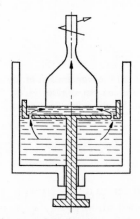

FIG. 2.14. Diagram of the floating-crucible technique.[23]

from the liquid contained in the movable crucible. This leads to a change in the concentration of foreign atoms in this part of the liquid. In the remaining part, the concentration of impurities is not altered, as diffusion through the small holes is insignificant. Owing to the motion of the crucible, the fresh liquid of unaltered composition flows in through these holes, thus ensuring the growth of homogeneous crystal.

In the Horn method, doped single crystals are obtained by using a homogeneous polycrystalline rod containing definite admixtures, or by employing a pure initial material, in which case the admixture is added to the liquid phase.

In the Verneuil method, doped crystals are prepared by introducing the foreign element to the powder, and in the floating zone method—by introducing foreign atoms to the liquid zone, near one of the ends of the polycrystalline rod. In the latter case the foreign element is distributed along the rod due to the passage of the liquid zone. The concentration of foreign atoms at a distance x from the end of the rod after one pass is given by the following formula:[3]

$$C_x^s = C_0 k_i \exp\left(-k_i x/l\right) \qquad (2.1)$$

where C_x^s is the concentration of foreign atoms in the crystal at a distance x, k_i is the distribution coefficient, C_0 is the initial concentration of the admixture in the liquid zone near the end of the rod, and l is the length of the liquid zone. The distribution of the admixture concentration along the rod, for the case when $k_i < 1$, after a single passage of the liquid zone is illustrated in Fig. 2.15. As seen from Fig. 2.15 the concentration of the admixture varies along the rod. These changes can be counterbalanced by passing the molten zone in the opposite direction.

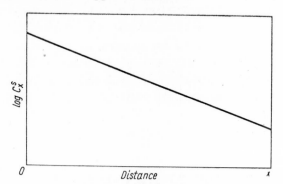

FIG. 2.15. Distribution of the admixture concentration in the semiconductor rod after a single passage of the liquid zone [cf. eq. (2.1)].

In the case of volatile admixtures it is recommended that the crystals be grown under conditions of equilibrium between the crystal and the gas phase, the latter containing admixture vapours of the appropriate partial pressure. This problem will be discussed in more detail in Chapter 7.

It should be noted that though the methods of crystal growth from liquids are most effective, they are not always applicable in the preparation of oxide crystals.

If a given oxide shows high vapour pressure at its melting point, or decomposes at this temperature, or else it appears in another polymorphic form, the crystallization should be performed at a temperature lower than its melting point. In such cases much better results are obtained by growing single crystals from solutions according to the *hydrothermal* and *molten salts methods*.

2.3. The Preparation of Single Oxide Crystals from Solutions

2.3.1. THE HYDROTHERMAL METHOD

This method of crystal growing was used as early as 1851 by De Senarmount, and in 1904 by Spezia. The hydrothermal method has not, however, been used for preparing semiconductor crystals. In recent years the interest in this technique has revived, since it was shown that the method yields good results in growing single oxide crystals.

The hydrothermal method takes advantage of the fact that oxides, which are insoluble in normal conditions, become soluble in water or in aqueous solutions, e.g. of NaOH, under conditions close to those of the critical point of water. A diagram of the hydrothermal system is shown in Fig. 2.16. The apparatus is composed of a steel autoclave, inside of which a container is placed, made of a material which does not contaminate the crystal (e.g. gold, platinum, or silver). The oxide material is then introduced into the container, and pure water, or more often an aqueous solution of sodium or potassium hydroxide is added. The container is filled to about 40–60% of its total volume. The more the container is filled, the faster the crystal growth; however, the perfection of

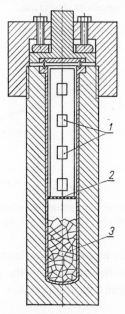

FIG. 2.16. Diagram of a hydrothermal set-up:[50] 1—crystal seeds, 2—diaphragm, 3—poly-crystalline oxide material.

the crystals is then affected. The aqueous solution is also introduced between the walls of the autoclave and the container. If the level of the solution is the same inside and outside the container, practically no pressure is exerted on the container walls, which therefore need not be thick.

Inside the container, at a certain height, a perforated diaphragm is placed, and in the upper part of the container crystal seeds are suspended on an appropriate frame. After closing the container and the autoclave, the bottom part of the whole system is heated to the required temperature, while at the same time the upper part is cooled. In this way two regions of aqueous solution, differing in temperature, are obtained. The temperature difference usually amounts to several dozen degrees. Thanks to the diaphragm, practically no temperature differences exist within the particular regions.

Owing to the relatively high temperature (*ca.* 670 K), the oxide in the lower part of the container is dissolved in the aqueous solution until saturation is reached. Because of the temperature difference existing between the upper and lower part of the container, the saturated solution passes to the upper part. Since the temperature in this part is lower, the solution becomes supersaturated, and the excess of the oxide crystallizes on the seeds. As a result of this process, the mass of the undissolved oxide is decreased at the expense of crystal growth. Crystals grown by this procedure are uniform in shape. The hydrothermal method may be also applied to the preparation, in a relatively simple manner, of doped crystals, by introducing foreign atoms or chemical compounds to the solution.

The hydrothermal method has the following advantages:

(1) It permits crystal growth at temperatures considerably lower than the melting point of the oxide.

(2) Owing to the very small temperature gradient, crystals contain fewer dislocations than in the case of growth from the melt.

(3) The relatively low temperature of crystal growth enables the application of this method to substances which show polymorphism.

(4) The closed system allows crystal growing in controlled—reducing or oxidizing conditions.

(5) The method ensures the rapid growth of crystals.

The disadvantage of the hydrothermal method is the necessity of using an autoclave which will withstand very high pressures. Another weak point of the method comes from the possibility of contamination, and from the fact that the process of crystal growth cannot be followed visually. In spite of these disadvantages, the hydrothermal method seems particularly promising for growing single crystals of oxides, both pure and doped. This method has produced single crystals of Al_2O_3, Cu_2O, Fe_3O_4, SiO_2, ZnO, etc. Many designs of the autoclave needed in this method have been reported. Some of them claim to stand pressures up to 2400 atm at the temperature of 1025 K. A detailed description of this method, the construction of the autoclave and the theoretical considerations involved may be found in papers by Ballman and Laudise,[50] and by Kremheller and Levine.[51]

2.3.2. THE MOLTEN SALT METHOD OF CRYSTAL GROWTH

As already mentioned in the preceding sections, metal oxides are hardly soluble in common solvents. They are, however, soluble in molten substances, or in molten mixtures of appropriate substances of determined composition. This permits the preparation of single crystals from solutions, by cooling or evaporation.

As an illustration, solvents of some oxides are given below:

Oxide	Solvent
Al_2O_3	PbO, PbF_2
Fe_2O_3	$Bi_2O_3 + Na_2CO_3$
TiO_2	$Li_2O + MoO_3$
ZnO	PbF_2

The molten salt method, also known as the *flux growth* (growth from the fluxed melt), was used as early as the end of the 19th century for the preparation of many refractory materials, such as sapphire and MgO. Like the hydrothermal method it has been used in the recent years more and more extensively for preparing single oxide crystals. Although it requires the use of higher temperatures than the hydrothermal method, these temperatures are none the less considerably lower (usually 1170–1570 K) than the melting points of oxides. Besides, this method is much simpler than the hydrothermal method.

Growth from the fluxed melt requires first of all an appropriately designed furnace, ensuring slow cooling and temperature control. A typical furnace used in this technique is shown in Fig. 2.17. The furnace is heated by means of a resistance heater of silicon carbide. The temperature inside the furnace is controlled by Pt–PtRh thermocouples.

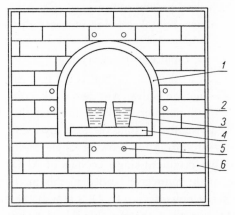

FIG. 2.17. Furnace for single crystal growth by the molten salt method:[52] 1—SiC muffle, 2—metal shield, 3—platinum crucible with the molten material, 4—ZrO_2 plate, 5—SiC heater, 6—firebrick.

An inorganic substance selected as a solvent is contained together with a determined amount of the oxide in a platinum crucible. In the case of volatile substances, a closed growth chamber is necessary. The crucible is then introduced into the furnace and heated to the required temperature. The solvent is melted in these conditions, dissolving the oxide. The temperature is adjusted in such a way that the resulting solution is not saturated. By slow cooling (usually 1 to 5 deg/hr), the solution becomes supersaturated, and the dissolved oxide begins to crystallize. Crystal seeds are formed on cooler parts of the crucible, which always occur in spite of efforts to maintain the same temperature over the whole surface. The number of seeds increases with increasing cooling rate. Hence, in order to obtain large single crystals, the rate of cooling should be reduced to a minimum, the lower limit of this rate being fixed by technical factors. The best results are obtained when introducing crystal seeds into the solution.

Another variant of the method under discussion consists in introducing a temperature gradient in the solution. This procedure resembles in some respects the hydrothermal method. The apparatus employed in this case is described by Laudise, Linares, and Dearborn.[53] A diagram is presented in Fig. 2.18. The lower part of the crucible, having a higher temperature, contains an excess of the oxide, and the solution here is saturated. When stirred, this solution passes to the upper part of the crucible, heated to a lower temperature. In these conditions the solution becomes supersaturated and the oxide crystallizes on the seeds fixed to the rod of the stirrer. The solutions of different temperatures are separated by a diaphragm.

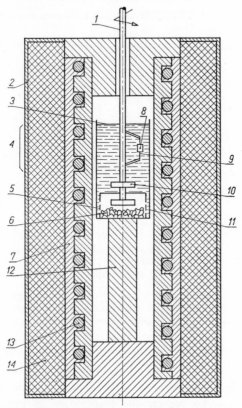

FIG. 2.18. Growth furnace with a temperature gradient:[53] 1—stirrer rod, 2—metal shield, 3—solution, 4—crystal growth zone, 5—diaphragm, 6—polycrystalline material, 7—alundum cement, 8—seed, 9—seed holder, 10—platinum stirrer, 11—platinum crucible, 12—firebrick, 13—platinum coil, 14—heat insulation.

A supersaturated solution can also be obtained by evaporating the solvent. By this technique single crystals of refractory oxides have been grown.[54, 55]

The molten salt method shows the following advantages:

(1) Simplicity of the apparatus.
(2) Easy selection of the appropriate solvent for a given oxide.
(3) High rate of crystal growth.

The disadvantages of this method arise from the possibility of crystal contamination with elements present in the solution, and the significantly higher temperature as compared with the hydrothermal method.

A technique intermediate between the molten salt and the floating zone methods is the *travelling solvent zone technique*. The latter consists in introducing a solvent layer between the crystal seed and polycrystalline rod. The whole set-up is positioned vertically, with the polycrystalline rod placed in the upper part. The zone containing the solvent is heated in a temperature gradient, which causes the dissolving of the poly-crystalline material, its diffusion into the liquid zone, and finally growth at a lower tempe-rature onto the seed crystal. As the single crystal is growing, the polycrystalline rod is moved downwards, so that fresh material may flow into solution. At the same time the growing crystal is lowered at the same rate.

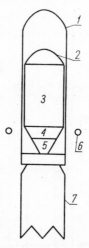

FIG. 2.19. Growth of ZnO single crystals by the travelling solvent zone technique:[56] 1—quartz tubing, 2—closed platinum tubing, 3—ZnO polycrystalline rod, 4—PbF$_2$ solvent, 5—ZnO crystal seed, 6—high-frequency induction coil, 7—shifting mechanism.

Figure 2.19 shows a diagram of the apparatus employed by Wolff and LaBelle[56] for the preparation of single ZnO crystals by this method. PbF$_2$ was used as a solvent, and the temperature of the hot zone was *ca.* 1170 K. The rate of passing the system down-wards was *ca.* 3·5 mm/day. To prevent the evaporation of PbF$_2$, the crystal growth was carried out in a closed platinum tube previously evacuated.

2.4. The Growth of Single Oxide Crystals from the Gas Phase

Crystal growth from the gas phase may be carried out according to three principal techniques:

(1) Oxide sublimation.
(2) Reaction in the gas phase.
(3) Transport reactions.

The first of these may be employed only for oxides which show high vapour pressure, and do not undergo decomposition on evaporating. Single crystals of oxides have been grown either in open or in closed systems. The temperature profile in such systems is illustrated by Fig. 2.20. A polycrystalline oxide is heated to a temperature at which it shows a sufficiently high vapour pressure. In the case of an open system, the oxide vapours are transported by inert gas to cooler parts of the tube, where single crystals are formed.

A similar process is observed in closed systems containing an inert gas, or preliminarily evacuated. In the initial stages of crystal growth, numerous seeds of crystallization are formed, some of which grow faster to yield finally several larger single crystals.

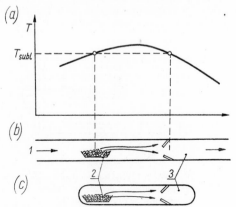

FIG. 2.20. Preparation of single crystals by the sublimation method:[57] (a) temperature profile, (b) open system, (c) closed system; 1—gas flow, 2—polycrystalline material, 3—crystal growth zone.

Since the crystals show a tendency to grow in the direction of the hotter zone, the tube in which the sublimation and condensation take place should be moved relatively to the furnace at a rate adjusted to the rate of crystal growth, or a special system of heating, ensuring only a small temperature gradient, should be applied. In the latter case crystal seeds may also be introduced. An important problem in this method is the selection of an appropriate material for the tube. In order to obtain the required purity of single crystals, it is advisable to use the same oxide, particularly in the cases when extremely high temperatures are applied.[58]

Doped crystals may be obtained by this method according to two techniques: either by introducing the foreign element into the polycrystalline material, or by introducing the vapours of the admixture into the oxide vapour. In the case of an open system, the vapours of the foreign element may be added to the inert carrier gas. If a closed system is chosen, the foreign element may be evaporated from a separate crucible heated to a suitably high temperature. For the preparation of homogeneous doped crystals, or of crystals having determined deviations from stoichiometry, the crystals should be grown under conditions of thermodynamic equilibrium between the crystal and the gas phase. This problem is considered in more detail in the second part of the present book.

The first technique has been applied recently by Savage and Dodson[59] to the preparation of single crystals of ZnO doped with copper and lithium. A schematic diagram of the apparatus used by these authors is shown in Fig. 2.21. Sintered, polycrystalline zinc oxide contained in the tube furnace was first reduced by hydrogen to zinc vapour, which was then reoxidized to form single crystal needles of zinc oxide in the hot zone. The doped single crystals of ZnO were obtained by adding a solution of the dopant to the polycrystalline oxide.

Single oxide crystals may be obtained more conveniently by a gas-phase reaction of the crystal components, or by a reaction of their volatile compounds. The preparation of single crystals of SnO_2 by this method, as reported by Nagasawa et al.,[60] is described below. $SnCl_4$ and H_2O were used as initial materials, as their vapour pressures at room temperature are relatively high.

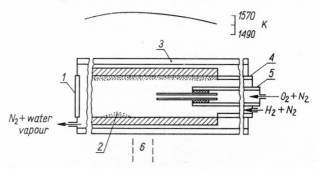

FIG. 2.21. Diagram of the growth furnace for preparing single crystals by the gas-phase reaction:[59] 1—silica window, 2—ZnO liner, 3—alumina porcelain tube, 4, 5—Purox alumina tubes, 6—region of crystal growth.

At suitably high temperatures these substances react in the gas phase to form SnO_2:

$$SnCl_4^{(g)} + 2H_2O^{(g)} \rightleftarrows SnO_2 + 4HCl \tag{2.2}$$

The experimental equipment used by these authors is given in Fig. 2.22. As is seen from this diagram, water and $SnCl_4$ were thermostated, thus maintaining constant

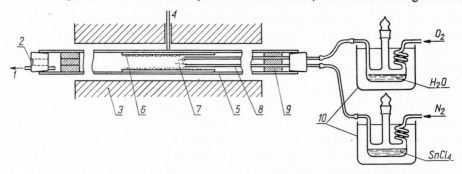

FIG. 2.22. Preparation of SnO_2 single crystals by reaction in the gas phase:[60] 1—gas outlet, 2—window, 3—furnace, 4—thermoelement, 5—Al_2O_3 tube, 6—quartz tube, 7—crystals, 8—quartz tubing, 9—Al_2O_3 block, 10—thermostat.

vapour pressures. The vapours were introduced into the reaction space by means of carrier gases. Nitrogen and oxygen were used as carrier gases; the presence of oxygen reduced the deviations from stoichiometry in SnO_2. The crystal growth took place under the following conditions:

(1) The temperature of the growth zone was 1370–1570 K.

(2) The temperature of the vapour supplying substances was contained in the range 290–320 K.

(3) The flow rate of the carrier gas was 25–150 cm^3/min. The size of the crystal obtained was $2 \times 5 \times 15$ mm. Quartz proved to be a good substrate on which the crystals could be grown.

Single crystals of SnO_2 of higher purity and with higher Hall mobility than previously reported have been grown from the vapour using the reaction

$$SnCl_4 + 2H_2 + O_2 \rightleftarrows SnO_2 + 4HCl \tag{2.3}$$

at 1320 K and 10 Tr*).[95]

When growing single zinc oxide crystals, we may take advantage of the reaction:

$$ZnCl_2^{(g)} + H_2O^{(g)} \rightleftarrows ZnO + 2HCl \tag{2.4}$$

The temperature of this reaction should be selected so that the vapours of zinc oxide thus produced do not become saturated. Single crystals may be grown by supersaturation of the oxide vapours in the colder part of the apparatus.

An interesting method of growing single crystals of non-volatile oxides from the gas phase takes advantage of transport reactions.[61, 62] This consists in introducing into the system a substance which, on reacting with the oxide, forms a volatile compound. If the chemical compound thus obtained shows a tendency to decompose, single crystals of oxides may be produced. As an example the transport reaction for beryllium oxide may be given:

$$BeO^{(s)} + H_2O^{(g)} \rightleftarrows Be(OH)_2^{(g)} \tag{2.5}$$

This reaction takes place at elevated temperatures. The vapours of beryllium hydroxide are passed, after equilibrium has been attained in the system, to the colder part of the apparatus, where they decompose into oxide and water vapour. The oxide can then crystallize on the crystal seed, placed there previously.

Another example of the application of this method is halide transport growth of single nickel oxide crystals, as described by Van de Stolpe.[63] This author made use of the following transport reactions:

$$NiO^{(s)} + 2HCl^{(g)} \rightleftarrows NiCl_2^{(g)} + H_2O^{(g)} \tag{2.6}$$

$$NiO^{(s)} + 2HBr^{(g)} \rightleftarrows NiBr_2^{(g)} + H_2O^{(g)} \tag{2.7}$$

$$NiO^{(s)} + Br_2^{(g)} \rightleftarrows NiBr_2^{(g)} + 1/2 O_2^{(g)} \tag{2.8}$$

The growth of NiO crystals took place in a quartz tube. In one of its ends a spectrally pure NiO powder was placed. After evacuation to a pressure of 10^{-6} Tr and introduction of a determined amount of carrier gas, the tube was closed. It was found that the optimum pressure of the carrier gas is *ca.* 20 Tr. The tube containing the NiO powder and the carrier gas was placed vertically in a furnace, thus ensuring the required temperature difference. Temperature T_1 of the lower part of the tube containing the NiO powder was 1170–1230 K. At these temperatures the equilibrium of the reactions (2.6)–(2.8) is shifted to the right. In the upper part of the tube, heated to a temperature T_2 lower than T_1, these reactions were shifted to the left, and hence the crystallization of nickel oxide took place in this part of the tube. During crystal growth the tube was moved upwards at a rate of *ca.* 1 mm/day.

In the table, given at the end of this book, the methods currently used for preparing single crystals of particular oxides are compiled.

---

*) 1 Tr = 1 Torr = 133·322 Pascal.

CHAPTER 3

PREPARATION OF THIN OXIDE FILMS

THE more and more extensive application of oxide films in technology, in particular in microelectronics, requires rapid progress in this field. This necessitates continuous improvement in methods of preparing thin films, and so accounts for the numerous studies on the conditions which will ensure the desired reproducible and controlled properties of these films. It may be observed that recent experimental techniques are well in advance of the theory in this field, and so the preparation of oxide films having good properties is to a great extent an art professed only by a few.

In this chapter we shall discuss in some detail the most important methods of preparing oxide films; these are:

(1) reactive sputtering,
(2) evaporation,
(3) anodic oxidation,
(4) plasma anodization,
(5) gas-phase reaction deposition.

3.1. Reactive Sputtering

The phenomenon of sputtering of a cathode metal in discharge tubes in rarefied gases was described independently by Grove in 1852 and Plücker in 1858. These workers observed a deposition of a metal layer on the walls of the discharge tube, due to the bombardment of the cathode by positive gas ions present in the tube. In 1877 Wright applied this phenomenon to preparation of metal films.

The application of this method to the preparation of oxide films was initiated in the fifties by the works of Helvig, Preston and Veszi on the sputtering of cadmium oxide. Veszi proposed a term *reactive sputtering* for the description of the oxide sputtering, as the process involves a chemical reaction. This method is at present extensively employed in preparing oxide films of controlled properties.

3.1.1. REACTIVE SPUTTERING IN THE TWO-ELECTRODE SYSTEM

The simplest experimental design of apparatus for the preparation of oxide films by sputtering is provided by the two-electrode system (Fig. 3.1). This consists of a metal or glass vacuum chamber in which two flat water-cooled electrodes, anode and cathode, are fixed. The vacuum chamber is fitted with a window, which makes it possible to observe the glow discharge.

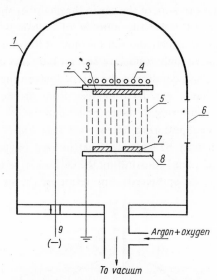

FIG. 3.1. Diagram of an experimental set-up for cathode sputtering: 1—bell jar, 2—cathode, 3—material to be sputtered, 4—water cooling system, 5—glow discharge, 6—window, 7—substrate, 8—anode, 9—high-tension lead.

The vacuum chamber is connected to a conventional vacuum system, by means of which the pressure in the chamber can be reduced to 10^{-6} Tr. Argon, containing a certain amount of oxygen, is usually used as the working gas, and hence the vacuum chamber is connected to argon and oxygen cylinders. Since the properties of oxide film depend on the composition of the surrounding atmosphere, gas flowmeters are incorporated into the gas line. In Fig. 3.2 a diagram of a simple flowmeter is presented: before the

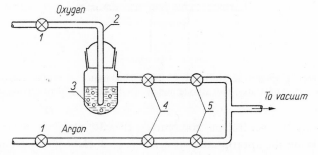

FIG. 3.2. Diagram of an oxygen flowmeter:[64] 1—reducing valves, 2—glass tubing, 3—silicone oil, 4—needle valves, 5—vacuum taps.

needle valve controlling the flow of oxygen, a small glass flask partly filled with silicone oil is placed. Purified oxygen is forced through the oil, the number of oxygen bubbles in unit time being the measure of the amount of oxygen introduced into the vacuum chamber. The partial pressure of argon can be regulated directly by means of the needle valve, since it is usually considerably higher than that of oxygen.

After evacuation of the chamber, a mixture of argon and oxygen in an appropriate ratio is admitted. The total pressure of the gas in the chamber should not exceed 10^{-1} Tr. At pressures higher than 10^{-1} Tr, the number of collisions between molecules and atoms or ions is too high, and their motion becomes diffusional. After the desired flow rate is established, a negative high-voltage of several kilovolts is applied to the cathode. The anode is earthed. In these conditions the rarefied gas in the chamber is ionized and the avalanche glow discharge can be observed. Bombardment of the cathode with positive ions leads to the sputtering of the cathode material.

The mechanism of oxide sputtering has not yet been fully elucidated. On the basis of experimental studies it may be supposed that ionized oxygen molecules (or atoms) combine with atoms of the metal constituting the cathode (the cathode is usually coated with the metal or alloy to be sputtered). Sputtering of the oxide layer thus formed is

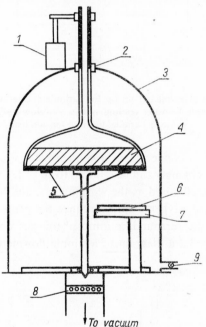

FIG. 3.3. Reactive sputtering apparatus:[67] 1—driving motor, 2—rotary seal, 3—bell jar, 4—refrigerant, 5—substrates, 6—cathode metal, 7—shield, 8—chevron baffle, 9—gas inlet.

performed by ions of a neutral gas bombarding the cathode. The sputtered oxide molecules then settle on an appropriate substrate (e.g. a glass plate) fixed to the anode, forming a thin layer of the oxide. It is also conceivable that the sputtered atoms of the metal react with oxygen during their flight in the chamber, or that adsorption of oxygen occurs during the growth of the thin oxide layer on the substrate.

Since bombardment with ions leads to the heating of the cathode the latter should be cooled. The rate of growth of the oxide layer is controlled by many factors, and primarily by the pressure of the gas and the electric power applied. Uniformity of the sputtered film is influenced by geometrical factors, e.g. the shape of the electrodes and their spacing.

The structure and physical properties of oxide films prepared by this method depend first of all on the composition of the gas phase and the temperature of the substrate. Strict control of these two parameters is therefore necessary. A detailed description of this method can be found in papers by Maissel[65] and Pleshivtsev.[66]

Below the apparatus used by Lieberman and Medrud[67] for preparing oxide films of eleven metals is described in detail, by way of example. The construction of the apparatus enables the simultaneous rotation and refrigeration of substrates during the sputtering. Substrates are cooled by liquid nitrogen to increase the possibility of obtaining amorphous films. The rotation of the substrates takes place in order to obtain films which are uniform in thickness, and also assists in the dissipation of heat from the surface of the substrate, since the substrates spend only a small fraction of each revolution in the plasma region. Moreover, rotation makes it possible to obtain mixed metal oxide films, by the simultaneous reactive sputtering of several independent cathodes. The basic sputtering equipment is shown schematically in Fig. 3.3. The main feature of the system is a liquid-nitrogen cooled vacuum flask made of stainless steel. The baseplate of this flask is a copper plate to which the glass substrates are screwed. The constant level of the liquid nitrogen in the flask is controlled automatically. An electric motor placed outside the vacuum system rotates the vacuum flask via a V-belt arrangement. Sector-shaped metal plates are used as cathodes in the sputtering. Water cooling is installed in the cathode supports. When multicathodic sputtering is applied the cathodes are placed adjacent to one another.

3.1.2. BIAS SPUTTERING

High-purity oxide films can be prepared by bias sputtering. Bias sputtering—one of the most useful versions on the thin film sputtering deposition method—may be defined as the technique of applying a small negative potential to the substrate. One of the first workers to report on the bias sputtering technique was Frerichs[214] in 1962. Since then this method was extensively employed in the preparation of both metal and oxide films.

There exist three basic types of laboratory apparatus, commonly used in bias sputtering. Diagrams of these three systems are given in Fig. 3.4. The first of them, the asymmetric a.c. system, resembles the two-electrode system described above, the only difference being that an asymmetric alternating potential is applied between the anode 3 and the cathode 1 (Fig. 3.4a). The substrate 2 is fixed to the anode. In the first half of the cycle the anode is earthed and a high negative potential is applied to the cathode. The sputtering mechanism is therefore analogous to that described previously, for the case in which a constant potential is applied. In the second half-cycle, a small negative potential is applied to the anode, while the cathode is the earthed electrode. The substrate is then bombarded with positive ions, and the surface of a film is cleaned as a result of the removal of adsorbed gas molecules.[68] Obviously the negative potential applied to the substrate should be lower than that applied to the cathode, since otherwise the

film could not grow. The ratio of the potentials commonly used is 1/4. The shape of
the potential is of no significance. It must be noted that both the cathode and the anode
should be made of the same material, in order to prevent contamination of the deposited
film.

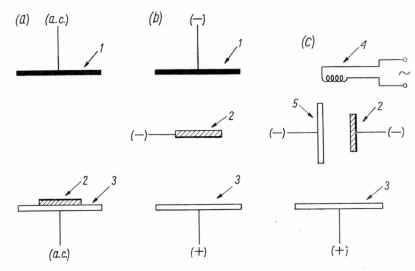

FIG. 3.4. Geometry of electrodes for bias sputtering:[69] (a) asymmetric a.c., (b) cold cathode d.c.,
(c) thermionic d.c.; 1—cathode, 2—substrate, 3—anode, 4—thermionic cathode (filament),
5—target.

The purification of the film surface may also be performed at constant voltage
(Fig. 3.4b). The system differs from that described in section 3.1.1 in that the substrate
constitutes a separate electrode and is located between the cathode and the anode.
A small potential, negative with respect to the plasma, is applied to this electrode, due
to which a part of the ions constantly bombards the growing film, thus purifying its
surface.

The d.c. bias sputtering system is more versatile than the a.c. system. In this case the
substrate is independent of the circuit required to maintain the gas discharge. The most
difficult problem consists here in the proper location of the substrate relative to the
cathode. Because of the high gas pressure (5×10^{-2} to 10^{-1} Tr) necessary to maintain
the discharge, the resulting mean free-path of the sputtered atoms or molecules is very
short. Thus the substrate must be placed extremely close to the cathode, making it
difficult to maintain uniformity in film thickness if a non-planar substrate is used.

The most effective method of preparing thin films under controlled conditions makes
use of the thermionic cathode (Fig. 3.4c). In this system a tungsten wire heated by low
voltage alternating current serves as the cathode 4, which is used only for the emission
of electrons. At the opposite side the anode 3 is placed, to which a positive potential
of several hundred volts is applied. This potential accelerates the electrons emitted from
the cathode, which, owing to the high energy thus obtained, ionize the gas in the chamber.
The positive ions formed bombard the target 5, to which a high negative potential has
been applied. The target material is sputtered and deposited on the substrate (Fig. 3.5).

Since the substrate is under a small potential, negative with respect to the plasma, a fraction of positive ions strikes the surface of the growing film, removing from it the adsorbed atoms or molecules of the gas. The contamination of the sputtering chamber with tungsten is prevented by placing the filament in a recessed heater. The substrate and the target can also be located anywhere else within the gas discharge space. The beam of electrons emitted by the thermionic cathode is much more intense than that emitted by the cold cathode, hence in the former case the gas pressure in the discharge chamber may be smaller, amounting to 10^{-4} to 10^{-3} Tr. Owing to this, the mean free-path of the sputtered atoms or molecules is considerably higher than in the case of the cold cathode, which makes it possible to obtain thin films of higher purity.

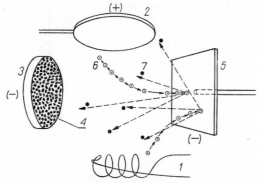

FIG. 3.5. Hot-cathode bias sputtering system:[69] 1—hot cathode, 2—anode, 3—substrate, 4—deposited thin film, 5—target, 6—argon ions, 7—sputtered atoms or molecules.

The greatest advantage of the thermionic cathode system consists, however, in that the target is independent of the plasma producing system. This makes possible a much better control of the conditions in which the thin film is formed. The plasma density may be controlled by varying the emission of the cathode and the pressure of the working gas in the chamber, and also by applying a magnetic field and then changing its intensity. A further advantage consists in the possibility of shaping the target to conform to the substrate geometry. The thermionic cathode d.c. sputtering system with a biased substrate is shown in Fig. 3.6.

All three types of apparatus entail the same difficulties in ensuring electrical contact with the substrate surface. If the substrate is a metal or a conductor, the bias leads may be attached by a simple wire wrap, soldering, brazing, welding, etc. If the substrate is a dielectric, it is usually necessary either to attach leads to a predeposited film, or to make a movable electrode which will contact the film after the first layer is deposited.

Many process variables are involved in the technique of ion sputtering, e.g. type of bombarding ion, ion energy and sputtering gas pressure.[70] In the case of bias sputtering, one may consider the following as particularly important parameters and variables:

(1) Target to substrate current density ratio.
(2) Pressure or concentration of the impurity gas.
(3) Substrate geometry.
(4) Nature of the target material (element or compound).

The first one is probably the most significant, as it determines the net deposition on the substrate, and governs the removal of impurities from the deposited film. Usually the 4:1 ratio is used, however, when adjusting it account should be taken of other factors.

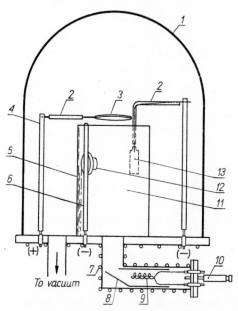

FIG. 3.6. Thermionic d.c. sputtering set-up with biased substrate:[69] 1—bell jar, 2—glass insulators, 3—anode, 4—electrode post, 5—glass chimney, 6—bias electrode, 7—water cooling coils, 8—heat shield, 9—thermionic cathode, 10—gas valve, 11—plasma region, 12—biased substrate, 13—target.

The impurity gas pressure or impurity concentration is important, as it indicates what density of the bombarding ion flux is required to maintain the purity of the deposited film.

Substrate geometry influences the net amount of material obtained from the target, particularly in cases when some parts of the substrate surface are only partially exposed to the target, but directly exposed to the ion plasma. If this is the case, the net deposition of the target material over the substrate will be variable. The nature of the target material, i.e. whether it is elemental or a compound, must be taken into account when it is desired to maintain stoichiometry of the deposited film.

As mentioned previously, the electrical properties of the resulting film are highly dependent on the accurate control of the composition of the sputtering atmosphere. If the system is properly balanced, a marked improvement in film stability over a wide temperature range and long periods of time may be achieved.[69, 71, 72]

3.1.3. R.F. SPUTTERING

Insulators cannot be sputtered by conventional d.c. techniques, because the accelerating potential cannot be directly applied to the insulator surface. This prevents neutraliz-

ing of the positive charge, which would accumulate on the surface during ion bombardment. This problem can be overcome by applying a high frequency potential to a metal
electrode behind the insulator. Power can be supplied to the plasma by applying the
displacement current through the dielectric material, and sputtering is realized due to
the alternative bombardment of the insulator by ions and electrons. The positive charge
which accumulates on the surface during the negative or sputter portion of each cycle
is neutralized by electrons in the positive part of the cycle.[78]

The principles of r.f. sputtering were described by Wehner in 1955.[73] In the following
years these methods have been developed by Wehner et al.,[74, 75] Davidse and Maissel,[76]
and others. Butler[77] studied the response of low pressure plasma, when an r.f. potential
was applied to a ring-shaped metal electrode placed externally against the glass wall
of the discharge tube. He established that the response voltage was self-biased negatively
with respect to the plasma. Without this negative bias, an excess electron current would
flow to the insulator during each cycle since the electron mobility is much greater than
the ion one, but this is not possible as the net d.c. current in the dielectric must be zero.

Davidse and Maissel[76] observed that a self-sustained r.f. glow discharge could be
maintained at pressures down to about 2×10^{-3} Tr. This pressure was further reduced
to about 1×10^{-3} Tr by superimposing a magnetic field perpendicular to the target.
For most applications, a conventional 1 kW generator can be used as a power supply
for r.f. sputtering. The current frequencies may vary from a few to about 30 Mc/s,
and the distance between the target and substrate from 2·5 to 3·0 cm.[78]

In general, the films obtained by r.f. sputtering have been found to be of higher quality
than insulator films produced by other low temperature deposition processes.[78]

A diagram of the system used by Pratt[79] is shown in Fig. 3.7. In Fig. 3.8 a diagram
of the r.f. sputtering apparatus is given after Holland, Putner, and Jackson.[80]

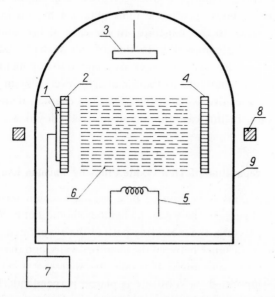

FIG. 3.7. Geometry of the r.f. sputtering set-up:[79] 1—metal, 2—dielectric, 3—anode, 4—substrate,
5—filament, 6—argon plasma, 7—r.f. power supply, 8—magnetic field coil, 9—bell jar.

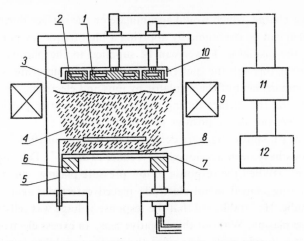

FIG. 3.8. Diagram of an apparatus for r.f. sputtering:[80] 1—water-cooled disc electrode, 2—water-cooled ring electrode, 3—dielectric plate, 4—plasma region, 5—screen, 6—soft steel, 7—substrate post, 8—substrate, 9—electromagnet coil, 10—glass casing, 11—control system, 12—r.f. power supply.

By capacitive coupling of the r.f. power supply to a metal or semiconductor electrode it is possible to obtain metal or semiconductor films by the same technique.[78, 81] Insulator films can also be produced at relatively high rates by r.f. reactive sputtering. For example, Al_2O_3 has been deposited at a rate of 330 Å/min.[78] The sputtering conditions were: diameter of the aluminium electrode 6·3 cm, r.f. power 350 watts, gas composition 90% Ar/10% O_2, and pressure $1·5 \times 10^{-2}$ Tr. This rate compares with that of 33 Å/min or less, reported for d.c. reactive sputtering of aluminium.[78]

The cathodic sputtering technique is undoubtedly one of the most effective methods for preparation of oxide films. The oxide films obtained by this method are uniform and show good adherence to the substrate. In the case of bias sputtering, the purity of the material obtained is comparable to that of films deposited under ultra-high vacuum. This method can also be relatively easily adapted to doping films, by introducing a determined amount of admixture to the metal. However, also in this case one may come across the difficulties discussed in the preceding chapter, if the admixture shows a high vapour pressure. In this case the metal must be alloyed with the admixture in a closed chamber.

3.2. The Preparation of Thin Oxide Films by Vacuum Evaporation

Evaporation of thin films is performed in a special vacuum set-up (Fig. 3.9). The pressure of the residual gases in the vacuum chamber should not exceed 10^{-5} Tr during evaporation. At such pressures the mean free-path of the evaporated atoms or molecules is usually larger than the distance between the chamber walls, and the atoms or molecules form a beam of a certain solid angle. If inside this angle—at a certain distance from the material that is evaporated—a substrate is placed perpendicularly to the trajectory of the molecules, the latter will be deposited on the substrate surface to form a thin film. The resulting film is stable and uniform if the substrate is heated.

The evaporating substance should be heated to the temperature at which its vapour pressure is between 10^{-1} to 10^{-2} Tr. Various methods of heating may be employed, e.g. resistance heating, bombardment with an electron beam, laser radiation, etc. Principally, this method cannot be employed directly to the preparation of thin oxide films, since at high temperatures in vacuum metal oxides decompose. In many cases

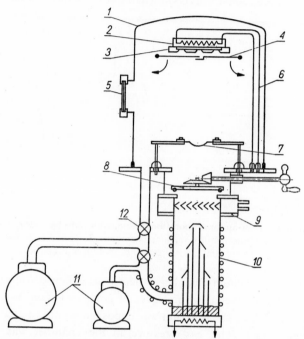

FIG. 3.9. Diagram of an apparatus for vacuum evaporation: 1—vacuum jar, 2—substrate heater, 3—substrate holder and substrate, 4—screen, 5—window, 6—power supply for the substrate heater, 7—source of vapour, 8—valve, 9—cold trap, 10—diffusion pump, 11—oil pump, 12—valve.

the dissociation pressure of an oxide is lower than the partial pressure of oxygen in the chamber, so that the complete decomposition is avoided; however, there always is the danger of partial reduction with formation of suboxides. There also exists a possibility of the reaction between the oxide and the crucible material leading to partial decomposition of the oxide. Such a reaction takes place near the crucible surface, however, the metal formed as a result of reduction may in turn react with the remaining oxide, producing suboxides. Moreover, such a reaction may lead to the formation of stable volatile oxides (e.g. WO_3 or MoO_3 when the crucible is made of tungsten or molybdenum), contaminating the films. Volatile metal compounds can be also formed via a reaction of the residual gases (e.g. water vapour) with the crucible material. It follows from the above considerations that by direct evaporation essentially only thin films of suboxides may be obtained. This pertains to the oxides which show low dissociation pressure at high temperatures. The method is unsuitable for preparing thin films of oxides which have high dissociation pressures.

Recently Rossi and Paul[82] prepared by this method thin films of nickel oxide, evaporating nickel in the atmosphere of oxygen at 10^{-4} Tr. Nickel was evaporated from
a graphite or alumina crucible using an electron beam. Plates of CaF_2, LiF and MgO
heated to about 820 K were used as substrates.

Recently Mandani and Nichols[83] used laser radiation in the evaporation of aluminium
oxide. The diagram of their apparatus is shown in Fig. 3.10. Laser radiation was admitted

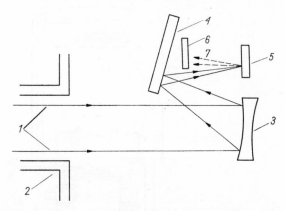

FIG. 3.10. Diagram of the set-up for evaporation of thin oxide films by laser radiation:[83] 1—CO_2
gas laser radiation, 2—window in the vacuum chamber, 3—concave mirror, 4—steel plate,
5—Al_2O_3 target, 6—substrate, 7—direction of motion of evaporated molecules.

through a window to a vacuum chamber, where it was focused on an alumina target
5 by a concave mirror 3 covered with a layer of gold, and stainless steel plate 4. The
silicon substrate 6, on which the thin film was deposited was fixed at a distance of 5 cm
from the alumina target. The gas pressure in the chamber was 3×10^{-6} Tr. No
distinct increase in the pressure during the evaporation was observed. The Al_2O_3 films
obtained by this method were 500–5000 Å thick and adhered well to the substrate.
The average time required for the preparation of a 2000 Å film was about 40 min.

The evaporating of oxide material by means of an electron beam or laser radiation
is advantageous, since the crucible is not necessary, and even in the case when the
substance to be evaporated is contained in a crucible, this latter is not heated directly,
which prevents contamination of the oxide films.

In cases when the evaporation method cannot be directly applied for preparing thin
films of a given oxide, these latter can be obtained by heating the evaporated films of
suboxides in the presence of oxygen or in air. The thin films of oxides can also be prepared by oxidation of deposited metal films; however, the films obtained in this way
usually are not uniform. The detailed description of the technique of evaporation of
thin films can be found in the monograph by Holland.[84]

3.3. Anodic Oxidation

Thin oxide films can be also obtained by anodic oxidation of metals or evaporated
thin metal films.[85] The principle of this method is as follows: when to an electrolyte

containing oxide ions, two electrodes are introduced and direct voltage is applied across them, the anions react with the anode material forming on its surface a thin film of an oxide. This film can grow only when oxygen ions of the electrolyte migrate through the oxide film to the oxide–metal interface where the reaction takes place, or when metal ions move in the opposite direction and the reaction proceeds at the outer surface of the oxide film (Fig. 3.11). Thus the film growth is determined by ionic conductance of the oxide. It depends then on the electric field in the oxide, and consequently on the voltage applied to the film. It is often assumed that the drop of potential in the thin oxide film is equal to the total voltage applied to the electrodes. However, taking into account the drop of potential at the phase boundary oxide–electrolyte and the resistance of the electrolyte, it should be noted that this assumption may be encumbered by large error, and for very thin films it may not be true at all.

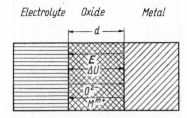

FIG. 3.11. Motion of ions in the process of anodic oxidation.

At the constant voltage, the film thickness is increased with time. This reduces the electric field in the oxide, and hence decreases the rate of the film growth. It has been shown that for not too long reaction times, the thickness of the oxide film is a function of the voltage applied to the system. Hence, the thickness of the oxide film is often expressed in Å/V. It should be remembered, however, that principally at the constant voltage the film thickness increases with time, the rate of oxide growth approaching zero. To ensure high rate of the film growth and also large thickness of the film, the voltage applied to the system should be sufficiently high. At too high voltage, however, the danger of break-down occurs.

Thin oxide films are usually produced either at the constant ionic current or at the constant voltage. In the former case, the voltage should be gradually risen during the film growth, in the latter case the ionic current is decreased with time.

Since, establishing of the constant ionic current requires large and rapid changes of the voltage, and the use of the constant voltage produces large and rapid changes of the ionic current, the control of the film growth may be effectuated by an appropriate electronic system. When the constant ionic current is applied, the film growth may be controlled either by switching off the current after a determined time, or after reaching the determined voltage between the cathode and anode.

This method has been applied to the preparation of uniform, thin oxide films of many metals, e.g. Al_2O_3, Ta_2O_3, etc. The detailed description of this method and its application to the preparation of thin oxide films can be found in the monograph by Young.[85]

3.4. Plasma Anodization

The method of plasma anodization was described in 1963 by Miles and Smith.[86] The principle of this method consists in the oxidation of a metal or a semiconductor element in oxygen plasma. It permits to obtain oxide films of high purity at relatively low temperatures, in some cases even below 370 K.

The diagram of a typical apparatus for plasma anodization is shown in Fig. 3.12. It consists of a vacuum bell jar containing a ring cathode made of aluminum, and a sample

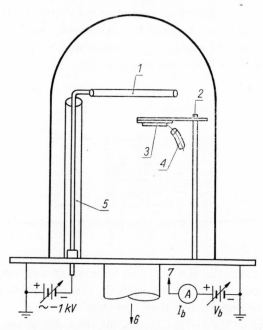

FIG. 3.12. Experimental set-up for plasma anodization:[87] 1—ring cathode, 2—sample holder, 3—sample, 4—electric connection to sample, shielded with quartz, 5—quartz shield, 6—to cold traps and pumps, 7—to sample, I_b—bias current, V_b—bias voltage.

holder. The earthed steel plate constitutes an anode. After pumping out the air from the chamber, oxygen under the pressure of 5×10^{-2} Tr is admitted. A negative potential of the order of 1 kV is then applied to the cathode and the glow discharge with the formation of the plasma is observed in the chamber.

To obtain a thin oxide film, a metal or a semiconductor sample fixed to a sample holder is placed in the negative glow, and the positive bias with respect to the anode is applied. At a small constant bias voltage, the thin oxide film is growing, the process of growth following the logarithmic rate law. The growth of the oxide film takes place due to the ionic and vacancy diffusion of either the metal or oxygen, or both, and depends upon the relative mobilities of the ions in the oxide considered (Fig. 3.13). The role of the positive or negative oxygen ions existing in the plasma in the process of the plasma oxidation is not as yet fully understood.[86-90]

Figure 3.14 shows the dependence of the thickness of the Al_2O_3 film on time at the constant bias voltage of 6 V, and the change in the current that flows through the sample, reported by Smith and Miles.[86] To prepare the film of larger thickness, the bias voltage should be gradually increased, however in such a way as to prevent the break-down of the film. The best conditions for the plasma anodization are ensured by applying the

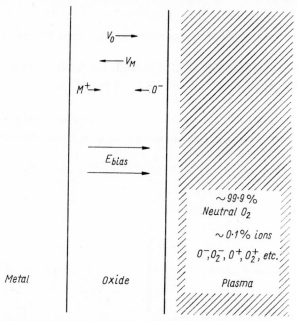

FIG. 3.13. Metal–oxide–plasma system during anodization.[87]

constant current density. In Fig. 3.15 the dependence of the voltage applied to the sample on the thickness of the Al_2O_3 film is presented.

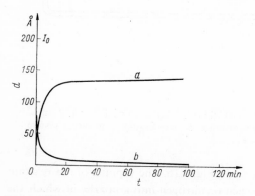

FIG. 3.14. Dependence of thickness of the Al_2O_3 film on time at the bias voltage 0·6 V, and the change in the current during plasma anodization:[86] a—thickness of the film, b—current.

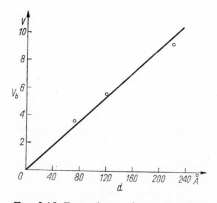

FIG. 3.15. Dependence of the bias voltage applied to the sample on the Al_2O_3 film thickness.[86]

The rate of the film growth is dependent on the oxygen pressure. For example, the maximum growth rate for Al_2O_3 films is obtained at the pressure of ca. 5×10^{-2} Tr.[87]

The method of plasma anodization can be applied to oxidation of the following metals: Al, Ta, Mg, Cr, Sb, Bi, Zr, Mn, U, Nb, Ti, Be, Ge, Si, La, Mo, and W.[87] The results of the studies on this method have been reviewed recently by O'Hanlon.[87]

3.5. Deposition of Oxide Films by Gas Phase Reactions

Thin oxide films can be prepared relatively simply by chemical reactions in the vapour phase. To illustrate this method we will describe below preparation of thin films of TiO_2, SiO_2 and SnO_2.

Preparation of thin films of TiO_2 by reaction in the gas phase was described by Feuersanger.[91] Titanium tetrachloride and water were used as initial materials. The diagram

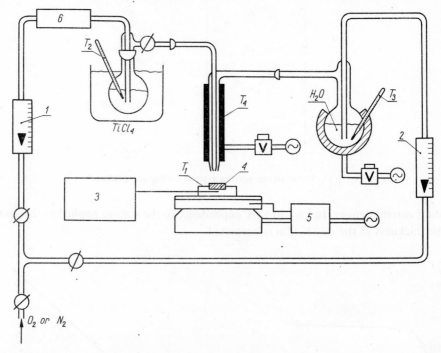

FIG. 3.16. An apparatus for preparation of thin TiO_2 films by chemical reaction:[91] 1, 2—flowmeters of the carrier gas, 3—compensator, 4—substrate, 5—temperature controlling system, 6—drier.

of the apparatus used by Feuersanger is shown in Fig. 3.16. The vapours of the reactant were introduced with aid of a stream of oxygen or nitrogen into a nozzle, in which the reaction:

$$TiCl_4 + 2H_2O = TiO_2 + 4HCl \tag{3.1}$$

took place. The resulting molecules of TiO_2 were deposited on the appropriate substrate, forming a thin film. The typical parameters of the process were as follows: the flow rates of the streams carrying $TiCl_4$ and H_2O were 0·2 and 1·4 l/min, respectively, the temperature of liquid $TiCl_4$ and H_2O being 283 and 313 K. The temperature of the substrate was 423 K, and that of the nozzle 433 K. The distance between the nozzle and the substrate was 1·5 cm. The rate of deposition of films in these conditions was 20 Å/s. Various materials were used as the substrates. It was found that the TiO_2 films obtained showed best electrical properties on germanium, silicon and platinum substrates.

Another example of this method is provided by preparation of SiO_2 films by the reaction:

$$SiH_4 + O_2 = SiO_2 + 2H_2 \tag{3.2}$$

described by Goldsmith and Kern[92], Hammond and Bowers[93] and also by Chu, Szedon and Gruber.[94] The schematic diagram of the apparatus used by Hammond and Bowers is shown in Fig. 3.17. Since the mixture of SiH_4 and O_2 is flammable, the vapour of

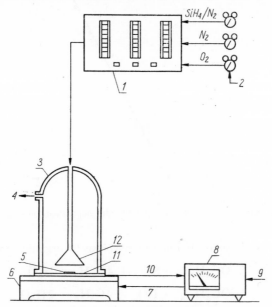

FIG. 3.17. Diagram of an apparatus for vapour deposition of SiO_2:[93] 1—gas flow control and mixing panel, 2—regulators, 3—bell jar, 4—exhaust, 5—substrate, 6—hot plate, 7—controlled power, 8—temperature controlling system, 9—power supply, 10—thermocouple, 11—aluminium heat spreader, 12—nozzle.

SiH_4 and oxygen were diluted with nitrogen. Water vapour had to be avoided to prevent formation of colloidal SiO_2. The ratio of $SiH_4 + O_2$ to N_2 was 1:50, whereas that of oxygen to SiH_4 was from 6 to 30. The flow rate was 10 1/min. It was found that when the ratio O_2/SiH_4 was smaller than 20, the rate of the film deposition was constant, whereas at the higher values of this ratio, this rate decreased while the film was growing. Silicon or aluminum were used as the substrates. Figure 3.18 shows the dependence of the rate of film deposition on temperature in the range 470–770 K.

Transparent thin films of SnO_2 of good electrical conductivity can be obtained by passing the $SnCl_2 \cdot 2H_2O$ vapour over the substrate heated to the temperature of 670–720 K. The reaction in this case is:

$$SnCl_2 \cdot 2H_2O = SnO_2 + 2HCl + H_2 \tag{3.3}$$

The detailed description of the preparation of SnO_2 films may be found in the paper by Livesey, Lyford and Moore.[96]

One of the problems which often arises with this technique is the subsequent translucent or milky appearance of the coated substrate. This can be avoided by conducting the film deposition in the atmosphere of dry oxygen, and by rapid cooling of the substrate after the process is terminated.[96]

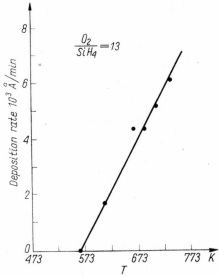

FIG. 3.18. Dependence of the rate of SiO_2 film deposition on temperature.[93]

Thin oxide films can be also obtained by pyrolysis of organic compounds, e.g.

$$Si(OC_2H_5)_4 \rightarrow SiO_2 + 4C_2H_4 + H_2O \tag{3.4}$$

$$Ti(OC_3H_7)_4 \rightarrow TiO_2 + 4C_3H_6 + 2H_2O \tag{3.5}$$

Pyrolytic decomposition of $Si(OC_2H_5)_4$ can be conducted in the presence of oxygen which lowers the substrate temperature to as low as 570 K. The degree of perfection of the films of SiO_2 obtained with this method is comparable with that of thermally grown films.[97]

The second of the above given reactions was used by Yokozawa et al.[98] for preparation of thin films of TiO_2. Vapours of $Ti(OC_3H_7)_4$ were introduced in a stream of nitrogen into the reaction chamber heated with infrared radiation. The vapours of $Ti(OC_3H_7)_4$ were decomposed and the resulting molecules of TiO_2 were deposited on the silicon substrate. The dependence of the growth rate of TiO_2 film on the reciprocal temperature for various partial pressures of oxygen is shown in Fig. 3.19. X-ray analysis and electron diffraction showed that the TiO_2 films prepared in the oxygen-free atmosphere had the anatase structure, and were amorphous when oxygen was present during the film growth.

The properties of the films prepared by reactions in vapour phase are strongly dependent on the conditions of the film deposition. For each reaction resulting in the formation of the thin film, there exists a minimal temperature below which the rate of deposition is insufficient. For example the minimal temperature for reaction (3.4) is about 970 K. Below this temperature, the rate of the film growth is very low. There exists also for each reaction a maximum temperature above which the properties of the films are

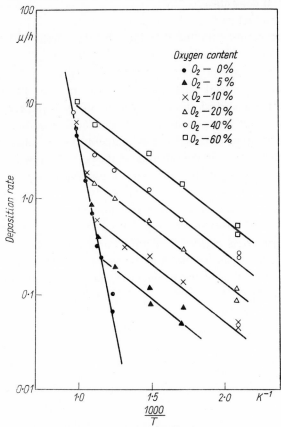

FIG. 3.19. Dependence of the deposition rate of TiO_2 film obtained by the chemical reaction method on temperature for various oxygen pressures.[98]

undesirable. The properties of thin films prepared by reactions in the gas phase depend on the composition of the mixture of gases and vapours, in particular on the presence of the vapours of impurities.

Recently Ohnishi, Yoshizawa and Ibuki[99] described a new method for preparing thin films of ZnO, based on the oxidation of vacuum-evaporated, thin films of ZnSe:

$$ZnSe^{(s)} + 3/2\ O_2^{(g)} = ZnO^{(s)} + SeO_2^{(g)} \tag{3.6}$$

at the temperature of about 670 K.

3.6. Epitaxial Growth of Thin Films

The term *epitaxy* denotes the process of orientated crystallization on a foreign monocrystalline substrate. The monocrystalline films obtained in this way are, however, imperfect, showing high concentration of dislocations, twin crystals, etc. The epitaxial growth of crystals depends on four principal factors:

(1) type of substrate,

(2) temperature of the substrate,

(3) rate of the film deposition,

(4) pressure of residual gases in the apparatus.

To obtain perfect monocrystalline thin films by this method, the substrate surface should be uniform and very pure.

The substrate temperature plays a main role in the process of film growth. At low temperatures the size of crystal seeds is small, their number being great. Owing to the low mobility of the adsorbed atoms, only some of them can reach the crystal seed. Large forces, acting during the condensation, lead to the formation of crystals of various orientation. Hence, the films obtained at low temperatures are imperfect, or polycrystalline. At too high temperatures, on the other hand, the crystals grow in the form of needles and plates. The best monocrystalline thin films are prepared at a determined temperature, corresponding to the conditions of the film growth of the given oxide.

The properties of the epitaxial films are also influenced by the rate of their growth and pressure of residual gases in the apparatus. At high growth rates, the crystals obtained, are as a rule, less perfect. The unfavourable influence of the residual gases on the quality of the films can be alleviated by using high vacuum.

A more detailed discussion of the problem of epitaxial growth of thin films can be found in the literature.[100-103]

PART TWO

CRYSTAL STRUCTURE AND IMPERFECTIONS OF OXIDE MATERIALS

CHAPTER 4

STRUCTURE AND DEFECTS OF OXIDE CRYSTALS

4.1. Crystal Structure of Oxides

Monoxides MO crystallize most often in the structure of the NaCl type, some of them, e.g. ZnO and BeO, show the structure of wurtzite.

Crystal lattice of the NaCl-type is composed of two face-centred cubic sublattices—the cation and anion sublattice. In this lattice each ion is surrounded by six others with opposite sign, the coordination number for both cations and anions being 6. The unit cell of the oxides of this structure is shown in Fig. 4.1. Crystal structure of the wurtzite

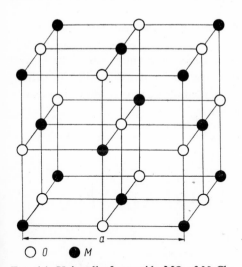

FIG. 4.1. Unit cell of an oxide MO of NaCl structure: a—lattice parameter.

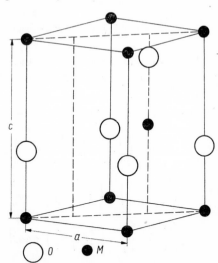

FIG. 4.2. Unit cell of an oxide MO of wurtzite structure: a and c—lattice parameters.

type has hexagonal symmetry. It contains two molecules of MO. The unit cell of this structure is given in Fig. 4.2. The coordinates of atoms in this structure are:

$$M: \quad (000), \quad \left(\frac{2}{3}\,\frac{1}{3}\,\frac{1}{2}\right)$$

$$O: \quad (00u), \quad \left(\frac{2}{3}\,\frac{1}{3}\,\frac{1}{2}+u\right)$$

In this type of structure, atoms of one kind are tetrahedrally bound to four atoms of another kind, the coordination number for both kinds of atoms being 4. In the ideal case, when the tetrahedral coordination is not perturbed, coordinate u is 3/8. The c/a ratio assumes the value of 1·63.

Dioxides MO_2 possess usually the crystal structure of fluorite or rutile. The fluorite structure is composed of close-packed, face-centred cubic sublattice of cations, in which all tetrahedral sites are occupied by anions. Each cation is tetrahedrally surrounded

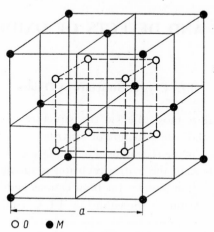

O 0   ● M

Fig. 4.3. Unit cell of an oxide MO_2 of fluorite type: a—lattice parameter.

by 8 anions, that are located in the corners of a cube, each anion has as its nearest neighbours four cations that form a tetrahedron. The coordination number of cations is then 8 and that of anions 4. The unit cell MO_2 of the fluorite type is shown in Fig. 4.3. The coordinates of cations and anions are as follows:

M: (000), $\left(\dfrac{1}{2}\,\dfrac{1}{2}\,0\right)$, $\left(\dfrac{1}{2}\,0\,\dfrac{1}{2}\right)$ and $\left(0\,\dfrac{1}{2}\,\dfrac{1}{2}\right)$

O: $\left(\dfrac{1}{4}\,\dfrac{1}{4}\,\dfrac{1}{4}\right)$, $\left(\dfrac{3}{4}\,\dfrac{1}{4}\,\dfrac{1}{4}\right)$, $\left(\dfrac{3}{4}\,\dfrac{3}{4}\,\dfrac{1}{4}\right)$, $\left(\dfrac{1}{4}\,\dfrac{3}{4}\,\dfrac{1}{4}\right)$, $\left(\dfrac{1}{4}\,\dfrac{1}{4}\,\dfrac{3}{4}\right)$,

$\left(\dfrac{3}{4}\,\dfrac{1}{4}\,\dfrac{3}{4}\right)$, $\left(\dfrac{1}{4}\,\dfrac{3}{4}\,\dfrac{3}{4}\right)$ and $\left(\dfrac{3}{4}\,\dfrac{3}{4}\,\dfrac{3}{4}\right)$

The fluorite structure is found with many oxides that possess four-valent cations of large radius such as (Zr, Hf, Ce, Pr, Tb, Po, Th, Pa, U, Np, Pu, Am) O_2. The anti-fluorite structure is shown by oxides of alkali metals: (Li_2, Na_2, K_2, Rb_2) O. In this latter structure cations occupy the positions which in the fluorite structure were occupied by anions, anions being located in the previous positions of cations.

The rutile structure has tetragonal symmetry. The unit cell in this case is given by a body-centred perpendicular parallelepiped, the centre and corners of which are occupied by cations (Fig. 4.4). Each cation is octahedrally coordinated by six anions, each of the latter being surrounded by three cations located in the corners of equilateral triangle.

The coordination numbers for cations and anions are 6 and 3, respectively, and the coordinates of ions:

M: (000), $\left(\dfrac{1}{2}\ \dfrac{1}{2}\ \dfrac{1}{2}\right)$

O: $\pm\ (uu0)$, $\left(\dfrac{1}{2}+u,\ \dfrac{1}{2}-u,\ \dfrac{1}{2}\right)$

For rutile, the c/a ratio is 0·644 and $u = 0·31$.

The rutile structure is found with oxides of four-valent metals, such as (Ti, Nb, Ta, Cr, Mo, W, Mn, Ru, Os, Ir, Ge, Sn, Pb, Te) O_2.

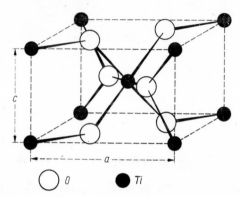

FIG. 4.4. Unit cell of an oxide MO_2 of rutile structure: a and c—lattice parameters.

Silica crystallizes in several modifications in all of which silicon and oxygen ions possess the same coordination. Eeach silicon ion is tetrahedrally coordinated by four oxygen ions, each oxygen ion is bound to two silicon ions, thus each oxygen ion is shared by two tetrahedra. The crystal structures of the SiO_2 modifications are rather complex and uncommon. The most important of these modifications are quartz, crystobalite and tridymite. Their densities are respectively 2·655, 2·30 and 2·27 g/cm³.

Many trioxides of the M_2O_3 type crystallize in the corundum structure (α-Al_2O_3). These include Bi_2O_3, Ga_2O_3, Cr_2O_3, α-Fe_2O_3 and others. The corundum structure belongs to a trigonal system, and resembles the rhombohedrally distorted NaCl structure, in which sodium or chloride ions are replaced by the Al_2O_3 groups. The unit cell of the corundum type is shown in Fig. 4.5.

Figure 4.6 shows a unit cell of cuprite type (Cu_2O). Each anion in this structure is tetrahedrally surrounded by four cations. The coordinates of anions and cations are:

M: $\left(\dfrac{1}{4}\ \dfrac{1}{4}\ \dfrac{1}{4}\right)$, $\left(\dfrac{3}{4}\ \dfrac{3}{4}\ \dfrac{3}{4}\right)$, $\left(\dfrac{3}{4}\ \dfrac{3}{4}\ \dfrac{1}{4}\right)$, $\left(\dfrac{1}{4}\ \dfrac{3}{4}\ \dfrac{3}{4}\right)$

O: (000), $\left(\dfrac{1}{2}\ \dfrac{1}{2}\ \dfrac{1}{2}\right)$

The crystal structure of the cuprite type is seldom found in nature. Beside cuprous oxide, also Ag_2O crystallizes in this form.

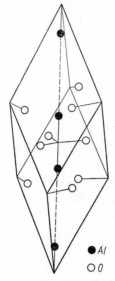

FIG. 4.5. Unit cell of M_2O_3 of corundum structure.

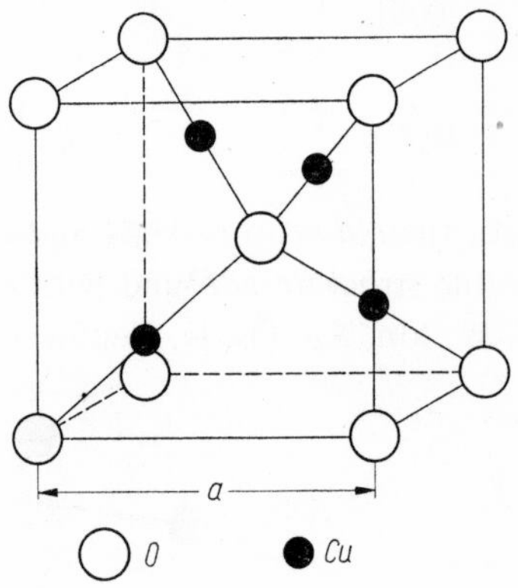

FIG. 4.6. Unit cell of M_2O of cuprite type.

4.2. Types of Defects in Oxide Crystals

An ideal crystal is the crystal of the perfectly ordered space lattice in which all interstitial positions are empty, all normal lattice sites are occupied by appropriate atoms or ions, and all valence electrons of these atoms are placed in the valence band filling it completely. The ideal crystal has thus the smallest internal energy and theoretically can exist only at the temperature of absolute zero. The real crystals existing in nature can never reach this ideal state, even at the temperature of absolute zero. They contain always some structural imperfections, which may be formed during the growth of crystals, or in the course of mechanical or thermal treatment of the grown crystals, and also by action of various radiation, etc.

The defects of the crystal lattice may be classified into two main groups:

(1) Defects of very small size called point defects, which can exist in equilibrium with the lattice and with another phase surrounding the crystal, for example with a gas phase, and

(2) Defects of larger size, e.g. dislocations and grain boundaries which cannot exist in equilibrium with the lattice and with another phase surrounding the crystal.

Point defects in the crystal lattice may be classified into:

A. Atomic defects:
    1. Native atomic defects
        (a) vacancies, i.e. empty lattice sites,
        (b) native interstitial atoms or ions,
        (c) antistructure defects formed by incorporation of misplaced native atoms into some lattice sites,
    2. Foreign atoms incorporated into the crystal lattice.

B. Electronic defects:
  1. Quasi-free electrons,
  2. Quasi-free holes.
C. Polarons.
D. Excitons.
E. Phonons.

Atomic defects, resulting from native disorder and from the presence of foreign atoms may be moreover divided into:

(1) neutral atomic defects, the effective charge of which with respect to the lattice is zero, and

(2) ionized atomic defects, which exhibit some effective charge with respect to the lattice.

The latter are created by ionization of neutral atomic defects. This process leads to the appearance of electronic defects: quasi-free electrons and holes. It should be noted that quasi-free electrons and holes can be also formed by transfer of valence electrons from the valence band to the conduction band. In oxides this process is of minor importance owing to the relatively large forbidden energy gaps in these compounds.

In part two, atomic and electronic defects in oxide crystals will be considered in detail from the point of view of thermodynamics and the band theory of crystals. From non-equilibrium defects, only most relevant to semiconducting properties, i.e. dislocations and grain boundaries and their interaction with atomic and electronic defects, will be discussed briefly. The properties of polarons will be reviewed in Chapter 9 pertaining to mobility of the current carriers.

Excitons constitute a separate subject beyond the scope of this book. The extensive discussion of these defects may be found in the monograph of Dexter and Knox.[104]

4.3. Dislocations and Grain Boundaries

Two basic types of dislocations may be distinguished: edge dislocations and screw dislocations.

The edge dislocation may be visualized as a line imperfection of the structure, created by inserting an additional atomic half-plane, as shown in Fig. 4.7. The boundary of

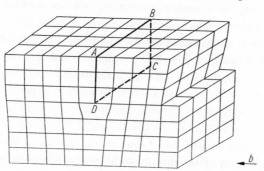

FIG. 4.7. A fragment of lattice with an edge dislocation: *ABCD*—additional atomic half-plane, *CD*—dislocation line, *b*—Burgers vector.

this additional half-plane constitutes a dislocation line. This line runs through the crystal and may be terminated on its surface or on other dislocations. The dislocation line need not be a straight line, nor it need lie in one plane. Two types of the edge dislocations may be distinguished: positive and negative edge dislocations.

The screw dislocation is considered also as a linear imperfection of the structure in which atoms of the crystal are shifted ones with respect to others in such a manner, that atomic planes are arranged in a helix characteristic of a screw, with a dislocation line as an axis (Fig. 4.8). The screw dislocation may have clockwise or anti-clockwise direction.

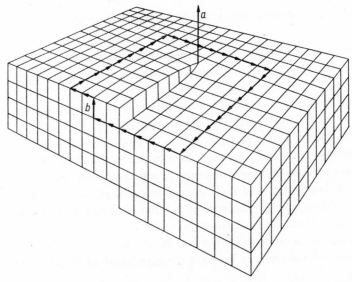

FIG. 4.8. A fragment of lattice with a screw dislocation and Burgers circuit: a—dislocation line, b—Burgers vector.

Dislocations in real crystals may be described in terms of so called Burgers circuit: around a dislocation, a closed circuit of arbitrary shape is described comprising all the crystal sites in the region of an undistorted crystal. The associated circuit is drawn in a perfect crystal, making use of one-to-one correspondence between atoms. In the latter case the circuit is not closed: the vector **b** necessary to close the circuit is independent of the shape of this latter and is called the *Burgers vector*.[105] The schematic presentation of the Burgers circuit is shown in Fig. 4.9. The Burgers vector is characteristic of a given dislocation and determines its type. An edge dislocation is perpendicular to its Burgers vector (cf. Figs. 4.7 and 4.9), whereas a screw dislocation is parallel to it (cf. Fig. 4.8). The problem, considered here only briefly, has been extensively discussed by Frank.[106]

A dislocation may move through the crystal under the action of small forces, which leads to a glide of certain part of the crystal in the vicinity of the dislocation past the other part. The mechanism of the motion of an edge dislocation may be explained by a simple model shown in Fig. 4.10, which shows a section of a crystal lattice of the NaCl type containing an edge dislocation.

Atom 2 is situated in the centre between its neighbours 4 and 5, placed in the adjacent atomic plane. If no external forces occur in the crystal under consideration, atom 2 situated on the dislocation line is attracted with the same force by atom 4 and 5, and is thus in equilibrium with the lattice. If some stresses exist in the crystal, formed for

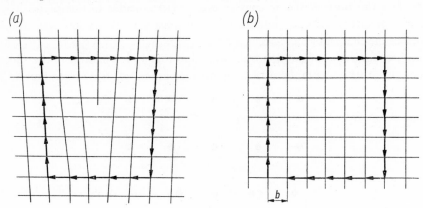

FIG. 4.9. Burgers circuit: (a) cross-section of a real crystal with an edge dislocation and the Burgers circuit, (b) corresponding part of an ideal crystal; b—Burgers vector.

instance by an action of an external force F as shown in Fig. 4.10, then atom 2 will be subjected to the net force directed to the left, which will tend to displace this atom so that it will be placed on the same line as atom 4.

The analogous forces will act upon atoms 1 and 3. As the result of this action atom 2 moves a little to the left, thus forming a new row of atoms (2, 4), and atom 1 at the

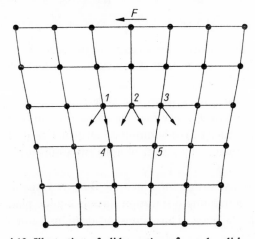

FIG. 4.10. Illustration of glide motion of an edge dislocation.

same time produces a new dislocation. It follows from the above considerations that the edge dislocation may be displaced to the new equilibrium position under the action of very small stresses. The smallest force necessary to glide the dislocation is called the *Peierls force*. It assumes the smallest value for planes of close packing of atoms. These planes are called the glide planes.

So far, we have discussed only the movement of an edge dislocation by a glide. Generally, it may be shown that a dislocation of any orientation can move in arbitrary direction perpendicular to the dislocation line. The movement of this dislocation may be resolved into two components: one along the glide plane determined by the dislocation line and the Burgers vector, and another, perpendicular to this plane. The first component describes the glide motion of the dislocation, the second one—the climb motion. For the climb motion to occur not only the existence of stresses but also diffusion of atoms are required. This motion is illustrated in Fig. 4.11. The edge of the additional half-plane of atoms is composed of a number of atoms of incomplete bonds. These

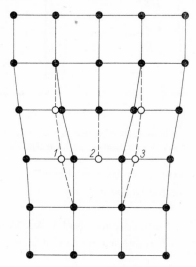

FIG. 4.11. Illustration of climb motion of an edge dislocation.

atoms may be hence relatively easily removed from the edge of the dislocation or added to it. The addition of atoms to the edge is equivalent to a local shift of the dislocation by one glide plane as shown in Fig. 4.11 (the dashed line 2). By analogy, the removal of atoms from the edge leads to a shift by one glide plane but in the opposite direction. Evidently the motion described above may be induced by diffusion of interstitial ions or vacancies towards the edge of the additional half-plane of atoms. The climb motion of a dislocation is accompanied by a shift of adjacent atoms in the crystal lattice (lines 1 and 3 in Fig. 4.11).

In the case of a screw dislocation for which the Burgers vector is parallel to the dislocation line, each plane containing dislocation lines is a glide plane and any motion of this dislocation becomes a glide. Thus screw dislocations cannot move by the climb motion.

The line imperfections discussed above occur in crystals in high concentrations. Crystals of metals and ionic compounds contain usually about 10^6 dislocations per cm^2 of their internal surface area. Covalent crystals are in most cases more perfect, showing about 10^4 dislocations per cm^2, or even less.

Dislocations may be created already in the process of formation of crystal as a result of growth faults, many of these defects are also formed during plastic deformation of crystals. The mechanism of the formation of dislocations was proposed by Frank and Read, and is known as the Frank–Read source.[107]

These authors described a dislocation source in the form of a mobile segment AB of the dislocation line, fixed at its ends with immobile points. Such points may be provided by atoms of impurities or by other immobile dislocations. Under the influence of the applied force F, perpendicular to the dislocation line, the segment AB begins to bow out in the glide plane as shown in Fig. 4.12. The force F produces the shear

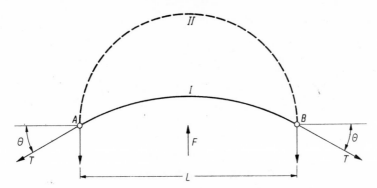

FIG. 4.12. Deformation of a fragment of an edge dislocation caused by an external force.

stress F/bL, where b is the Burgers vector of this dislocation and L is the length of the segment AB. On the other hand, creation of a dislocation requires certain energy, necessary for surmounting interatomic forces and for breaking some bonds. This energy is proportional to the length of the dislocation line. It may be thus said that there exists tension of the dislocation line T, tangent to this line, which counteracts the increase in its length.

Let us consider now the position of the section of a dislocation line denoted by I in Fig. 4.12. The force F producing the bend of the dislocation line is balanced by components of two tensions T of the line segment, thus $F = 2T \sin \theta$. The shear stress in this case is:

$$\tau = \frac{2T}{bL} \sin \theta \qquad (4.1)$$

Let us assume that the shear stress increases so that the line segment adopts the form II. The shear stress in this case is:

$$\tau_c = \frac{2T}{bL} \qquad (4.2)$$

since $\theta = \pi/2$. The stress τ_c is termed a critical stress.

With the further increase in τ the external force F is not balanced by tension T of the line. Thus for $\tau < \tau_c$, the segment AB is bowed out, whereas at $\tau > \tau_c$ it expands dynamically.

Figure 4.13 shows the successive forms from 1 to 5 of the segment AB for $\tau > \tau_c$. As seen from this figure, fragments of the dislocation line denoted by 1 and 2 move in the opposite directions in the same glide plane to join finally together. As the result of this, a loop 5a is formed which increases further and the initial segment *AB* is regenerated (segment 5b). It follows from the above considerations that this segment may act as a constant source of dislocation loops. It is recognized that the Frank–Read

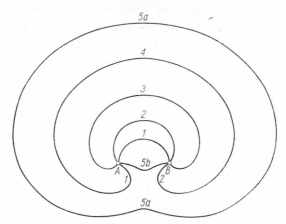

FIG. 4.13. The Frank–Read source.

source is the most important source of dislocations in crystals subjected to plastic treatment. Obviously this source begins to operate when the stress τ is higher than the critical stress.

Other non-equilibrium defects relevant to semiconducting properties are provided by grain boundaries.

They may be formed during crystallization, when this process commences in two or more points. There are formed then two or more crystals growing independently one of another. Crystallographic axes of these crystals have as a rule different orientations, so that when the crystals come into contact they cannot be matched completely in the atomic scale. The defect of structure thus formed is called a *grain boundary*. It follows from the above discussion that the grown crystalline material may be composed of aggregates of grains, each of which is a single crystal separated from an adjacent grain by a grain boundary. The most successful model of these defects proposed by Burgers[108] and Bragg[109] and also by Shockley and Read[110] assumes that the grain boundary is in reality nothing else but a system of dislocations.

Figure 4.14 shows a cross-section of a cubic crystal composed of two single crystals, and the dislocation model of the grain boundary, illustrating clearly that the grain boundary in this case is composed of several edge dislocations.

In recent years increasing attention has been paid to the free surface of a crystal. This surface constitutes a special type of a defect and in many cases exerts an essential influence on the properties of semiconductors. Even a perfect surface of a crystal of the ideal ordering of atoms constitutes a defect in the sense that continuity of atomic planes of the crystal lattice is broken on it. The real surface which is usually obtained is far from being ideal and disorder among the atoms may range even several hundreds of the atomic distance deep in the crystal. Moreover, the atoms of the surface are chemically active and hence the free surface may adsorb atoms from the surrounding atmosphere or react with them. In the latter case, a mono- or multi-atomic layer of another chemical compound is formed on the crystal surface.

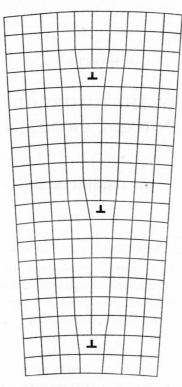

FIG. 4.14. Dislocation model of a grain boundary.

The detailed review of non-equilibrium defects can be found in monographs by Rhodes,[111] Van Bueren, [112] Shockley and co-workers[113] and Read.[114]

CHAPTER 5

FOUNDATIONS OF THE THEORY OF POINT DEFECTS IN OXIDE CRYSTALS

5.1. Historical Outline

The problem of composition of inorganic compounds arose already at the time when foundations of modern chemistry were being developed.

At the turn of the 18th and 19th centuries this problem was the subject of a strong controversy between two French chemists, Proust and Berthollet. Proust put forward a hypothesis, stating that in a chemical compound the component elements occur in strictly defined proportions which can be expressed by the ratio of small integers, these ratios being constant for a given compound. For instance in the case of ferrous oxide, the appropriate chemical formula was, according to Proust, FeO and not $Fe_{0.99}O$ or $Fe_{0.95}O$. Berthollet claimed controversially that elements can react in varying proportions.

The atomic theory of Dalton turned in 1807 the tide of the battle to Proust and his followers, and his hypothesis became one of the basic laws of chemistry, known as the *law of constant proportions*, and unquestioned throughout the whole 19th century. At the beginning of the 20th century, the Russian chemist Kurnikov observed that a great number of inorganic compounds did not obey this law. Kurnikov suggested a name *berthollides* to distinguish these compounds from so-called *daltonides* for which the deviations from the law of constant proportions were not found at that time.

The present state of knowledge gives grounds for the presumption that all inorganic compounds may exhibit smaller or larger deviations from stoichiometry, although for the prevailing majority of these substances the range of their stability is not as yet established. Hence, the term "non-stoichiometry in chemical compounds" appears more correct than "non-stoichiometric compounds", as it was suggested earlier by Libowitz.[115] Obviously, the deviations from stoichiometry in chemical compounds are conceivable only owing to the presence of atomic defects in crystals. Oxides and sulphides are commonly quoted as examples of the compounds which show large deviations from stoichiometry.

The first theoretical approach to the problem of atomic and electronic defects in ionic crystals is due to Wagner and Schottky.[116, 117] Employing the laws of statistical thermodynamics, these authors derived in 1930–5 general relationships between equili-

66

brium concentrations of the point defects, and dependences of these concentrations on temperature and partial pressures of crystal components present in the gas phase surrounding the crystal.

The same authors proved also that the analogous relationships may be derived by applying the law of mass action to various quasi-chemical reactions which describe, in a formal way, processes of formation of point defects, regarding the latter species (e.g. cationic or anionic vacancies, electron holes and electrons) as chemical molecules. Thus Wagner and Schottky originated the first theoretical method for studying point defects in ionic crystals, by applying the law of mass action to these defects.

The method proposed by Wagner and Schottky contains however certain inexactness, resulting from the assumption that all the electrons not involved in chemical bonds are quasi-free. The band model of solids, on the other hand, shows that such an assumption is justified only in cases in which donor levels are situated very close to the bottom of a conduction band and acceptor levels—very close to the upper part of a valence band.[118] The band theory and experimental data point out instead that in semiconducting compounds, the energy levels which appear due to the presence of defects in the crystals lattice may be situated in various parts of the forbidden energy gap,[225] and then the Wagner–Schottky theory cannot explain satisfactorily the structure of point defects and physical properties of the considered crystals.

The band structure of energy levels in crystals was taken into account in the extended theory of defect structure proposed by Kröger and Vink.[119,120] These authors employed the approximate graphical method of solving the defect equilibria equations suggested by Brouwer.[121]

The extended theory of point defects was based however on the law of mass action, i.e. on the same theoretical bases as the theory of Wagner and Schottky, disregarding the fact that the latter theory was concerned with a particular case of complete ionization of point defects.

It was thus necessary to prove in terms of statistical thermodynamics and the band theory the applicability of the law of mass action to processes of ionization of atomic defects for cases when the structure of energy levels in the forbidden energy gap was complex. In particular, limits of applicability of this law to defect equilibria demanded an examination. This problem was considered theoretically by Brebrick[122] for a simple binary compound, assuming that the atomic defects were provided by the vacancies in both sublattices of the crystal. It has been shown that in this case the law of mass action can be applied to the atomic and electronic defects, provided that the following conditions are fulfilled:

(1) deviations from stoichiometry are small, and
(2) electron or hole gas is non-degenerate.

The extended theory of point defects proposed by Kröger and Vink is at present extensively employed for interpretation of a number of physical properties of crystals which exhibit deviations from stoichiometry, and it affords the adequate explanation of these properties.

It should be noted, however, that the development of this branch of science is hindered by experimental difficulties. These are encountered both in preparation of very pure single crystals and in measurements required for determination of physical properties influenced by defects, since these measurements have to be performed in the wide range of high temperatures and partial pressures of the crystal components present in the gas phase surrounding the crystal.

5.2. Types of Electrically Neutral Atomic Defects in Oxide Crystals and Quasi-chemical Reactions of Defects

The system of symbols used throughout this book is that proposed by Kröger and Vink,[120,229] which is at present supplanting the other systems from the literature. According to the Kröger and Vink system, all normal constituents of a crystal lattice are regarded as if they were atoms, irrespectively of the type of a crystal (covalent or ionic). In the case of a covalent crystal, obviously such a system is adequate, whereas in ionic crystals only the effective charge of a centre is of importance and thus writing down a normal ionic charge in all reactions seems indispensable. In the latter case, the charges of ions can be readily supplemented if necessary.

Theoretical considerations concerning atomic and electronic defects in oxide crystals will be carried out taking as an example a hypothetical oxide MO of the cubic structure of NaCl type, where M indicates a more positive element (a metal or a semiconducting element) and O denotes oxygen. Electrically neutral with respect to the lattice atomic defects in a pure crystal of the MO type are:

(1) Neutral vacancies in the sublattice M: vacant lattice sites in the sublattice M, indicated by the symbol V_M^x. Thus in an ionic lattice, for example in NiO, V_{Ni}^x indicates a defect of the structure resulting from the removal of a Ni^{2+} ion, together with two electrons, from the cationic sublattice.

(2) Neutral vacancies in the oxygen sublattice: vacant lattice sites in this sublattice denoted by V_O^x. The symbol V_O^x denotes the defect formed by the removal of an oxygen atom (not an O^{2-} ion) from the oxygen sublattice. Defects V_M^x and V_O^x are illustrated in Fig. 5.1.

(3) Neutral interstitial atoms denoted by the symbols M_i^x and O_i^x. For example in a ZnO crystal Zn_i^x denotes a defect formed by incorporation of a Zn atom into the interstitial site (Fig. 5.2).

(4) Neutral antistructure defects: by these are meant the defects created by incorporation of oxygen atoms into some lattice sites of the sublattice M, and incorporation of M atoms into some sites of the oxygen sublattice. They are indicated by the symbols O_M^x and M_O^x, respectively (Fig. 5.3).[†]

The defects enumerated above may be distributed in a crystal statistically, or they may form complexes by the process of association. Electrically neutral with respect to the lattice associated centres are indicated by brackets, e.g. $(V_M V_O)^x$, $(V_M M_i)^x$ $(V_O O_i)^x$, $(M_O O_M)^x$. As seen, in the Kröger and Vink system the defects are denoted

---

† One may find in the literature also such names as Frenkel and Schottky defects. These names have rather the historical meaning at present, and will not be introduced in this book.

by symbols determining their nature, whereas the subscripts indicate the position of defects. The asterisk stresses the fact of the effective neutrality with respect to the lattice. The concentration of defects is denoted usually by bracketing a given symbol. For example $[M_i^x]$ indicates the concentration of interstitial atoms M_i^x.

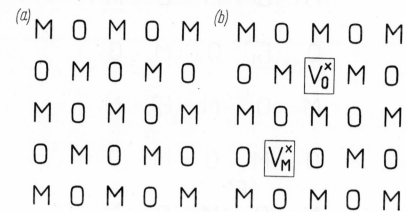

FIG. 5.1. Vacancies in a hypothetical crystal MO: (a) a perfect crystal, (b) neutral vacancies V_M^x and V_O^x in a crystal MO.

All the point defects given above and their associates are called *native atomic defects*.

In the crystals containing impurities there occur beside native defects also other point defects created due to the presence of foreign atoms. These atoms may be incor-

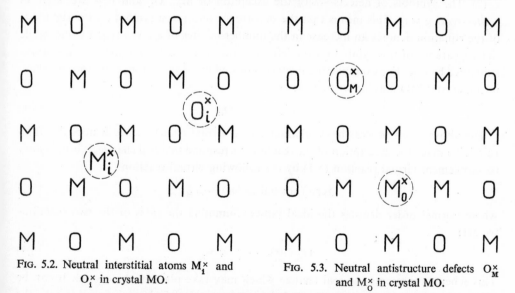

FIG. 5.2. Neutral interstitial atoms M_i^x and O_i^x in crystal MO.

FIG. 5.3. Neutral antistructure defects O_M^x and M_O^x in crystal MO.

porated either into normal lattice sites or into interstitial spaces. The symbols assigned to them are F_M^x or F_O^x for the former case and F_i^x for the latter one (Fig. 5.4).

Formation of various types of point defects by thermal vibrations of atoms or ions in the crystal lattice may be described schematically with the aid of equations of quasi-

chemical reactions. Since the correct formulation of these reactions is of essential importance in the theory of defects, it seems appropriate to present the rules which should be
observed in the description of the defect reactions. They are:

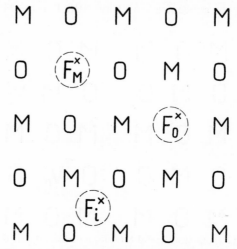

FIG. 5.4. Neutral foreign atoms F_M^x, F_O^x and F_i^x incorporated into crystal lattice MO.

(1) A number of sites in the sublattice M of a crystal MO should be equal to the
number of sites in the sublattice O. Obviously the total number of the sites may change.

(2) The symbols of defects—with the exception of M_i^x, O_i^x and F_i^x—are used in
a *site-creating* way. This means that the occurrence of a given symbol on the right side
of the equation denotes an increase in the number of sites of a given type by one, while
the appearance of this symbol on the left side, a decrease in the number of sites in this
sublattice by one. For example, the incorporation of an oxygen atom from the gas phase
into a crystal MO may be written as:

$$1/2 \, O_2^{(g)} \rightarrow O_O^x \tag{5.1}$$

The above given process has a character of a virtual change, since it does not fulfil
rule 1. To make the description of the reaction correspond to a real change, it is necessary
to supplement virtual reaction (5.1) by the following virtual reaction:

$$\text{zero (normal order)} \rightarrow V_M^x \tag{5.2}$$

where normal order denotes the ideal lattice. Summing the sides of the two reactions
we get:

$$1/2 \, O_2^{(g)} \rightarrow O_O^x + V_M^x \tag{5.3}$$

This scheme represents the real change which may take place in the crystal. It can be
easily shown that the real reaction of the incorporation of aluminium oxide into the
crystal lattice of zinc oxide can be resolved into two virtual reactions:

$$Al_2O_3 \rightarrow 2\,Al_{Zn}^x + O_2^{(g)} + 1/2 \, O_2^{(g)} \tag{5.4}$$

$$O_2^{(g)} \rightarrow 2\,O_O^x \tag{5.5}$$

The overall reaction may be written as:

$$Al_2O_3 \rightarrow 2Al_{Zn}^x + 2O_O^x + 1/2 O_2^{(g)} \tag{5.6}$$

It follows from the above given considerations that the real reactions involved in the formation of defects may be represented by a combination of virtual reactions.

(3) Mass conservation is the third rule that must be observed when writing down the defect reactions. This means that sums of masses on the both sides of the reaction equation should be equal. Vacancies have mass equal to zero.

(4) If interstitial atoms are present in the crystal, interstitial spaces should be, for the sake of the exactness, treated separately by introducing a concept of an interstitial vacancy V_i^x. If, for example, an atom $M^{(g)}$ from the gas phase is incorporated into interstitial space of the crystal MO, the corresponding process should be written down as the reaction:

$$M^{(g)} + V_i^x \rightarrow M_i^x \tag{5.7}$$

If no interstitial atoms occur in the crystal, introduction of interstitial vacancies is not necessary. This problem will be considered later at the discussion of chemical potential of defects.

In the description of *quasi*-chemical reactions representing the formation of ionized atomic defects and electronic defects, one more and very important condition should be taken into account, namely the condition of electrical neutrality of the lattice. This will be dealt with in the forthcoming section.

5.3. Factors Determining the Equilibrium Concentration of Defects

As already mentioned in the introduction, a perfect crystal has the minimal internal energy at the temperature of absolute zero. At this temperature all atoms or ions occupy normal lattice sites, remaining immobile. At the higher temperatures, atoms in the crystal perform vibrations around the lattice sites, the mean energy of which is proportional to the absolute temperature. The energy of this vibrational motion shows, however, fluctuations owing to which single atoms or groups of atoms may acquire energy considerable higher than the mean energy. Such fluctuations of thermal motion may lead to the formation of native atomic defects, e.g. vacancies or interstitial atoms.

The vacancies may be originated at the surface of a crystal and then migrate to its bulk by diffusion. The crystal surface constitutes thus the inexhaustible source of vacancies. Real crystals possess more efficient sources of vacancies in the bulk of crystals such as non-equilibrium defects, most often dislocations, and in the case of polycrystalline substances—grain boundaries. The vacancies may also migrate from the bulk of a crystal to its surface or to non-equilibrium defects to be annihilated there.

Interstitial atoms may be created by the displacement of an atom from a lattice site to an interstitial position, or they may be incorporated into the crystal from the gas phase. The fluctuations of energy of vibrations may induce also the formation of anti-structure defects. The direct exchange of positions of atoms M and O is of low probability for geometrical and energetic reasons. The same reasons determine also the type of defects, predominating in a given crystal under definite thermodynamic conditions.

Let us consider now the factors which determine the concentration of point defects at thermodynamic equilibrium.

According to the laws of chemical thermodynamics,[234] every spontaneous process occurring in a crystal at a constant external pressure is accompanied by a decrease in the Gibbs free energy of the whole crystal; thus for $T = $ const the following condition must be fulfilled:

$$\Delta g = \Delta h - T\Delta s < 0 \tag{5.8}$$

where Δg is the change in the Gibbs free energy, Δh and Δs are respectively the changes of the enthalpy and entropy of the crystal brought about by a given process. The change of the enthalpy at the constant external pressure is given by:

$$\Delta h = \Delta u + p\Delta v \tag{5.9}$$

where Δu denotes the change of the internal energy, p is the external pressure and Δv is the change of volume of the crystal due to the process occurring in it.

The formation of point defects produces only very small changes in the crystal volume and hence the term $p\Delta v$ can be neglected and the enthalpy change may be regarded as approximately equal to the change of the internal energy of the crystal. Thus, when discussing the structure of point defects one may consider the notations of enthalpy and energy as interchangeable.

Let us take now a hypothetical crystal MO which exhibits a tendency to form neutral complexes of the $(V_M V_O)^\times$ type, and let us denote the Gibbs free energy of this crystal

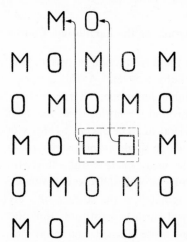

FIG. 5.5. Formation of complex defects $(V_M V_O)^\times$ in a hypothetical oxide MO.

at 0 K by $g(N, 0) = h(N, 0)$, where N is the total number of pairs of lattice sites in the crystal MO. The formation of these complexes at higher temperatures is accompanied by the increase in the enthalpy of the crystal, since the creation of each such complex requires the performance of work necessary for the transfer of the atoms M and O from the bulk of the crystal to its surface, as shown in Fig. 5.5. (The total number of atoms M and O in the crystal is not changed, but appearance of each single complex $(V_M V_O)^\times$ increases the number of sites in either sublattice by one). Therefore with the increase in the total number of the considered defects, the enthalpy of the whole crystal MO increases.

The increase in the number of complexes $(V_M V_O)^\times$ leads to the increase also in the crystal entropy, since randomness of distribution of atoms in the lattice sites is increased. The total entropy in crystal may be resolved into configurational entropy s_c and vibrational entropy s_v. The first one represents the randomness of distribution of complexes $(V_M V_O)^\times$ in the crystal and can be described by the following formula:

$$s_c = k \ln \frac{N!}{n!(N-n)!} \tag{5.10}$$

where N is a number of sites in one sublattice of the crystal MO, n is a number of complexes $(V_M V_O)^\times$ in the crystal, k is the Boltzmann constant. The expression $N!/n!(N-n)!$ is the number of ways of distributing n complexes among N lattice sites (thermodynamic probability of the system).

Vibrational entropy represents randomness of location of atoms in the crystal, which results from their vibrations. The $(V_M V_O)^\times$ complexes cause the increase in the vibrational entropy of the crystal, since the amplitude of oscillations of atoms adjacent to them is higher than the average amplitude of other atoms in the crystal.

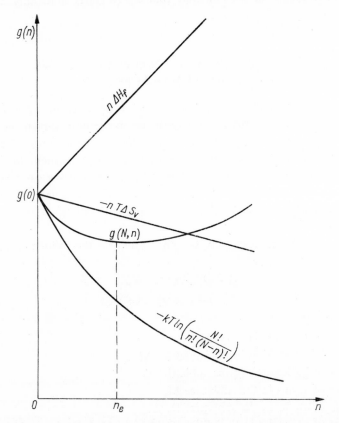

FIG. 5.6. Dependence of Gibbs free energy and its component terms on the concentration of defects.

Thus according to eq. (5.8) the Gibbs free energy of the crystal MO depends on the total number of the complexes. Let us denote the function corresponding to a given number n of the complexes by $g(N, n)$. The dependence of the change in the Gibbs free energy Δg, induced by the presence of the complexes, on their total number can be then described by:

$$\Delta g = g(N, n) - g(N, 0) = n\Delta H_f - nT\Delta S_v - kT \ln \frac{N!}{n!(N-n)!} \qquad (5.11)$$

where ΔH_f is the enthalpy of formation of one complex, ΔS_v is the change in vibrational entropy of the crystal caused by the presence of one complex. It should be noted that in the case under consideration both N and n are the variables, whereas the numbers of atoms M and O are constant.

Figure 5.6 shows how each of the terms of eq. (5.11) is dependent on the total number of complexes in the crystal. As seen from this figure, $g(N, n)$ assumes a minimum value at a certain definite values of N_e and n_e, corresponding to thermodynamic equilibrium.

The conclusions drawn from the simple example considered above are of more general character and can be applied to all types of defects. At given conditions, this type of the defects is predominating, for which the minimum of the Gibbs free energy has the smallest value. It should be remembered that eq. (5.11) is valid only if the number of defects in the crystal is very small.

5.4. Chemical Potential of Neutral Atomic Defects.
Law of Mass Action

Let us consider now a more complex case, which is provided by a crystal MO having the tendency to form electrically neutral vacancies in the both sublattices. Such a case may occur when a crystal exchanges its atoms with the surrounding gas phase. Owing to the higher volatility of oxygen as compared with that of element M, it is assumed that oxygen atoms can be exchanged between the crystal and the gas phase. It is also assumed that the concentration of defects in the crystal is so small that the vacancies V_M^x and V_O^x are distributed randomly, do not interact with each other and do not form complexes.

Formation of these vacancies may be represented by the following quasi-chemical reactions:

$$1/2\, O_2^{(g)} \rightarrow O_O^x + V_M^x \qquad (5.12)$$

$$\text{zero} \rightarrow V_M^x + V_O^x \qquad (5.13)$$

illustrated in Fig. 5.7.

Let us introduce the following symbols:

N_1 — a number of lattice sites in the sublattice M,
N_2 — a number of lattice sites in the sublattice O,
n_M — a number of atoms in the sublattice M,
n_O — a number of atoms in the sublattice O,
n_1 — a number of vacancies in the sublattice M,
n_2 — a number of vacancies in the sublattice O,

interrelated by:

$$N_1 = n_M + n_1; \qquad N_2 = n_0 + n_2 \tag{5.14}$$

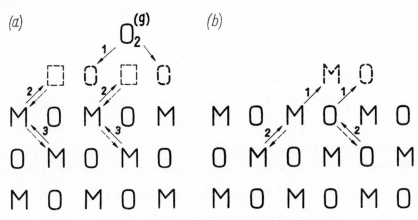

FIG. 5.7. Formation of neutral vacancies in a crystal MO: (a) according to reaction (5.12), (b) according to reaction (5.13).

In the real MO crystal, the number of sites in the both sublattices is the same, thus $N_1 = N_2$. The different notation of these numbers is introduced since the virtual processes will be considered in the forthcoming section.

The Gibbs free energy of the whole crystal may be in the case under consideration resolved into three parts, namely into a term involving normal constituents of the crystal: M_M^x and O_O^x, a term resulting from the presence of vacancies in sublattice M, and finally a term due to the presence of vacancies in the oxygen sublattice. Regarding n_M, n_0, n_1 and n_2 as variables, we get the change of the Gibbs free energy of the crystal MO caused by processes (5.12) and (5.13):

$$\Delta g = g(n_M, n_0, n_1, n_2) - g(n_M, n_0, 0, 0)$$
$$= \Delta g' + [n_1(\Delta H_f)_1 - T\Delta s_1] + [n_2(\Delta H_f)_2 - T\Delta s_2] \tag{5.15}$$

where $g(n_M, n_0, n_1, n_2)$ and $g(n_M, n_0, 0, 0)$ are the Gibbs free energy of the crystal with vacancies and without defects at the same temperature, $\Delta g'$ indicates the change in the Gibbs free energy caused by incorporation of the additional atoms of oxygen, $(\Delta H_f)_1$ is the enthalpy of formation of a vacancy V_M^x equal to the work necessary to displace an atom M from the normal lattice site in the bulk of the crystal to the analogous surface site, $(\Delta H_f)_2$ is the enthalpy of formation of a vacancy V_O^x, which is defined similarly like the vacancy in the sublattice M, Δs_1 and Δs_2 are the changes of the entropy of the crystal due to the presence of vacancies V_M^x and V_O^x, respectively.

The changes of entropy Δs_1 and Δs_2 may be written as

$$\Delta s_1 = n_1(\Delta S_v)_1 + k \ln \frac{N_1!}{n_1!(N_1 - n_1)!} \tag{5.16}$$

$$\Delta s_2 = n_2(\Delta S_v)_2 + k \ln \frac{N_2!}{n_2!(N_2 - n_2)!} \tag{5.17}$$

where $(\Delta S_v)_1$ and $(\Delta S_v)_2$ are the changes in the vibrational entropy of the crystal, resulting from the presence of one vacancy V_M^x and one V_O^x, respectively.

The first terms of the above formulae represent the contribution of vibrational entropy, while the second ones—the contribution of configurational mixing entropy.

By using Stirling's approximation:

$$\ln n! = n \ln n - n \tag{5.18}$$

eqs. (5.16) and (5.17) can be simplified to:

$$\Delta s_1 = n_1 (\Delta S_v)_1 + k[N_1 \ln N_1 - n_1 \ln n_1 - (N_1 - n_1) \ln (N_1 - n_1)] \tag{5.19}$$

$$\Delta s_2 = n_2 (\Delta S_v)_2 + k[N_2 \ln N_2 - n_2 \ln n_2 - (N_2 - n_2) \ln (N_2 - n_2)] \tag{5.20}$$

Substituting eqs. (5.19) and (5.20) into eq. (5.15) the Gibbs free energy of the crystal MO containing electrically neutral vacancies in both sublattices can be written as:

$$g(n_M, n_O, n_1, n_2) = g(n_M, n_O) + n_1 [(\Delta H_f)_1 - T(\Delta S_v)_1] + n_2 [(\Delta H_f)_2 -$$
$$- T(\Delta S_v)_2] - k T[N_1 \ln N_1 + N_2 \ln N_2 - n_1 \ln n_1 - n_2 \ln n_2 -$$
$$- (N_1 - n_1) \ln (N_1 - n_1) - (N_2 - n_2) \ln (N_2 - n_2)] \tag{5.21}$$

where $g(n_M, n_O) = g(n_M, n_O, 0, 0) + \Delta g'$ is the total Gibbs free energy of all the atoms M_M^x and O_O^x in the crystal MO at a definite temperature T.

In our discussion, we regard the crystal MO as an entity composed of constitutents M_M^x and O_O^x, arranged in lattice positions and of vacancies V_M^x and V_O^x. They may be called the elements of structure of the crystal MO. We shall consider now thermodynamic properties of the crystal MO in terms of chemical potentials of these elements.

A chemical potential of the structural elements is defined by analogy to homogeneous mixtures as:

$$\xi = \left(\frac{\partial g}{\partial n_i} \right)_{p, T, n_{j \neq i}} \tag{5.22}$$

where ξ is the chemical potential of ith element of the structure, g is the Gibbs free energy of the system, n_i is the number of elements of structure of ith type, p denotes the external pressure, T the temperature. According to the above given formula, the chemical potential of the ith element of structure is equal to the increase in the Gibbs free energy of the system when n_i is increased by one, the number of the remaining elements of the structure, the pressure and temperature being unchanged. The chemical potential of the elements of structure defined in such the manner does not reflect, however, the real changes in the crystal, since the change in the number of the structural elements of one type produces always the change in the number of other elements, to fulfill the condition of the equality of number of sites in the both sublattices. The chemical potential defined in the above way is named *a virtual chemical potential*.

According to the definition given by eq. (5.22), the virtual chemical potential of atoms M_M in the crystal MO is equal:

$$\xi_M = \left[\frac{\partial g(n_M, n_O, n_1, n_2)}{\partial n_M} \right]_{p, T, n_O, n_1, n_2} \tag{5.23}$$

Differentiating eq. (5.21) with n_M as a variable at constant p, T, n_0, n_1 and n_2, and taking into account eq. (5.14) we get:

$$\xi_M = \xi_M^o + kT \ln x_M \qquad (5.24)$$

where

$$\xi_M^o = \left[\frac{\partial g(n_M, n_0)}{\partial n_M} \right]_{p,T,n_0,n_1,n_2}$$

and $x_M = n_M/N_1$ is a site fraction of atoms M_M^x in the crystal lattice MO.

ξ_M^o is the standard virtual chemical potential of an atom M_M^x in the crystal MO at the temperature T when $x_M = 1$. This potential can be resolved into two terms:

$$\xi_M^o = \Delta H_M - T(\Delta S_v)_M \qquad (5.25)$$

where ΔH_M is the change of the enthalpy of the crystal resulting from the incorporation of one atom M into the surface site of the M sublattice, $(\Delta S_v)_M$ is the change of the vibrational entropy of the crystal caused by the addition of one atom M. The enthalpy of atoms M and O, occupying normal lattice sites of the crystal MO is calculated with respect to the state of free atoms of M and molecules of O_2, which is taken as the standard state. Thus ΔH_M is equal to the work necessary for the transfer of an atom M from infinity to a normal surface site in the sublattice M.

In the analogous manner we can derive the expression for the virtual chemical potential of atoms O_O^x in the crystal MO:

$$\xi_O = \left[\frac{\partial g(n_M, n_0, n_1, n_2)}{\partial n_0} \right]_{p,T,n_M,n_1,n_2} \qquad (5.26)$$

and

$$\xi_O = \xi_O^o + kT \ln x_O \qquad (5.27)$$

where

$$\xi_O^o = \left[\frac{\partial g(n_M, n_0)}{\partial n_0} \right]_{p,T,n_M,n_1,n_2}$$

and $x_O = n_0/N_2$ is a site fraction of atoms O_O^x in the crystal lattice MO.

ξ_O^o is the virtual standard chemical potential of an atom O_O^x in the crystal MO at temperature T when $x_O = 1$. This potential is equal:

$$\xi_O^o = \Delta H_O - T(\Delta S_v)_O \qquad (5.28)$$

where ΔH_O is half of the work required for the transfer of an oxygen molecule from infinity to the surface of the crystal, splitting this molecule into oxygen atoms and incorporation of these atoms into the surface sites of the oxygen sublattice.

$(\Delta S_v)_O$ is the change of the vibrational entropy of the crystal MO accompanying the addition of one oxygen atom.

The expressions for the virtual chemical potentials ξ_1 and ξ_2 of vacancies V_M^x and V_O^x are derived in a similar way:

$$\xi_1 = \left[\frac{\partial g(n_M, n_0, n_1, n_2)}{\partial n_1} \right]_{p,T,n_M,n_0,n_2} \qquad (5.29)$$

and

$$\xi_1 = \xi_1^\circ + kT \ln x_1 \tag{5.30}$$

where:

$$\xi_1^\circ = (\Delta H_f)_1 - T(\Delta S_v)_1 \tag{5.31}$$

and $x_1 = n_1/N_1$ is a site fraction of vacancies in the sublattice M. ξ_1° is the virtual standard chemical potential of a vacancy V_M^x at temperature T and at external pressure p when $x_1 = 1$;

$$\xi_1 = \left[\frac{\partial g(n_M, n_O, n_1, n_2)}{\partial n_2} \right]_{p,T,n_M,n_O,n_1} \tag{5.32}$$

and

$$\xi_2 = \xi_2^\circ + kT \ln x_2 \tag{5.33}$$

where

$$\xi_2^\circ = (\Delta H_f)_2 - T(\Delta S_v)_2 \tag{5.34}$$

and $x_2 = n_2/N_2$ is a site fraction of vacancies in the oxygen sublattice.

ξ_2° is the virtual standard chemical potential of a vacancy V_O^x at temperature T and at external pressure p when $x_2 = 1$.

In reality, the incorporation of an additional atom of oxygen to the crystal lattice MO produces always, according to eq. (5.12), one vacancy V_M^x, and hence the real chemical potential of oxygen μ_O in the compound MO is equal to the sum of the virtual chemical potentials of constituents O_O^x and V_M^x.

$$\mu_O = \xi_O + \xi_1 \tag{5.35}$$

The real chemical potential of oxygen μ_{O_2} in the gas phase may be also written in the form analogous to the virtual potential considered above:

$$\mu_{O_2} = \mu_{O_2}^\circ + kT \ln P_{O_2} \tag{5.36}$$

oxygen pressure being introduced here instead of a molar fraction. $\mu_{O_2}^\circ$ denotes the standard chemical potential of oxygen at temperature T, when $P_{O_2} = 1$ atm.

The chemical potential in eq. (5.36) is calculated per one molecule of oxygen. $\mu_{O_2}^\circ$ can be resolved into two terms:

$$\mu_{O_2}^\circ = \Delta H_{O_2}^\circ - T \Delta S_{O_2}^\circ \tag{5.37}$$

where $\Delta H_{O_2}^\circ$ and $\Delta S_{O_2}^\circ$ are respectively the standard values of the enthalpy and entropy of the oxygen molecule in the gas phase at temperature T and at $P_{O_2} = 1$ atm.

The change of the thermodynamic potential Δg_1 accompanying reaction (5.12) can be written in the form:

$$\Delta g_1 = \xi_O + \xi_1 - \frac{1}{2} \mu_{O_2} \tag{5.38}$$

In the same manner the change of the thermodynamic potential Δg_2 resulting from reaction (5.13) may be given as:

$$\Delta g_2 = \xi_1 + \xi_2 \tag{5.39}$$

When the crystal is in the state of thermodynamic equilibrium with the surrounding oxygen, the increments of the thermodynamic potential Δg_1 and Δg_2 are equal to zero. For this case combining eqs. (5.27), (5.30), (5.36) and (5.38) yields:

$$\frac{x_0 x_1}{P_{O_2}^{1/2}} = K_1 = \exp\left[-\frac{\xi_0^\circ + \xi_1^\circ - \frac{1}{2}\mu_{O_2}^\circ}{kT}\right] \tag{5.40}$$

In the analogous way, from eqs. (5.30), (5.33) and (5.39) we obtain:

$$x_1 \cdot x_2 = \exp\left[-\frac{\xi_1^\circ + \xi_2^\circ}{kT}\right] \tag{5.41}$$

Making use of eqs. (5.28), (5.31), and (5.37) and assuming that $x_0 \approx 1$ which is true for small deviations from stochiometry, eq. (5.40) may be presented in the form:

$$x_1 = K_1 P_{O_2}^{1/2} = P_{O_2}^{1/2} \exp\left[\frac{\Delta S_1}{k}\right] \exp\left[-\frac{\Delta H_1}{kT}\right] \tag{5.42}$$

where

$$\Delta S_1 = (\Delta S_v)_0 + (\Delta S_v)_1 - \frac{1}{2}\Delta S_{O_2}^\circ \tag{5.43}$$

$$\Delta H_1 = \Delta H_0 + (\Delta H_f)_1 - \frac{1}{2}\Delta H_{O_2}^\circ \tag{5.44}$$

Similarly from eqs. (5.31) and (5.34):

$$x_1 \cdot x_2 = K_2 = \exp\left[\frac{\Delta S_2}{k}\right] \exp\left[-\frac{\Delta H_2}{kT}\right] \tag{5.45}$$

where

$$\Delta S_2 = (\Delta S_v)_1 + (\Delta S_v)_2 \tag{5.46}$$

$$\Delta H_2 = (\Delta H_f)_1 + (\Delta H_f)_2 \tag{5.47}$$

From eqs. (5.42) and (5.45) one can readily derive the relation between the equilibrium site fraction of electrically neutral oxygen vacancies and temperature and oxygen pressure:

$$x_2 = \frac{K_2}{K_1} P_{O_2}^{-1/2} = P_{O_2}^{-1/2} \exp\left[\frac{\Delta S_2 - \Delta S_1}{k}\right] \exp\left[-\frac{\Delta H_2 - \Delta H_1}{kT}\right] \tag{5.48}$$

In the special case when the crystal MO does not show deviations from stoichiometry, i.e. when $x_1 = x_2 = x_s$, the equilibrium site fraction of vacancies in the both sublattices is given by the formula:

$$x_s = K_2^{1/2} = \exp\left[\frac{\Delta S_2}{2k}\right] \exp\left[-\frac{\Delta H_2}{2kT}\right] \tag{5.49}$$

In physics of semiconductors, the amount of point defects is expressed usually in terms of concentration in cm^{-3} rather than in site fractions. From the formulae for the site fractions, the expressions for concentrations can be readily obtained by multiplying both sides of eqs. (5.42), (5.48), and (5.50) by a number of sites in a given sublattice encompassed in 1 cm³ of a crystal. In further discussion symbol [ ] will denote the concentration expressed in cm^{-3}.

It results from the above considerations that in the case of the crystal MO which shows small deviations from stoichiometry, the expressions derived for the dependence of site fractions of neutral vacancies in both sublattices on temperature and oxygen pressure are identical with those obtained on applying the law of mass action to reactions (5.12) and (5.13). Constants K_1 and K_2 may be hence named the equilibrium constants of these quasi-chemical reactions.[234]

Obviously the analogous results can be obtained for other types of neutral atomic defects, e.g. interstitial atoms or antistructure defects, provided that the deviations from stoichiometry are small.

Application of chemical thermodynamics to the systems under consideration is substantiated by the fact that real crystals containing various types of atomic defects may be regarded as solid solutions, in which elements of structure constitute the solvent and atomic defects are the solute.

It should be, however, remembered that the above considerations are valid only for ideal solutions, i.e. for crystals in which no interaction between the defects occurs, these latter being distributed randomly in the crystal. One may suppose that in cases in which deviations from stoichiometry and hence the defect concentration are small, this assumption is held with a good approximation.

If, however, the concentration of defects in a given crystal is so high that their interactions cannot be neglected, defect activities instead of defect concentrations should be introduced into quasi-chemical reactions, according to the formula:

$$a_i = f_i [\ ] \tag{5.50}$$

where a_i is the activity of the ith element of the structure, [ ] denotes its concentration, and f_i is the activity coefficient. The methods of calculation of the activity of defects are described in works by Teltow,[123, 124] Liliard,[125] and Libowitz.[126, 127] For the same reasons, one can also introduce a fugacity into eq. (5.36), which determines the dependence of the chemical potential of oxygen on its pressure.[128]

5.5. Structure of Electronic Defects

5.5.1. ELECTRONIC DEFECTS IN CRYSTALS NOT CONTAINING ATOMIC DEFECTS

The solution of the problem of structure of point defects in crystals amounts to the solving of the Schrödinger equation involving all possible interactions between electrons and between these latter and nuclei. Principally we could derive in this way all possible values of the energy of electrons in the crystal and also the wave functions corresponding to these energies. Hence the distribution of probability of all possible space locations of nuclei at a given internal energy of the crystal would be obtained and the crystal structure and the distribution of electrons within the crystal could be described.

This solution involves however the problem of many-bodies, which cannot be solved mathematically. Hence the only possible approach is to introduce a number of simplifying assumptions to the Schrödinger equation. It is then assumed that the state of electrons in the filled electron shells is not changed when an assembly of isolated atoms is brought together to form a crystal. A crystal is then visualized as an entity composed of positive ions and a cloud of valence electrons, the state of these electrons being essentially different from that in isolated atoms. Further, it is assumed that the positive ions are immobile in lattice sites of an ideal crystal lattice. Each electron moves in the averaged potential field of all positive ions and the remaining valence electrons. The potential energy of the valence electrons varies periodically with positions due to periodic distribution of electric charge in the crystal lattice. The variation of potential energy of an electron with a distance for a one-dimensional crystal is shown in Fig. 5.8.

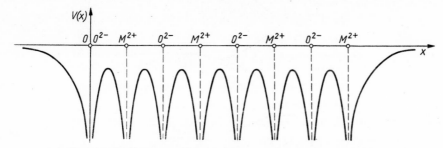

FIG. 5.8. Periodic potential energy of electron in one-dimensional crystal MO.

At the assumptions given above, the Schrödinger equation can be solved by a one-electron approximation. In this method the wave function of all valence electrons in a crystal is derived from wave functions of individual valence electrons. Bloch has shown that in the case of the periodic potential energy, the total wave function which is the solution of the Schrödinger equation assumes the following form:

$$\Psi = u_k(\mathbf{r}) \exp(i\mathbf{kr}) \qquad (5.51)$$

where $u_k(\mathbf{r})$ is a periodic function of the distance r, $\mathbf{k}$ is the wave vector. The solution of the Schrödinger equation obtained at the simplifying assumptions may be found in the text books on the quantum theory of semiconductors. In this book we shall consider only some conclusions resulting from the application of wave mechanics to crystals, which will be necessary for explaining the structure of electronic defects in semiconducting compounds.

Let us consider an assembly of N atoms M (e.g. sodium) and N atoms X (e.g. chlorine) placed at such a distance that each of these atoms can be regarded as isolated. When these atoms are brought together to form a crystal, the forces of attraction between the electrons and the nuclei of the adjacent atoms are increased. This electrostatic interaction causes the weakening of the attraction forces between the valence electrons and their own nuclei, and hence leads to the lowering of the potential barriers between the atoms, the decrease in their ionization energy, and also to the shift of the energy levels of the valence electrons with respect to these levels in the isolated atoms. The shift of the electron energy levels in one-dimensional crystal of sodium chloride is shown in Fig. 5.9.

As seen from this figure, the shift of the energy levels is the higher, the smaller is the distance between the atoms. At the distances close to interatomic distances in a crystal, the interactions of electric fields between individual atoms give rise to splitting of each energy level into N different levels. Hence instead of separate levels characteristic of individual atoms, there are formed in crystal energy bands.

For instance, in NaCl the level $3s$ of isolated chlorine atoms is splitted into N levels forming a band $3s$ Cl (Fig. 5.9). Each of these levels can accommodate, according to

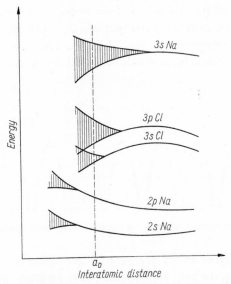

FIG. 5.9. Dependence of the position of energy levels in NaCl on the interatomic distance. a_0 indicates a normal lattice parameter.

the Pauli principle, two electrons and thus at the temperature of absolute zero this band is completely filled. In the analogous manner each of the three $3p$ levels of chlorine and the $3s$ levels of sodium form $3p$ Cl and $3s$ Na bands. Since the $3s$ Na band lies higher than the $3p$ Cl band (Fig. 5.9), the electrons of the former band occupy the levels of the partly filled $3p$ Cl band, and hence at the temperature of absolute zero this latter is completely filled ($6N$ electrons), the $3s$ Na band (the uppermost band) being at this temperature empty. The energy band completely filled at the temperature of absolute zero (e.g. $3p$ band Cl in sodium chloride) is called the *valence band*, and the higher-lying, empty at this temperature band (e.g. $3s$ Na in NaCl) is called the *conduction band*. Obviously above the conduction band there may be present other empty bands arising from excited levels.

The width of the bands is independent of the size of a crystal and hence the larger is the crystal the smaller is the spacing of the energy levels within a band. The bands are separated by forbidden energy gaps. If, in a given solid the forbidden energy gap is large, such a solid behaves as an insulator, if it is smaller we have a semiconductor. Finally, when the valence band is not filled completely, or when the conduction band and the valence band overlap, we have a metal. The schematic drawing of the energy bands in a semiconductor is shown in Fig. 5.10. In the same figure the periodic changes of potential energy of an electron in the crystal are also shown.

According to eq. (5.51), the wave function of an electron in the crystal is spread over many potential wells, having a maximum within one well. Thus, although the highest probability of finding an electron occurs in only one potential well, it is not however equal to zero within the adjacent wells. It results from the above that the electrons can be present not only in the potential wells peculiar to their own atoms, but also inside

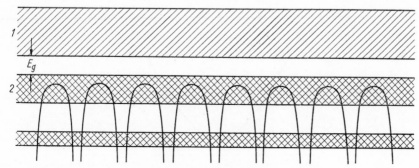

FIG. 5.10. Model of energy bands and periodic potential energy in a crystal; 1—conduction band, 2—valence band; E_g—forbidden energy gap.

the potential barriers and in the adjacent wells (cf. Fig. 5.10). They can hence penetrate through the potential barriers without changing their total energy. This phenomenon, according to the laws of wave mechanics, is known as the *tunnel effect*.

The total energy of an electron E is a periodic function of the wave vector $\mathbf{k}$. As the potential energy function is even, energy $E(\mathbf{k})$ is also an even function. In one-dimensional crystal the period of this function is $2\pi/a$, where a is the period of the potential energy $V(x)$. In three-dimensional crystal, in which the unit cell is a perpendicular parallelepiped with sides a_1, a_2 and a_3 parallel to axes x, y, z, respectively, the electron energy is a periodic function of k_x, k_y and k_z with periods $2\pi/a_1$, $2\pi/a_2$ and $2\pi/a_3$, respectively. The values of k_x, k_y and k_z are usually limited to the range: $-\pi/a_1 \leqslant k_x \leqslant \pi/a_1$; $-\pi/a_2 \leqslant k_y \leqslant \pi/a_2$ and $-\pi/a_3 \leqslant k_z \leqslant \pi/a_3$.

The region bounded by values of $\mathbf{k}$ lying within the limits $\pm\pi/a$ is usually called the *first Brillouin zone*. The shape of this zone depends on the structure of the crystal. The simplest model of the band structure in semiconductors has been proposed by Wilson. This model assumes a single minimum of the $E(\mathbf{k})$ function in the middle of the Brillouin zone for the conduction band and the maximum of this function in the middle of the Brillouin zone for the valence band. If we assume additionally that the crystal has the regular structure then in the first case:

$$E(\mathbf{k}) = E_c + \frac{h^2}{8\pi^2 m_e^*}(k_x^2 + k_y^2 + k_z^2) \tag{5.52}$$

whereas in the second case:

$$E(\mathbf{k}) = E_v - \frac{h^2}{8\pi^2 m_h^*}(k_x^2 + k_y^2 + k_z^2) \tag{5.53}$$

where E_c and E_v are the energies of the bottom of the conduction band and the top of the valence band respectively, m_e^* and m_h^* are effective masses of electrons and holes respectively, h is the Planck constant.

In the model under discussion we obtain spherical surfaces of constant energies in **k** space. Hence, such the energy bands are called *spherical bands*. In Fig. 5.11 the dependence of electron energy on wave number k_x for direction x is shown for a spherical energy band. The model discussed above describes the simplest of the band structures. Unfortunately no semiconductor of such the structure is known. Theoretical calculation

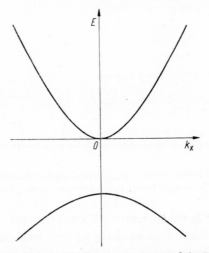

FIG. 5.11. Spherical energy bands near the centre of the Brillouin zone.

of the $E(\mathbf{k})$ function is difficult even for the simplest crystal structures. This problem has been so far solved for only few semiconductors, e.g. germanium and silicon. Therefore in many cases it is convenient to employ the Wilson model for interpretation of experimental data, in particular in the initial stages of the studies, e.g. in cases of oxides, where the band structure is usually unknown.

Let us consider now how the electronic defects can be formed in semiconductor crystals which do not contain atomic defects. As already mentioned, at the temperature of 0 K the valence band is completely filled, and the conduction band is empty. Thus at 0 K the crystal does not show any electronic defects. At higher temperatures, however, some electrons from the valence band may acquire the energy sufficient for their transfer to the conduction band by thermal excitation.

This process can be described by the following reaction:

$$\text{zero} \rightleftarrows e' + h^{\cdot} \tag{5.54}$$

According to the Kröger–Vink notation e' denotes a quasi-free electron in the conduction band having a negative charge (indicated by a dash), and $h^{\cdot}$ is a positive hole in the valence band formed by the removal of an electron. The positive charge of the hole is denoted by a point in the superscript. Thus as the result of the process (5.54), the electronic defects: quasi-free electrons in the conduction band and the holes in the valence band, appear in the crystal. These defects can participate in conduction of electrical current.

To calculate the concentration of these defects at a given temperature we should know the number of energy states in a unit volume of the crystal comprised in the range $E-(E+\mathrm{d}E)$, both for the conduction and valence band, and also the probability of occurrence of process (5.54).

According to the Wilson model, the numbers of levels in the conduction band and in the valence band can be described by the following functions:

$$g_c(E)\mathrm{d}E = 2\pi\left(\frac{2m_e^*}{h^2}\right)^{3/2}(E-E_c)^{1/2}\mathrm{d}E \tag{5.55}$$

$$g_v(E)\mathrm{d}E = 2\pi\left(\frac{2m_h^*}{h^2}\right)^{3/2}(E_v-E)^{1/2}\mathrm{d}E \tag{5.56}$$

where $g_c(E)\mathrm{d}E$ and $g_v(E)\mathrm{d}E$ denote the numbers of energy states per unit volume lying between E and $E+\mathrm{d}E$, in the conduction and valence bands, respectively. The functions g_c and g_v are called the *density of states* in the conduction and valence band, respectively.

The probability that a state of energy E in the conduction band is occupied is given by the Fermi–Dirac distribution function:

$$f(E) = \frac{1}{\exp\left(\dfrac{E-E_F}{kT}\right)+1} \tag{5.57}$$

where E_F is a parameter called the Fermi energy or the Fermi level. Statistical thermodynamics shows that this level is just the chemical potential of electrons (and holes).

In typical semiconductors the concentration of charge carriers is contained within the limits 10^{10} to 10^{18} cm^{-3}. This means that $f(E) \ll 1$, and hence $\exp(E-E_F)/kT \gg 1$. Hence we can neglect unity in the denominator in eq. (5.57), thus obtaining the classical Maxwell–Boltzmann distribution:

$$f_1(E) = \exp\left(-\frac{E-E_F}{kT}\right) \tag{5.58}$$

The distribution functions described by eqs. (5.57) and (5.58) are shown in Fig. 5.12. It results from Fig. 5.12 that:

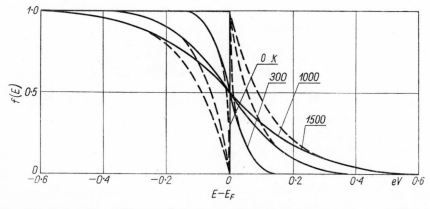

FIG. 5.12. Probability of filling energy levels at various temperatures; ———— the Fermi–Dirac distribution function, — — — — the Maxwell–Boltzmann distribution function.

(1) the probability that a state of energy $E = E_F$ is occupied by an electron is $1/2$,

(2) the plot of the distribution function is symmetrical about the Fermi level,

(3) the classical Maxwell–Boltzmann distribution can be applied only when $|E-E_F| > 2kT$ (at the room temperature $kT = 0.025$ eV). In other cases the function given by eq. (5.57) should be used. The crystal to which the latter function is applicable is called a *degenerate semiconductor*.

For non-degenerate semiconductors, the concentration of electrons in the conduction band is given by:

$$n = 2 \int_{E_c}^{E_1} g_c(E) f_1(E) dE = 2 \left(\frac{2\pi m_e^* k T}{h^2} \right)^{3/2} \exp \left(\frac{E_F - E_c}{kT} \right) = N_c \exp \left(\frac{E_F - E_c}{kT} \right) \quad (5.59)$$

where E_1 is the energy of the top of the conduction band. Factor 2 results from the spin degeneracy. In the similar manner we can calculate the concentration of holes in the valence band, the difference being in that the probability of occupying the level E by a hole is given by the function $[1-f_1(E)]$:

$$p = 2 \int_{E_2}^{E_v} g_v(E) [1 - f_1(E)] dE = 2 \left[\frac{2\pi m_h^* k T}{h^2} \right]^{3/2} \exp \left(\frac{E_v - E_F}{kT} \right) = N_v \exp \left(\frac{E_v - E_F}{kT} \right) \quad (5.60)$$

E_2 is the energy of the bottom of the valence band.

Assuming that the effective masses of electrons and holes are equal to the mass of an electron, the values of N_c and N_v at the room temperature amount to about 2.5×10^{19} cm^{-3}.

The product of eqs. (5.59) and (5.60) gives the very important equation for the defect theory:

$$np = K_i = N_c N_v \exp \left(- \frac{E_g}{kT} \right); \quad E_g = E_c - E_v \quad (5.61)$$

where E_g is the energy gap. When a semiconductor does not contain atomic defects, the concentration of electrons in the conduction band is equal to the concentration of holes in the valence band and hence:

$$n = p = 2 \left(\frac{2\pi k T}{h^2} \right)^{3/2} (m_e^* \, m_h^*)^{3/4} \exp \left(- \frac{E_g}{2kT} \right) \quad (5.62)$$

From eqs. (5.59) and (5.60) we can derive the dependence of the Fermi level position on the concentration of electrons in the conduction band or on the concentration of holes in the valence band:

$$E_F = E_c + kT \ln \frac{n}{N_c} \quad (5.63)$$

$$E_F = E_v - kT \ln \frac{p}{N_v} \quad (5.64)$$

In the case under discussion $n = p$, and hence the position of the Fermi level in such a semiconductor calculated from eqs. (5.63) and (5.64) is:

$$E_F = \frac{E_g}{2} + \frac{3kT}{4} \ln \frac{m_h^*}{m_e^*} \qquad (5.65)$$

It follows from eq. (5.65) that when the effective masses of electrons and holes are equal, the Fermi level lies in the middle of the forbidden energy gap (Fig. 5.13).

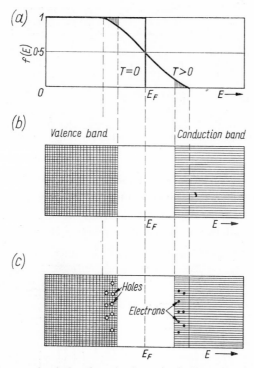

FIG. 5.13. Filling of energy levels by electrons in an intrinsic semiconductor: (a) distribution function, (b) filling of the states at 0 K, (c) filling of the states when $T > 0$ K.

5.5.2. Electronic Defects in Crystals with Atomic Disorder

In this section we shall consider electronic defects in a hypothetical crystal MO, arising due to the presence of atomic defects. Let us consider a crystal MO which contains foreign atoms which substitute atoms M in the sublattice M. The valency of these atoms is higher by one than the valency of atoms M. In this case one electron of the admixture does not contribute to the binding, and the positive charge of the admixture ion is greater by one from the charge of an ion M. Such an atomic defect exhibits hence elementary effective positive charge with respect to the lattice, which creates an additional coulombic field, perturbing the periodic potential energy in the crystal. The excess electron is thus bound to its parent ion and revolves around it, similarly like an electron moves around a proton in a hydrogen atom. The situation resembles then the hydrogen-like problem, the solution of which gives a number of energy levels situated below the conduction band. The valence electrons of the parent lattice atoms, and the electrons of the admixture which participate in the binding fill then the valence band, and the excess electron occupies a level lying below the conduction band (Fig. 5.14).

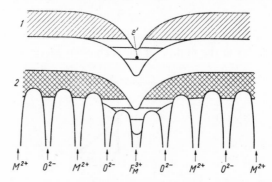

FIG. 5.14. Deformation of the periodic potential energy and energy bands in the vicinity of a donor foreign atom in a crystal MO: 1—conduction band, 2—valence band, e′—electron localized at a donor level.

The analogous system of levels is obtained in the case of an interstitial atom M (Fig. 5.15), or when the crystal MO contains a vacancy in the oxygen sublattice (Fig. 5.16). In this latter case, the valence electrons of the excess atom M are captured by oxygen vacancies that behave as effective positive charges, creating an additional

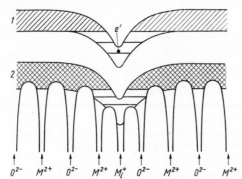

FIG. 5.15. Deformation of the periodic potential energy and energy bands in the vicinity of an interstitial atom in a crystal MO: 1—conduction band, 2—valence band, e′—electron localized at a donor level.

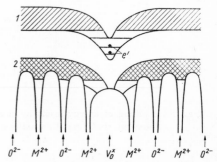

FIG. 5.16. Deformation of the periodic potential energy and of energy bands in the vicinity of an oxygen vacancy: 1—conduction band, 2—valence band, e′—electron localized at a donor level.

coulombic field. This field perturbs the periodicity of the potential energy of the crystal similarly like in the cases considered above.

The energy levels lying below the conduction band are called donor levels, and an oxide which has the defects mentioned above is a semiconductor of n-type. The distance of donor levels from the bottom of the conduction band (the ionization energy of donors) is usually small and hence even small thermal excitation is sufficient for the transfer of an electron from these levels to the conduction band, i.e. for detaching the electron from the donor defect.

Processes of ionization of the donor defects in a crystal MO can be described by the following quasi-chemical reactions:

$$F_M^x \rightleftarrows F_M^\bullet + e' \qquad (5.66)$$

$$M_i^x \rightleftarrows M_i^\bullet + e' \qquad (5.67)$$

$$V_O^x \rightleftarrows V_O^\bullet + e' \qquad (5.68)$$

Obviously, the singly-ionized atomic defects can undergo further ionization according to the reactions:

$$M_i^\bullet \rightleftarrows M_i^{\bullet\bullet} + e' \qquad (5.69)$$

$$V_O^\bullet \rightleftarrows V_O^{\bullet\bullet} + e' \qquad (5.70)$$

The point in the superscript denotes here an effective elementary positive charge with respect to the lattice, the dash the analogous negative charge.

Since the crystal as a whole has no electric charge, the reactions of charged defects must observe the condition of electroneutrality. This means that the total effective charge of the defects written on the right-hand side of the reaction equation must be equal to the total effective charge of the defects on the left-hand side.

Let us assume that a crystal MO has donor defects of only one kind, denoted by a symbol D. Their presence in the crystal is accompanied by the appearance of an occu-

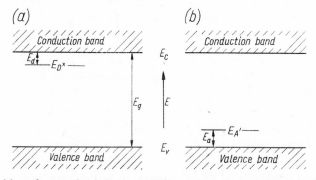

FIG. 5.17. Position of energy levels in the forbidden energy gap: (a) donor levels, (b) acceptor levels; E_d—ionization energy of donors, E_a—ionization energy of acceptors.

pied energy level E_{D^x} in the energy gap as shown in Fig. 5.17a. At temperature $T > 0\,\text{K}$ a fraction of the donors is ionized according to the reaction:

$$D^x \rightleftarrows D^\bullet + e' \qquad (5.71)$$

giving off electrons to the conduction band.

As shown in section 5.1, in cases of non-degenerate semiconductors the equilibria of the reactions describing ionization of defects can be considered in terms of the law of mass action and hence we obtain:

$$\frac{[D^\bullet]n}{[D^x]} = K_d \qquad (5.72)$$

where n is the concentration of electrons in the conduction band and K_d is the equilibrium constant.

The concentration of non-ionized donors is equal to the product of the total concentration of donors in the crystal [D], and the probability of occupying a donor level $E_{D^\times}$ by an electron:[118]

$$[D^\times] = \cfrac{[D]}{1 + \cfrac{1}{2}\exp\left(\cfrac{E_{D^\times} - E_F}{kT}\right)} \tag{5.73}$$

The denominator in (5.73) gives the probability of occupying a donor level by an electron that has one of the two possible values of spin.

Taking into account the condition: $[D] = [D^\times] + [D^\cdot]$, from eq. (5.73) we obtain the following expression for the dependence of the Fermi level position on the concentration of neutral and ionized donors:

$$E_F = E_{D^\times} + kT\left[\ln\frac{[D^\times]}{[D^\cdot]} + \ln\frac{1}{2}\right] \tag{5.74}$$

Equations (5.59)–(5.64) derived in section 5.5.1 remain valid for a semiconductor which contains atomic defects, provided that it is not degenerate.

Comparing eqs. (5.63) and (5.74) and taking into account eq. (5.72) we obtain the following expression for the temperature dependence of the equilibrium constant of reaction (5.71):

$$K_d = \frac{[D^\cdot]n}{[D]} = \frac{N_c}{2}\exp\left[-\frac{E_d}{kT}\right] \tag{5.75}$$

where $E_d = (E_c - E_{D^\times})$ is the ionization energy of donors.

Let us consider now a crystal MO containing foreign atoms F in the sublattice M, the valency of which is lower by one from the valency of atoms M. In such a case there is a deficit of one electron in the binding. An ion of such an admixture exhibits hence an effective negative charge with respect to the lattice, creating an additional coulombic field which produces a deformation of the periodic potential energy as shown in Fig. 5.18. To explain the defect situation created in this way, let us imagine that an additional electron is introduced to an atom F_M to saturate the binding. This electron

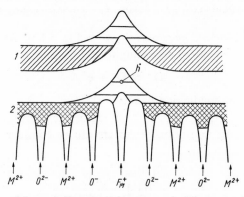

FIG. 5.18. Deformation of the periodic potential energy and of the energy bands in the vicinity of an acceptor foreign atom in a crystal MO: 1—the conduction band, 2—the valence band, $h^\cdot$—a hole localized on an acceptor level.

is obviously more weakly bound to its parent ion than the other valence electrons. It occupies an energy level lying higher than the top of the valence band. It is seen from the above considerations that atoms of the admixture of lower valency than the parent atoms introduce into the forbidden energy gap energy levels (or a level) which lie above the valence band. They are called *acceptor levels*. At the temperature of absolute zero the acceptor levels are empty, since all valence electrons involved in the binding fill completely the valence band situated below. At higher temperatures, the electrons of this band can jump to the acceptor levels by thermal excitation. As the result of this transfer, the valence band has empty energy levels called *holes* which can migrate quasi-freely in this band. The model of the energy levels for this case is shown in Fig. 5.18.

The analogous system of the energy levels is obtained when a crystal MO contains vacancies in the sublattice M (Fig. 5.19). Each of these vacancies constitutes a localized negative charge, similarly like the foreign atom considered above. At the same time

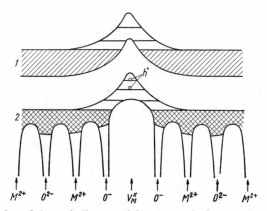

FIG. 5.19. Deformation of the periodic potential energy and of energy bands in the vicinity of a cationic vacancy in a crystal MO: 1—conduction band, 2—valence band, h•—hole localized on an acceptor level.

the adjacent oxygen atom has incomplete bonds. In this situation we observe the appearance of the acceptor levels above the valence band. Thus an oxide containing foreign atoms of the valency lower than atoms M, or cationic vacancies, behaves as a *p*-type semiconductor. Ionization of these defects can be described by the reactions:

$$F_M^x \rightleftarrows F_M' + h^\bullet \tag{5.76}$$

$$V_M^x \rightleftarrows V_M' + h^\bullet \tag{5.77}$$

$$V_M' \rightleftarrows V_M'' + h^\bullet \tag{5.78}$$

Let us assume now that acceptor defects: foreign atoms or cationic vacancies, denoted generally by A, are the only defects in a crystal MO. They give rise to an acceptor level $E_{A'}$ in the energy gap, as shown in Fig. 5.17b. At temperature higher than absolute zero this level is partly filled by electrons coming from the valence band, according to the reaction:

$$A^x \rightleftarrows A' + h^\bullet; \qquad \frac{[A'][h^\bullet]}{[A^x]} = K_a \tag{5.79}$$

By analogy to the case of donor defects discussed above, the concentration of non-ionized acceptors is given by:

$$[A^\times] = [A] [1 - P(E)] \tag{5.80}$$

where $[A] = [A'] + [A^\times]$ and $P(E)$ is the probability that the acceptor level is occupied by two electrons of the opposite spins. It can be shown that this probability is:[118]

$$P(E) = \frac{1}{1 + 2 \exp\left(\dfrac{E_{A'} - E_F}{kT}\right)} \tag{5.81}$$

Hence the concentration of non-ionized acceptors can be written as:

$$[A^\times] = \frac{[A]}{1 + \dfrac{1}{2} \exp\left(\dfrac{E_F - E_{A'}}{kT}\right)} \tag{5.82}$$

Rearranging eq. (5.82) we obtain the following expression which describes the dependence of the Fermi level position on the concentration of ionized and non-ionized acceptors:

$$E_F = E_{A'} + kT\left[\ln \frac{[A']}{[A^\times]} + \ln 2\right] \tag{5.83}$$

From eqs. (5.63) and (5.83) we can readily derive the temperature dependence of the equilibrium constant K_a:

$$K_a = \frac{[A']p}{[A^\times]} = \frac{N_v}{2} \exp\left(-\frac{E_a}{kT}\right) \tag{5.84}$$

where $E_a = E_{A'} - E_v$.

In an n-type semiconductor $n \gg p$, and hence according to eqs. (5.62) and (5.63), the Fermi level lies in the upper part of the energy gap, being the closer to the bottom of the conduction band the higher is the concentration of the electrons in this band. If the concentration of the electrons in the conduction band attains the value such that $|E_c - E_F| < 2kT$, the semiconductor is said to be degenerate. The dividing line between degenerate and non-degenerate semiconductors is called the *degeneracy concentration*.

In a p-type semiconductor, $p \gg n$, and the Fermi level is situated in the lower part of the energy gap, the closer to the top of the valence band, the higher is the concentration of holes. By analogy to the n-type semiconductor, the hole gas is degenerate when $|E_F - E_v| < 2kT$.

It follows from the above considerations that the position of the Fermi level in the forbidden energy gap is determined by the concentration of donors and acceptors in the crystal, and hence on the concentration of atomic defects, both native and foreign atoms. Figure 5.20 shows the dependence of the Fermi level position on the concentration of donors and acceptors for a case in which a donor level lies near the bottom of the conduction band and an acceptor level near the top of the valence band. In this case we can assume that all donors and acceptors are ionized and thus $n = [D]$ and $p = [A]$.

If the classical distribution function cannot be applied, the Fermi–Dirac distribution should be used in eqs. (5.58) and (5.59). In this case, the concentrations of electrons and holes are given by the following formulae:

$$n = \frac{4\pi(2m_e^* k T)^{3/2}}{h^3} F_{1/2}(E_F^*)$$ (5.85)

$$p = \frac{4\pi(2m_h^* k T)^{3/2}}{h^3} F_{1/2}(E_F^*)$$ (5.86)

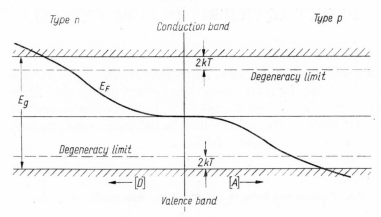

FIG. 5.20. The Fermi level vs. concentration of donors and acceptors.

where $F_m(E_F^*)$ is the Fermi integral:

$$F_m(E_F^*) = \int_0^\infty \frac{x^m \, dx}{\exp(x - E_F^*) + 1}$$ (5.87)

in which $x = E/kT$ is the reduced energy of an electron, $E_F^* = \dfrac{E_F}{kT}$ is the reduced Fermi level.

CHAPTER 6

DEFECT EQUILIBRIA IN PURE CRYSTALS

OWING to the limited size of this book, the problem of defect equilibria in pure crystals will be considered only for some selected types of defect situations. The conclusions, formulated on the basis of these examples, will be however of general character, and the method of treatment of the subject will enable the reader to apply the theory discussed to any combination of various types of defects.

6.1. Equilibrium between a Crystal and Surrounding Gas Phase

Chemical composition of semiconducting compounds is strictly determined by the equilibrium between a solid and other phases, in particular a gas phase (systems solid–gas are most frequently encountered in practice). Hence, in both theoretical and experimental studies on physical properties of crystals, one should consider the fact that these pro- perties are dependent on composition and parameters of the gas phase surrounding the solid. Not always, however, can this influence be controlled. At not too high tempe- ratures motion of defects in crystals is so slow that establishment of thermodynamic equilibrium between the bulk of a crystal and the gas phase required a very long time, which cannot be as a rule realized in practice. At these temperatures, only the surface equilibrium is established, physical properties of the bulk of the crystal being determined by so called history of the material.

At high temperatures, on the other hand, the thermodynamic equilibrium between the whole crystal and its environment can be attained in a relatively short time.[†] There- fore, it is only at high temperatures that physical properties of crystals are determined uniquely by thermodynamic conditions in which the solid is present and are independent of the history of the samples. The further discussion will be concerned with the high- temperature equilibria in the solid–gas systems.

The equilibrium in the solid–gas system will be considered for a hypothetical crystal MO which has reached the state of thermodynamic equilibrium with the surrounding vapour, the latter containing atoms $M^{(g)}$ and molecules $O_2^{(g)}$.

[†] It is generally assumed that for the compounds of MO type the boundary between moderate and high temperatures corresponds to 0.7 of melting point of a given compound in Kelvin scale, and is named the *Tammann temperature*.

For simplicity, we assume that the crystal MO shows a tendency to form solely neutral vacancies V_M^x and V_O^x, which are distributed randomly and do not interact ones with the others. Although such a case is not fully conceivable owing to ionization of defects, it permits us to formulate some interesting conclusions.

The equilibrium between a crystal MO and its vapour may be described by the following formulae:

$$MO \equiv M_M^x + O_O^x \rightleftarrows MO^{(g)} \qquad (6.1)$$

$$M_M^x + O_O^x \rightleftarrows M^{(g)} + 1/2\, O_2^{(g)} \qquad (6.2)$$

Applying the law of mass action to the above reactions we obtain:

$$\frac{P_{MO}}{[M_M^x][O_O^x]} = K_1' \qquad (6.3)$$

$$\frac{P_M P_{O_2}^{1/2}}{[M_M^x][O_O^x]} = K_2' \qquad (6.4)$$

Since the concentrations of the defects are small, one may assume that $[M_M^x]$ and $[O_O^x]$ are approximately constant, and write eqs. (6.3) and (6.4) in the form:

$$P_{MO} = K_1'[M_M^x][O_O^x] = K_1 \qquad (6.5)$$

$$P_M P_{O_2}^{1/2} = K_2'[M_M^x][O_O^x] = K_2 \qquad (6.6)$$

According to the phase rule, the system under discussion has two degrees of freedom, as there are two components and two phases. It follows from this, that at the fixed temperature either P_{O_2} or P_M can be varied arbitrarily. This makes possible to change the concentration of defects by the following reactions:

$$M^{(g)} \rightleftarrows M_M^x + V_O^x \qquad (6.7)$$

$$1/2\, O_2^{(g)} \rightleftarrows O_O^x + V_M^x \qquad (6.8)$$

According to the law of mass action, from the above relation one may get:

$$\frac{[M_M^x][V_O^x]}{P_M} = K_3' \qquad (6.9)$$

$$\frac{[O_O^x][V_M^x]}{P_{O_2}^{1/2}} = K_4' \qquad (6.10)$$

Applying the approximation, similarly like in the case of eqs. (6.5) and (6.6), the concentrations of vacancies in the sublattices M and O may be written as:

$$[V_O^x] = \frac{K_3'}{[M_M^x]} P_M = K_3 P_M \qquad (6.11)$$

$$[V_M^x] = \frac{K_4'}{[O_O^x]} P_{O_2}^{1/2} = K_4 P_{O_2}^{1/2} \qquad (6.12)$$

Equations (6.6), (6.11) and (6.12) can be combined to:

$$[V_M^x][V_O^x] = K_2 K_3 K_4 \equiv K_s \qquad (6.13)$$

The equilibrium constant $K_S = K_2 K_3 K_4$ is named the *Schottky constant*, as it describes the equilibrium of the reaction:

$$\text{zero} \rightleftarrows V_M^x + V_O^x \tag{6.14}$$

The relationships described by eqs. (6.6), (6.11) and (6.12) are plotted in Fig. 6.1 on a logarithmic scale.

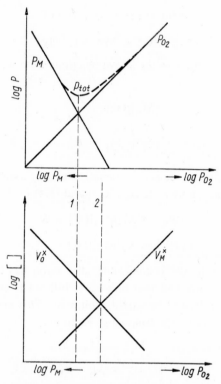

FIG. 6.1. Dependence of total pressure and concentration of neutral vacancies in both sublattices of crystal MO on composition of the gas phase at constant temperature. Symbol [ ] denotes concentration of defects of a given type: 1—minimum total pressure, 2—stoichiometric composition.

As seen from the plot in Fig. 6.1 there exist two ranges of pressures P_M and P_{O_2}. In the first of them (low pressure P_M and high P_{O_2}), some of molecules $O_2^{(g)}$ from the gas phase are incorporated into the crystal forming new vacancies V_M^x and filling vacancies V_O^x. As the result of these processes, with the increase in P_{O_2}, the concentration of vacancies V_O^x is decreased and that of vacancies V_M^x is increased. In this range of pressures vacancies V_M^x are hence predominating in the crystal. In the second range of pressures (high P_M and low P_{O_2}), atoms $M^{(g)}$ incorporating from the gas phase into the crystal give rise to vacancies in the sublattice O and occupy vacancies V_M^x. Thus the concentration of vacancies V_O^x in the crystal MO is increased and that of vacancies V_M^x is decreased when P_M is increased. In this range of pressures vacancies V_O^x are thus prevailing.

A special situation is obtained in the case when $[V_M^x] = [V_O^x]$ which indicates that the crystal has the stoichiometric composition. The pressures of $M^{(g)}$ and $O_2^{(g)}$ corresponding to this composition, denoted by $(P_M)_{st}$ and $(P_{O_2})_{st}$, obey the following condition resulting from eqs. (6.11) and (6.12):

$$(P_M)_{st} = \frac{K_4}{K_3} (P_{O_2}^{1/2})_{st} \tag{6.15}$$

The pressures $(P_M)_{st}$ and $(P_{O_2})_{st}$ may be expressed by the equilibrium constants. Namely from eqs. (6.11), (6.12) and (6.13) we get:

$$[V_M^x]_{st} = [V_O^x]_{st} = K_s^{1/2} \tag{6.16}$$

$$(P_M)_{st} = \frac{K_s^{1/2}}{K_3} \tag{6.17}$$

$$(P_{O_2})_{st} = \frac{K_s}{K_4^2} \tag{6.18}$$

Another interesting case concerns the minimum vapour pressure over the crystal, which is an important parameter in selection of experimental conditions. The total vapour pressure is given by:

$$P_{tot} = P_M + P_{O_2} + P_{MO} \tag{6.19}$$

Substituting $P_{MO} = K_1$ from eq. (6.5) and P_{O_2} calculated from eq. (6.6) into eq. (6.19) one obtains:

$$P_{tot} = P_M + K_2^2 P_M^{-2} + K_1 \tag{6.20}$$

To derive the minimum vapour pressure the differential $\partial P_{tot}/\partial P_M$ is then calculated and equalized to zero. The value $(P_M)_{min}$ obtained in this way is:

$$(P_M)_{min} = (2K_2^2)^{1/3} \tag{6.21}$$

Calculated in the similar manner $(P_{O_2})_{min}$ is found to be:

$$(P_M)_{min} = 2(P_{O_2})_{min} \tag{6.22}$$

It follows from the above discussion that properties of a crystal can be controlled only when at sufficiently high temperature one varies the pressures P_M or P_{O_2} in such a way that $P_M > (P_M)_{min}$ or $P_{O_2} > (P_{O_2})_{min}$. If for instance the partial pressure of oxygen over an oxide crystal is reduced below the value $(P_{O_2})_{min}$ of this compound, the oxide begins to dissociate. Due to this latter process the pressure of oxygen is increased to the value corresponding to the minimum value of the total pressure.

There exist several other factors limiting the range of changes of partial pressures in the atmosphere surrounding the crystal. The lower limit of the oxygen pressures is dependent on the following factors:

(1) dissociation pressure of an oxide, and also on

(2) formation of an oxide of lower valency, e.g. Cu_2O when CuO is investigated. The upper limit of the oxygen pressures is determined by:

(1) technological factors, e.g. material strength of the experimental set-up, and also

(2) formation of an oxide of higher valency, e.g. Fe_2O_3 when FeO is investigated. In the case of changes of P_M the latter cannot exceed the vapour pressure over the pure metal.

The pressure of non-dissociated molecules in the gas phase P_{MO} need not be known as a rule, with the exception of the cases in which knowledge of the total mass of the gas is required.

6.2. Equilibria of Fully Ionized Vacancies, Electrons and Holes

Discussion of this problem is a continuation of considerations presented in section 1 of the present chapter. The assumptions, pertaining to the composition of the atmosphere surrounding the crystal and to the occurence of vacancies in the both sublattices as the only type of defects, remain then valid. In the present section the electronic defects resulting from ionization of these vacancies will be discussed.

For simplicity we assume that only some of donor and acceptor levels are situated in the forbidden energy gap as shown in the scheme presented in Fig. 6.2, and that all

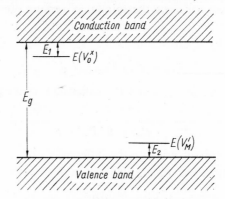

FIG. 6.2. Diagram of energy levels in crystal MO containing vacancies in both sublattices.

donor and acceptor levels are completely ionized. This latter assumption is frequently fulfilled in practice, since in many chemical compounds donor levels are so close the conduction band, and acceptor levels so close the valence band that at sufficiently high temperatures the complete ionization of these levels can be realized.

In accordance to the assumptions, the processes which occur in a crystal MO can be described by the following quasi-chemical reactions:

$$M^{(g)} \rightleftarrows M_M^x + V_o^\bullet + e' \tag{6.23}$$

$$1/2\,O_2^{(g)} \rightleftarrows O_o^x + V_M' + h^\bullet \tag{6.24}$$

$$zero \rightleftarrows e' + h^\bullet \tag{6.25}$$

The equilibrium given by eq. (6.25) describes a spontaneous process, consisting in a transfer of some electrons from the valence band to the conduction band by thermal excitation. For the full description of the defect situation in the crystal under discussion one must obviously take into account eqs. (6.2) and (6.6). Finally the neutrality condition should be fulfilled since the crystal as a whole has no electrical charge. This condition may be written in the form of the following equation:

$$n + [V_M'] = p + [V_o^\bullet] \tag{6.26}$$

The considered defects are then adequately described by four equilibrium equations [eqs. (6.2), (6.23), (6.24) and (6.25)], and the neutrality condition [eq. (6.26)].

Making use of the law of mass action, eqs. (6.23)–(6.25) may be written in the form:

$$\frac{[M_M^x][V_O^{\cdot\cdot}]n}{P_M} = K_5'$$ (6.27)

$$\frac{[O_O^x][V_M']p}{P_{O_2}^{1/2}} = K_6'$$ (6.28)

$$n \cdot p = K_i$$ (6.29)

As results from the discussion in section 6.1, eqs. (6.27) and (6.28) can be simplified to give:

$$[V_O^{\cdot\cdot}] \cdot n = \frac{K_5'}{[M_M^x]} P_M = K_5 P_M$$ (6.30)

$$[V_M'] \cdot p = \frac{K_6'}{[O_O^x]} P_{O_2}^{1/2} = K_6 P_{O_2}^{1/2}$$ (6.31)

We obtain hence 5 equations [(6.6), (6.26), (6.29)–(6.31)] with 7 variables: $n, p, [V_M']$, $[V_O^{\cdot\cdot}]$, P_M, P_{O_2} and T, where T is the absolute temperature of the system.

In the case of high-temperature isothermal processes the system has one degree of freedom, i.e. one variable can be varied arbitrarily. The pressure P_{O_2} is commonly taken as this variable.

Taking P_{O_2} as the independent variable, P_M should be eliminated. For this, in the further discussion we will consider instead of eqs. (6.6) and (6.30) the expression:

$$[V_M'][V_O^{\cdot\cdot}] = K_2 K_5 K_6/K_i = K_{S_1}.$$ (6.32)

which is obtained from eqs. (6.6), (6.29)–(6.31).

The system of eqs. (6.26), (6.29), (6.31) and (6.32) enables us to derive with the analytical method the concentrations of all defects discussed so far as dependent on the partial pressure P_{O_2} and on equilibrium constants, the solutions obtained are however complex (in particular in the cases of more complicated defect situations). Therefore for solving this system of equations we will apply the approximate graphical method proposed by Brouwer.[121] The system of equations given above is solved according to this method by making use of the approximate formulae for the neutrality condition. The whole range of the partial oxygen pressures is subdivided into the regions in which the two types of defects occurring in the neutrality condition predominate. However, to make this subdivision it is necessary either to know—at least approximately—the values of the equilibrium constants at a given temperature, or to assume them a priori.

The concentrations of defects are then expressed as a function of the equilibrium constants and of the adjusted partial pressure of oxygen in particular regions, in which the approximate conditions of electroneutrality can be employed. Taking logarithms of the expressions obtained, we get the system of linear equations. Finally plots of logarithms of concentrations of defects against the logarithm of oxygen pressure are drawn for various regions of pressure. Usually the plots show different slopes in various pressure regions, the limits of these regions being determined by points of intersection of the straight lines.

For illustration, the Brouwer method will be applied to a hypothetical case in which the value of the equilibrium constant K_i is considerably smaller than the value of K_{S_1}. At very low values of P_{O_2}, the vacancies in the oxygen sublattice are the prevailing defects. Their ionization gives rise to ionized centres $V_O^{\cdot}$ and quasi-free electrons in the conduction band. The neutrality condition for this case can be written:

$$n = [V_O^{\cdot}] \gg p, [V_M'] \qquad (6.33)$$

With the increase in the pressure P_{O_2}, $[V_O^{\cdot}]$ is decreased and $[V_M']$ is increased. Thus, in a certain range of pressures, acceptor levels $E(V_M')$ will be filled by the electrons originating from donor levels $E(V_O^x)$ (see Fig. 6.2). The intrinsic process may be neglected since $K_i \ll K_{S_1}$ and the neutrality condition assumes the form:

$$[V_M'] = [V_O^{\cdot}] \gg n, p \qquad (6.34)$$

Finally, at high pressures P_{O_2}, vacancies V_M^x predominate in the crystal. Their ionization gives rise to ionized centres V_M' and holes in the valence band. The neutrality condition is then:

$$p = [V_M'] \gg n, [V_O^{\cdot}] \qquad (6.35)$$

Having derived the electroneutrality conditions, the solutions of the system of eqs. (6.29), (6.31) and (6.32) can be obtained for particular ranges of the pressure P_{O_2}. These solutions are presented in Table 1.

TABLE 1. CONCENTRATIONS OF DEFECTS IN CRYSTAL MO CONTAINING SINGLY-IONIZED VACANCIES IN BOTH SUBLATTICES AS A FUNCTION OF OXYGEN PRESSURE AT DIFFERENT SIMPLIFIED CONDITIONS OF ELECTRONEUTRALITY

Simplified conditions of electro-neutrality	Range I	Range II	Range III
	$n = [V_O^{\cdot}]$	$[V_M'] = [V_O^{\cdot}]$	$p = [V_M']$
n	$K_i^{1/2} K_{S_1}^{1/2} R^{-1/2}$	$K_i K_{S_1}^{1/2} R^{-1}$	$K_i R^{-1/2}$
p	$K_i^{1/2} K_{S_1}^{-1/2} R^{1/2}$	$K_S^{-1/2} R$	$R^{1/2}$
$[V_O^{\cdot}]$	$K_i^{1/2} K_{S_1}^{1/2} R^{-1/2}$	$K_{S_1}^{1/2}$	$K_{S_1} R^{-1/2}$
$[V_M']$	$K_{S_1}^{1/2} K_i^{-1/2} R^{1/2}$	$K_{S_1}^{1/2}$	$R^{1/2}$
		$R = K_6 P_{O_2}^{1/2}$	

Taking logarithms of these solutions we obtain three systems of linear equations which express logarithms of concentrations of all defects occurring in the crystal under discussion, as a function of log R. The relations thus obtained assume different form in various regions of R. Their graphical presentation gives a number of intersecting lines (Fig. 6.3). The points of the intersection determine approximately the limits of the pressures P_{O_2} in which the chosen approximate neutrality conditions can be used. On passing from one region of pressure to another, the given neutrality condition ceases to hold and is replaced by another one. It is understandable that the approximate solutions of the system of eqs. (6.26), (6.29), (6.31) and (6.32) compiled in Table 1 are close to the solutions derived with the analytical method only in the vicinity of the centre of each range of pressure, and they deviate most at the limits of this pressure

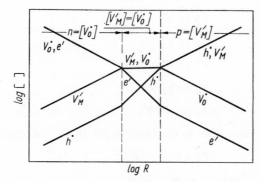

FIG. 6.3. Log concentration of defects in crystal MO containing singly ionized vacancies in both sublattices as a function of log R at constant temperature for the case $K_{S_1} \gg K_i$.

ranges. However, in spite of the approximate character of graphical method of the solution, the Brouwer method is of great merit owing to its simplicity both in theoretical and experimental studies on interrelations between concentrations of defects in crystals. The accurate analytical solutions are so intricate particularly in the case of more complicated defect systems that their practical use is only limited.

6.3. Equilibria of Neutral and Ionized Vacancies, and Electrons and Holes

In this section a more general and at the same time more complex case of defect equilibria will be considered. The model of energy levels in this case is given in Fig. 6.4.

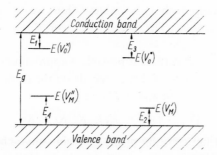

FIG. 6.4. Diagram of energy levels in crystal MO containing vacancies in both sublattices.

The complete ionization of the defects is not assumed in this case; however, the other assumptions given in section 1 of this chapter remain valid.

The defect reactions for such a crystal are:

$$MO \equiv M_M^x + O_O^x \rightleftarrows M^{(g)} + 1/2 O_2^{(g)} \qquad (6.36) = (6.2)$$

$$M^{(g)} \rightleftarrows M_M^x + V_O^x \qquad (6.37) = (6.7)$$

$$\text{zero} \rightleftarrows V_M^x + V_O^x \qquad (6.38) = (6.14)$$

$$V_M^x \rightleftarrows V_M' + h^{\cdot} \qquad (6.39)$$

$$V_M' \rightleftarrows V_M'' + h^{\cdot} \qquad (6.40)$$

$$V_O^x \rightleftarrows V_O^{\cdot} + e' \qquad (6.41)$$

$$V_O^{\cdot} \rightleftarrows V_O^{\cdot\cdot} + e' \qquad (6.42)$$

$$\text{zero} \rightleftarrows e' + h^{\cdot} \qquad (6.43) = (6.25)$$

Applying the law of mass action to reactions (6.36)–(6.43), we obtain:

$$P_M \cdot P_{O_2}^{1/2} = K_2 \qquad (6.44) = (6.6)$$

$$[V_M^x] = K_4 P_{O_2}^{1/2} = R_1 \qquad (6.45) = (6.12)$$

$$[V_M^x] \cdot [V_O^x] = K_S \qquad (6.46) = (6.13)$$

$$\frac{[V_M']p}{[V_M^x]} = K_7 \qquad (6.47)$$

$$\frac{[V_M''] \cdot p}{[V_M']} = K_8 \qquad (6.48)$$

$$\frac{[V_O^{\cdot}] \cdot n}{[V_O^x]} = K_9 \qquad (6.49)$$

$$\frac{[V_O^{\cdot\cdot}] \cdot n}{[V_O^{\cdot}]} = K_{10} \qquad (6.50)$$

$$n \cdot p = K_i \qquad (6.51) = (6.29)$$

The neutrality condition in this case assumes the form:

$$n + [V_M'] + 2[V_M''] = p + [V_O^{\cdot}] + 2[V_O^{\cdot\cdot}] \qquad (6.52)$$

We obtain thus 9 equations with 11 variables. Thus, in isothermal processes the system has one degree of freedom. The pressure P_{O_2}, or R_1 is taken as the independent variable.

It follows from eq. (6.52) that there is possible 9 approximated conditions of electroneutrality. The selection of some of them depends on the equilibrium constants.

From eqs. (6.44), (6.47), (6.49), and (6.51) we get:

$$[V_M'] \cdot [V_O^{\cdot}] = K_S K_7 K_9 / K_i \equiv K_{S_2} \qquad (6.53)$$

where K_{S_2} is the equilibrium constant of the following quasi-chemical reaction:

$$\text{zero} \rightleftarrows V_M' + V_O^{\cdot} \qquad (6.54)$$

From eqs. (6.48), (6.50), (6.51) and (6.53) we get:

$$[V_M''] \cdot [V_O^{\cdot\cdot}] = K_{S_2} K_8 K_{10} / K_i \equiv K_{S_3} \qquad (6.55)$$

where K_{S_3} is the equilibrium constant of the following quasi-chemical reaction:

$$\text{zero} \rightleftarrows V_M'' + V_O^{\bullet\bullet} \tag{6.56}$$

The system of eqs. (6.44)–(6.52) will be solved, at the assumption that $K_{S_3} > K_i^2 > K_{S_2}$.

At very low partial pressure of oxygen, the crystal under discussion shows a tendency to form vacancies mainly in the oxygen sublattice. They give rise to donor levels $E\ (V_O^x)$ and $E\ (V_O^{\bullet})$ in the forbidden energy gap (cf. Fig. 6.4). If the concentration of oxygen vacancies is very high one can assume that these donors are only partially ionized supplying quasi-free electrons to the conduction band. This leads to the formation of mainly singly-ionized oxygen vacancies, i.e. positive centres $V_O^{\bullet}$. The process of formation of doubly-ionized vacancies $V_O^{\bullet\bullet}$ can be neglected. In this case the simplified condition of electroneutrality may be written as:

$$n = [V_O^{\bullet}] \tag{6.57}$$

At higher pressures P_{O_2}, a certain number of vacancies in the sublattice M is created, involving the appearance of acceptor levels $E\ (V_M')$ and $E\ (V_M'')$ as shown in Fig. 6.4. The number of vacancies in the oxygen sublattice is reduced, though their concentration is still much larger than the concentration of vacancies in the sublattice M. In this situation, one can assume that oxygen vacancies are fully ionized. Thus, for this pressure range, the neutrality condition is given by:

$$n = 2\ [V_O^{\bullet\bullet}] \tag{6.58}$$

With the further increase in the oxygen pressure, the concentration of vacancies in the oxygen sublattice is further reduced. Bearing in mind the assumed condition $K_{S_3} > K_{S_2}$, one may consider that in the third pressure range, the doubly-ionized vacancies are prevailing in the both sublattices. This is due to the fact, that in this pressure range, the concentration of vacancies in the oxygen sublattice is approximately equal to that in the sublattice M, their ionization being effectuated mainly by the electron transfer from levels $E\ (V_O^x)$ and $E\ (V_O^{\bullet})$ to levels $E\ (V_M')$ and $E\ (V_M'')$.

The simplified neutrality condition in this case assumes the form:

$$[V_O^{\bullet\bullet}] = [V_M''] \tag{6.59}$$

At still higher oxygen pressures, the concentration of vacancies in the sublattice M prevails over the concentration of vacancies in the oxygen sublattice. In this case, the electrons from the valence band fill mainly the acceptor levels $E\ (V_M')$ and $E\ (V_M'')$, the simplified neutrality condition being:

$$p = 2[V_M''] \tag{6.60}$$

Finally, at sufficiently high oxygen pressures, the vacancies occur mainly in the sublattice M. Their ionization involves the filling of the acceptor level $E\ (V_M')$ by electrons of the valence band. The neutrality condition in this case may be written:

$$p = [V_M'] \tag{6.61}$$

The solutions of the system of eqs. (6.44)–(6.51), obtained taking into account the above given neutrality conditions are listed in Table 2.

TABLE 2. CONCENTRATIONS OF DEFECTS IN CRYSTAL MO CONTAINING NEUTRAL, SINGLY- AND DOUBLY-IONIZED VACANCIES IN BOTH SUBLATTICES AS A FUNCTION OF OXYGEN PRESSURE AT DIFFERENT SIMPLIFIED CONDITIONS OF ELECTRONEUTRALITY

Simplified conditions of electro-neutrality	Range I $n = [V_O^\bullet]$	Range II $n = 2[V_O^{\bullet\bullet}]$	Range III $[V_O^{\bullet\bullet}] = [V_M'']$	Range IV $p = 2[V_M'']$	Range V $p = [V_M']$
n	$K_9^{1/2} R_1^{-1/2}$	$(2K_9 K_{10})^{1/3} R_1^{-1/3}$	$(K_9 K_{10})^{1/2} K_{S_3}^{-1/4} R_1^{-1/2}$	$K_i(2K_7 K_8 K_S)^{-1/3} R_1^{-1/3}$	$K_i(K_S K_7)^{-1/2} R_1^{-1/2}$
p	$K_i K_9^{-1/2} R_1^{1/2}$	$K_i(2K_9 K_{10})^{-1/3} R_1^{1/3}$	$K_i(K_9 K_{10})^{-1/2} K_{S_3}^{1/4} R_1^{1/2}$	$(2K_7 K_8 K_S)^{1/3} R_1^{1/3}$	$(K_S K_7)^{1/2} R_1^{1/2}$
$[V_M']$	$K_{S_2} K_i K_9^{-1/2} R_1^{1/2}$	$K_{S_2}(2K_{10})^{1/3} K_9^{-2/3} R_1^{2/3}$	$K_{S_2} K_9^{-1/2} K_{10}^{1/2} K_{S_3}^{-1/4} R_1^{1/2}$	$K_{S_2} K_i K_9^{-1}(2K_7 K_8 K_S)^{-1/3} R_1^{2/3}$	$(K_S K_7)^{1/2} R_1^{1/2}$
$[V_M'']$	K_{10}	$K_{S_3}\left(\frac{1}{4} K_9 K_{10}\right)^{-1/3} R_1^{1/3}$	$K_{S_3}^{1/2}$	$\left(\frac{1}{4} K_7 K_8 K_S\right)^{1/3} R_1^{1/3}$	K_8
$[V_M^x]$	$K_S R_1$	$K_S R_1$	$K_S R_1$	$K_S R_1$	$K_S R_1$
$[V_O^\bullet]$	$K_9^{1/2} R_1^{-1/2}$	$K_9^{2/3}(2K_{10})^{-1/3} R_1^{-2/3}$	$K_9^{1/2} K_{10}^{-1/2} K_{S_3}^{1/4} R_1^{-1/2}$	$K_9(2K_7 K_8 K_S)^{1/3} K_i^{-1} R_1^{-2/3}$	$K_{S_2}(K_S K_7)^{-1/2} R_1^{-1/2}$
$[V_O^{\bullet\bullet}]$	$K_{S_3} K_{10}^{-1}$	$\left(\frac{1}{4} K_9 K_{10}\right)^{1/3} R_1^{-1/3}$	$K_{S_3}^{1/2}$	$K_{S_3}\left(\frac{1}{4} K_7 K_8 K_S\right)^{-1/3} R_1^{-1/3}$	$K_{S_3} K_8^{-1}$
$[V_O^x]$	R_1^{-1}	R_1^{-1}	R_1^{-1}	R_1^{-1}	R_1^{-1}

$R_1 = (K_2 K_3)^{-1} P_{O_2}^{1/2}$

It follows from the above considerations, that the whole region of P_{O_2} (or R_1) can be divided into five smaller regions, in each of which one of the five selected, simplified conditions of electroneutrality (i.e. one of the solutions given in Table 2) is held. As seen from Fig. 6.5, the limits of these regions can be determined by plotting log concentrations of a given type of defects as a function of log R_1 with the assumed values of the equilibrium constants. The plots of the above functions, namely, with the exception of those for non-ionized defects, have different slopes in different regions of R_1, intersecting at these limits. From the plots: log defect concentration vs. log R_1 one can

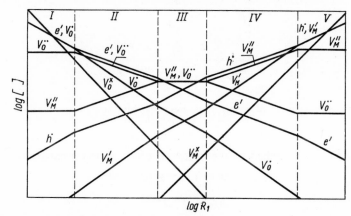

FIG. 6.5. Dependence of log defect concentration in crystal MO containing neutral, singly-, and doubly-ionized vacancies in both sublattices on log R_1 at constant temperature for the case
$$K_{S_3} > K_i^2 > K_{S_2}.$$

predict, in a relatively simple way, some properties of the crystal in various thermodynamic conditions. In particular, it follows from Fig. 6.5 that at high values of P_{O_2} the crystal will behave as a p-type semiconductor, and at high values of P_M as an n-type semiconductor. At intermediate pressures, both holes and electrons will be the current carriers in the crystal, the ratio of their concentration being dependent on the partial pressure P_{O_2} in the atmosphere surrounding the crystal. By appropriate selection of P_{O_2} we can obtain the value of this ratio equal to 1. The knowledge of the oxygen partial pressure is then of particularly great importance for the process of preparation of materials, since by adjusting this parameter we can obtain the material of the controlled physical properties. It must be, however, remembered that this is possible only when the temperature of the sample preparation is sufficiently high to ensure the equilibrium between the crystal and the surrounding gas phase.

6.4. Equilibria of Vacancies, Interstitial Atoms, and Electrons and Holes

We will consider now a defect situation, encountered frequently in practice, consisting in the presence of vacancies and interstitial atoms in only one sublattice of the crystal.

It is assumed that a hypothetical crystal MO shows a tendency to form the interstitial atoms and vacancies in the sublattice M. Thus only levels $E(M_i^x)$ and $E(V_M')$ are present in the energy gap as shown schematically in Fig. 6.6. It is also assumed that the concentration of the defects is small, so that they are distributed randomly in the crystal, not interacting and not forming associates. The composition of the atmosphere surrounding the crystal is the same as in the cases considered previously.

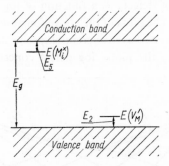

FIG. 6.6. Schematic diagram of energy levels in crystal MO, containing interstitial atoms and vacancies in sublattice M.

Such a case can be described by the following quasi-chemical reactions:

$$M^{(g)} + V_i^x \rightleftarrows M_i^x \tag{6.62}$$

$$M_M^x + V_i^x \rightleftarrows M_i^x + V_M^x \tag{6.63}$$

$$M_i^x \rightleftarrows M_i' + e' \tag{6.64}$$

$$V_M^x \rightleftarrows V_M' + h^\cdot \tag{6.65}$$

$$\text{zero} \rightleftarrows e' + h^\cdot \tag{6.66}$$

Application of the law of mass action to reactions (6.62)–(6.66) yields:

$$\frac{[M_i^x]}{[V_i^x] \cdot P_M} = K_{11}' \tag{6.67}$$

$$\frac{[M_i^x][V_M^x]}{[M_M^x][V_i^x]} = K_F' \tag{6.68}$$

$$\frac{[M_i']n}{[M_i^x]} = K_{12} \tag{6.69}$$

$$\frac{[V_M']p}{[V_M^x]} = K_7 \tag{6.70} = (6.47)$$

$$n \cdot p = K_i \tag{6.71} = (6.29)$$

The electroneutrality condition in this case is:

$$n + [V_M'] = p + [M_i'] \tag{6.72}$$

In the case of very small concentrations of the defects, the concentration of interstitial vacancies V_i^x is approximately equal to the concentration of lattice sites in the sublattice M. Equations (6.67) and (6.68) may be thus written as:

$$[M_i^x] = K_{11}'[V_i^x]P_M = K_{11} P_M = R_2 \tag{6.73}$$

$$[M_i^x][V_M^x] = K_F'[M_M^x][V_i^x] = K_F \tag{6.74}$$

The equilibrium constant K_F is called the *Frenkel constant*. We obtain thus six indepen-
dent equations [(6.69)–(6.74)] with eight variables: n, p, $[M_i^x]$, $[M_i^{\cdot}]$, $[V_M^x]$, $[V_M^{\prime}]$, T
and P_M (or R_2). At high-temperature isothermal processes, the system has then again
one degree of freedom. In this case R_2 is taken as the independent variable.[†]

It follows from eq. (6.72) that in the case under discussion there exist four possible
approximated conditions of electroneutrality. Three of them will be employed in the
further considerations.

At low pressures P_M, the vacancies in the sublattice M will be the predominating
defects. Some of them undergo ionization by transfer of electrons from the valence
band to acceptor level E ($V_M^{\prime}$). The filling of the acceptor level gives rise to ionized
centres $V_M^{\prime}$ and quasi-free holes in the valence band. The neutrality condition in this
pressure range is:

$$p = [V_M^{\prime}] \tag{6.75}$$

When the partial pressure of the component M in the atmosphere surrounding the
crystal is high, then the interstitial atoms are the predominating defects. Part of these
defects become ionized, supplying quasi-free electrons to the conduction band and
forming singly-ionized positive centres $M_i^{\cdot}$. The simplified neutrality condition assumes
the form:

$$n = [M_i^{\cdot}] \tag{6.76}$$

In the intermediate range of pressure P_M the concentrations of interstitial atoms and
vacancies in the crystal are comparable.

To derive the simplified condition of neutrality for the intermediate pressures P_M,
the equilibrium constant of the reaction:

$$\text{zero} \rightleftarrows V_M^{\prime} + M_i^{\cdot} \tag{6.77}$$

should be known.

Applying the law of mass action to the above reaction we get:

$$[V_M^{\prime}][M_i^{\cdot}] = K_{F_1} = K_F K_{12} K_7 / K_i \tag{6.78}$$

The value of constant K_{F_1} is calculated from eqs. (6.69), (6.70), (6.71) and (6.74). The
selection of the neutrality condition in this pressure range depends on whether the
constant K_{F_1} is larger or smaller than K_i. If $K_{F_1} > K_i$, then of the four types of defects
involved in the neutrality condition, only two will predominate, namely $M_i^{\cdot}$ and $V_M^{\prime}$.
This means, that ionization of these defects takes place by transfer of some electrons
from the donor level $E(M_i^x)$ to the acceptor level $E(V_M^{\prime})$. The neutrality condition
in this case may be thus written in the simplified form:

$$[M_i^{\cdot}] = [V_M^{\prime}] \tag{6.79}$$

If, on the other hand $K_i > K_{F_1}$, then the transfer of some electrons from the valence
band to the conduction band will be prevailing, as the result of which quasi-free electrons
and holes will predominate in the crystal. The neutrality condition for this case is:

$$n = p \tag{6.80}$$

[†] It should be remembered that pressure P_M is related to P_{O_2} by relation (6.6).

OXIDE SEMICONDUCTORS

In the case of oxides, the forbidden energy gap is relatively large, and hence condition (6.80) is usually not held. Thus in the further discussion the condition (6.79) is accepted as the one which is valid in the crystal.

The solutions of the system of equations (6.69)–(6.74), derived taking into account the simplified conditions of electroneutrality described by eqs. (6.75), (6.76) and (6.79), are listed in Table 3. In Fig. 6.7 logarithms of concentrations of particular types

TABLE 3. CONCENTRATIONS OF DEFECTS IN CRYSTAL MO CONTAINING NEUTRAL AND SINGLY-IONIZED INTERSTITIAL ATOMS AND VACANCIES IN SUBLATTICE M AS A FUNCTION OF PRESSURE P_M AT DIFFERENT SIMPLIFIED CONDITIONS OF ELECTRONEUTRALITY

Simplified conditions of electro-neutrality	Range I	Range II	Range III
	$p = [V'_M]$	$[M_i^•] = [V'_M]$	$n = [M_i^•]$
n	$K_i K_F^{-1/2} K_7^{-1/2} R_2^{1/2}$	$K_i^{1/2} K_{12}^{1/2} K_F^{-1/2} K_7^{-1/2} R_2$	$K_{12}^{1/2} R_2^{1/2}$
p	$K_7^{1/2} K_F^{1/2} R_2^{-1/2}$	$K_F^{1/2} K_7^{1/2} K_i^{1/2} K_{12}^{1/2} R_2^{-1}$	$K_i K_{12}^{-1/2} R_2^{-1/2}$
$[V'_M]$	$K_F^{1/2} K_7^{1/2} R_2^{-1/2}$	$K_F^{1/2} K_7^{1/2} K_{12}^{1/2} K_i^{-1/2}$	$K_F K_7 K_{12}^{1/2} K_i^{-1} R_2^{-1/2}$
$[M_i^•]$	$K_F^{1/2} K_7^{1/2} K_{12} K_i^{-1} R_2^{1/2}$	$K_F^{1/2} K_{12}^{1/2} K_7^{1/2} K_i^{-1/2}$	$K_{12}^{1/2} R_2^{1/2}$
$[V_M^x]$	$K_F R_2^{-1}$	$K_F R_2^{-1}$	$K_F R_2^{-1}$
$[M_i^x]$	$R_2 = K_{11} P_M$	R_2	R_2

of defects are plotted schematically as a function of $\log R_2$. If the ionization energies of donor and acceptor levels E_5 and E_2 (Fig. 6.6) are very small, both the donors and acceptors are completely ionized. In this case reactions (6.62) and (6.64) may be replaced by the following equation:

$$M^{(g)} + V_i^x \rightleftarrows M_i^• + e' \tag{6.81}$$

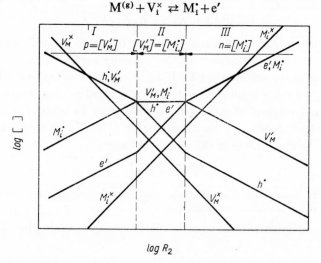

$\log R_2$

FIG. 6.7. Log concentration of defects in crystal MO, containing neutral and singly-ionized interstitial atoms and vacancies in sublattice M as a function of $\log R_2$ at constant temperature.

and reactions (6.63) and (6.65) by reaction (6.77). The law of mass action, applied to reaction (6.81) yields:

$$[M_i^{\cdot}] \cdot n = K_{13}' [V_i^{x}] P_M = K_{13} P_M = R_3 \qquad (6.82)$$

Thus all independent relations between the concentrations of defects may be described by eqs. (6.71), (6.72), (6.78) and (6.82).

Assuming that in the crystal under discussion there are held successively the simplified neutrality conditions described by equations (6.75), (6.76) and (6.79), we may readily

TABLE 4. CONCENTRATIONS OF DEFECTS IN CRYSTAL MO CONTAINING FULLY IONIZED INTERSTITIAL ATOMS AND VACANCIES IN SUBLATTICE M AS A FUNCTION OF PRESSURE P_M AT DIFFERENT CONDITIONS OF ELECTRONEUTRALITY

Simplified conditions of electro-neutrality	Range I $p = [V_M']$	Range II $[M_i^{\cdot}] = [V_M']$	Range III $n = [M_i^{\cdot}]$
n	$K_i^{1/2} K_{F_1}^{-1/2} R_3^{1/2}$	$K_{F_1}^{-1/2} R_3$	$R_3^{1/2}$
p	$K_i^{1/2} K_{F_1}^{1/2} R_3^{-1/2}$	$K_i K_{F_1}^{1/2} R_3^{-1}$	$K_i R_3^{-1/2}$
$[V_M']$	$K_i^{1/2} K_{F_1}^{1/2} R_3^{-1/2}$	$K_{F_1}^{1/2}$	$K_{F_1} R_3^{-1/2}$
$[M_i^{\cdot}]$	$K_{F_1}^{1/2} K_i^{-1/2} R_3^{1/2}$	$K_{F_1}^{1/2}$	$R_3^{1/2}$

express the concentrations of various defects as a function of R_3 and of the equilibrium constants. These functions are listed in Table 4, and their plots on the double logarithmic scale are shown in Fig. 6.8.

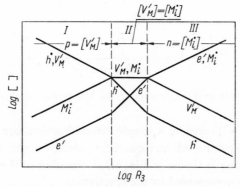

FIG. 6.8. Log concentration of defects in crystal MO, containing fully ionized interstitial atoms and vacancies in sublattice M as a function of R_3 at constant temperature, for $K_{F_1} > K_i$.

6.5. The Temperature Dependence of Concentration of Point Defects

In the preceding sections, isothermal equilibria of some types of point defects occurring most often in oxide crystals have been considered. This section will be concerned with the temperature dependence of the concentration of point defects at constant oxygen pressure, for the crystal MO that exhibits very small deviations from stoichiometry.

The equilibrium constant of a given defect situation may be written in the form:

$$K = \exp\left[\frac{\Delta S^\circ}{nk}\right] \exp\left[-\frac{\Delta H^\circ}{nkT}\right] \tag{6.83}$$

where ΔS° and ΔH° denote respectively the changes of standard entropy and enthalpy of the system for a given defect situation, and n is a small integer, e.g. 1, 2 or 3 (cf. Chapter 5). Essentially the values of ΔS° and ΔH° are temperature dependent. Hence, $\log K$ is not a linear function of the reciprocal of absolute temperature. Instead of real values of the entropy and enthalpy changes one may, however, adjust effective (averaged) values of ΔS^* and ΔH^*, such that $\log K$ is the linear function of $1/T$. Equation (6.83) may be then written:

$$\ln K = \frac{\Delta S^*}{nk} - \frac{\Delta H^*}{nk}\frac{1}{T} \tag{6.83a}$$

where ΔS^* and ΔH^* are constant.

Making use of the graphical method of Brouwer, we may express log concentrations of various types of defects occurring in a given crystal as a function of the reciprocal temperature, at constant P_{O_2}, and at adjusted simplified neutrality conditions, similarly as it was done in the discussion of isothermal dependence of concentration of point defects on the partial pressure of oxygen.

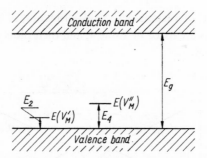

FIG. 6.9. Electronic energy level diagram for crystal MO containing vacancies in sublattice M.

For illustration, we will consider a simple defect situation, consisting in the presence of vacancies in the sublattice M and quasi-free electrons and holes. The scheme of energy levels for this case is shown in Fig. 6.9. Formation of the defects in this crystal at high temperatures is represented by the reactions:

$$1/2\ O_2^{(g)} \rightleftarrows O_O^x + V_M^x, \Delta H_V; \qquad [V_M^x] = K_4 P_{O_2}^{1/2} \qquad (6.84) = (6.12)$$

$$V_M^x \rightleftarrows V_M' + h^\cdot, E_2; \qquad [V_M']p = K_4 K_7 P_{O_2}^{1/2} \qquad (6.85) = (6.47)$$

$$V_M' \rightleftarrows V_M'' + h^\cdot, E_4; \qquad \frac{[V_M'']p}{[V_M']} = K_8 \qquad (6.86) = (6.48)$$

$$\text{zero} \rightleftarrows e' + h^\cdot, E_g; \qquad n \cdot p = K_i \qquad (6.87) = (6.29)$$

The neutrality condition in this case is:

$$n + [V'_M] + 2[V''_M] = p \tag{6.88}$$

As follows from eq. (6.88), we can consider three simplified electroneutrality conditions: $n = p$, $2\,[V''_M] = p$ and $[V'_M] = p$. Since the energy gap E_g in oxides is usually larger than the energy of formation of native atomic defects, the first condition is not held, and the last two conditions are valid. Solutions of the system of eqs. (6.84)–(6.87),

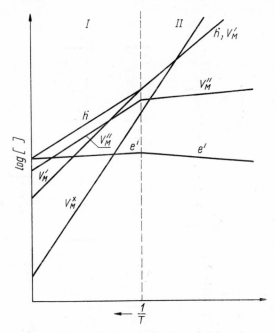

FIG. 6.10. Temperature dependence of the concentration of defects in crystal MO containing vacancies in sublattice M.

obtained taking into account successively these two conditions, are given in Table 5, and their graphical representation in Fig. 6.10. Principally, the choice of the simplified conditions of electroneutrality is determined by the value of the forbidden energy gap, energy of formation of atomic defects, and ionization energy of these defects.

6.6. Other Types of Defects

In the preceding sections we have considered only two types of point defects, called often the Schottky and Frenkel defects. The anti-structure defects have been so far neglected, as the probability of occurrence of these types of defects in oxides appears very small for geometrical and energetic reasons. For illustration we will write down some reactions involved in formation of these defects, at the assumption that no other defects occur in the crystal:

$$2M^{(g)} \rightleftarrows M^x_M + M^x_O \tag{6.89}$$

$$M^x_M + O^x_O \rightleftarrows M^x_O + O^x_M \tag{6.90}$$

TABLE 5. CONCENTRATIONS OF DEFECTS IN CRYSTAL MO CONTAINING VACANCIES IN THE SUBLATTICE M AS A FUNCTION OF TEMPERATURE AT DIFFERENT SIMPLIFIED CONDITIONS OF ELECTRONEUTRALITY

Approx. neutrality condition	Range I $2[V''_M] = p$	Range II $[V'_M] = p$
n	$(K_i^\circ)^{1/3}(2K_4^\circ K_7^\circ K_8^\circ)^{-1/3} P_{O_2}^{-1/6} \exp\left[-\dfrac{E_g - \Delta H_V - E_2 - E_4}{3kT}\right]$	$K_i^\circ (K_4^\circ K_7^\circ)^{-1/2} P_{O_2}^{-1/4} \exp\left[-\dfrac{2E_g - \Delta H_V - E_2}{2kT}\right]$
p	$(2K_4^\circ K_7^\circ K_8^\circ)^{1/3} P_{O_2}^{1/6} \exp\left[-\dfrac{\Delta H_V + E_2 + E_4}{3kT}\right]$	$(K_4^\circ K_7^\circ)^{1/2} P_{O_2}^{1/4} \exp\left[-\dfrac{\Delta H_V + E_2}{2kT}\right]$
$[V'_M]$	$(2K_8^\circ)^{-1/3}(K_4^\circ K_7^\circ)^{2/3} P_{O_2}^{1/3} \exp\left[-\dfrac{2\Delta H_V + 2E_2 - E_4}{3kT}\right]$	$(K_4^\circ K_7^\circ)^{1/2} P_{O_2}^{1/4} \exp\left[-\dfrac{\Delta H_V + E_2}{2kT}\right]$
$[V''_M]$	$\left(\dfrac{1}{4} K_4^\circ K_7^\circ K_8^\circ\right)^{1/3} P_{O_2}^{1/6} \exp\left[-\dfrac{\Delta H_V + E_2 + E_4}{3kT}\right]$	$K_8^\circ \exp\left[-\dfrac{E_4}{kT}\right]$
$[V^x_M]$	$K_4^\circ P_{O_2}^{1/2} \exp\left[-\dfrac{\Delta H_V}{kT}\right]$	$K_4^\circ P_{O_2}^{1/2} \exp\left[-\dfrac{\Delta H_V}{kT}\right]$

The presence of defects M_O^x and O_M^x may be accompanied by the appearance of donor and acceptor levels in the forbidden energy gap, which in turn may lead to the following reactions:

$$M_O^x \rightleftarrows M_O' + h^{\cdot} \tag{6.91}$$

$$O_M^x \rightleftarrows O_M^{\cdot} + e' \tag{6.92}$$

In real crystals there is always a certain probability of occurrence of the defect association. If the concentration of complexes formed due to this latter process cannot be neglected, one must take into consideration the equilibrium between single and associated defects. If we assume that only two types of defects (A and B) associate, this process may be described by:

$$nA + mB \rightleftarrows (A_n B_m) \tag{6.93}$$

where n and m are respectively the numbers of defects forming a complex. When the concentration of the complexes is small, and they are distributed in the crystal randomly, we may apply the law of mass action to reaction (6.93):

$$\frac{[(A_n B_m)]}{[A]^n [B]^m} = K_{AB} \tag{6.94}$$

It should be noted, that the defect situations in oxide crystals may be much more complex than it results from the described above limiting cases. One may also expect more numerous energy levels in the forbidden energy gap. In such cases the discussion on interrelations between the concentrations of various types of defects, involves larger number of equilibria, and hence more equations obeying the law of mass action. This makes the problem more complex, in particular in the case of numerous energy levels occurring near the valence and conduction bands. Formulation of the simplified conditions of electroneutrality becomes then a difficult problem.

The above discussion is concerned with the cases in which the defect concentrations in the crystal are so small, that no interaction between the defects occur, and hence the systems may be regarded as ideal solutions. If, however, the defect concentrations are not small and interactions between the defects cannot be neglected, the concentrations should be replaced by activities.

Finally it should be mentioned, that we may consider in the analogous manner, the defect equilibria in crystals of the general formula $M_a O_b$. The description of the defect reactions in this case is only modified, and thus the relations obtained by applying the law of mass action to these equilibria are slightly altered.

6.7. Deviations from Stoichiometry

Deviations from stoichiometry in chemical compounds are due to the presence of native atomic defects.

When a hypothetical oxide MO has a tendency to form vacancies as the only defects in the both sublattices, the deviation from stoichiometry y is equal:

$$y = \frac{[\overline{V}_M] - [\overline{V}_O]}{N_0} \tag{6.95}$$

where $[\overline{V}_M]$ and $[\overline{V}_O]$ are the total concentration of vacancies in the sublattice M and O respectively, e.g. $\overline{V}_O = [V_O^x] + [V_O^\cdot] + [V_O^{\cdot\cdot}]$, and N_0 is the number of lattice sites in the sublattice M or O in 1 cm^3. In the special case, when $[\overline{V}_O] = [\overline{V}_M]$, the deviation from stoichiometry is zero, in spite of the existence of atomic native defects in the crystal.

If the crystal shows a tendency to form interstitial atoms and vacancies in only one sublattice, e.g. in the sublattice M, the deviation from stoichiometry is given by:

$$y = \frac{[\overline{V}_M] - [\overline{M}_i]}{N_0} \tag{6.96}$$

where $[\overline{M}_i]$ is the total concentration of interstitial atoms of the component M.

In the general case, when all possible non-associated native atomic defects are present in the crystal, the deviation from stoichiometry may be described by the formula:

$$y = \frac{[\overline{O}_i] + [\overline{O}_M] + [\overline{V}_M] - [\overline{M}_i] - [\overline{M}_O] - [\overline{V}_O]}{N_0} \tag{6.97}$$

where dashed symbols of defects denote respectively the total concentrations of defects of the same group. An oxide that shows the deviation from stoichiometry is usually denoted by the formula MO_{1+y}.

If the oxide MO has an excess of oxygen (deficit of the component M), the deviation from stoichiometry is positive: $y > 0$, in the opposite case when the oxide shows a deficit of oxygen (an excess of component M), $y < 0$.

The question now arises, in what manner the deviation from stoichiometry is related to the oxygen pressure. In the case when neutral vacancies prevail in the both sublattices of the crystal MO (cf. section 6.1) and the value of y is small, this relation can be obtained in the following way. Substituting eqs. (6.11) and (6.12) into eq. (6.95) and taking into account eq. (6.6) we get:

$$y = \frac{K_4 P_{O_2}^{1/2} - K_2 K_3 P_{O_2}^{-1/2}}{N_0} \tag{6.98}$$

Multiplying eq. (6.98) by $P_{O_2}^{1/2}$ and rearranging its terms we obtain:

$$K_4 P_{O_2} - y N_0 P_{O_2}^{1/2} - K_2 K_3 = 0 \tag{6.99}$$

Solving the above equation one gets:

$$P_{O_2}(y) = \left[\frac{N_0 y \pm \sqrt{N_0^2 y^2 + 4 K_2 K_3 K_4}}{2 K_4} \right]^2 \tag{6.100}$$

At the stoichiometric composition $y = 0$, thus:

$$P_{O_2}(0) = K_2 K_3 / K_4 \tag{6.101}$$

Moreover at this composition [cf. eq. (6.13)]:

$$[V_M^x]_{st} = [V_O^x]_{st} = (K_2 K_3 K_4)^{1/2} = \delta \tag{6.102}$$

Finally from eqs. (100)–(102) we get:

$$\frac{P_{O_2}(y)}{P_{O_2}(0)} = 1 + \frac{N_0^2 y^2 + N_0 y \sqrt{N_0^2 y^2 + 4 \delta^2}}{2 \delta^2} \tag{6.103}$$

In Fig. 6.11 the dependence of the ratio $\dfrac{P_{O_2}(y)}{P_{O_2}(0)}$ on y at the constant temperature is shown for some values of δ. As seen from the plots in Fig. 6.11, the higher is the value of δ the smaller change in the ratio $P_{O_2}(y)/P_{O_2}(0)$ is needed for creation in the crystal

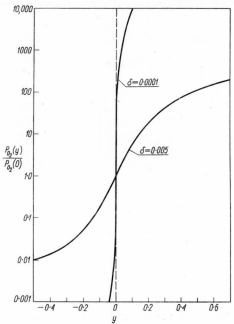

FIG. 6.11. Dependence of ratio $P_{O_2}(y)/P_{O_2}(0)$ on deviation from stoichiometry in crystal MO at constant temperature.[115]

MO a determined deviation from stoichiometry. In other words, if the stoichiometric crystal MO has a very small number of point defects (δ is very small), the formation of an excess of one component in this compound requires the application of large changes in the oxygen pressure. At high δ, already small change in the oxygen pressure may cause large deviation from stoichiometry. Obviously δ is increased with the increase in temperature, and thus deviation from stoichiometry at a given oxygen pressure is increased with the increasing temperature.

In the case of occurrence of ionized defects, the dependence of the deviation from stoichiometry on the pressure of one of the crystal components is similar, although much more complex mathematically. However, applying the graphical method of Brouwer one may obtain relatively simple relationships also in this case.

To explain this problem, the relation between the deviation from stoichiometry and the partial pressure of the component M will be considered for a pure crystal that shows a defect situation discussed in section 6.4. The deviation from stoichiometry in this case is given by:

$$|N_0 y| = |[M_i^x] + [M_i^{\cdot}] - [V_M^x] - [V_M']| \tag{6.104}$$

The dependence of y on the pressure P_M is shown in Fig. 6.12 on a double logarithmic scale. It follows from the plot that in various regions of the pressure P_M, the plot has different slopes. At low pressures P_M, the crystal contains an excess of atoms O, and y is positive. At the higher pressures the crystal has an excess of atoms M and hence y is negative. At moderate pressures there exists a certain value of P_M at which y changes the sign from the negative to positive values. This change takes place stepwise. The very small deviations from stoichiometry cannot be then determined. In the case under

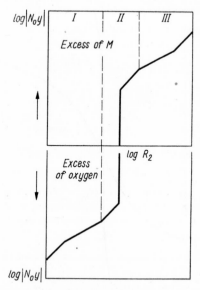

FIG. 6.12. Log deviation from stoichiometry in crystal MO as a function of log R_2 for the defect situation shown in Fig. 6.7.

consideration the point at which y is changed corresponds to the point at which the hole conduction is changed into the electronic conduction. The two points do not always coincide however.

In the writing of Chapter 6, the author depended to a great extent on the basic work by Kröger and Vink.[120]

CHAPTER 7

DEFECT EQUILIBRIA IN CRYSTALS CONTAINING ADMIXTURES

SEMICONDUCTOR physics shows that the presence of foreign atoms in crystals may lead to essential changes in their physical and chemical properties. In semiconductor elements and in compounds of nearly stoichiometric composition, the control of their properties is realized by introducing into the crystal admixtures of either donor or acceptor character. The problem is different in the case of oxides, which, as a rule, have the tendency to deviate from stoichiometry. The donors or acceptors in oxides are provided by both native defects and foreign atoms incorporated into the crystal lattice. Therefore, to obtain the controlled properties, the interrelations between the concentrations of native defects and of foreign atoms in oxides should be known. In order to explain some basic aspects of this problem we will consider some simple cases of defect equilibria in oxide crystals containing admixtures.

7.1. Mechanism of Incorporation of Foreign Atoms into the Crystal Lattice

There exist three possible ways of incorporating foreign atoms into the crystal lattice of a hypothetical oxide MO. The foreign atoms may namely occupy lattice sites in the sublattice $M (F_M)$, lattice sites in the oxygen sublattice (F_O), or interstitial positions (F_i). In the first two cases, the foreign atoms show a tendency to incorporate into such lattice sites that are normally occupied by atoms of similar electronegativity. Thus metal atoms are incorporated usually into the sites of the sublattice M, and atoms of a non-metal into the sites in the oxygen sublattice. If, however, the electronegativity of foreign atoms has the intermediate values, geometrical factors have the decisive role.

As already mentioned, incorporation of foreign atoms into a crystal is accompanied by the appearance of energy levels in the forbidden energy gap. Location of these levels depends on the type of the foreign atoms and on the nature of the matrix components of the lattice. The general rule concerning the distribution of the energy levels in the forbidden energy gap states as follows: if an atom F_M or F_O has the higher number of the valence electrons than a matrix atom M or O, the incorporation of an atom F_M or F_O gives rise to a donor level (or levels). If, on the other hand, an atom F_M or F_O has fewer valence electrons than an atom M or O, its incorporation is accompanied by the appearance of an acceptor level (or levels). In the case of interstitial atoms (both foreign and misplaced basic components of the lattice), more electropositive of them act as donors, and more electronegative as acceptors.

When considering the effect of the gas atmosphere on the defect structure in the crystal, one should obviously take into account the pressure (or fugacity) of a given admixture in the gas phase and its solubility in the matrix material at a given temperature. For illustration we will consider now nickel oxide NiO, the compound of low volatility, doped with chromium oxide Cr_2O_3 of even lower volatility, and with lithium oxide Li_2O which shows high volatility.

If we introduce a small amount of Cr_2O_3 into nickel oxide we can expect that practically all chromium oxide will become incorporated into the lattice of NiO, and the amount of Cr_2O_3 in the gas phase will be negligible. One can thus assume that the number of Cr atoms incorporated into the NiO crystal will be practically equal to the double number of the Cr_2O_3 molecules and will be independent of the partial pressures of the components of the gas phase. With the increase in the amount of chromium oxide introduced into the matrix crystal, the number of chromium oxide molecules in the gas phase will increase and hence the vapour pressure (or fugacity) of this oxide will increase. At certain amount of this admixture, the equilibrium between the amount of chromium oxide in the gas and solid phase will be attained. This means that the concentration of chromium in the solid phase reached the value equal to its solubility in the matrix material. The further increase in the amount of Cr_2O_3 at a given temperature will not increase the concentration of chromium in the solid phase, neither it will increase its partial pressure in the gas phase, but the oxide will begin to precipitate in the form of a separate solid phase. Obviously solubility of the admixture depends both on the temperature and on the oxygen pressure.

Another situation exists in the case of doping NiO with lithium oxide which has high volatility. If the amount of lithium oxide in the NiO–gas phase system is smaller than its solubility in the solid phase, the concentration of lithium in the matrix crystal will depend on the conditions in which the doping is performed. If, for instance, the experiments are carried out at the flow of gas over the solid phase, this concentration is influenced by the flow rate of the gas, the time of heating and also by the temperature. In this case the concentration of lithium in the crystal of nickel oxide should be determined experimentally after the process of doping has been terminated. If, however, the system under discussion contains certain excess of lithium oxide in the form of a separate phase, the concentration of lithium in NiO is equal to the solubility of lithium in nickel oxide and is related to partial pressures of the components of the gas phase and to the temperature by thermodynamic laws. In this case, the parameter that determines the amount of the incorporated lithium in NiO may be, for instance, the pressure of lithium in the gas phase and the pressure of nickel or oxygen.

7.2. Interrelations between Concentrations of Native Defects and of Foreign Atoms

It has been shown in Chapter 6 that the concentrations of all types of native defects in the crystal are interrelated. Similar relations exist also between the concentrations of native defects and of foreign atoms, since both foreign atoms and native defects must fulfil the electroneutrality condition. These relations may also result from the processes of association of foreign atoms with native defects which yield complexes, e.g. $(V_M F_M)$.

When considering the defect equilibria in a crystal containing admixtures, one should take into account the following processes:

(1) all quasi-chemical reactions describing the defect situations in a pure crystal (cf. Chapter 6),

(2) formation of complexes by association of foreign atoms with native defects,

(3) ionization of foreign atoms.

Moreover, one should also consider two conditions: (a) the sum of concentrations of foreign atoms ionized, non-ionized and associated is equal to the total concentration of foreign atoms in the crystal, and (b) the full condition of electroneutrality involving also the ionized foreign atoms.

By applying the law of mass action to processes (1)–(3) we obtain a set of equations. These equations and the two conditions mentioned above may be used for deriving by a graphical method described in Chapter 6 the values of concentrations of all types of defects occurring in the crystal containing admixtures, and their dependences on the partial pressures of the components of the gas phase. It should be noted that the analytical method is not suitable for solving this set of equations, since it involves ardous calculations.

The graphical method, described in Chapter 6, will be now employed for the description of the defect equilibria in a crystal MO containing admixtures, at the assumption that the crystal has native defects (cf. section 6.4) that do not associate with the atoms of the admixture, the latter atoms being distributed randomly. The composition of the gas phase is the same as that in the case given in section 6.4. It is also assumed that the element F or its compounds with oxygen show a very low vapour pressure, so that all atoms F are present in the solid phase. To simplify the discussion it will be moreover assumed that the forbidden energy gap contains only three energy levels as shown in Fig. 7.1. The level $E\,(F_M^x)$ is due to the presence of foreign atoms in the crystal.

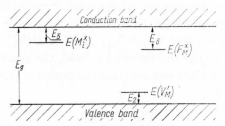

FIG. 7.1. Schematic diagram of electronic energy levels in crystal MO containing interstitial atoms and vacancies in sublattice M and donor foreign atoms.

At the assumptions made above, all equations given in section 6.4 for a pure crystal remain valid also in the case under discussion. Thus:

$$[M_i^x] = K_{11} P_M = R_2 \tag{7.1}$$

$$[M_i^x][V_M^x] = K_F \tag{7.2}$$

$$\frac{n[M_i^\bullet]}{[M_i^x]} = K_{12} \tag{7.3} = (6.69)$$

$$\frac{p[V_M']}{[V_M^x]} = K_7 \tag{7.4} = (6.70)$$

$$np = K_i \tag{7.5}$$

Ionization of the foreign atoms is described by the equilibrium:

$$F_M^x \rightleftarrows F_M^\bullet + e' \tag{7.6}$$

and by the equation:

$$\frac{n[F_M^\bullet]}{[F_M^x]} = K_{15} \tag{7.7}$$

The following two equations describe respectively the condition of conservation of the total number of foreign atoms in the crystal, and the electroneutrality condition:

$$[F_M^x] + [F_M^\bullet] = [F_M]_{tot} \tag{7.8}$$

$$n + [V_M'] = p + [M_i^\bullet] + [F_M^\bullet] \tag{7.9}$$

The defect equilibria in the case under consideration can be thus described by eight equations [(7.1)–(7.5) and (7.7)–(7.9)] with nine variables: n, p, $[M_i^x]$, $[V_M^x]$, $[M_i^\bullet]$, $[V_M']$, $[F_M^x]$, $[F_M^\bullet]$ and R_2. By applying the graphical method of Brouwer, the concentrations of all types of defects can be expressed as a function of R_2.

When the partial pressure P_M is very small and the concentration of foreign atoms is not too high, the concentration of vacancies in the sublattice M is higher that the concentration of foreign atoms in the crystal. The concentration of interstitial atoms can be neglected, and hence the simplified electroneutrality condition assumes the form:

$$p = [V_M'] \gg n, [M_i^\bullet], [F_M^\bullet] \tag{7.10}$$

High concentration of the vacancies, a considerable fraction of which is ionized, causes the shift of the Fermi level towards the valence band. It can be thus assumed that practically all centres F_M become ionized, as a result of the transfer of electrons from the donor level E (F_M^x) to the acceptor level E (V_M'). The level E (V_M') is filled by the electrons of both the donor level E (F_M^x) and the valence band, the contribution of the electrons from this donor level being however insignificant. Equation (7.8) can be thus simplified by neglecting the term $[F_M^x]$:

$$[F_M^\bullet] = [F_M]_{tot} \tag{7.11}$$

With the increase in P_M, the concentration of the vacancies is decreased, and hence the ratio $[F_M^\bullet]/p$ is increased. At a certain value of P_M this ratio becomes ≈ 1. At the pressures higher than this value the electroneutrality condition assumes the form:

$$[F_M^\bullet] = [V_M'] \gg n, p, [M_i^\bullet] \tag{7.12}$$

The condition given by eq. (7.11) remains still valid.

At still higher pressures P_M, the concentration of the vacancies becomes much smaller than the concentration of the foreign atoms, and hence only a small fraction of these atoms undergoes the ionization by transfer of electrons from the level $E\,(F_M^x)$ to the level $E\,(V_M')$. Also only a small number of foreign atoms is ionized by the electron transfer from the level $E\,(F_M^x)$ to the conduction band, since the ionization energy E_6 is large (cf. Fig. 7.1). Hence in the third range of pressures the electroneutrality condition (7.12) is unchanged; however, eq. (7.8) assumes the simplified form:

$$[F_M^x] = [F_M]_{tot} \tag{7.13}$$

With the further increase in the pressure P_M, the concentration of the vacancies is so small, that the transfer of some electrons from the level $E\,(F_M^x)$ to the conduction band becomes the predominating process, and the neutrality condition is:

$$n = [F_M^\bullet] \gg p, [V_M'], [M_i^\bullet] \tag{7.14}$$

The condition described by eq. (7.13) remains unchanged.

In the fifth range of high pressures P_M, interstitial atoms M_i are the predominating defects in the crystal. A fraction of them undergoes ionization by the electron transfer from the donor level $E\,(M_i^x)$ to the conduction band. Hence the neutrality condition in this pressure range has the form:

$$n = [M_i^\bullet] \gg p, [V_M'], [F_M^\bullet] \tag{7.15}$$

the condition (7.13) being still held.

We have obtained then five regions of P_M or R_2, in each of which a different simplified condition of electroneutrality is held, and in each of which different simplified conditions of conservation of the total concentration of foreign atoms are valid. Solving the set of equations: (7.1)–(7.5) and (7.7) with taking into account particular pairs of the given above conditions, we obtain five systems of equations which express the concentrations of various types of defects in the crystal as a function of P_M or R_2. In Fig. 7.2 these functions are plotted on a double logarithmic scale. As seen from Fig. 7.2 the foreign atoms have the predominating effect only in the regions of the intermediate pressures P_M, however, even at these pressures the semiconducting properties of the system depend on the composition of the gas phase surrounding the crystal (with the exception of regions II and IV).

In region II, the concentration of ionized vacancies in the sublattice M is determined by the concentration of foreign atoms in the crystal and is independent of the partial pressure P_M. In this range of pressures we deal with a solid solution $MO + FO_2$. This is equivalent to the presence in the crystal of the same number of vacancies in the sublattice M as the number of foreign atoms F. Hence in this pressure range we deal with the so called mechanism of controlled atomic defect structure.

In region IV, the concentration of the electrons is independent of the composition of the gas phase, and is determined by the concentration of foreign atoms. In this region the process of the admixture incorporation is governed by the so called mechanism of the controlled electronic defect structure. The width of this region can be readily calculated. In the case under consideration it amounts to:

$$\Delta \log R_2 = \log\left([F_M]_{tot} \cdot K_{15}/K_{F_1}\right) \tag{7.16}$$

where K_{F_1} is given by eq. (6.78) (cf. Chapter 6).

We will consider now a similar defect situation, in which the incorporated atoms F have fewer valence electrons than atoms M. All the equilibrium constants have the same

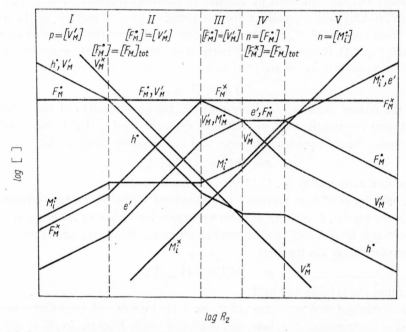

FIG. 7.2. Interrelations between concentrations of atoms and vacancies in sublattice M and of donor foreign atoms in crystal MO at constant temperature.

values as those given previously. The scheme of the energy levels in the forbidden energy gap for this case is shown in Fig. 7.3. The native defects in the crystal are described

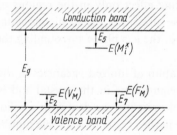

FIG. 7.3. Schematic diagram of electronic energy levels in crystal MO containing interstitial atoms and vacancies in sublattice M and acceptor foreign atoms.

by eqs. (7.1)–(7.5). However eqs. (7.6) and (7.7) are replaced by the following expressions:

$$F_M^x \rightleftarrows F_M' + h^\bullet \tag{7.17}$$

$$\frac{p \, [F_M']}{[F_M^x]} = K_{16} \tag{7.18}$$

The conditions of electroneutrality and conservation of the total concentration of foreign atoms assume the form:

$$n + [V'_M] + [F'_M] = p + [M_i^{\cdot}] \tag{7.19}$$

$$[F_M^{\times}] + [F'_M] = [F_M]_{tot} \tag{7.20}$$

The simplified conditions of electroneutrality and conservation of the total concentration of the admixtures are as follows:

(1) At very low pressure P_M

$$p = [V'_M] \gg n, [F'_M], [M_i^{\cdot}] \tag{7.21}$$

Since ionization energy E_7 of the acceptor level E (F'_M) (cf. Fig. 7.3) is relatively high, only a small number of foreign atoms F is ionized, and hence

$$[F_M^{\times}] = [F_M]_{tot} \tag{7.22}$$

(2) In the second region of pressures P_M, $[V_M]_{tot}$ is smaller than $[F_M]_{tot}$ since the total concentration of the vacancies is decreased with the increase in P_M, and hence:

$$p = [F'_M] \gg n, [V'_M], [M_i^{\cdot}] \tag{7.23}$$

The second condition is unchanged.

(3) In the third region of P_M, the crystal contains already a considerable number of interstitial atoms, which introduce to a forbidden energy gap a donor level E ($M_i^{\times}$). The electrons of this level pass to the acceptor level E (F'_M), and the electroneutrality condition is given by:

$$[M_i^{\cdot}] = [F'_M] \gg n, [V'_M], p \tag{7.24}$$

Since, however, the concentration of interstitial atoms in this region is considerably smaller than that of the foreign atoms, the second condition is the same as in the previous regions.

(4) In the fourth region of P_M the electroneutrality condition remains unchanged, but the condition of conservation of the total concentration of foreign atoms assumes the form:

$$[F'_M] = [F_M]_{tot} \tag{7.25}$$

Owing to the high concentration of interstitial atoms, nearly all atoms F_M are ionized as the result of the electron transfer from the donor level E ($M_i^{\times}$) to the acceptor level E (F'_M).

(5) Finally, in the last region of P_M, the electroneutrality condition is:

$$n = [M_i^{\cdot}] \gg p, [V'_M], [F'_M] \tag{7.26}$$

since ionization of the interstitial atoms takes place mainly by the electron transfer from the level E ($M_i^{\cdot}$) to the conduction band. The second condition is unchanged.

Solving the system of eqs. (7.1)–(7.5) and (7.18) with allowance for the pairs of simplified conditions of electroneutrality and conservation of the total concentration of the foreign atoms, we obtain five systems of equations which represent the dependence of concentrations of a given type of defects on R_2. These functions are shown in Fig. 7.4

plotted on the double logarithmic scale. It is readily seen that some fragments of the plot given in Fig. 7.4 are a mirror reflection of the analogous fragments of the plots in Fig. 7.2.

It follows from Fig. 7.4 that also in this case, we deal with the region of the controlled electronic defect structure (region II) and the region of the controlled atomic structure (region IV). The mechanism of the incorporation of the foreign atoms is however different. In region IV namely, each ionized atom F_M is balanced by an ionized interstitial

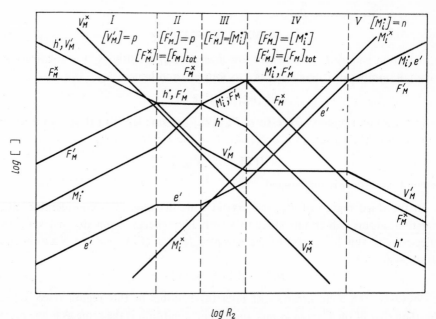

$$\log R_2$$

FIG. 7.4. Interrelations between concentrations of interstitial atoms and vacancies in sublattice M and of acceptor foreign atoms in crystal MO at constant temperature.

atom $M_i^{\bullet}$, and the solid solution formed has the composition: MO + F, whereas at lower pressures P_M, the solid solution contains MO + FO. The region of the controlled electronic defect structure is the most relevant for semiconducting properties. The width of this region is given by eq. (7.16) in which the equilibrium constant K_{15} is replaced by the constant K_{16} (eq. 7.18).

It should be noted that at high temperature in many cases all donor and acceptor levels are fully ionized. To describe this case it is assumed that the ionization energies E_5, E_2 and E_6 are practically equal to zero (cf. Fig. 7.1).

In this latter case, the defect equilibria are described by the following equations (cf. section 6.4):

$$n[M_i^{\bullet}] = K_{14} P_M \equiv R_3 \qquad (7.27) = (6.82)$$

$$[M_i^{\bullet}] [V_M'] = K_{F_1} \qquad (7.28)$$

$$np = K_i \qquad (7.29)$$

$$[F_i^{\bullet}] = [F_M]_{tot} \qquad (7.30)$$

$$n + [V_M'] = p + [M_i^{\bullet}] + [F_M^{\bullet}] \qquad (7.31)$$

The simplified conditions of electroneutrality are obviously the same as those given previously, and hence in the case under consideration we obtain four regions of R_2, and thus four systems of equations describing the defect concentration as a function of the pressure P_M. These functions are shown in Fig. 7.5. Similarly like in the cases

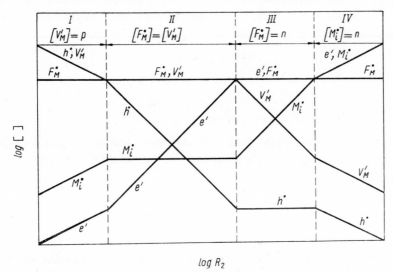

FIG. 7.5. Interrelations between concentrations of interstitial atoms and vacancies in sublattice M and of donor foreign atoms in crystal MO at constant temperature for the case when all these defects are ionized.

considered previously, also in the case of full ionization of the donor and acceptor levels there exists the region of the controlled atomic defect structure (region II) and the region of the controlled electronic defect structure (region III). Simple calculations show that the width of this latter region is given by:

$$\Delta \log R_3 = \log \frac{[F_M]_{tot}^2}{K_{F_1}} \tag{7.32}$$

7.3. Other Types of Defect Situation in Crystals Containing Admixtures

The description of defect equilibria in a crystal containing vacancies in the both sublattices is not different essentially from the description of the equilibria considered in the preceding section. The defect situation of this type is described by eqs. (6.45)–(6.51) and relations which describe ionization of foreign atoms and conservation of their total concentration, e.g. eqs. (7.7) and (7.8) or eqs. (7.18) and (7.20). Moreover, the general condition of electroneutrality should be taken into account. In the case under discussion this condition has the form:

$$n + [V_M'] + 2[V_M''] = p + [V_O^{\bullet}] + 2[V_O^{\bullet\bullet}] + [F_M^{\bullet}] \tag{7.33}$$

or

$$n + [V_M'] + 2[V_M''] + [F_M'] = p + [V_O^{\bullet}] + 2[V_O^{\bullet\bullet}] \tag{7.34}$$

Selecting the simplified conditions of electroneutrality and conservation of the total concentration of foreign atoms, we may draw, in the analogous manner as in the preceding section, the plots of defect concentration as a function of the pressure P_M.

The defect situations encountered in practice are usually more complex than those described above. The foreign atoms may be incorporated not only into the lattice sites but also into the interstitial space. In the latter case we must consider also the reaction of transfer of an atom F from a lattice site to the interstitial space:

$$V_i^x + F_M^x \rightleftarrows F_i^x + V_M^x \tag{7.35}$$

and the equilibrium constant corresponding to this reaction:

$$\frac{[F_i^x][V_M^x]}{[F_M^x][V_i^x]} = K_{17} \tag{7.36}$$

It may be assumed that the mole fraction of interstitial vacancies is equal to unity.

If the interstitial atoms F_i undergo ionization, one should also take into account the following reactions:

$$F_i^x \rightleftarrows F_i^{\cdot} + e' \tag{7.37}$$

or

$$F_i^x \rightleftarrows F_i' + h^{\cdot} \tag{7.38}$$

Depending on whether the atoms F_i are more positive or more negative we obtain the following equations:

$$\frac{n[F_i^{\cdot}]}{[F_i^x]} = K_{18} \tag{7.39}$$

or

$$\frac{p[F_M']}{[F_M^x]} = K_{19} \tag{7.40}$$

If the foreign atoms associate with other defects, or if there are formed complexes of atoms F situated in various positions, we should consider also the reactions which describe these processes, e.g.

$$F_M^{\cdot} + V_M' \rightleftarrows (F_M V_M)^x \tag{7.41}$$
$$F_M^x + F_i^x \rightleftarrows (F_M F_i)^x \tag{7.42}$$

and the equilibrium constants corresponding to these reactions:

$$\frac{[(F_M V_M)^x]}{[F_M^{\cdot}][V_M']} = K_{20} \tag{7.43}$$

$$\frac{[(F_M F_i)^x]}{[F_M^x][F_i^x]} = K_{21} \tag{7.44}$$

In the complex defect situations the condition of conservation of the total concentration of foreign atoms in crystal is modified. This condition may be written in the following form:

$$\sum [F_i^k] + \sum [F_i^m] = [F]_{tot} \tag{7.45}$$

where l denotes M or O, and k and m are the effective charges of the defect.

Obviously this sum should comprise concentrations of all admixtures, irrespectively of the manner of their distribution (whether they are distributed as single defects or as complexes).

Finally the electroneutrality condition should involve all concentrations of defects, both native and foreign atoms possessing an effective charge.

By applying the approximate graphical method we can calculate the concentrations of all defects at thermodynamic equilibrium, even in complex cases involving many equations of defect equilibria, provided that all equilibrium constants are known.

7.4. Solubility of Foreign Atoms in Crystals

The discussion presented in sections 7.2 and 7.3 was based on the assumption that the amount of the admixture F in the gas phase is negligible and hence the total concentration of the foreign atoms in the crystal is constant.

In this section this assumption will be omitted and the equilibrium between the amount of atoms F in the solid and gas phase will be taken into account in the further considerations. In this case the total concentration of foreign atoms in the crystal attains the value maximal in given thermodynamic conditions and is called the solubility of the element F in the crystal MO. If we assume additionally that the element F occurs in the gas phase also in the form single atoms $F^{(g)}$, then its solubility in the crystal at a fixed temperature will be, according to the phase rule, a function of two parameters: P_M and P_F or P_{O_2} and P_F. If the mechanism of incorporation of foreign atoms into the crystal is not changed, this function can be written in the form:

$$[F]_{tot} = K P_M^r P_F^s \tag{7.46}$$

or

$$[F]_{tot} = K P_{O_2}^q P_F^s \tag{7.47}$$

where K, r, q and s are constants.

For illustration we will consider the following examples:

(1) In the solid solution MO + F_2O, the prevailing defects are F_M' and $V_O^{\cdot}$. The reaction between the atoms $F^{(g)}$ from the gas phase and the crystal, and the electroneutrality condition in this case are given by the following equations:

$$F^{(g)} \rightleftarrows F_M' + V_O^{\cdot} \tag{7.48}$$

$$[F_M'] = [V_O^{\cdot}] \tag{7.49}$$

$$[F_M]_{tot} \cong [F_M'] \tag{7.50}$$

Applying the law of mass action to eq. (7.48) we obtain:

$$\frac{[F_M'][V_O^{\cdot}]}{P_F} = K_{2\dot{2}} \tag{7.51}$$

Taking into account the conditions given by eqs. (7.49) and (7.50) we get finally:

$$[F]_{tot} = K_{2\dot{2}}^{1/2} P_F^{1/2} \tag{7.52}$$

Thus in the case considered $r = 0$, $s = 1/2$, $K = K_{2\dot{2}}^{1/2}$

(2) The defects F_M are the sole defects occurring in the crystals. Their formation can be described by:

$$F^{(g)} + M_M^{\times} \rightleftarrows F_M^{\times} + M^{(g)} \tag{7.53}$$

The law of mass action applied to this reaction yields:

$$\frac{[F_M^{\times}] P_M}{[M_M^{\times}] P_F} = K_{23} \tag{7.54}$$

$$[F]_{tot} = [F_M^{\times}] \tag{7.55}$$

The function (7.46) assumes in this case the form:

$$[F]_{tot} = K P_M^{-1} P_F \tag{7.56}$$

where $K = K_{23}[M_M^{\times}]$, $r = -1, s = 1$.

(3) Complexes $(F_M V_O)'$ and $V_O^{\bullet}$ are the predominating defects in the crystal, the gas phase contains molecules $F_2^{(g)}$. The process of defect formation in this case is represented schematically by the following equation:

$$\frac{1}{2}(F_2)^{(g)} + M^{(g)} \rightleftarrows (F_M V_O)' + V_O^{\bullet} + M_M^{\times} \tag{7.57}$$

The electroneutrality condition assumes the form:

$$[(F_M V_O)'] = [V_O^{\bullet}] \tag{7.58}$$

$$[F]_{tot} = [(F_M V_O)'] \tag{7.59}$$

The law of mass action applied to eq. (7.57) gives:

$$\frac{[(F_M V_O)'][V_O^{\bullet}][M_M^{\times}]}{P_{F_2}^{1/2} P_M} = K_{24} \tag{7.60}$$

Equation (7.46) assumes the form:

$$[F]_{tot} = K P_M^{1/2} P_{F_2}^{1/2} \tag{7.61}$$

and the constants in eq. (7.46) are $K = K_{24}/[M_M^{\times}], r = 1/2\ s = 1/4$.

(4) The prevailing defects are F_M' and $V_O^{\bullet\bullet}$, the gas phase contains molecules $F_2^{(g)}$. The formation of these defects is given by:

$$F_2^{(g)} + \frac{1}{2} O_2^{(g)} \rightleftarrows 2F_M' + V_O^{\bullet\bullet} + O_O^{\times} \tag{7.62}$$

The electroneutrality condition in this case assumes the form:

$$[F_M'] = 2[V_O^{\bullet\bullet}] \tag{7.63}$$

$$[F]_{tot} = [F_M'] \tag{7.64}$$

By applying the law of mass action to eq. (7.62) we get:

$$\frac{[F_M']^2 [V_O^{\bullet\bullet}][O_O^{\times}]}{P_{F_2} P_{O_2}^{1/2}} = K_{25} \tag{7.65}$$

and hence:

$$[F]_{tot} = K P_{O_2}^{1/6} P_{F_2}^{1/3} \tag{7.66}$$

The constants in eq. (7.47) have the values: $K = (2K_{25}/[O_O^{\times}])^{1/3}$, $q = 1/6, s = 1/3$.

It follows from the examples considered above that the dependence of the solubility of a given element in the crystal MO on the composition of the gas phase[†] is determined by the type of defects occurring in the crystal and by their degree of ionization. The value of the solubility is dependent on the changes of the entropy and enthalpy accompanying the reactions of the defect formation. It is also influenced by temperature since the equilibrium constant is a function of this latter parameter (the solubility increases with the increasing temperature).

It should be noted, however, that the solubility changes are limited. The limitations result from the fact of formation of new phases. Moreover, the pressures P_M and P_F or P_{O_2} and P_F cannot be always varied independently one of another. If atoms F react in the gas phase with oxygen atoms to form, for example, a compound FO:

$$F^{(g)} + \frac{1}{2} O_2^{(g)} \rightleftarrows FO^{(g)} \tag{7.67}$$

the pressures P_F and P_{O_2} are interrelated by:

$$\frac{P_{FO}}{P_F P_{O_2}^{1/2}} = K_{26} \tag{7.68}$$

The considerations presented in sections 7.2 and 7.3 are based on the original paper by Kröger and Vink.[120]

[†] At higher pressures, when interactions between the molecules cannot be neglected, the pressures should be replaced by fugacities.

CHAPTER 8

CONCENTRATION OF DEFECTS AT LOW AND INTERMEDIATE TEMPERATURES

The discussion of defect situations in oxide crystals presented in the foregoing chapters pertained to thermodynamic equilibrium in the solid–gas system. Hence the conclusions drawn from the theoretical considerations given above can be applied only to the investigations carried out at high temperatures. In practice, however, the oxide materials are used usually at the temperatures considerably lower than those at which thermodynamic equilibrium can be attained in relatively short time. Interpretation of physical and chemical properties of oxides at these temperatures presents some difficulties and more detailed discussion of this problem would be beyond the scope of this review. We shall confine then our considerations to describing some special, simplified cases. However, the approach to the problem which will be shown in the present chapter should enable the reader to interpret the properties of oxide crystals at low and intermediate temperatures, providing at the same time certain general conclusions as regards the rational method of carrying experimental studies on these crystals.

To advance our considerations on defect situations in oxide crystals at low and intermediate temperatures we must first assume that the material under study has been prepared or has undergone the final thermal treatment in the conditions of thermodynamic equilibrium, as the result of which its physical and chemical properties are independent of its history. If this is the case then these properties depend on thermodynamic conditions under which the material has been prepared or subjected to the final thermal treatment and on the conditions of cooling of the material. When discussing the effect of cooling we should consider three essential cases:

(1) When a crystal is rapidly cooled from the temperature of its preparation to the lower temperature, we can assume that the total concentration of atomic defects is not changed, since such a change would involve diffusional motion of atoms in the crystal lattice. The latter process, as it is known, requires relatively high activation energy. We may hence assume that the atomic defects become frozen. Essentially different behaviour is observed for quasi-free electrons and holes. If donor levels are close to the bottom of the conduction band and acceptor levels close to the top of the valence band, the distribution of conduction electrons and holes among the energy levels in cooled oxide crystals corresponds to the state of equilibrium at a given lower

temperature. Thus in this case the concentration of atomic defects in the cooled crystal will correspond to high-temperature equilibrium and the concentration of electronic defects—to low-temperature equilibrium. It should be noted that although total concentration of atomic defects is not changed by cooling, the concentrations of particular types of defects both neutral and ionized will be different in the cooled crystals and only their sum remains constant. If, however, the crystal has deep-lying energy levels in the forbidden band, the time required for establishing the equilibrium of electronic defects is long, and hence electrons and holes remain in the metastable state.[129]

(2) When the time of cooling is very long, and activation energy for diffusion of atoms in the crystal lattice is not too high, then the concentrations of both atomic and electronic defects will correspond to the low-temperature equilibrium (provided that the energy levels are not too deep).

(3) In the intermediate case, the properties of crystals at low temperatures are not strictly defined.

It follows from the above considerations that only two extremal cases can be interpreted quantitatively. Since, however, the second situation is very difficult or even impossible to be realized in practice, only the first case will be dealt with in more detail. Sufficiently short time, necessary for quenching atomic defects is not alwyas attainable in practice. The time of cooling will obviously depend on the experimental conditions. The operation of cooling requires the assurance of good thermal contact between the crystal being cooled and the refrigerant. This latter should show high thermal conductivity and large specific heat. The time of cooling is dependent not only on the experimental conditions but also on the type of the crystal. Albers, Haas and Vink[130] have shown that the shortest cooling time which can be attained at the most favourable experimental conditions is determined by thermal properties of the specimen and by its size, and is given by the following formula:

$$\tau_c = \frac{c_p d^2}{\varkappa} \tag{8.1}$$

where τ_c is the shortest time of cooling [s], c_p is the specific heat of the crystal [cal/cm^3 K], d is the smallest dimension of the specimen [cm], $\varkappa$ is the thermal conductivity of the sample [cal/cm s K].

If time τ_c is longer than the time sufficient for diffusion to take place, τ_D, the atomic defects cannot be frozen completely.

Generally, it can be assumed that the total concentration of atomic defects in crystals at low and intermediate temperatures is the closer to the value corresponding to high-temperature equilibrium, the shorter is the time of cooling. It should be remembered, however, that rapid cooling may cause the formation of dislocations.[131]

Metastable states of electrons mentioned above have relatively short life time for deep-lying energy levels, with the exception of dielectrics which have very deep lying energy levels. It can be then assumed that equilibrium of electrons and holes in semiconductors may be attained at any temperature.

For better illustration of defect situation in crystals after their cooling we shall consider the following example.

A crystal MO has been prepared under the conditions of equilibrium at high temperature, T_1, and at a determined composition of the gas phase. The crystal has a tendency to form vacancies in the oxygen sublattice. It is assumed moreover that in the forbidden zone there is present only one level V_O^x close to the bottom of the conduction band. After rapid cooling to low temperature T_2, the defect situation in the crystal may be described by the following expressions:

$$V_O^x \rightleftarrows V_O^{\cdot} + e', \qquad \frac{[V_O^{\cdot}]n}{[V_O^x]} = K = f(T_2) \qquad (8.2)$$

$$\text{zero} \rightleftarrows h^{\cdot} + e', \qquad np = K_i = f(T_2) \qquad (8.3)$$

Owing to the freezing of the atomic defects, the total concentration of all vacancies—both neutral and ionized—is not changed and will be the same as that at temperature T_1, though concentrations $[V_O^x]$ and $[V_O^{\cdot}]$ at the temperature T_2 will be different than at T_1. Hence:

$$[V_O^x] + [V_O^{\cdot}] = [V_O]_{tot} \qquad (8.4)$$

When temperature T_2 is sufficiently low, the value of $[V_O^{\cdot}]$ is very small and $[V_O^x] \approx [V_O]_{tot}$.

The electroneutrality condition for this case assumes the form:

$$[V_O^{\cdot}] + p = n \qquad (8.5)$$

with all concentrations in eq. (8.5) corresponding to temperature T_2. In oxides the energy gap E_g is usually large and hence the electroneutrality condition can be written in the form:

$$n = [V_O^{\cdot}] \qquad (8.6)$$

Assuming that only a small fraction of the vacancies is ionized ($[V_O^x] \approx [V_O]_{tot}$), one obtains from eqs. (8.2) and (8.3):

$$n = [V_O^{\cdot}] = K^{1/2}[V_O]_{tot}^{1/2} \qquad (8.7)$$

$$p = K_i K^{-1/2}[V_O]_{tot}^{-1/2} \qquad (8.8)$$

It results from the above that the concentrations of electronic defects present in the crystal depend both on the measurement temperature and on the temperature of preparation of the material.†

To illustrate the changes in the structure of defects in a crystal occurring during its cooling, let us consider the case already discussed in section 6.4. To avoid the problems connected with ionization of defects, it is assumed that the crystal is cooled to 0 K.††
The discussion of this problem will involve full conditions of electroneutrality which are held at high-temperature processes, thus in the case under consideration the condition given by eq. (6.72).

---

† Since $[V_O]_{tot}$ is dependent on the temperature of material preparation.
†† Distribution of electrons among the energy levels for temperatures higher than 0 K can be determined by methods described in books on physics of semiconductors.

At very low pressures P_M (region I, cf. section 6.4), only the concentrations of electrons can be neglected and hence the electroneutrality condition assumes the form:

$$p + [M_i^{\cdot}] = [V_M']$$ (8.9)

On rapid cooling to the temperature of 0 K all electron holes are captured by acceptor centres V_M'. Hence the concentration of ionized vacancies is reduced to the value $[V_M'] = [M_i^{\cdot}]$. All interstitial atoms are ionized since $[V_M]_{tot}$ is much higher than $[M_i]_{tot}$. The total concentrations of both vacancies and interstitial atoms are the same as those at high temperatures.

In the middle of region II, the total concentration of the vacancies is equal to the concentration of interstitial atoms and hence all the vacancies have negative and interstitial atoms positive charge. On the left-hand side of region II there is present the excess of the vacancies and thus the condition given by eq. (8.9) remains valid. In this part of region II again $[V_M'] = [M_i^{\cdot}]$, since the remaining fraction of ionized vacancies recombine with the holes forming neutral centres V_M^x. In the right-hand side of region II the interstitial atoms are in excess and condition (8.9) should be replaced by:

$$n + [V_M'] = [M_i^{\cdot}]$$ (8.10)

The electrons which at high temperatures occupy the conduction band recombine on cooling with centres $M_i^{\cdot}$ forming neutral defects M_i^x and accordingly, also in this part of region II $[V_M'] = [M_i^{\cdot}]$.

In region III the neutral interstitial atoms are predominant. However, in this range of pressures P_M a small number of vacancies is observed which get ionized by jumping of electrons from level M_i^x to V_M^x. Hence also in this region $[V_M'] = [M_i^{\cdot}]$, though the concentrations of ionized defects are low and decrease with the increase in P_M. Figure 8.1

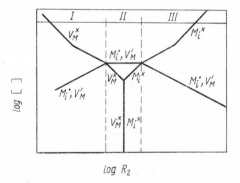

FIG. 8.1. Concentrations of defects in a crystal MO at temp. 0 K corresponding to defect situation at high temperatures given in Fig. 6.7.

shows concentrations of defects in the crystals cooled to the temperature of 0 K as a function of pressure P_M, plotted on the double logarithmic scale. The plots correspond to the model of defect situation at high temperature equilibrium presented in Fig. 6.7.

In the similar manner we may consider other types of defect situations in cooled pure crystals. It should be noted, however, that in practice the total concentration of atomic defects in crystals at low and intermediate temperatures is somewhat lower than that corresponding to the high temperature equilibrium, since even on very rapid cooling, these equilibria undergo certain shift towards the low temperature situation.

Finally we shall discuss defect situations in impure crystals cooled to the temperature of 0 K, for the case when foreign atoms are the electron donors (Fig. 7.2). The high-temperature equilibria in these crystals in the crystal–gas system has already been dealt with in section 7.2. It was assumed there that the rate of cooling was sufficiently high to freeze the atomic defects.

Accordingly, similarly like in the case discussed above, the total concentrations of particular types of atomic defects are at 0 K the same as at high temperatures:

$$[F_M]_{tot} = [F_M^x] + [F_M^{\cdot}] = const \qquad (8.11)$$

$$[V_M]_{tot} = [V_M^x] + [V_M'] = const \qquad (8.12)$$

$$[M_i]_{tot} = [M_i^x] + [M_i^{\cdot}] = const \qquad (8.13)$$

Distribution of electrons among various energy levels, on the other hand, is essentially changed, since their state corresponds to the temperature of 0 K. At this temperature all electrons of the conduction band and holes of the valence band recombine either with each other or with ionized defects forming in this way the neutral defects. Since in the case under discussion level V_M^x is the lowest-lying one in the forbidden zone, electrons from the higher levels of this zone, i.e. from levels M_i^x and F_M^x (cf. Fig. 7.1), will fill this level.

At low pressures P_M vacancies in the sublattice M are the dominant defects and hence all centres M_i^x and F_M^x become ionized. Since, however, the concentration of interstitial atoms in this range of pressure P_M is very low, they are not significant. The excess of vacancies will be obviously non-ionized. With the increase in the pressure P_M the total concentration of vacancies is decreased, but at the same time, the concentration of interstitial atoms M_i^x is still small. Thus beginning from certain value of P_M, the foreign atoms in a crystal will outweigh the vacancies. The excess of the foreign atoms will occur in the form of neutral centres F_M^x. Since level M_i^x lies higher than level F_M^x, all interstitial atoms are ionized.

At still higher pressures P_M the concentration of the vacancies is already so small that neutral centres F_M^x begin to prevail. At the same time with the increase in the pressure P_M the electrons of level M_i^x are more and more involved in the filling of levels V_M' since the concentration of interstitial atoms increases rapidly. With the further increase in pressure P_M, we reach the value at which the concentration of vacancies becomes equal to the concentration of interstitial atoms. From this pressure upwards, levels V_i^x are filled solely by the electrons of level M_i^x. Hence the concentration of negatively ionized vacancies becomes equal to the concentration of positively ionized interstitial atoms. All foreign atoms remain neutral. The crystal possess also non-ionized interstitial atoms which at still higher pressures P_M will prevail over foreign atoms. The discussed above defect situation occurring at 0 K is illustrated in Fig. 8.2 (cf. Fig. 7.2).

Figure 8.3 illustrates quenched defects in impure crystal MO for the case when foreign atoms act as acceptors. The corresponding high-temperature defect equilibria have been considered in section 7.2 (cf. Fig. 7.4). The detailed discussion of this situation does not seem necessary due to analogies with the situation discussed above.

It follows from the above considerations that the defect structure in a crystal cooled to the temperature of 0 K depends on the temperature of the material preparation and on the composition of the gas phase surrounding the crystal during this process. The state of the crystal at 0 K can be regarded as a starting point in the interpretation of the semiconducting properties of the crystals which show native defects at temperatures

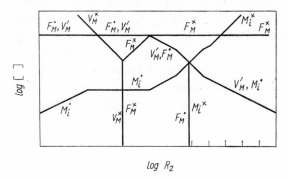

FIG. 8.2. Concentration of defects in a crystal MO containing donor impurities at 0 K; the plots correspond to defect situation at high temperatures given in Fig. 7.2.

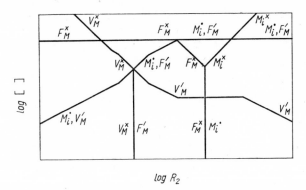

FIG. 8.3. Concentration of defects in a crystal MO containing acceptor impurities at temp. 0 K corresponding to high temperature defect situation given in Fig. 7.4.

higher than 0 K, e.g. at room temperature. It becomes hence evident that at temperatures higher than 0 K the properties are strictly determined by thermodynamic conditions under which the crystals have been prepared (if the cooling was sufficiently short) since these conditions determine the nature of donors and acceptors and their concentrations, i.e. the number and distribution of energy levels in the forbidden energy gap. It is obvious that the properties of such the semiconductor depend also on the temperature of the measurement, since distribution of the electrons among the various energy levels and hence also the concentration of quasi-free electrons in the conduction band and concentration of holes in the valence band are temperature dependent.

Thus the control over the properties of a semiconductor showing a tendency to form native defects is possible only when crystals of this compound have been grown (or heated) in the conditions of thermodynamic equilibrium at high temperatures and at a determined composition of the gas phase. In the case of impure crystals also the total concentration of foreign atoms in the crystal should be known. It should be borne in mind, however, that if the crystals previously quenched are used at temperatures higher than the room temperature, the energy of thermal motion may attain the value of the activation energy for diffusion of atoms in the crystal. This may alter the concentration of atomic defects and as a result may cause the instability of semiconducting properties. The probability of an atom acquiring the thermal energy equal to the activation energy of the diffusion is the higher the higher is the temperature. Since, however, the activation energy of the diffusion is, in the compounds under discussion, relatively high, this effect becomes significant only at temperatures considerably higher than the room temperature. If the crystal were heated to such temperatures and then cooled to the room temperature or below, its properties would undergo appreciable but uncontrolled change.

PART THREE

DEFECT STRUCTURE, ELECTRICAL AND ATOMIC TRANSPORT PHENOMENA IN SELECTED OXIDES

CHAPTER 9

ELECTRONIC AND ATOMIC TRANSPORT PHENOMENA — FUNDAMENTALS

9.1. Electronic Transport Phenomena

Electronic transport in semiconductors involves such phenomena as electrical conductivity, Hall effect and Seebeck effect (thermoelectric power).

For oxides of wide energy bands, e.g. ZnO, CdO, Cu_2O, SnO_2, these phenomena can be explained in terms of the band approximation and the theory of defects. The band structure of oxide semiconductors has not been as yet adequately described. The transport properties in these materials are usually interpreted in terms of simple model of Wilson and Sommerfeld[118, 132] which assumes spherical symmetry of energy surfaces, although in reality the structure of the energy levels in oxides may be more complex. In this approach, the transport properties are determined by introducing certain parameters such as energy gap (or forbidden band width) E_g, scalar effective masses of electrons m_e^* and holes m_h^*, mobility of electrons μ_e and of holes μ_h, concentrations of donors [D] and of acceptors [A] and ionization energies of donors and acceptors E_d and E_a.

When the model assuming spherical symmetry of spatial distribution of energy and scalar effective masses is applicable, the electrical conductivity is also a scalar and is given by:

$$\sigma = \sigma_e + \sigma_h \tag{9.1}$$

where

$$\sigma_e = en\mu_e \tag{9.2}$$

$$\sigma_h = ep\mu_h \tag{9.3}$$

σ_e and σ_h denote electron and hole conductivity, respectively, e is an electron charge, n and p are concentrations of respectively electrons and holes.

The Hall coefficient R is given by the following formula:

$$R = \frac{R_e\sigma_e^2 + R_h\sigma_h^2}{\sigma^2} \tag{9.4}$$

where

$$R_e = -\frac{r_e}{ne} \tag{9.5}$$

$$R_h = \frac{r_h}{pe} \tag{9.6}$$

and r_e and r_h are the scattering coefficients.

For non-degenerate semiconductors in which the current carriers are scattered by thermal vibrations of the lattice constituents the theoretical considerations yield the following values for coefficients r_e and r_h: in covalent crystals $r_e = r_h = 3\pi/8 = 1\cdot18$; in ionic crystals $r_e = r_h = 1$ for $T \ll \theta$ and $r_e = r_h = 15/16 \times 3\pi/8 = 1\cdot1$ for $T \gg \theta$, where θ is the Debye temperature.

For scattering on charged point defects $r_e = r_h = 315\pi/512 = 1\cdot93$. Finally the Seebeck coefficient is defined by the following expression:

$$\alpha = \frac{\alpha_e \sigma_e + \alpha_h \sigma_h}{\sigma} \tag{9.7}$$

where

$$\alpha_e = \left(-\frac{k}{e}\right)\left(A_e + \frac{E_{F_1}}{kT}\right) \tag{9.8}$$

$$\alpha_h = \left(\frac{k}{e}\right)\left(A_h + \frac{E_{F_2}}{kT}\right) \tag{9.9}$$

α_e and α_h are Seebeck coefficients respectively for n- and p-type semiconductors, k is the Boltzmann constant, A_e and A_h are constants depending on the mode of scattering of the current carriers, E_{F_1} and E_{F_2} denote the Fermi level measured with respect to the bottom of conduction band and the top of valence band, respectively (Fig. 9.1).

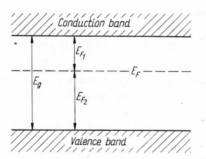

FIG. 9.1. The Fermi level position with respect to the bottom of conductance band and top of the valence band.

From discussion presented in Chapter 5 it follows that for non-degenerate semiconductors parameters E_{F_1} and E_{F_2} are related to temperature and concentrations of carriers by the following equations:

$$\frac{E_{F_1}}{kT} = \ln \frac{N_c}{n} \tag{9.10}$$

$$\frac{E_{F_2}}{kT} = \ln \frac{N_v}{p} \tag{9.11}$$

where

$$N_c = 2(2\pi m_e^* k T/h^2)^{3/2} \tag{9.12}$$

$$N_v = 2(2\pi m_h^* k T/h^2)^{3/2} \tag{9.13}$$

The values of constants A_c and A_h in eqs. (9.8) and (9.9) are determined by the dependence of the mean free path of current carriers on their energy. Generally the mean free path l is related to the energy of current carriers by: $l \sim E^s$ where s is a constant dependent on the type of the crystal lattice and the manner of scattering. For non-degenerate semiconductors $A = A_e = A_h = s+2$. In covalent crystals $s = 0$ and $A = 2$, in ionic crystals $s = 0.5$ and $A = 2.5$ for $T \ll \theta$ and $s = 1$ and $A = 3$ for $T \gg \theta$. For scattering on the charged defects $s = 2$ and $A = 4$.

In many cases the concentration of current carriers in oxide materials is so high that electron or hole gas is partially or completely degenerated. For degenerate semiconductors eqs. (9.1) to (9.7) remain valid, the scattering coefficient in the Hall effect assumes, however, the value of 1. Equations (9.8) to (9.13) cannot by applied to these materials. The temperature dependence of the carrier concentration and thermoelectric power in degenerate materials are represented by more general formulae resulting from the necessity of applying the Fermi–Dirac statistics in the calculations:

$$n = \frac{4\pi(2m_e^* k T)^{3/2}}{h^3} F_{1/2}(E_F^*) \tag{9.14}$$

$$p = \frac{4\pi(2m_h^* k T)^{3/2}}{h^3} F_{1/2}(E_F^*) \tag{9.15}$$

$$\alpha_e \text{ (or) } \alpha_h = \pm \frac{k}{e} \left[\frac{s+2}{s+1} \frac{F_{s+1}(E_F^*)}{F_s(E_F^*)} - E_F^* \right] \tag{9.16}$$

where $F_m(E_F^*)$ is the Fermi integral

$$F_m(E_F^*) = \int_0^\infty \frac{x^m dx}{\exp(x - E_F^*) + 1} \tag{9.17}$$

$x = E/kT$ is the reduced energy of electron, and E_F^* is the reduced Fermi energy.

Equation (9.1) which represents the relation between the concentration of the current carriers and their mobility is a fundamental equation describing the processes involved in the transport of current carriers in semiconductors.

The influence of the preparation conditions of semiconducting oxides on the concentration of the current carriers is discussed in part two of the present book. At present we shall consider another fundamental parameter of eq. (9.1), i.e. the mobility of current carriers. This can be defined as:

$$\mu_c = \frac{v_c}{E} \tag{9.18}$$

where v_c is the drift velocity component directed towards electric field, E is the intensity of this field.

The parameter μ_c defined in this way is called the *drift mobility*. More frequently the term *Hall mobility* is used. This latter is given by:

$$\mu_H = R\sigma \tag{9.19}$$

From eqs. (9.6) and (9.7) we get:

$$(\mu_H)_e = r_e(\mu_c)_e \tag{9.20}$$

$$(\mu_H)_h = r_h(\mu_c)_h \tag{9.21}$$

In the further discussion it is assumed that $r_e \approx 1$ and $r_h \approx 1$, subscripts H and c being dropped.

The carrier mobility depends on the scattering mechanism.[118, 132] In oxides three scattering processes are of importance:

(1) scattering by acoustic phonons,
(2) scattering by optical phonons,
(3) scattering by charged point defects.†

Displacements of atoms in one-dimensional crystal corresponding to acoustic and optical vibrations are illustrated schematically in Figs. 9.2 and 9.3, respectively.

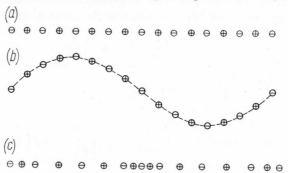

FIG. 9.2. Displacements of elements of one-dimensional ionic crystal lattice over one wavelength in the case of acoustical vibrations: (a) ionic lattice at 0 K, (b) transverse vibrations, (c) longitudinal vibrations; $\ominus$—anions, $\oplus$—cations.

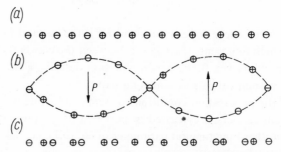

FIG. 9.3. Displacements of elements of one-dimensional ionic crystal over one wavelength in the case of optical vibrations: (a) ionic lattice at 0 K, (b) transverse vibrations, (c) longitudinal vibrations; $\oplus$—cation, $\ominus$—anion.

---

† In single crystals having a great number of dislocations an appreciable role may be acquired by scattering of carriers on these line defects. In polycrystalline samples the scattering on the grain boundaries may also occur.

For scattering of conduction electrons by acoustic phonons the following expression has been derived:[118, 132]

$$\mu_1 = \frac{2^{3/2}\pi^{1/2}e\hbar^4\rho v^2}{3(m_e^*)^{5/2}E_1^2(kT)^{3/2}} \tag{9.22}$$

where ρ is the density of the material, v is the velocity of motion of phonons in the crystal, $E_1 = \Delta E_c \times V_0/\Delta V$, ΔE_c is the change in the energy of the bottom of conduction band, caused by a small change ΔV of the initial volume V_0 of the considered crystal.

The mobility of holes is given by the analogous expression, the effective mass of holes m_h^* replacing m_e^* and E_1 is replaced by a value corresponding to the top of the valence band.

In ionic crystals, in which scattering on optical phonons predominates, the mobility of electrons and holes depends on the temperature range.

At low temperatures $(T \ll \theta)$ the mobility is represented by:

$$\mu_2 = \frac{a^3}{2\sqrt{2\pi}e^3}\frac{M}{(m^*)^{3/2}}\frac{(h\nu_0)^{3/2}}{\gamma^2 Z^2}\exp\left[\frac{h\nu_0}{kT}\right] \tag{9.23}$$

where a is the lattice constant, Ze is the ion charge, M denotes the mass of an ion, γ is a coefficient involving polarizability of ions in collective electric field, m^* is the effective mass of the current carriers, ν_0 is the frequency of lattice vibrations.

At sufficiently high temperatures $(T \gg \theta)$ the expression for the mobility of the current carriers in the ionic crystals assumes the following form:

$$\mu_2 = \frac{4a^3}{3\pi e^3}\frac{M}{(m^*)^{3/2}}\left(\frac{h\nu_0}{\gamma Z}\right)^2\frac{1}{\sqrt{2\pi kT}} \tag{9.24}$$

The scattering on charged point defects has a different character. In this case theoretical analysis yields the following expression for the temperature dependence of the mobility:

$$\mu_3 = \frac{64\pi^{1/2}\varepsilon^2(2kT)^{3/2}}{NZ^2e^3(m^*)^{1/2}}\frac{1}{\ln\left[1+\left(\frac{12\pi\varepsilon kT}{Ze^2N^{1/3}}\right)^2\right]} \tag{9.25}$$

where N is the concentration of ionized defects, ε is a dielectric constant, m^* is the effective mass of electrons and holes.

It follows from the above survey that the temperature dependence of mobility of current carriers in semiconductors is different for different scattering mechanisms. For scattering on acoustic phonons: $\mu_1 \sim T^{-3/2}$, scattering on optical phonons gives: $\mu_2 \sim \exp(h\nu_0/kT)$ at $T \ll \theta$ and $\mu_2 \sim T^{-1/2}$ at $T \gg \theta$. For scattering by charged point defects: $\mu_3 \sim T^{3/2}$.

If all the scattering mechanisms outlined above occur simultaneously, the total mobility of the current carriers is given by:

$$\frac{1}{\mu} = \frac{1}{\mu_1} + \frac{1}{\mu_2} + \frac{1}{\mu_3} \tag{9.26}$$

The temperature dependence of mobility in this case may be very complex, being dependent on the per cent of contribution of various mechanisms to the overall process of scattering.

In transition metal oxides of very narrow energy bands or of localized energy levels, we may deal with so called *hopping mechanism* of the mobility consisting in jumps of electrons or small polarons[133-140] from one ion in the crystal lattice to another. In this case the mobility has an activated character and according to the simplest hopping mechanism is given by the following formula:

$$\mu_4 = \mu_0 \exp\left[-\frac{\Delta H_m}{kT}\right] \tag{9.27}$$

where μ_0 is a constant and ΔH_m is the activation enthalpy of motion of current carriers. Heikes and Johnston[141] obtained somewhat different expression for the temperature dependence of the mobility considered in terms of the hopping mechanism:

$$\mu_4 = \frac{\mu_0}{T} \exp\left[-\frac{\Delta H_m}{kT}\right] \tag{9.28}$$

Holstein[133] on the basis of the small polaron theory deduced the following formula:

$$\mu_4 = \frac{\mu_0}{T^{3/2}} \exp\left[-\frac{\Delta H_m}{kT}\right] \tag{9.29}$$

The experimental data on oxides available at present do not permit a decision as to which of the three equations (eqs. (9.27), (9.28) or (9.29)) is correct.

9.2. Self-diffusion and Chemical Diffusion Coefficients

Several possible mechanisms of self-diffusion in solids have been postulated.[142-144] In the light of the current results it is assumed that in majority of oxide crystals three mechanisms of diffusion play the decisive role:

(1) vacancy mechanism,
(2) interstitial mechanism, and
(3) interstitialcy mechanism.

These three mechanisms are illustrated in Figs. 9.4, 9.5 and 9.6, respectively. They may occur both in the sublattice M and in the oxygen sublattice of a hypothetical oxide MO, depending on the structure of point defects in a given oxide.

The self-diffusion coefficient is defined as a proportionality coefficient in the first Fick's law when the concentration gradient of the diffusing species is zero:

$$D_i^s = \lim_{|dc/dx| \to 0} \left(\frac{J}{dc/dx}\right) \tag{9.30}$$

where D_i^s is the self-diffusion coefficient of the ith diffusing species, J and dc/dx are flux and concentration gradient of the diffusion species.

When the concentration gradient or more generally—the gradient of chemical potential occurs in the crystal, we deal with so-called *intrinsic diffusion coefficient* D_i^I of ith species. Under the influence of a chemical potential gradient, the diffusivity is increased, the intrinsic diffusion coefficient, D_i^I, being defined by:

$$D_i^I = D_i^s[\partial \ln a_i / \partial \ln N_i] \tag{9.31}$$

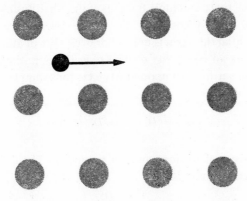

FIG. 9.4. Interstitial mechanism, elementary jump.

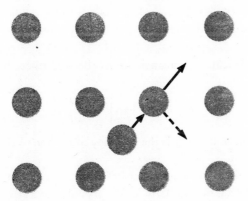

FIG. 9.5. Interstitialcy mechanism. The solid arrows show displacements of the diffusing atoms during the elementary jump in a collinear interstitialcy mechanism. The dotted arrow shows an alternative (noncollinear) motion for the lattice atom.

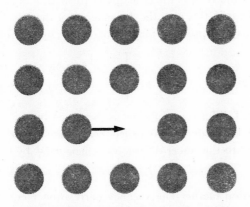

FIG. 9.6. Vacancy mechanism, elementary jump.

where a_i and N_i are the activity and mole fraction of the ith diffusing species, respectively, and the term $\partial \ln a_i / \partial \ln N_i$ is known as the *thermodynamic factor*. In the region of constant chemical potential this term is unity. For every flux of atoms moving by a defect mechanism, there occurs an equal flux of defects in the opposite direction. In the case of the vacancy mechanism in a compound $M_{1-y}O$, for example, the vacancy diffusion coefficient D_{V_i} is defined[145] as:

$$D_{V_i} = D_i^s \frac{n_i}{n_{V_i}} = D_i^s \frac{1-y}{y} \tag{9.32}$$

where n_i, n_{V_i} are numbers of ith ions and ith vacancies. The definition of D_{V_i} is not unanimous: D_{V_i} is often given as:[146]

$$D_{V_i} = \frac{D_i^s}{N_{V_i}} \tag{9.33}$$

where N_{V_i} is the mole fraction of vacancies often taken as being equal to y. If half the sites are vacant $D_{V_i} = D_i^s$ and thus eq. (9.32) seems to be valid. As y approaches zero, eq. (9.32) reduces to eq. (9.33), which is accordingly applicable at low concentrations of the vacancies.

The diffusion coefficient of vacancies may be described by the following formula:[142-144]

$$D_{V_i} = D_{V_i}^\circ \exp\left[-\frac{\Delta H'_m}{kT} \right] \tag{9.34}$$

where D_{V_i} is a constant and $\Delta H'_m$ is the enthalpy of motion of the predominant atomic defects.

The dependence of the mole fraction of defects N_{V_i} on temperature and the oxygen pressure at various defect situations in oxide crystals have been considered in detail in Chapters 5 and 6. When singly ionized vacancies in the sublattice M are the predominant defects, for example, then N_{V_i} is given by:

$$N_{V_i} = K^\circ P_{O_2}^{1/4} \exp\left[-\frac{\Delta H_f}{2kT} \right] \tag{9.35}$$

where K° is a constant and ΔH_f is the enthalpy of formation of singly ionized vacancies in the sublattice M. Thus in this case the dependence of the self-diffusion coefficient on temperature and the oxygen pressure may be described by the following formula:

$$D_i^s = D_{V_i}^\circ K^\circ P_{O_2}^{1/4} \exp\left[-\frac{\frac{1}{2}\Delta H_f + \Delta H'_m}{kT} \right] \tag{9.36}$$

In most cases the self-diffusion coefficient is measured by the tracer methods, hence the allowance should be made for so called *correlation factor*.[142] The self-diffusion coefficient D_i^s is related to the tracer diffusion coefficient D_i^T by the following formula:

$$D_i^T = f D_i^s \tag{9.37}$$

where f is the correlation factor. The vacancy correlation factor for a dilute solution of vacancies in face-centred cubic lattice is 0·78146.

As seen from the above brief considerations, the measurements of the dependence of self-diffusion coefficients on temperature and on the oxygen pressure provide valuable information about the structure of point defects in oxide materials.

The chemical, or inter-diffusion coefficient in a compound MX is defined as the proportionality constant in the Fick's law for the case when mass transport occurs under a chemical potential gradient and both species move:

$$\tilde{J} = J_1 - J_2 = -\tilde{D} \cdot \partial \tilde{c} / \partial x \qquad (9.38)$$

where the $\tilde{J}$'s denote the fluxes of the two diffusion species through a given plane normal to the diffusion direction and $\tilde{c}$ is the absolute value of the excess concentration of one component. It may be regarded as the flow of the deviation from stoichiometry through the crystal to restore a uniform composition. The inter-relations of $\tilde{D}$, D_i^s and the deviation from stoichiometry have been considered by many authors. Below, we shall present a short survey of various equations relating these terms.

The first of them was derived by Wagner[147,148] from a consideration of tarnishing reaction between a metal M and non-metal X, and gave a relation between the electrical conductivity σ with chemical diffusion coefficient. This equation applies to an electronic semiconductor with a small deviation from stoichiometry [cf. eq. (9.38)]:

$$\tilde{J} = \frac{300}{96\,500} \frac{(t_M + t_X) t_e \sigma}{e} \frac{1}{|z_M|} \frac{\partial \mu_M}{\partial \tilde{c}} \frac{\partial \tilde{c}}{\partial x} \qquad (9.39)$$

Here t_M, t_X, t_e are the transport numbers of the metal, the non-metal, and the electronic carrier, respectively, $\tilde{c}$ is the absolute excess concentration of one species in equivalents per cm³, x is the distance variable, μ_M is the chemical potential of the metal, and z_M the metal valence. $\tilde{D}$ can also be related to the self-diffusion coefficients by the Nernst–Einstein equation which applies to dilute solutions of defects. In the case of metal deficient oxides, $D_M^s \gg D_O^s$ and the expression for $\tilde{D}$ becomes:

$$\tilde{D} = (1 + |z_M|) D_M^s \frac{N_M}{N_{v_M}} \qquad (9.40)$$

From eq. (9.32) we get the following expression for a binary, electronic semiconductor, $M_{1-y}X$, both M and X being divalent elements:

$$\tilde{D} = \frac{3(1-y)}{y} \frac{D_M^T}{f} \qquad (9.41)$$

The factor 3 in the above equation is due to the diffusion potential, $1 + z_M$. An equation similar to eq. (9.40) may be also derived by considering the fluxes in the solid oxide:[149]

$$\tilde{D} = (1 + m) D_{v_M} \qquad (9.42)$$

The above equation, given by Wagner, shows the dependence of $\tilde{D}$ on the vacancy diffusivity using the effective charge of the vacancy m instead of the cationic charge.

Another equation given by Brebrick[150] pertains to a univalent ionic semiconductor with a close-to-stoichiometry composition:

$$\tilde{D} = k_X \lambda^2 \left\{ 1 + \left(\frac{k_M}{k_X} - 1 \right) \right\} \frac{n_{v_M}}{n_{v_M} + n_{v_X}} \left\{ 1 + \left(\frac{y^2 + 4 K_S}{y^2 + 4 K_i} \right)^{1/2} \right\} \qquad (9.43)$$

where k_X and k_M are related to D_X^s and D_M^s by Nernst–Einstein equation, which for D_M^s can be written as:

$$D_M^s = k_M \cdot \lambda^2 \frac{n_{V_M}}{S} \tag{9.44}$$

where λ is the mean distance of ion jump, k_M is the frequency of the cation jump, n_{V_M} is the number of cation vacancy sites, and S is the total number of sites in a given sublattice at a given vacancy concentration. In eq. (9.43) n_{V_X} is the number of anion vacancy sites, y is the deviation from stoichiometry, K_S is the Schottky constant and K_i the intrinsic constant.

When the concentration of cation vacancies is much greater than that of the anion vacancies $n_{V_M}/(n_{V_M}+n_{V_X}) \to 1$ and the deviation from stoichiometry is large enough that $y^2 \gg 4K_S, 4K_i$, eq. (9.43) reduces to:

$$\tilde{D} = 2D_M^s \frac{S}{n_{V_M}} \tag{9.45}$$

Similar equation is held when $n_{V_X} \gg n_{V_M}$. Using eq. (9.33) for D_{V_M} we come to Wagner's equation for a univalent compound $(1+z_M = 2)$. Brebrick's equation, however, assumes complete ionization of the vacancies, and its application at low defect concentration requires a knowledge of the Schottky and intrinsic constants and also the mean ion jump distance and the jump frequency.

Another equation describing interdiffusion in binary alloys is due to Darken[151], who derived it from empirical considerations:

$$\tilde{D} = N_X D_M^I + N_M D_X^I \tag{9.46}$$

From eq. (9.43) and bearing in mind that:

$$\frac{\partial \ln a_M}{\partial \ln N_M} = \frac{\partial \ln a_X}{\partial \ln N_X} = \frac{\partial \ln a_i}{\partial \ln N_i} \tag{9.47}$$

for a binary compound we obtain:

$$\tilde{D} = (N_X D_M^s + N_M D_X^s)\frac{\partial \ln a_i}{\partial \ln N_i} \tag{9.48}$$

which for $D_M^s \gg D_X^s$ is reduced to:

$$\tilde{D} = N_X D_M^s \frac{\partial \ln a_i}{\partial \ln N_i} \tag{9.49}$$

where the thermodynamic factor $\partial \ln a_i/\partial \ln N_i$ comprises the driving force for material transport derived at a composition N_X. The latter factor may be obtained from the plots of the experimental activity vs. composition, or it may be also derived in the form of the analytical expression if $\ln a_M$ and $\ln N_M$ can be written in a suitable form.

Considering the atomistic mechanism of vacancy diffusion Manning[152] obtained expressions for the intrinsic diffusion coefficients in metals which allow for a net vacancy flow. He arrived at the Darken expression with an additional term :

$$D_i^I = D_i^s \left(\frac{\partial \ln a_i}{\partial \ln N_i}\right) s \tag{9.50}$$

where

$$s = 1 + \frac{\partial N_M / \partial x}{\partial N_i / \partial x} \frac{2N_i(D_M^s - D_X^s)}{M(N_M D_M^s + N_X D_X^s)} \tag{9.51}$$

In this equation M is a constant related to the correlation factor, which for face centred cubic crystals amounts to 7·15. For interdiffusion eq. (9.48) becomes:

$$\tilde{D} = (N_M D_X^s + N_X D_M^s) \left\{ \frac{\partial \ln a_i}{\partial \ln N_i} \right\} s' \tag{9.52}$$

where s' is given by:

$$s' = 1 + \frac{2N_M N_X (D_M^s - D_X^s)^2}{M(N_M D_X^s + N_X D_M^s)(N_M D_M^s + N_X D_X^s)} \tag{9.53}$$

When $D_M^s \gg D_X^s$, s' reduces to 1·28. Hence:

$$\tilde{D} = 1 \cdot 28 N_X D_M^s \frac{\partial \ln a_i}{\partial \ln N_i} \tag{9.54}$$

Price[153] assumed that the measured chemical diffusion coefficient considered in studies on interphase equilibration was an intrinsic cation vacancy diffusion coefficient D_{V_M}. Taking into account the expressions for the thermodynamic factor and mole fractions of vacancies and cations, he obtained the following equation for the compound of the $M_{1-y}O$ type:

$$\tilde{D} = D_{V_M} = D_M^s(m+1) \frac{(1-y)}{y^2} \tag{9.55}$$

Equation (9.55) differs from Wagner's eq. (9.41) or eq. (9.42) in that it contains an extra factor: the inverse of the vacancy fraction.

CHAPTER 10

NICKEL OXIDE, NiO

10.1. Electronic Transport in Nickel Oxide
at Low and Intermediate Temperatures

Nickel oxide, NiO, is regarded as a model semiconductor for oxides of the $3d$ transition metals which show very low mobility of current carriers. Although fundamental transport properties of NiO such as electrical conductivity, Hall effect and Seebeck effect have been in the last twenty years a subject of intense studies, many problems related to these properties have not been as yet satisfactorily explained and still remain a subject of discussion.

The model character of NiO impels us to consider its properties in more detail. In section 10.1 we shall present results of studies on electronic transport in nickel oxide at low and intermediate temperatures. Section 10.2 will describe the works concerned with investigations of these properties at high temperatures and with the structure of point defects in NiO. A survey of studies on self- and chemical diffusion in NiO will be given in section 10.3. In section 10.4 some physico-chemical properties of nickel oxides will be outlined and finally in section 10.5 the properties of thin films of this oxide will be discussed.

Above about 470 K NiO shows a cubic structure of NaCl type: its lattice constant is 4·2 Å.[184] Below this temperature a very small rhombohedral distortion is observed and 0·15% contraction along a (111) axis.[154] The electrical measurements seem to indicate that this distortion occurs at 390 K.[155] The density of NiO is 7.45 g/cm³, and its m.p. is about 2230 K. Nickel oxide is a p-type semiconductor.

Pure and almost stoichiometric nickel oxide is an insulator with the room temperature resistivity of approximately 10^{13} ohm cm. The resistivity can be lowered to about 1 ohm cm by the addition of lithium (Fig. 10.1).

Verwey and de Boer[158, 159] were the first to explain this fact, by assuming that conduction in NiO is due to the presence of Ni^{3+} ions. These ions may be formed e.g. by appearance in the crystal lattice of NiO nickel vacancies or by incorporation of mono-valent atoms, e.g. of lithium. According to Verwey and de Boer introduction of Li into the crystal lattice of NiO gives rise to acceptor centres Li^+-Ni^{3+}. At low temperatures the Ni^{3+} holes formed in this way are bound to lithium ion which has an effective negative charge. At higher temperatures these holes can detach from the Li^+-Ni^{3+} centres and move quasi-freely in the crystal by exchange of electrons between

Ni^{3+} and adjacent Ni^{2+} ions. According to this model the activation energy of the conductivity is equal to the energy necessary for detaching the hole from Li$^+$ ion, whereas no energy is required for the exchange of electrons between the nickel ions. The model outlined above had been generally accepted and not disputed to about 1951.

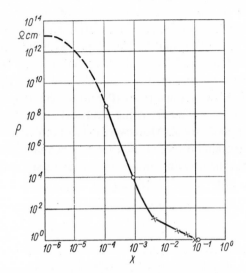

FIG. 10.1. Room temperature resistivity of Li$_x$Ni$_{1-x}$ O as a function of the lithium content: o—after Morin,[156] ×—after Verwey.[157]

Examination of the temperature dependence of electrical conductivity and Seebeck effect in Li-doped nickel oxide, reported by Morin[156, 160-163] and Parravano[164] and Heikes and Johnston[141] seemed to indicate that the Verwey and de Boer model did not account for the observed properties of nickel oxide. Analysing the data of Seebeck coefficient, Morin assumed that the density of states in NiO was constant and was equal to the concentration of lattice sites in the cationic sublattice of this compound. He assumed further that the transport term in the expression for the Seebeck coefficient was zero. It turned out that the mobility of current carriers in NiO, calculated at these assumptions, increased exponentially with the temperature, and the activation energy of the hole movement amounted to about 0·1 eV. Accordingly, Morin put forward a new hypothesis claiming that the temperature dependence of conduction in NiO reflected in the first place the change in mobility and only to the very small extent the changes in carrier concentration.

Morin and Heikes and Johnston explained this fact by assuming thermally activated-diffusive mechanism of conduction in NiO, called a *hopping mechanism*, which consists in jumping of current carriers from one lattice site to another. The activation energy of this diffusional process comes from the trapping of the holes by lattice polarization this latter being caused by the holes themselves.

The subsequent studies seemed to confirm the hopping mechanism of conduction in nickel oxide.[165-169] The value of the mobility at the room temperature obtained by various authors was very small, ranging from 10^{-3} to 10^{-6} cm²/Vs. The Hall effect measurements carried out by Fujime et al.[167] at the room temperature also corroborated this model. The value of the Hall mobility in NiO reported by this author was of the order of 10^{-4} cm²/Vs, being thus in accordance with the values obtained from the studies of electrical conductivity and Seebeck effect.

The hopping model of the hole movement in NiO was not questioned till 1963. Re-examination of electrical conductivity and Hall and Seebeck effects carried out by Ksendsov et al.[170] for polycrystalline NiO doped with lithium and studies of Zhuze and Shelykh,[171] Roilos and Nagels[172] on single crystals of NiO threw a new light on the mechanism of the hole transport in this oxide. According to these workers, the Hall mobility of holes in NiO is contained from 10^{-2} to 0·4 cm²/Vs, and is thus appreciably higher than that calculated earlier from the electrical conductivity and Seebeck effect data assuming the hopping model. Moreover, it has been found that above the room temperature the Hall mobility does not increase exponentially with increasing temperature as anticipated from the hopping model, but it decreases with increasing temperature. Accordingly the last results contradict the hopping model pointing out to the

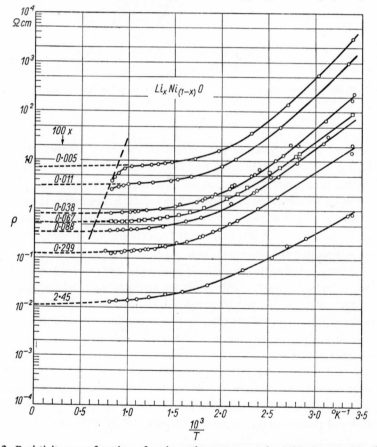

FIG. 10.2. Resistivity as a function of reciprocal temperature for NiO doped with different amounts of Li.[176] The dashed line represents the resistivity of pure NiO in equilibrium with oxygen (1 atm) measured on single crystal.[177]

mechanism of hole transport in the narrow band. This latter conclusion was confirmed by the subsequent investigations of transport properties in NiO.[173-175]

Extensive studies on electrical conductivity and Seebeck effect in ceramic samples of NiO doped with lithium were performed by Bosman and Crevecoeur.[176] The temperature range covered in these studies was from 100 to 1300 K. Figure 10.2 gives the temperature dependence of electrical resistivity obtained by these workers for samples of NiO with different Li content. The dashed line pertains to the corresponding dependence at thermodynamic equilibrium.[177] Only at very low lithium concentrations

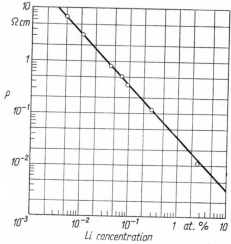

FIG. 10.3. Resistivity at high temperature as a function of the Li concentration. The values of the resistivity are obtained from Fig. 10.2 by extrapolating the measurements to $1/T = 0$.[176]

the effect of the deviations from stoichiometry on conductivity in NiO was observed. The values of the conductivity at high temperatures are proportional to the concentration of lithium in the crystal lattice of NiO as shown in Fig. 10.3. Figure 10.4 shows the temperature dependence of the Seebeck coefficient obtained by Bosman and Crevecoeur for NiO containing 0·088 at. % Li. At temperatures below 140 K the Seebeck coefficient increases rapidly with the increasing temperature, reaching a maximum around 140 K, and then slowly decreases to a minimum at about 900 K.

Such courses of the ϱ vs. $1/T$ and α vs. T dependence are interpreted by the authors as follows. It is assumed that the electrical conductivity of NiO is a sum of the conductivity resulting from the presence of holes σ_h and the conductivity induced by impurities:

$$\sigma = \sigma_h + \sigma_i \tag{10.1}$$

At temperatures higher than 140 K the first term of eq. (10.1) predominates, whereas at lower temperatures the conductivity involving impurities prevails.

In the first case the Seebeck coefficient may be expressed by the formula (cf. Chapter 9):

$$\alpha = \frac{k}{q} \ln\left(\frac{N_v}{p} + A\right) = 2 \cdot 3 \frac{k}{q} \log\left(\frac{N_v e^A}{p}\right) \tag{10.2}$$

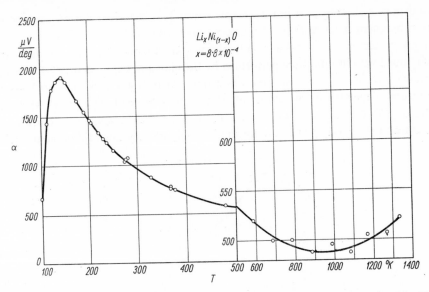

FIG. 10.4. Thermoelectric power as a function of temperature for NiO containing $8 \cdot 8 \times 10^{-2}$
at. % Li.[176]

where k is the Boltzmann constant, q is an electron charge, N_v denotes the density of states, p is the concentration of holes and A is a term involving kinetic energy of quasi-free holes. On the other hand

$$\log \rho = \log \frac{1}{pq\mu} \tag{10.3}$$

where ρ is resistivity and μ mobility of the current carriers. Since A is constant, and $N_v = 2(2\pi m_h^* kT/h^2)^{3/2}$ where m_h^* is the effective mass of holes and h is the Planck constant, then if the mobility of holes in NiO increased exponentially with the increasing temperature, $\log \rho$ would decrease faster with the increasing $1/T$ than $\alpha q/2 \cdot 3k$. In Fig. 10.5 the plots of $\log \rho$ and $\alpha q/2 \cdot 3k$ vs. reciprocal of the absolute temperature are presented. As seen from this figure, above 170 K the both dependences are almost identical. Hence, we may conclude that the temperature dependence of electrical conductivity of NiO results from the change in the concentration of holes and not from the change in their mobility. The results of Bosman and Crevecoeur contradict the hopping model. They can be, however, explained in terms of the mechanism of movement of holes in a narrow band.

Ksendzov, Avdeenko and Makarov[178] studied the temperature dependence of electrical resistivity and Hall and Seebeck effect in single crystals of NiO doped with lithium. The results obtained by them in measurements of the resistivity and the Hall coefficient are shown in Fig. 10.6. As seen from this figure, the temperature dependence of the Hall constant in the vicinity of the Néel point distinctly departs from the exponential relationship. The authors ascribed this fact to the influence of the anomalous Hall constant and obtained the following expression for the normal Hall constant R_0 in antiferromagnetics (like NiO):

$$R_0 = \frac{R_H}{1 - 4\pi a \varkappa} = R_H + 4\pi \varkappa R_a \qquad (10.4)$$

where R_H is the experimental Hall constant, $a = \text{const}$, R_a is anomalous Hall constant, and $\varkappa$ is the magnetic susceptibility of the material under examination.

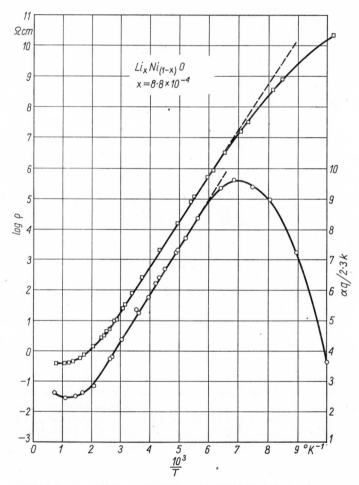

Fig. 10.5. Resistivity and thermoelectric power as a function of reciprocal temperature for NiO doped with $8 \cdot 8 \times 10^{-2}$ at. % Li.[176]

Parameter R_a can change its sign in the vicinity of the Néel point, whereas the sign of R_0 does not change. Such the change in the sign of the Hall constant was observed in works [173–175], whereas Ksendzov and co-workers found the positive sign of this constant in the entire range of the temperatures covered in their studies. They estimated the value of a and knowing $\varkappa$ determined constant R_0. The normal Hall constant in NiO was found to be 1·5 to 2 times larger than the value of R_H. The temperature dependence of R_0 obtained by Ksendzov and co-workers for crystal 2 is shown by the dotted line in Fig. 10.6.

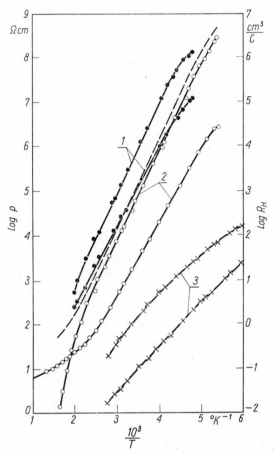

FIG. 10.6. Resistivity and Hall coefficient of lithium-doped NiO as a function of temperature.[178] 1, 2—samples doped during the growth of single crystals with the Li content of 0·02 and 0·05 at. %, respectively, 3—sample doped by diffusion containing 1% Li; the upper curve of each pair pertains to the Hall coefficient R_H, the lower curve to the resistivity ρ. The dotted line shows the normal Hall constant R_0 for crystal 2.

Figure 10.7 presents the temperature dependence of the Hall mobility obtained by Ksendzov for the three samples of NiO (cf. Fig. 10.6). The mobility of holes in sample 2 obeys the equation:

$$\mu_h = \mu_0 \exp \frac{E}{kT} \tag{10.5}$$

where $E = 0.073$ eV is practically equal to the energy of longitudinal optical phonons (0·076 eV): the value of μ_0 obtained by extrapolation amounts to about 0·01 cm²/Vs.

The mobility of current carriers in crystal 3 passes through a maximum at the same temperature at which the dependence of the conductivity on the current frequency was observed. The authors believe that the effect of the electron component of the current may account for this fact.

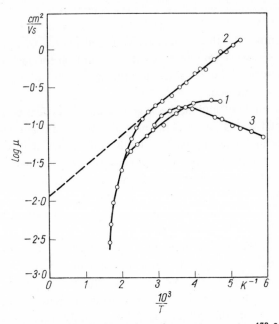

FIG. 10.7. Hall mobility in Li-doped NiO as dependent on temperature[178] for three samples of different lithium content: 1—0·02 at. %, 2—0·05 at. %, 3—1 at. %.

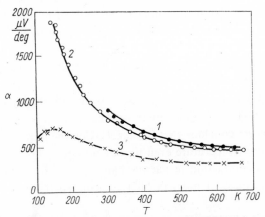

FIG. 10.8. The temperature dependence of the Seebeck coefficient in Li-doped NiO:[178] 1—0·02 at. % Li, 2—0·05 at. % Li, 3—1 at. % Li.

The temperature dependence of the Seebeck coefficient for the three samples of NiO under study is shown in Fig. 10.8. The Seebeck coefficient of NiO decreases with the increasing temperature and with the increase in the lithium concentration. In the case of crystal 3 containing relatively high concentration of lithium, α reaches a maximum at 140 K. As already mentioned, Bosman and Crevecoeur[176] observed at the same temperature the maximum value of the Seebeck coefficient for polycrystalline samples of NiO. Thus the results of studies on transport properties in single crystals of NiO obtained by Ksendzov and coworkers are in accordance with the earlier data of Bosman and Crevecoeur, indicating the band character of the motion of current carriers in NiO. In particular they show that the carriers are scattered mainly by optical phonons. The authors believe that the scattering on native defects and on foreign atoms in NiO need not to be taken into consideration, since no influence of the addition concentration on the mobility has been observed.

Extensive studies on Hall and Seebeck effects and electrical conductivity in single crystals of NiO doped with Li were performed also by Austin and co-workers.[179] They found that in the temperature range 150–400 K, the electrical resistivity is the exponential function of the temperature, the activation energy of the resistivity decreasing with the increasing lithium content. Above the Néel point the rapid decrease of the activation energy was observed similar to that observed earlier by Koide.[168] The Hall effect measurements showed that in the temperature range 240–400 K the Hall coefficient changes exponentially with the temperature, the activation energy of this process being somewhat higher than the activation energy of the resistivity (Fig. 10.9).

The temperature dependence of the Hall mobility in NiO obtained by Austin and co-workers is shown in Fig. 10.10. As seen from this figure, above 250 K in all NiO samples the Hall mobility decreases with increasing temperature. However, in some samples μ_H attains a maximum around 200–300 K. Finally, Fig. 10.11 shows the results of the Seebeck effect measurements reported by Austin *et al.* The latter results were used for estimation of the concentration of holes and for calculation of the drift mobility in NiO. The temperature dependence of the drift mobility obtained is shown in Fig. 10.12. In the same figure the analogous dependence of the Hall mobility obtained by Austin *et al.*, Bosman *et al.*,[174] and Roilos and Nagels[172] is also given. The value of the drift mobility at room temperature obtained by Austin *et al.* is 0·4 cm²/Vs and remains constant at temperatures from 250 to 500 K. At higher temperatures the drift mobility in NiO decreases with the increasing temperature. The Hall mobility is one order magnitude smaller than the drift mobility, also decreasing with the increase in temperature. Above Néel point the Hall constant alters its sign.

Austin and co-workers conclude that in nickel oxide the impurity conduction predominates up to the room temperature even in the samples without lithium addition, and suggest small polaron conduction in narrow band. From the simple band model they estimated the effective mass of holes in NiO as being *ca.* $12m_0$ where m_0 is the mass of an electron.

Makarov and co-workers[180] measured drift mobilities of both holes and electrons in NiO. The values obtained were: for holes *ca.* 0·3 cm²/Vs and for electrons *ca.* 0·14 cm²/Vs. The Hall mobility obtained by van Daal and Bosman[181] is at room temperature about 0·2 cm²/Vs and decreases with the increasing temperature changing its sign around 600 K. In the temperature range 670–1000 K Hall mobility remains constant with the value of about 0·004 cm²/Vs.

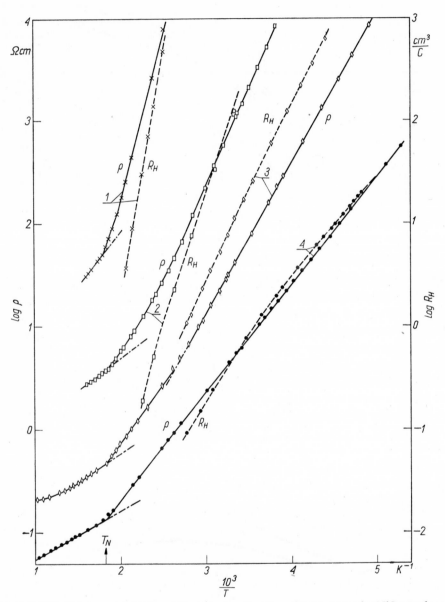

FIG. 10.9. Resistivity ρ and Hall coefficient R_H as a function of temperature for NiO samples of different lithium content:[179] 1—pure NiO, 2—0·029 at. % Li, 3—0·202 at. % Li, 4—0·537 at. %. The continuous line represents the resistivity, the dashed line the Hall coefficient.

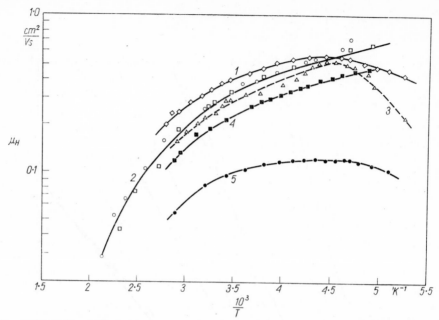

FIG. 10.10. Hall mobility in Li-doped NiO for the samples of different lithium concentrations:[179] 1—0·202 at. %, 2—0·029 at. %, 3—0·144 at. %, 4—0·211 at. %, 5—0·537 at. %.

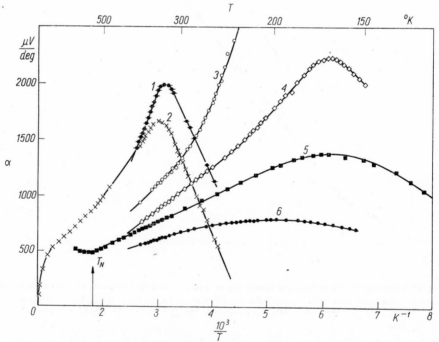

FIG. 10.11. Seebeck coefficient in NiO as a function of reciprocal temperature:[179] 1, 2—pure NiO, 3—0·032 at. % Li, 4—0·202 at. % Li, 5—0·211 at. % Li, 6—0·537 at. % Li.

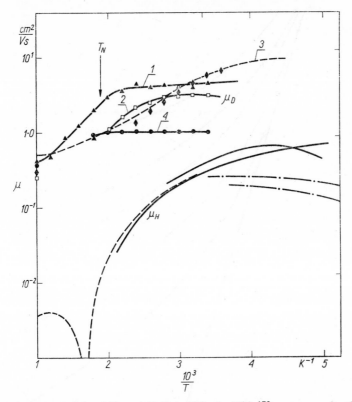

FIG. 10.12. Comparison of the drift and Hall mobility in NiO:[179] ————— Austin and co-workers,[179] — — — — Bosman *et al.*[174] — · — · — · — · Roilos and Nagels.[172] Lithium content: 1—0·03 at. %, 2—0·21 at. %, 3—0·202 at. %, 4—0·537 at. %.

Aiken and Jordan[182] measured the dependence of the electrical conductivity of NiO simple crystals with various amounts of the excess oxygen on temperature and on the current frequency. It was found that the activation energy of the conductivity decreased with the increasing concentration of the excess oxygen. The temperature dependence of the conductivity for different current frequencies is shown in Fig. 10.13. Analogous studies were performed by Kabashima and Kawakubo[183] on single crystals of NiO doped with lithium. Some of their results obtained for the samples containing 1·2 ppm Li are given in Fig. 10.14.

It follows from the survey of works given above that beginning from 1963 almost all the results of studies on electron transport in NiO indicate the narrow band conduction mechanism. At low temperatures the impurity conduction prevails in nickel oxide, both donors and acceptors being present. The compensation of acceptors by donors at low temperatures is observed in all studies described above.

The influence of the donor impurities on electrical properties of NiO at intermediate temperatures has been recently investigated by Osburn and Vest.[554] The cited authors have observed that the addition to nickel oxide of a few hundred parts per million of donor elements considerably increases the activation energy for conduction. Further-

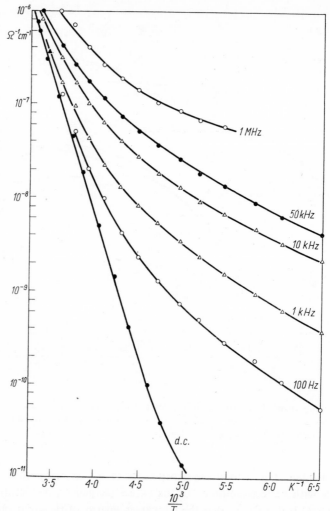

FIG. 10.13. Variation of the d.c. conductivity of NiO and the real part of the a.c. conductivity at fixed frequencies with reciprocal temperature.[182]

more, these donors decrease the magnitude of conductivity at 670 K from 10^{-1} to 10^{-8} ohm^{-1}cm^{-1}. The electrical conductivity of pure NiO was found to be almost independent of temperature in the region of 570 to 1270 K. Seebeck effect measurements carried out by Osburn and Vest confirm that the carrier concentration, rather than the mobility, decreases with decrease of temperature. The Hall mobility is also found to be almost independent of temperature.

However, the energy level structure of NiO has not been elucidated till now and is still a matter for discussion. Some authors[184, 186, 555, 556] assume that the nickel $3d$ levels are the only states in the vicinity of the Fermi energy in NiO, and form either localized states or a narrow $3d$ band because the ions are relatively far apart and there is electrostatic repulsion between the $3d$ electrons. This may suggest that in nickel oxide the $3d$ level conduction is due to small polarons.[133,140,179,185,556,559]

On the other hand, many investigators[176, 178, 181, 236, 561, 562] considered NiO to be a broad-band semiconductor. Here it is suggested that the oxygen $2p$ band is primarily responsible for the electrical transport phenomena in this compound.[187, 561, 562] Taking into account the polar bonding in NiO, large-polaron conduction may be expected in this oxide.[140]

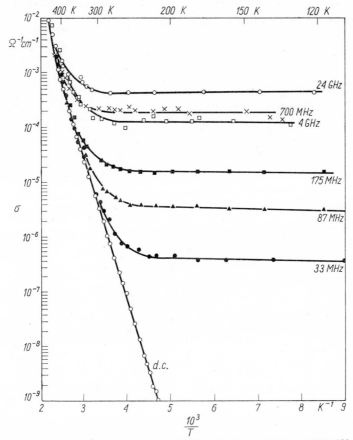

FIG. 10.14. The d.c. and h.f. conductivities of 1·2 ppm Li-doped NiO.[183]

Really Bosman and Van Daal[236] have shown that in the temperature range of 100 to 1200 K the electrical properties of the oxide under consideration are difficult to explain on the grounds of the small-polaron theory. Instead, these authors believe that the properties of this compound are in accordance with theory of large-polaron band conduction.

Adler and Feinleib[561] arrived at a similar conclusion in the case of the temperature range of 200 to 1000 K. On the basis of calculations of the latter authors it seems that in the case of NiO large-polaron conduction in the oxygen $2p$ band is more probable than the small-polaron mechanism in the $3d$ levels of this oxide.

Newman and Chrenko[188] found on the basis of optical absorption measurements that the energy gap in NiO amounts to 3·9 eV. Very similar value of 3·7 eV was reported also by Ksendzov and Drabkin[189] from the photoconductivity measurements.

10.2. Defect Structure and Electronic Transport in NiO
at High Temperatures

The first studies on electrical conductivity of polycrystalline nickel oxide were performed by Baumbach and Wagner[190] over the temperature range 1173–1273 K and in the oxygen pressure range of 2×10^{-4}–1 atm. They found that the electrical conductivity was proportional to the fourth root of the oxygen pressure.

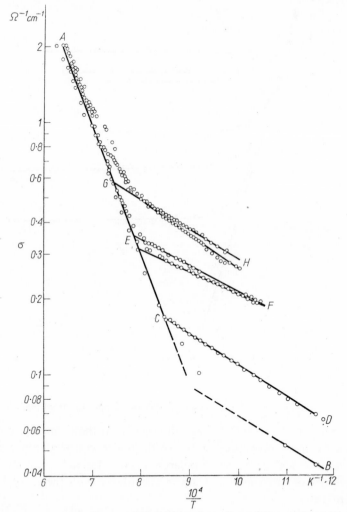

Fig. 10.15. Log electrical conductivity of NiO at 1 atm of oxygen pressure as a function of reciprocal temperature.[177]

Fig. 10.15 shows the results of the electrical conductivity measurements obtained by Mitoff[177] in the temperature range 823–1573 K and the oxygen pressure of 1 atm. Curve A–B represents the dependence of $\log \sigma$ on $1/T$ obtained during very slow cooling of the specimen (two weeks) from the temperature of 1573 to 823 K. As follows from Fig. 10.15

the thermodynamic equilibrium between NiO and O_2 was attained only at temperatures higher than 1170 K. Curve C–D was obtained as follows: the specimen was annealed at the temperature corresponding to point C for 20 hr and then cooled for 4 hr to the temperature of point D. Each of the plots E–F and G–H is composed of two curves, one of which pertains to the conductivity changes during the cooling, while another during the heating. The cooling or heating times in these cases were short amounting to about 2 hr. It was found that at temperatures higher than 1320 K the specimen attained equilibrium after 2 hr. The activation energy of the conductivity at high temperatures (i.e. at thermodynamic equilibrium) calculated from the formula:

$$\sigma = \sigma_0 \exp\left[-\frac{E_c}{kT}\right] \tag{10.5}$$

was 1·01 eV, and at intermediate temperatures 0·24 eV.

Mitoff examined also the dependence of the conductivity of NiO on the oxygen pressure in the range 10^{-4}–1 atm. He observed $\partial \log \sigma / \partial \log P_{O_2} = 1/6$; however, the scatter of the experimental points was so great that the slope of the plot $\log \sigma$ vs. $\log P_{O_2}$ could be as well taken as equal to 1/4.

Mitoff's interpretation of his results is based on two assumptions:

(1) doubly ionized nickel vacancies and holes formed according to the reaction:

$$1/2 O_2^{(g)} \rightleftarrows O_O^x + V_{Ni}'' + 2h^{\boldsymbol{\cdot}}; \quad (\Delta H_f)_2 \tag{10.6}$$

are the predominant point defects in NiO in the studied range of oxygen pressures, and

(2) high-temperature behaviour of NiO may be considered in terms of the Heikes and Johnston model of hole mobility outlined in Chapter 9.

With these assumptions the high-temperature conductivity in NiO is described by the following formula (cf. Chapter 9):

$$\sigma = \frac{C}{T} P_{O_2}^{1/6} \exp\left[\left(\frac{(\Delta H_f)_2}{3kT} + \frac{\Delta H_m}{kT}\right)\right] \tag{10.7}$$

where σ is the electrical conductivity, C is a constant, $(\Delta H_f)_2$ is the enthalpy of formation of doubly ionized nickel vacancies, ΔH_m is the activation enthalpy for motion of the holes, k and T have the usual meaning. Thus, according to Mitoff, the value of $[(\Delta H_f)_2/3 + \Delta H_m]$ is equal to the activation energy of the conductivity at high temperatures (1·01 eV) and ΔH_m is equal to the activation energy of conductivity at intermediate temperatures (0·24 eV) at which as it is assumed the nickel vacancies are completely frozen in the crystal lattice. Hence $(\Delta H_f)_2 = 3·2$ eV.

But his interpretation of the results of electrical conductivity measurements is based on the *a priori* assumption that at temperatures lower than 1170 K the charge carrier concentration $p = $ const. In our opinion, however, it seems that in the temperature range, where the atomic defects (foreign atoms and native defects) are frozen, p increases exponentially with T because these defects become ionized, and the function $\sigma(T)$ at temperatures lower than 1170 K is related mainly to the function $p(T)$ and not to $\mu(T)$.

Pizzini and Morlotti [191] measured the electrical conductivity of sintered nickel oxide in the temperature range 1073–1373 K and at the oxygen pressure from 10^{-2} to 1 atm. The NiO specimens were sintered in air at 1773 K in the Super Kanthal furnace. The measurements were done in a double-electrode system. To improve electric contact between the platinum electrodes and the specimen, the side faces of this latter were covered with a layer of gold or platinum. The layer of gold was deposited by vacuum evaporation and the platinum layer by cathode sputtering. The required oxygen pressure was obtained by varying the ratio of nitrogen to oxygen in the mixture of these gases passing over the specimen. The composition of the gas mixture was determined by mass spectrometry. The flow rate was several cm^3/min. The measurements were done on several different samples containing different amounts of various impurities. The activation energy of the conductivity derived from eq. (10.5) was different for different samples depending on the content of impurities, especially on the content of iron. At the oxygen partial pressure of 10^{-2} to 10^{-1} atm, the value of $\partial \log \sigma / \partial \log P_{O_2}$ was $1/6$. At higher oxygen pressures the departures from the dependence $\sigma \sim P_{O_2}^{1/6}$ towards the higher values of the exponent were observed.

Similarly like Mitoff, Pizzini and Morlotti explain their results assuming that the nickel vacancies in NiO are doubly ionized. The departures from the dependence: $\sigma \sim P_{O_2}^{1/6}$ at oxygen pressures higher than 10^{-1} atm are ascribed to the presence of the $(V_{Ni} Ni_i V_{Ni})'$ complexes which would give the dependence $\sigma \sim P_{O_2}^{1/4}$.

Uno[192] studied the electrical conductivity of NiO single crystals obtained by the Verneuil method: the temperature range was 1270–1520 K and the pressure range 10^{-3}–152 mm Hg. The activation energy of the conductivity reported by him was 0·96 eV at the oxygen pressure of 152 mm Hg. At low oxygen pressures this energy was considerably higher and at 10^{-3} mm Hg amounted to about 1·4 eV.

Uno believes that electrical conductivity of NiO at low oxygen pressures is determined mainly by impurities and not by native defects. Hence he considers the dependence of $ogl(G-G_0)$ on the $\log P_{O_2}$, where G is the conductance at a given oxygen pressure and G_0 conductance at the pressure of 10^{-3} mm Hg. In the pressure range from about 10^{-2} to about 1 atm he obtained the following relationship: $G-G_0 \sim P_{O_2}^{1/n}$ where n was from 3·7 to 3·9. The author suggests that singly ionized nickel vacancies and holes formed according to the reaction:

$$1/2 O_2^{(g)} \rightleftarrows O_O^x + V'_{Ni} + h^\cdot; \quad (\Delta H_f)_1 \tag{10.8}$$

are the predominant defects in NiO.

Bransky and Tallan[193] measured the electrical conductivity of single crystals and polycrystalline samples of NiO in the temperature range 1273–1873 K and in the oxygen pressure range 10^{-6}–1 atm. The single crystals were prepared by the method described by Cech and Alessandrini[194] consisting in epitaxial growth of NiO on the MgO substrate. Polycrystalline samples were obtained by oxidation of spectrally pure nickel foil 0·14 mm thick. The nickel foil was oxidized in air at 1723 K for 240 hr. The electrical conductivity was measured at a.c. The platinum wires were fixed to the single crystal specimens with platinum paste, whereas in experiments with the poly-crystalline samples the wires were soldered to the nickel foil. The samples were suspended in a vertical tube furnace. Various partial pressures of oxygen were obtained by using the flow of the mixture of O_2 and Ar or of CO and CO_2. No dependence of the electrical conductivity of NiO on the current frequency was observed up to 20 kHz.

The data on resistivity of single crystal and polycrystalline samples at 1 atm of oxygen obtained by Bransky and Tallan are plotted as a function of the reciprocal of temperature in Fig. 10.16. The activation energy calculated with the least squares method from

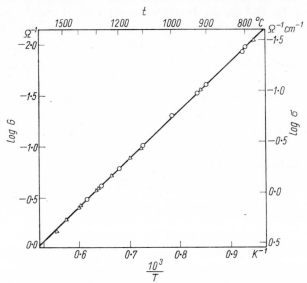

FIG. 10.16. Log conductivity of single crystal (o) and log conductance of polycrystalline (△) NiO as a function of reciprocal temperature in $P_{O_2} = 1$ atm.[193]

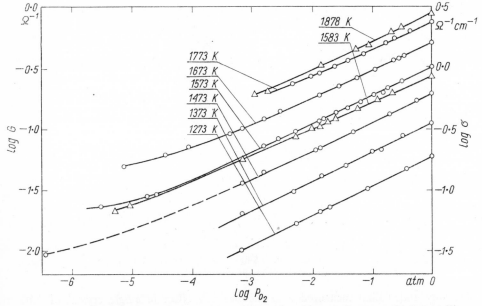

FIG. 10.17. Log electrical conductivity of single crystal (o) and log conductance of polycrystalline (△) NiO as a function of log oxygen pressure at various temperatures.[193]

eq. (10.5) is identical for the single crystal and polycrystalline sample amounting to 0.92 ± 0.02 eV. In Fig. 10.17 is shown the dependence of conductivity of single crystal and conductance of the polycrystalline sample on the oxygen pressure plotted on the logarithmic scale. In the range of the oxygen partial pressures of 10^{-3} to 1 atm the electrical conductivity is proportional to the fourth root of the oxygen pressure.

The authors explain their results similarly like Uno, assuming that in the studied range of temperatures and oxygen pressures, singly ionized nickel vacancies and holes are the dominant defects, i.e. they accept the occurrence of reaction (10.8) which leads to such a relation between the electrical conductivity and the oxygen pressure.

Bransky and Tallan note, however, that the above dependence of σ on P_{O_2} may be also derived if NiO contains impurities of the valency different than 2. For example, when NiO contains trivalent impurities incorporated into the cation sublattice and compensated by doubly ionized nickel vacancies, and reaction (10.6) takes place, then in the special case when the electroneutrality condition has the form:

$$2[V_{Ni}''] \cong [F_{Ni}^{\cdot}] \cong [F_{Ni}]_{tot} \tag{10.9}$$

one obtains the relationship:

$$\sigma = P_{O_2}^{1/4}[F_{Ni}]_{tot}^{-1/2} \tag{10.10}$$

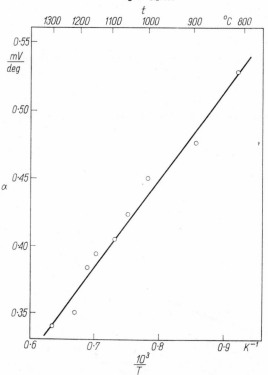

FIG. 10.18. The Seebeck coefficient of NiO single crystal relative to platinum at $P_{O_2} = 1$ atm as a function of reciprocal temperature.[193]

Bransky and Tallan measured also the Seebeck effect in single crystal of NiO as a function of temperature. The results obtained are presented in Fig. 10.18.

The Seebeck coefficient of p-type semiconductors is given by the following formula (cf. Chapter 9):

$$\alpha = \frac{k}{q}\left[\ln\frac{N_v}{p} + A\right] \tag{10.11}$$

where A is a constant related to the kinetic energy of the current carriers and N_v is the density of states. For very narrow energy bands $A \ll 1$.

If then the energy levels are localized on cationic sites without formation of a band, i.e. when the transport of current carriers may be described in terms of the hopping model, we may assume $A = 0$ and N_v equal to the concentration of cations in the crystal lattice which for NiO is 5.5×10^{22} cm^{-3}.

Substituting into eq. (10.11) the expression for p obtained by applying the law of mass action to reaction (10.8) and differentiating, Bransky and Tallan derived the following equation, which makes possible to calculate the enthalpy of formation of singly ionized nickel vacancies $(\Delta H_f)_1$:

$$q \left(\frac{d\alpha}{d\frac{1}{T}} \right) = \frac{1}{2} (\Delta H_f)_1 \qquad (10.12)$$

From the slope of the plot α vs. $1/T$ illustrated in Fig. 10.18 they obtained $(\Delta H_f)_1 = 1.32$ eV. q is the electronic charge.

On the basis of the results of the conductivity and Seebeck effect measurements, Bransky and Tallan discuss the character of current carrier mobility in NiO. Similarly like Mitoff and Uno they assume hopping mechanism of conductance in NiO as the one operating in the temperature range under study. The simplest version of the hopping model leads to the following expression for the mobility:

$$\mu_p = \mu_0 \exp \left[- \frac{\Delta H_m}{kT} \right] \qquad (10.13)$$

Hence in the case when singly ionized nickel vacancies and electron holes are the predominating defects in NiO, and their concentrations are small, the electrical conductivity in NiO is given by (cf. Chapter 9):

$$\sigma = C P_{O_2}^{1/4} \exp \left[- \left(\frac{(\Delta H_f)_1}{2kT} + \frac{\Delta H_m}{kT} \right) \right] \qquad (10.14)$$

where C is a constant.

As already noted, the activation energy of the conductivity calculated by Bransky and Tallan is 0.92 eV. Substituting the value of $(\Delta H_f)_1 = 1.32$ eV derived from the Seebeck coefficient data into eq. (10.14) Bransky and Tallan estimated the enthalpy of hole motion in NiO, ΔH_m, to be 0.26 eV. They also confronted their results with the model of mobility proposed by Heikes and Johnston and Holstein (cf. Chapter 9). The linear dependence of $\log \sigma T$ on $1/T$ for the Heikes and Johnston model and $\log \sigma T^{3/2}$ on $1/T$ for the Holstein mechanism were obtained. The activation energy of the conductivity derived from these two plots was, however, slightly higher than 0.92 eV derived from the slope of the plot $\log \sigma$ vs. $1/T$, amounting to 1.03 and 1.09 eV for the Heikes and Johnston, and Holstein model, respectively. The corresponding values of ΔH_m were 0.37 and 0.43 eV. Bransky and Tallan suggest the mechanism proposed by Heikes and Johnston as the one which operates in NiO, thus accepting $\Delta H_m = 0.37$ eV.

Making use of the thermogravimetric data presented by Mitoff they calculated the mobility of holes at 1667 K to be 0·25 cm²/Vs. They propose the following expression for the temperature dependence of hole mobility in NiO:

$$\mu_p = \frac{5959}{T} \exp\left[-\frac{0·37}{kT}\right] \quad \text{cm}^2/\text{Vs} \tag{10.15}$$

However, the above inferences with regard to mobility behaviour in NiO are in disagreement with those drawn from Seebeck effect and resistivity data at the temperatures lower than about 1270 K as described in section 10.1.

Furthermore, the experimental results concerning the Seebeck effect measurements, obtained by Bransky and Tallan,[193] have been questioned by Bosman and Van Daal.[236]

Eror and Wagner[195] measured the electrical conductivity of single crystals of NiO in the temperature range 1170–1470 K and in the oxygen pressure range from 10^{-4} to 1 atm. In this pressure range and at temperatures from 1220 to 1470 K the conductivity of NiO was proportional to the fourth root of the oxygen pressure, which may indicate, similarly like the results of Bransky and Tallan and Uno, reaction (10.8) as the main process involved in defect formation in NiO. The results obtained by Eror and Wagner are shown in Fig. 10.19.

According to the Eror's and Wagner's interpretation of the results given in Fig. 10.19 (similarly as Mitoff[177]) the sum of enthalpy of defect formation and enthalpy of activation of the hole motion in NiO is constant in the studied range of the oxygen pressure. The enthalpy of activation of the hole motion, however, increases with the decreasing oxygen pressure thus obeying the so called *Meyer–Neldel relationship*. The dependence of the enthalpy of the hole motion on the fourth root of the oxygen pressure is shown in Fig. 10.20. Eror and Wagner explain this problem as follows: at low concentrations of holes, the majority of them are trapped on lattice defects, e.g. on dislocations, which leads to an extra equilibrium process not considered by other workers:

immobile electronic defect

$\rightleftarrows$ mobile electronic defect at dislocation site + free dislocation site   (10.16)

At high concentrations of defects, the total number of holes in the NiO crystal may outweigh the number of the defects, e.g. dislocations, which capture the electronic defects and the Meyer–Neldel relationship may not be observed, which was confirmed by the experiment.

The electrical conductivity of polycrystalline NiO was measured by Cox and Quinn[196] in the high oxygen pressures from 10^{-2} to 750 atm. According to their studies nickel oxide is stable at 1223 K in the above pressure range. They obtained the relationship $\sigma \sim P_{O_2}^{1/5}$. Cox and Quinn suppose hence that nickel oxide contains nickel vacancies both singly and doubly ionized.

Similar relationship between the electrical conductivity of NiO and the oxygen pressure was observed recently by Jarzębski et al.[197] in the temperature range 1220–1470°K and the oxygen pressure range 10^{-3}–1 atm. Both polycrystalline samples and single crystals prepared from the same initial material were examined. In polycrystalline samples the equilibrium was attained after relatively short time of several to several tens minutes depending on temperature, whereas for single crystals this time was longer amount-

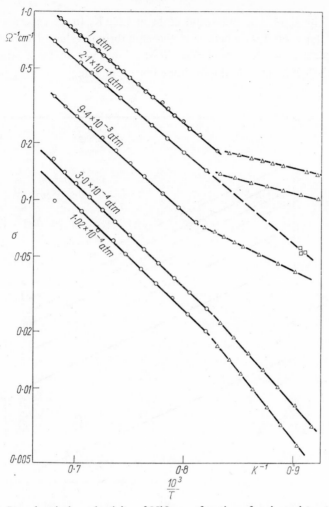

FIG. 10.19. Log electrical conductivity of NiO as a function of reciprocal temperature.[195]

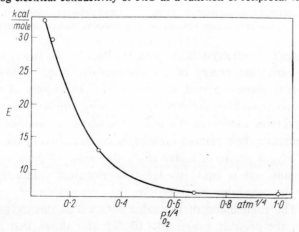

FIG. 10.20. Oxygen partial pressure dependence of the activation energy for electrical conductivity in NiO.[195]

ing to about 8 hr at 1473 K and about 25 hr at 1223 K. In all experiments the linear dependence of $\log \sigma$ on $1/T$, where σ is the equilibrium value of the conductivity at a given temperature, was observed. For illustration some of these straight lines are shown in Fig. 10.21, the continuous lines corresponding to polycrystalline samples

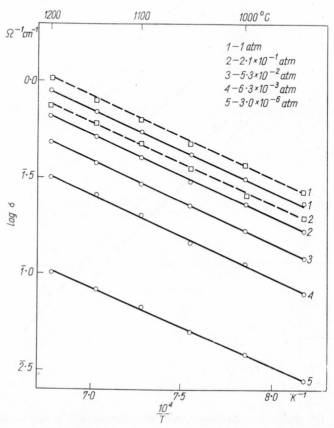

FIG. 10.21. Log electrical conductivity of single crystal and polycrystalline NiO as a function of temperature:[197] continuous line—polycrystalline samples, broken line—single crystal.

and the broken lines to single crystals. As seen, the lines for the two types of the samples are parallel, the activation energy of the conductivity being (0.86 ± 0.02) eV. This value is very close to those reported in other works. The values of the conductivity for poly- and mono-crystalline samples are also very similar, which indicates that scattering of the current carrier on the grain boundaries of sintered polycrystallites has only a slight effect on the measured value of the conductivity. In the whole range of temperature and oxygen pressures under study the value of $\partial \log \sigma / \partial \log P_{O_2}$ is approximately constant and is equal to $1/5$. The electrical conductivity of the two types of the samples was also measured in the atmosphere of argon, at $P_{O_2} = 3 \times 10^{-6}$ atm. The comparison of the value obtained at this oxygen pressure with those recorded in the pressure range 6.3×10^{-3}–1 atm shows that at lower oxygen pressures the exponent is smaller than $1/5$.

Recently Volpe and Reddy[198] observed also the approximated dependence $\sigma \sim P_{O_2}^{1/5}$ in single crystals of NiO. Their results are shown in Fig. 10.22. Volpe and Reddy interpreted the temperature dependence of the hole mobility in NiO in accordance with Heikes and Johnston (cf. section 9.1), hence the dependence in Fig. 10.22 is plotted as $\log \sigma T$ vs. $\log P_{O_2}$.

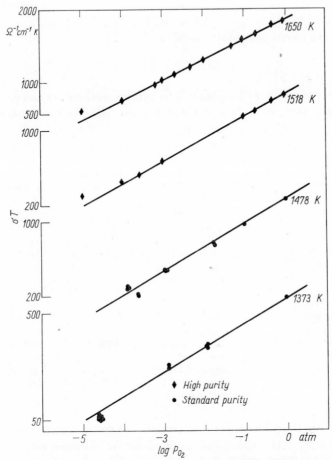

Fig. 10.22. Log (σT) vs. log P_{O_2} for different temperatures.[198]

The results obtained by Cox and Quinn,[196] Jarzębski et al.,[197] and Volpe and Reddy[198] may be explained as follows. If we assume namely in NiO an intermediate range of oxygen pressures in which both singly and doubly ionized nickel vacancies exist, then we may write down the following processes of incorporation of oxygen into the crystal lattice of NiO occurring in this pressure range:

$$\frac{1}{2} O_2^{(g)} \rightleftarrows O_O^x + V_{Ni}' + h^{\cdot}; \quad (\Delta H_f)_1 \tag{10.17}$$

$$\frac{1}{2} O_2^{(g)} \rightleftarrows O_O^x + V_{Ni}'' + 2h^{\cdot}; \quad (\Delta H_f)_2 \tag{10.18}$$

where $(\Delta H_f)_1$ and $(\Delta H_f)_2$ are the enthalpy changes respectively for reaction (10.17) and (10.18). These two processes may be described in the form of the following overall process:

$$O_2^{(g)} \rightleftarrows 2O_O^x + V'_{Ni} + V''_{Ni} + 3h^\cdot; \quad \Delta H_f \tag{10.19}$$

where ΔH_f is the enthalpy change for reaction (10.19). Obviously: $\Delta H_f = (\Delta H_f)_1 + (\Delta H_f)_2$.

If we assume additionally that $[V'_{Ni}] \approx [V''_{Ni}] \approx [V_{Ni}]/2$, where $[V_{Ni}] = [V'_{Ni}] + [V''_{Ni}]$, which leads to the electroneutrality condition:

$$3/2[V_{Ni}] = p \tag{10.20}$$

then we obtain $\sigma \sim P_{O_2}^{1/5}$.

The values of the exponent $1/n$ obtained by various workers are compared in Table 6. As seen from this table the values of $1/n$ of 1/4 was found in four works, the value of

TABLE 6.   HIGH-TEMPERATURE ELECTRICAL CONDUCTIVITY OF NiO

Year	Authors	Material	Temperature range K	Oxygen pressure atm	$1/n$
1934	Baumbach and Wagner[190]	polycrystalline	1070–1270	10^{-3} to 1	1/4
1961	Mitoff[177]	single crystals	1170–1620	10^{-4} to 1	1/6
1967	Pizzini and Morlotti[191]	polycrystalline	1070–1370	10^{-2} to 10^{-1}	1/6
1967	Uno[192]	single crystals	1270–1520	10^{-2} to 1	1/4
1968	Bransky and Tallan[193]	single crystals polycrystalline	1270–1870	10^{-3} to 1	1/4
1969	Eror and Wagner[195]	single crystals	1220–1470	10^{-4} to 1	1/4
1969	Cox and Quinn[196]	polycrystalline	1220	10^{-2} to 750	1/5
1970	Volpe and Reddy[198]	single crystals	1450–2030	10^{-6} to 1	1/5
1970	Tripp and Tallan[488]	polycrystalline	1070–1370	10^{-4} to 10^{-1}	1/5
1971	Jarzębski et al.,[197]	single crystals polycrystalline	1220–1470	10^{-3} to 1	1/5
1971	Osburn and Vest[563]	single crystals polycrystalline	1170–1670	10^{-4} to 1	1/6

1/6 was reported in three and 1/5 in four papers. The recent studies on deviations from stoichiometry in $Ni_{1-y}O$ carried out by coulometric titration indicate the relation $y = \text{const} P_{O_2}^{1/6}$.[16, 17] Thus some of the papers concerned with the defect structure in NiO indicate the presence of singly ionized defects, whereas the other show them to be doubly ionized. The results published in the last two years may also show that the range of the oxygen pressures of 10^{-3} to 1 atm is the intermediate region for NiO in which both singly and doubly ionized nickel vacancies may exist.

Analysing the results of studies on defect structure in NiO, Jarzębski and Mrowec[201] have proposed a model of the defect structure in pure NiO for the entire range of its homogeneity. According to them, at very low oxygen pressures doubly ionized interstitial nickel atoms and doubly ionized nickel vacancies are the predominant defects. At intermediate pressures the doubly ionized nickel vacancies prevail and at high pressures either singly ionized nickel vacancies of singly ionized complexes $(V_{Ni} Ni_i V_{Ni})'$ dominate.

The mobility of holes in NiO at high temperatures has been little discussed in the literature, although its activation character has been generally accepted.[177, 192, 193, 195, 197, 198] Van Daal and Bosman [181] and Tallan and Tannhauser[202] measured the Hall mobility in NiO at 1280 K obtaining the values of the order of 10^{-3} cm²/Vs. They found, however, that the Hall coefficient is negative, whereas, as generally recognized, the conductivity in NiO is of p-type. Van Daal and Bosman account for this fact by assuming the effect of induced magnetization on current carriers in NiO, whereas Tallan and Tannhauser suppose that at high temperatures the holes in NiO are localized and hence their Hall mobility is several orders of magnitude smaller than the drift mobility. If this is the case the Hall mobility of electrons may outweigh the Hall mobility of holes leading to the negative sign of the Hall effect.

No data on the Hall mobility in NiO at temperatures higher than 1280 K are available in the literature. This is understandable if we bear in mind experimental difficulties encountered in measurements of the Hall effect at such high temperatures. At these temperatures the mobility in non-stoichiometric compounds is usually calculated from the data of the deviations from stoichiometry and the electrical conductivity, assuming at the same time that all dominant defects occurring in the crystal are ionized. Such an assumption is fully justified for high temperatures.

The deviation from the stoichiometric composition y in NiO at equilibrium conditions may be given by the following formula:

$$y = y_0 P_{O_2}^{1/n} \exp\left(-\frac{E_y}{kT}\right) \qquad (10.21)$$

where y_0 is a constant and E_y may be called the activation energy for deviation from the stoichiometric composition. The values of n, y_0 and E_y obtained by different authors are given in Table 6a.

TABLE 6a. DEVIATION FROM THE STOICHIOMETRIC COMPOSITION IN NiO

Year	Authors	Samples and methods	Temperature range K	Oxygen pressure range atm	$1/n$	y_0	E_y eV
1961	Mitoff[177]	single crystals; thermogravimetry	1400–1800	1	—	0.77	1.04 ± 0.35
1968	Sockel, Schmalzried[16]	polycrystalline; coulometric titration	1470	10^{-6}–10^{-3}	1/6	—	—
1969	Tretyakov, Rapp[17]	polycrystalline; coulometric titration	1100–1370	10^{-4}–1	1/6	$0.51^{+0.21}_{-0.15}$	0.83 ± 0.4
1970	Tripp, Tallan[488]	polycrystalline; thermogravimetry	1070–1370	10^{-4}–10^{-1}	1/5	0.168	0.86 ± 0.15

Dereń, Jarzębski and Rusiecki[203] attempted to estimate the hole mobility in NiO from the results of Tretyakov and Rapp (cf. Fig. 10.23 and Table 6a). They also made use of these results in calculations of the diffusion coefficient of defects in NiO.

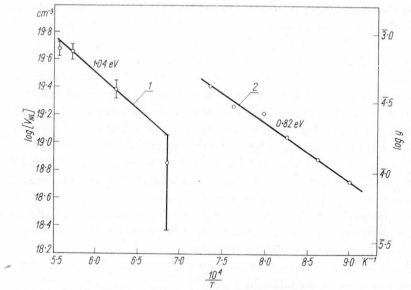

FIG. 10.23. Log concentration of nickel vacancies in NiO as a function of reciprocal temperature: 1—after Mitoff,[177] 2—after Tretyakov and Rapp.[17]

The hole mobility μ_p in NiO was calculated from the formula:

$$\mu_p = \frac{\sigma}{q[V'_{\text{Ni}}]} \tag{10.22}$$

where σ is the conductivity, q is an electron charge, $[V'_{\text{Ni}}]$ is the concentration of singly ionized nickel vacancies in cm^{-3}. It is assumed that in the temperature range under study the nickel vacancies in NiO are singly ionized. The values of electrical conductivity in single crystals of NiO at 1 atm of oxygen used in the calculations, were taken from various works (Fig. 10.24).

The calculated values of hole mobility in NiO in the temperature from 1070 to 1370 K and at the oxygen pressure of 1 atm range from 0·06 to 0·18 cm^2/Vs. The activation enthalpy ΔH_m of the hole motion calculated according to the formula: $\mu_p = \mu_p^0 \exp(-\Delta H_m/kT)$ is small, being contained in the range from 0 to about 2 eV.

The large differences in the values of mobility and its activation energy are due to the discrepancies of the values of conductivity, obtained by different authors, and the above mentioned errors in the measurements of deviation from the stoichiometric composition. The activation energy of the motion of holes has been found to be much smaller than the values of ΔH_m estimated by Mitoff, Bransky and Tallan, and Eror and Wagner.

Jarzębski[204] has recently carried out a detailed analysis of the high-temperature electrical properties, deviation from the stoichiometric composition and the defect structure of NiO in order to explain the mechanism of electrical transport phenomena

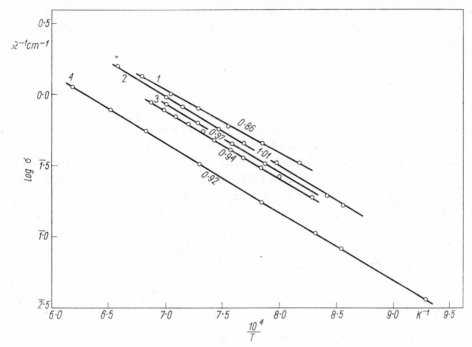

FIG. 10.24. Log electrical conductivity of single crystals NiO at 1 atm of oxygen as a function of reciprocal temperature according to various authors: 1—after Dereń, Jarzębski, Mrowec, Walec,[197] 2—after Mitoff,[177] 3—after Eror, Wagner,[195] 4—after Bransky, Tallan.[193] The values indicate the activation energy of conductivity (E_c) in eV, calculated from the dependence

$$\sigma \sim \exp\left[-\frac{E_c}{kT}\right]$$

in this oxide at temperatures above 1200 K. It has been found that in the 1200 to 1800 K range the charge carrier mobility in nickel oxide is almost independent of temperature. The obtained values of μ change from $(0\cdot27\pm0\cdot15)$ to $(0\cdot54\pm0\cdot15)$ cm^2/Vs for different assumed degrees of ionization of nickel vacancies. It has been ascertained that this is not evidence of small-polaron conduction in NiO at high temperatures.

This conclusion, drawn on the basis of an analysis of the data given by many authors, has been recently supported by the experimental results (electrical conductivity and deviation from the stoichiometric composition) obtained by Osburn and Vest.[563] In the 1170 to 1670 K range these authors found that for the very pure samples the activation energy of conductivity is equal to the activation energy of deviation from the stoichiometric composition, and according to the dependence: $\sigma \sim \exp\left[-\dfrac{E_c}{kT}\right]$ amounts to $(0\cdot81\pm0\cdot04)$ eV. They also ascertained that the mobility in NiO in the studied temperature range is almost independent of temperature and equals $0\cdot53$ cm^2/Vs. Hence, the value of mobility obtained by Osburn and Vest[563] is approximately equal to the values calculated by Jarzębski.[204]

Thus, is seems that the charge carrier phenomena in this oxide at low and intermediate temperatures (cf. 10.1) as well as at high temperatures can be explained either by the large-polaron theory, or else NiO has transitional electrical properties which may be exactly elucidated on the basis of a new intermediate model between the large and small polaron models.

10.3. Self-diffusion and Chemical Diffusion in NiO

In this section we shall describe briefly the results of studies on self-diffusion of nickel and oxygen in nickel oxide and on chemical diffusion in this compound.

Shim and Moore[205] studied the temperature dependence of self-diffusion of nickel in polycrystalline and single crystals of NiO over the temperature range of 1273–1673 K. The polycrystalline samples were prepared by oxidation of nickel foil in air at 1523 K, the time of oxidation being 88 hr. After oxidation and rapid cooling at the liquid nitrogen temperature the specimens were homogeneous and had no cracks. They were then heated at 1520 K for 88 hr and again rapidly cooled. The single crystals were obtained by the Verneuil method. Isotope Ni[63] was used as a tracer. The layer of Ni[63] was deposited on a NiO sample by vacuum evaporation. The thickness of the radioactive layer was 440 Å. During the diffusion the specimens were placed in a platinum boat heated with the platinum resistance furnace. No evaporation of the isotope layer was observed. The temperature dependence of D_{Ni} obtained by Shim and Moore may be described by the following equations:
for single crystal:

$$D_{Ni} = 3.9 \times 10^{-4} \exp\left[-\frac{1.93 \text{ eV}}{kT}\right] \tag{10.23}$$

for polycrystalline samples:

$$D_{Ni} = 5.0 \times 10^{-4} \exp\left[-\frac{1.93 \text{ eV}}{kT}\right] \tag{10.24}$$

Since the values of D_{Ni} for single crystals and polycrystalline samples do not differ much, Shim and Moore assume that diffusion along the grain boundaries plays only a minor role in the case of nickel oxide samples prepared by oxidation of nickel.

Lindner and Åkerström[206] measured D_{Ni} in NiO using the same method and the similar material. The values of D_o and ΔH obtained by them differ significantly from those reported by Shim and Moore, being:

$$D_{Ni} = 1.72 \times 10^{-2} \exp\left[-\frac{2.4 \text{ eV}}{kT}\right] \tag{10.25}$$

To explain this difference Choi and Moore[207] re-examined their earlier data. The measurements of D_{Ni} were carried out on single crystals over the temperature range 1273–1743 K. The plot of $\log D_{Ni}$ vs. $1/T$ obtained by Choi and Moore is shown in Fig. 10.25, the temperature dependence of D_{Ni} is described by:

$$D_{Ni} = 1.83 \times 10^{-3} \exp\left[-\frac{1.98 \text{ eV}}{kT}\right] \tag{10.26}$$

Klotsmann, Timofeyev and Traktenberg[208] studied the self-diffusion of nickel in single crystals of NiO over the temperature range 1463–1673 K. They estimated D_0 and ΔH to be $4 \cdot 8 \times 10^{-4}$ cm^2/s and $2 \cdot 07$ eV, respectively.

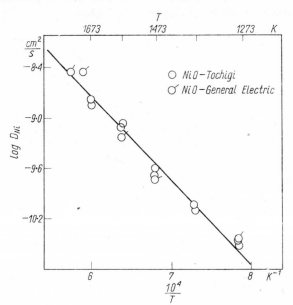

FIG. 10.25. Log diffusion coefficient of nickel in NiO as a function of reciprocal temperature.[207]

Wang[209] reports the values: $D_0 = 1 \cdot 26 \times 10^{-5}$ cm^2/s and $\Delta H = 2$ eV, obtained in the studies on sintering of NiO from the measurements of the electrical conductivity. The value of ΔH obtained by Wang by entirely different method is close to the value derived by Choi and Moore.

Recently Volpe and Reddy[198] have published the results of studies on self-diffusion of nickel in NiO obtained in the temperature range 1450–2030 K and in the oxygen pressure range from 5×10^{-7} to 1 atm (Fig. 10.26). The diffusion coefficient of nickel was measured by a tracer method. When the diffusion took place in the atmosphere of pure oxygen the following temperature dependence of the nickel diffusion coefficient was obtained:

$$D_{\text{Ni}} = (4 \cdot 77 \pm 1 \cdot 3) \times 10^{-2} \exp\left[- \frac{2 \cdot 65 \pm 0 \cdot 03}{kT} \right] \qquad (10.27)$$

In pure CO$_2$ the same dependence had the form:

$$D_{\text{Ni}} = (2 \cdot 06 \pm 0 \cdot 4) \times 10^{-2} \exp\left[- \frac{2 \cdot 73 \pm 0 \cdot 02}{kT} \right] \qquad (10.28)$$

Volpe and Reddy observed $D_{\text{Ni}} \sim P_{O_2}^{1/n}$, where $n = 6$ at 1518 K and $n = 5$ at 1653 K. Similar increase of the exponent $1/n$ with the increase in temperature was found also by Fueki and Wagner[211] in their studies on kinetics of nickel oxidation.

As can be seen from above considerations the values of ΔH obtained by Volpe and Reddy are much larger than those given in previous papers.

Volpe *et al.*[564] have determined the isotope effect for cation self-diffusion in NiO crystals by simultaneous diffusion of ^{57}Ni and ^{66}Ni tracers in the temperature range from 1474 to 1951 K. The cited authors have shown that their results are consistent only with cation self-diffusion by a vacancy mechanism.

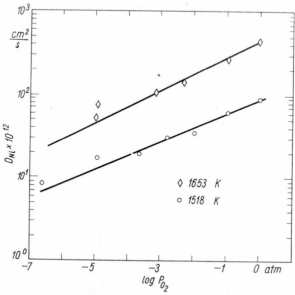

FIG. 10.26. Log diffusion coefficient of nickel in NiO as a function of log oxygen pressure.[198]

Self-diffusion of oxygen in NiO was studied by O'Keeffe and Moore.[210] They determined the coefficient D_O in NiO by the method of oxygen exchange between the sample and the surrounding oxygen-containing atmosphere enriched in isotope O^{18}. The results obtained by O'Keffe and Moore are shown in Fig. 10.27. They report the following temperature dependence of the oxygen diffusion coefficient in NiO:

$$D_O = 6 \cdot 2 \times 10^{-4} \exp\left[-\frac{2 \cdot 47 \text{ eV}}{kT}\right] \tag{10.29}$$

observed over the temperature range 1370–1770 K. They found also that the diffusion coefficient of oxygen in NiO increases with the increasing oxygen pressure, which excludes the mechanism of the diffusion via oxygen vacancies. The obtained dependence of D_O on P_{O_2} would indicate the diffusion of oxygen via interstitial atoms or ions of oxygen, which, however, is little probable if we bear in mind the large atomic radius of oxygen. O'Keeffe and Moore propose also another mechanism of the oxygen diffusion in NiO, namely the diffusion through the complexes of the ($V_{Ni} V_O V_{Ni}$) type. If this were true the oxygen diffusion coefficient would increase with the increase in the oxygen pressure. The ratio D_{Ni}/D_O at 1500 K has been found to be about 2000 which would constitute the proof for the defect structure in nickel oxide being limited practically only to the cation sublattice.

The oxygen self-diffusion in NiO has been studied more recently by Hoch and Szwarc[565] by means of sintering kinetics method. They observed that these oxygen diffusion coefficient measurements are in agreement with data obtained by other techniques. Hoch and Szwarc found also that doping NiO with lithium increased the D_o, instead addition of trivalent chromium decreased the oxygen diffusion coefficient in this oxide, although the effect was not so great as in the case of lithium doping.

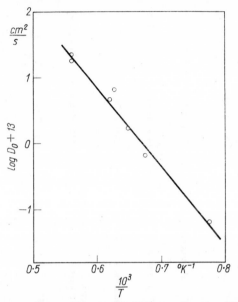

FIG. 10.27. Log diffusion coefficient of oxygen in NiO as a function of reciprocal temperature at $P_{O_2} = 50$ Tr.[210]

The data on chemical diffusion coefficient in NiO have been published in the papers of Price and Wagner,[212] Morlotti,[489] and Jarzębski et al.[213] In all those works the electrical conductivity method was applied. In the temperature range of 1270–1470 K Jarzębski et al. obtained the values of this coefficient ranging from 10^{-7} to 6.3×10^{-7} cm^2/s. The activation enthalpy of the process of chemical diffusion in NiO given by Price and Wagner[212] is 0.95 eV. Instead in the two last works these values are much higher and amount to 1.35 and 1.46 eV, respectively.

The data on self-diffusion and chemical diffusion coefficients, and the conditions of the measurements in which they were obtained, are collected in Table 7.

10.4. Physico-chemical Properties of Nickel Oxide

Bielański, Dereń, Haber and co-workers[13, 215-222] have carried out a thorough study on physico-chemical properties of NiO including also its defect structure.

It has been found[13] that in polycrystalline samples of NiO obtained by calcination of nickel salts, the deviation from stoichiometry in surface layers of the polycrystallites differs considerably from that in the bulk of the crystallites. The analytical method described by these authors made possible to distinguish between the concentration of defects in these two regions of the crystallites. According to these studies the earlier

TABLE 7. SELF-DIFFUSION AND CHEMICAL DIFFUSION COEFFICIENTS IN NiO

Year	Authors	Diffusing element	Material	Method	Temperature range K	D_o cm²/s	ΔH eV
1957	Shim and Moore[205]	Ni	polycrystalline single crystal	Ni[63] radiotracer	1270–1670	$5{\cdot}0 \times 10^{-4}$ $3{\cdot}9 \times 10^{-4}$	$1{\cdot}93 \pm 0{\cdot}14$
1957	Lindner and Åkerström[206]	Ni	polycrystalline single crystal	Ni[63] radiotracer	970–1670	$1{\cdot}72 \times 10^{-2}$	2·43
1962	Choi and Moore[207]	Ni	single crystal	Ni[63] radiotracer	1270–1670	$1{\cdot}83 \times 10^{-3}$	1·98
1962	Klotsmann et al.[208]	Ni	single crystal	Ni[63] radiotracer	1460–1670	$4{\cdot}8 \times 10^{-4}$	$2{\cdot}1 \pm 0{\cdot}10$
1965	Fueki and Wagner[211]	Ni	polycrystalline	oxidation kinetics	1270–1670	—	1·95
1966	Wang[209]	Ni	polycrystalline	electrical study of sintering shrinkage	550–1000	$1{\cdot}26 \times 10^{-5}$	2·02
1970	Volpe and Reddy[198]	Ni	single crystal	Ni[57] and Ni[63] radiotracer	1450–2030	$(4{\cdot}77 \pm 1{\cdot}3) \times 10^{-2}$	$2{\cdot}64 \pm 0{\cdot}03$
1961	O'Keeffe and Moore[210]	O	single crystal	O[18] mass spec.	1370–1770	$6{\cdot}2 \times 10^{-4}$	2·5
1966	Price and Wagner[212]	chemical	single crystal	electrical conductivity	1070–1370	—	0·95
1969	Morlotti[489]	chemical	single crystal	electrical conductivity	1020–1270	14	1·35
1971	Jarzębski et al.[213]	chemical	single crystal	electrical conductivity	1270–1470	—	1·46

data on deviation from stoichiometry in NiO gave the sum of defect concentration in the bulk and at the surface and hence they could not be employed in evaluation of extent of disorder in NiO. It turned out that the major part of the deviation from stoichiometry in NiO fell to the surface layer of the crystallites and could be related to processes of oxygen chemisorption. A good illustration of this finding is provided by the data compared in Table 8,[216] which show the influence of the temperature of NiO preparation from basic nickel carbonate on the magnitude of the deviation from stoichiometry in NiO.

TABLE 8. TOTAL AMOUNT OF EXCESS OXYGEN IN NiO AND AMOUNT OF OXYGEN INCORPORATED TO CRYSTAL LATTICE IN THIS COMPOUND AT DIFFERENT TEMPERATURES[216]

Heat treatment temperature K	Total amount of excess oxygen at. %	Amount of excess oxygen incorporated to crystal lattice at. %
673	2·23	0·59
773	1·55	0·58
798	0·97	0·57
823	0·89	0·42
873	0·15	0·04
1073	0·06	0·03
1273	less than 0·01	less than 0·01

The further investigations of these workers were concerned with the effect of ions, introduced into the host lattice of NiO, on its properties. They comprise primarily the examination of the effect of lithium addition as a monovalent ion on physicochemical and electronic properties of NiO. The mechanism of incorporation of large quantities of lithium is not disputable and can be described by the following equation:

$$\frac{1}{2} O_2^{(g)} + Li_2O \rightleftarrows 2O_O^x + 2Li'_{Ni} + 2h^{\bullet} \tag{10.30}$$

Bielański and co-workers have shown, however,[216, 217] that at small concentrations of lithium of the order of 1 at. %, the mechanism of its incorporation is essentially different. As seen from the data collected in Table 9, the first portions of incorporated

TABLE 9. THE INFLUENCE OF LITHIUM ON EXCESS OXYGEN CONCENTRATION IN NiO

No. of samples	Concentration of Li at. %	Concentration of excess oxygen		Amount of oxygen desorbed in vacuum number of atoms/m²
		total: in lattice and on the surface at. %	in lattice at. %	
1	pure NiO	not detected		—
2	0·025	0·01	not detected	$1·6 \times 10^{18}$
3	0·07	0·03	not detected	$4·7 \times 10^{18}$
4	0·13	0·05	0·03	$2·7 \times 10^{18}$
5	0·24	0·12	0·07	$7·6 \times 10^{18}$
6	0·38	0·19	0·15	$7·7 \times 10^{18}$
7	0·85	0·37	0·33	$8·3 \times 10^{18}$
8	3·40	1·93	1·70	$53·8 \times 10^{18}$

lithium do not cause the appearance of Ni^{3+} ions in the crystal lattice of the parent oxide (samples 2 and 3). This implies that the hole concentration ($h^\bullet = Ni^{3+}$) is smaller than 0·01 at. %, the latter value being the detectability limit in determination of the defect concentration. The other samples of lithium doped nickel oxide showed the presence of the excess oxygen, its total concentration being, however, in all the samples somewhat smaller than that resulting from eq. (10.30). The only exception was sample 8 containing 3·40 at. % Li in which the concentration of the excess oxygen was higher than the concentration corresponding to eq. (10.30).

The figures in the last column of Table 9 give the content of the excess oxygen desorbable in vacuum at 673 K. It has been proved that the oxygen excess is due to chemisorption. This oxygen is then equivalent to cationic vacancies in the near-to-surface layers of the crystal. For pure nickel oxide and the doped samples containing about 0·1 at. % Li, the thickness of this layer is of the order of the lattice constant. This indicates that the amount of chemisorbed oxygen covering the surface of these samples do not exceed one atomic layer. The number of oxygen atoms in this monolayer is about 11×10^{18} m^{-2}. In sample 8 the amount of oxygen which can be desorbed is ca. 5 times larger. Thus in this case, the desorption at 673 K removes not only the chemisorbed oxygen but also certain amount of the excess oxygen from the bulk of the crystal lattice. Analogous results were obtained also for the samples containing 1·4 and 2·5 at. % Li.

Moreover, the results of the above studies indicate that as the concentration of lithium increases, which is equivalent to the increase in the concentration of cationic vacancies, the mobility of components of the crystal lattice and hence the rate of self-diffusion are also increased. The above results are consistent with those of Keier[223] who found that the increase in lithium concentration enhanced the ability to isotopic exchange of oxygen between the crystal lattice and the gas phase.

Parravano and Boudart[224] assume that the formation of the solid solution NiO–Li_2O at small concentrations of lithium oxide involves the filling of cationic vacancies in the lattice of NiO by lithium ions. The cationic vacancies may be formed in the process which can be schematically described as:

$$1/2 O_2^{(g)} \rightleftarrows O_O^x + V_{Ni}'' + 2h^\bullet \tag{10.31}$$

The filling of these vacancies is represented by the equation:

$$Li_2O + 2V_{Ni}'' + 2h^\bullet \rightleftarrows 2Li_{Ni}' + 1/2 O_2^{(g)} \tag{10.32}$$

It follows from the above equation that the first portions of lithium which is being incorporated should produce not an increase but the decrease in concentration of holes and cationic vacancies.

Such the mechanism cannot account however for the absence of the excess oxygen in samples 2 and 3, as according to eq. (10.30) the excess oxygen should be absent only when the lithium concentration is smaller than 0·01 at. %. Accordingly Bielański, Dereń and co-workers[13, 215, 216, 222] proposed another mechanism for incorporation of first portions of lithium which can be represented schematically by the equation:

$$Li_2O \rightleftarrows Li_{Ni} + Li_i + O_o \tag{10.33}$$

Equation (10.33) is simplified: it implies that lithium atom in interstitials is non-ionized, and lithium in the lattice site has an effective charge of 2. The authors assume the formation of complexes of the type $(Li'_{Ni}h^{\cdot})$ and $(Li_i^{\cdot}e')$ (interstitial lithium ion and monovalent nickel ion, and lithium ion in the normal lattice site and trivalent nickel ion).

The incorporation of lithium into NiO lattice may be also described by another equation:

$$Li_2O \rightleftarrows 2Li'_{Ni} + O_o^{x} + V_o^{\cdot\cdot} \qquad (10.34)$$

The decision which of the mechanisms is correct is possible on the basis of measurements of the lattice constant of the oxide as a function of the addition concentration: we

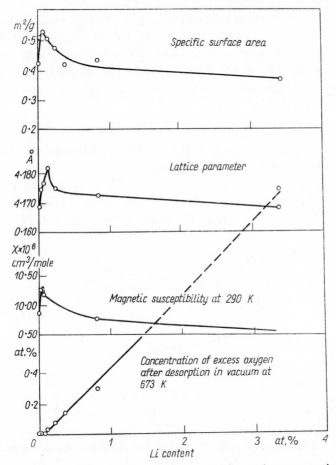

FIG. 10.28. Dependence of various physico-chemical properties on the concentration of lithium.

would expect namely the increase in the lattice constant if the mechanism described by eq. (10.33) operates, and the decrease if mechanism given by eq. (10.34) is valid. Figure 10.28 illustrates the dependence of the lattice constant of the solid solution NiO–Li₂O on the lithium concentration. As seen from this figure the first portions of lithium produce an increase of the lattice constant, whereas the further portions its decrease. Such the behaviour indicates the complexity of the process of lithium incorporation into the NiO lattice. At low lithium concentrations mechanism (10.33) predominates, at its higher concentrations it is replaced by mechanism (10.34). The authors suggest that the incorporation of lithium into interstitials (eq. 10.33) is probably a transition stage in the process of formation of the solid solution NiO–Li$_2$O.

Figure 10.28 shows also the changes of the surface area, magnetic susceptibility and concentration of the excess oxygen in the crystal lattice plotted as a function of the lithium concentration. The course of changes in the specific surface area indicates distinct changes in the rate of sintering caused by the presence of the addition. It is interesting to note a close correlation between the change in the lattice constant and the magnitude of the specific surface area.

Subsequent studies of Dereń and co-workers[218–221] were concerned with electronic properties of the NiO–Li$_2$O system. They included the measurement of the electron work function, Seebeck coefficient and electrical conductivity over the temperature range 373–673 K in the controlled atmosphere. The measurements of the Seebeck effect enable to determine the position of the Fermi level with respect to the $3d^8$ level from the simple relationship:

$$E_F = \alpha T q \qquad (10.35)$$

where E_F is the Fermi level, α is the Seebeck coefficient, T denotes the absolute temperature and q is an electron charge [cf. eq. (9.9)].

Dereń and co-workers have shown that eq. (10.34) can be with good approximation applied to polycrystalline systems, the data hence obtained being related to the bulk of the crystal. The measurements of the electron work function, on the other hand,

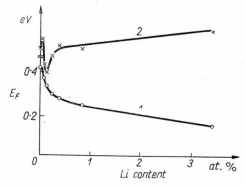

FIG. 10.29. Position of Fermi level in NiO as a function of incorporated lithium: 1—calculated from the Seebeck coefficient measurements, 2—derived from electron work function measurements.

determine the position of the Fermi level at the crystal surface with respect to a fixed but indeterminable zero level. The latter measurements provide thus information solely about the relative changes of the Fermi level position at the crystal surface. The dependence of the negative values of the electron work function ϕ and the Seebeck coefficient α on the lithium concentration are shown in Fig. 10.29. The curves 1 and 2 in this figure illustrate the course of the Fermi level changes in the bulk of the crystals and at their surface, respectively. According to these results the Fermi level in the bulk is lowered monotically with the increase in the lithium concentration. At very small content of lithium this level slightly raises, which may be due to the different degree of ionization of donor centres as compared with the acceptors. Such the centres may be provided by the previously mentioned complexes formed by the reaction (10.33): donors by complex $(Li_i^{\cdot} e')$ and acceptors by $(Li'_{Ni} h^{\cdot})$. The analogous course is revealed by the curve of the electrical conductivity changes as a function of the addition concentrations.

The curve illustrating the position of the Fermi level at the surface of the NiO–Li$_2$O crystals shows an essentially different course. Only at low lithium content of about 0·1 at. % Li the course of this curve corresponds to that of the work function changes. At higher lithium concentrations the Fermi level at the crystal surface increases with the increasing concentration of the addition. On the basis of these results a simplified energy model for lithium doped nickel oxide has been postulated.[223] (Fig. 10.30).

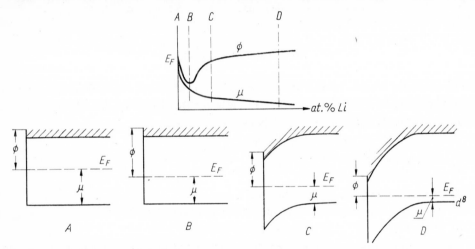

FIG. 10.30. Energy level of NiO doped with Li; schemes from A to D correspond to lithium concentrations denoted in the upper plot.

According to this model the presence of small quantities (up to about 0·1 at. % Li) gives rise to the parallel shift of the Fermi level with respect to $3d^8$ level at the surface and in the bulk of the crystal. At these concentrations the acceptor centres are formed both in the bulk and at the surface. On passing to higher concentrations of the addition, the Fermi level at the crystal surface is raised relative to the $3d^8$ level, whereas it is lowered in the bulk. At these lithium concentrations, the introduction of lithium gives rise to acceptor centres, in the bulk of the crystals according to eq. (10.33). At the surface, on the other hand, the formation of the donor centres is observed. The nature of these latter centres cannot be described at present. The existence of such centres may account, however, for catalytic and chemisorptive properties of the system.

According to the electronic theory of chemisorption, the lowering of the Fermi level at the surface should lead to the decrease in the surface coverage, whereas the raising of this level should have the opposite effect (Fig. 10.31). The comparison of the curve given in Fig. 10.31 with curve 2 in Fig. 10.30 indicates the changes in the chemisorption with the changes in the Fermi level position in agreement with the theory.

The presented results of studies in NiO depict a classical example of the problem widely discussed recently in the literature of essential differences occurring between the electronic properties of the bulk of semiconducting crystals and of their surface.

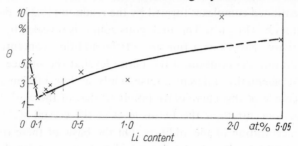

FIG. 10.31. Coverage of NiO surface with oxygen θ as a function of concentration of incorporated lithium; adsorption time 100 min, $P_{O_2} = 2\cdot2\text{--}2\cdot8 \times 10^{-2}$ Tr.

10.5. Thin Films of NiO

The extensive studies on methods of preparation of nickel oxide thin films and on their properties have been carried out recently by Rossi and Paul.[82] They used the following methods for preparation of NiO films:

(1) evaporation of NiO in high vacuum,
(2) flash evaporation of NiO,
(3) oxidation of nickel films,
(4) chemical transport and reaction via a gas,
(5) electron beam evaporation of nickel in an oxygen atmosphere,
(6) sputtering of nickel in an oxygen atmosphere.

In the evaporation method powdered NiO was heated in a tungsten boat in vacuum of the order of 10^{-6} Tr. The substrate was placed on a tantalum plate heated by a special heater of tantalum wire. NiO evaporates relatively easily at 1870 K. This method was found, however, unsuitable for preparation of thin films of NiO since the oxide decomposed under these conditions and the evolved nickel formed an alloy with the boat material. The alloy oxidized in the further course of the experiment.

In the flash evaporation method the NiO powder was dropped continuously onto the heated tungsten boat. The temperature of the boat was 2070 to 2270 K. It turned out that at the pressure of 5×10^{-6} Tr only nickel films were formed. NiO films could be obtained by this method in an oxygen atmosphere under the pressure of 2×10^{-4} Tr. LiF was used as a substrate. It was heated to 770–820 K.

Optical studies of the films revealed, however, that also other oxides, most probably tungsten oxide, evaporate together with nickel oxide contaminating the thin films of this latter.

Oxidation of thin nickel layers in an oxygen atmosphere led to NiO films of variable composition.

Thin films of nickel oxide were also prepared by the method described by Cech and Alessandrini[194] which consists in growth of epitaxial thin films of the oxide on the MgO substrate. The film grows due to decomposition of nickel halide in the atmosphere of water vapour at the temperature of about 970 K. This method yields thin films of NiO of good quality.

Evaporation of nickel from an alundum or graphite crucible was also realized by heating with an electron beam. The oxygen pressure in the chamber was 10^{-4}Tr. Under these conditions pure films of NiO can be prepared on the substrate heated to 820 K.

Finally, thin nickel oxide layers can be obtained by cathodic reactive sputtering in the atmosphere of oxygen and argon.

Katada et al.[567] have prepared thin films of single crystal of NiO by the method initiated by Cech and Alessandrini. The films were heated at 1670 to 1870 K in air and were examined by means of electron microscopy and electron diffraction. The authors observed many particles of a second phase in the matrix film of NiO. They have a defect structure of Ni-deficient NiO, which is of spinel type.

CHAPTER 11

OXIDES OF COBALT, IRON AND MANGANESE

11.1. Cobaltous Oxide, CoO

Cobaltous oxide is a p-type semiconductor of low current carrier mobility resembling in this respect nickel oxide. At high and intermediate temperatures CoO has a NaCl structure with a lattice constant of 4·26 Å. Below 284 K, a 2% tetragonal distortion occurs, the c-axis contracting relative to the other two axes.[154, 226, 227] There is evidence that there is also a small 0·06% rhombohedral distortion leading to monoclinic symmetry in this plane.[228] The density of CoO is 6·43 g/cm³, the m.p. 2080 K. Similarly like NiO cobaltous oxide is an antiferromagnetic with the Néel temperature of 292 K.

According to the Bloch–Wilson theory of electrical conduction, this oxide, similarly as NiO, should show a metallic $3d$ band whereas pure and nearly stoichiometric CoO is an insulator at low temperatures.[172, 184]

A p-type conductivity, observed in cobaltous oxide, appears owing to atomic defects (acceptors) which are both foreign atoms with valency smaller than that of the host one (e.g. Li atoms), incorporated in the cobalt sublattice or native atomic defects due to deviation from the stoichiometric composition, y, defined by the chemical formula $Co_{1-y}O$.

From measurements of y it is well known that the excess of oxygen atoms is comparatively high in CoO which has been heated at not too low oxygen pressure.[18, 19, 233, 239, 557] For example, this oxide can contain up to 1·2 at. % of excess oxygen atoms if it is prepared at 1570 K and $P_{O_2} = 1$ atm.[18, 557] Hence, in such CoO samples, which besides were not doped intentionally, the concentration of native atomic defects would be much higher than the concentration of any impurities.

The high resistivity observed in Li-doped CoO at low and medium temperatures was initially explained by Verwey et al.[558] in terms of a model of localized $3d$ electrons and by the controlled valency method. Namely, these authors assumed that the activation energy of conductivity is due to ionization of the Li^+–Co^{3+} acceptors. The quasi-free holes created in this way can move through the lattice by an interchange of electrons between Co^{2+} and Co^{3+} ions without any activation energy of motion.

Later investigations of Heikes and Johnston[141] have shown that the temperature dependence of CoO conductivity is entirely due to the drift mobility of holes, which increases exponentially with temperature.

Such an increase of the Hall mobility in CoO with increasing temperature has also been observed by Austin et al.[560] These results could point to the occurrence in this oxide of the mechanism of small-polaron conduction in a hopping regime.[133, 140] However, in other works an evolution of opinions on electrical transport phenomena in CoO is observed, namely, from the hopping to narrow-band model. For instance, Roilos and Nagels[172] have shown that the electrical conductivity of single crystals of CoO at room temperature varies between 10^{-8}–10^{-15} ohm^{-1}cm^{-1} and the activation energy of the conductivity between 0·73–1·35 eV, which is undoubtedly due to impurities and also to the point defects. Roilos and Nagels report also that the addition of about

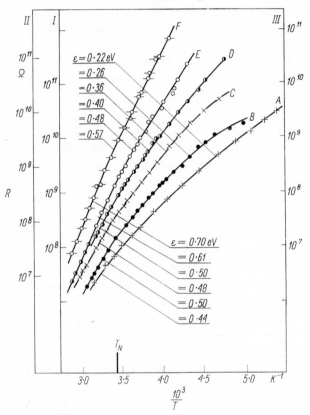

FIG. 11.1. The resistance of CoO_{1+y} as a function of reciprocal temperature for different y:[18] Curve A—$CoO_{1.013}$, Curve B—$CoO_{1.008}$, Curve C—$CoO_{1.006}$, Curve D—$CoO_{1.004}$, Curve E—$CoO_{1.002}$, Curve F—$CoO_{1.001}$. Curves A, B and C belong to Scale I; Curves D and E belong to Scale II, and Curve F belongs to Scale III.

1% of Li to CoO increases its room temperature conductivity to 10^{-4} ohm^{-1}cm^{-1}. These authors observed the linear dependence of the logarithm of electrical conductivity on the reciprocal of absolute temperature, the slope of the log σ vs. $1/T$ plot changing in the vicinity of the Néel temperature. A similar change of the slope was also reported by Fisher and Tannhauser[18] for polycrystalline cobaltous oxide, but these authors assume a hopping model for this oxide. The results obtained by Fisher and Tannhauser are shown in Fig. 11.1. As may be seen from this figure, the activation energy of conductivity amounts to 0·5 eV above the Néel point, and is lower by about 0·1 eV below this temperature.

Zhuze and Shelykh[231] concluded from the measurements of μ_H that cobaltous oxide shows indeed the small-polaron conduction but in the intermediate region between the hopping and narrow-band models.

Austin et al.[179] measured the electrical conductivity, Hall effect and Seebeck effect in single lithium-doped CoO crystals over the temperature range 150–1100 K. Their results are presented in Figs. 11.2 to 11.4.

As seen from Fig. 11.3, the Hall mobility is practically constant in the temperature range studied. In the temperature range 300–500 K the drift mobility is also approximately constant. The results of Austin et al. indicate compensation at low temperatures which is in agreement with the earlier data of Johnston et al.[230] The effective mass of the holes in CoO was estimated by Austin et al.[179] at about $20m_0$. These authors have not given any evidence of small-polaron hopping conduction in the oxide considered here. They interpreted their investigations of conductivity and Seebeck and Hall effects in terms of the Holstein theory (cf. Ref. 133) of narrow-band small-polaron conduction.

Irrespective of some differences in interpretation of the transport phenomena in CoO, all the authors mentioned above agree that this compound is a small-polaron semiconductor. On the other hand, Shelykh et al.[232] have shown that this oxide may be considered to be a band semiconductor. This conclusion has been drawn from measurement results of electrical conductivity and Seebeck effect, carried out on single CoO crystals in the temperature range of 900–1500 K.

A similar conclusion has been drawn by Bosman and van Daal[181] from the Hall mobility measurements in polycrystalline CoO in a very extended range of temperatures from 210 to 1500 K. They found the Hall mobility to have a constant value over a wide range of temperatures from 200 to 1500 K (Fig. 11.5). These authors believe that such data seem to militate against the supposition that cobaltous oxide is a small-polaron semiconductor. They assume that the exponential dependence of the electrical conductivity on temperature is due to the hole concentration rather than to the exponential increase of the mobility with temperature.

Bosman and Crevecoeur[235] recently measured the electrical conductivity and Seebeck effect coefficient of lithium-doped ceramic cobaltous oxide over a temperature range of 150 to 1300 K. Their results are shown in Figs. 11.6–11.9. They deduce that the temperature dependence of the electrical conductivity of CoO is due to the change of concentration of the current carriers. The ionization energy of the Li^+–Co^{3+} acceptors is about 0·43 eV, and decreases to 0·29 eV with increasing lithium concentration. The drift mobility of holes in CoO, calculated from the measurements of σ and α, changes only slightly with temperature as compared with the change in the carrier concentration. As seen from Fig. 11.8, the character of the temperature dependence of the drift mobility in CoO is determined by the choice of the parameters appearing in the Seebeck coefficient formula, and thus by the conductivity mechanism assumed for this oxide.

If it is assumed that the density of states N_v is constant (hopping model), the mobility increases significantly with temperature above 500 K, which may indicate the hopping mechanism and small-polaron conduction in CoO. On the other hand, if it is accepted

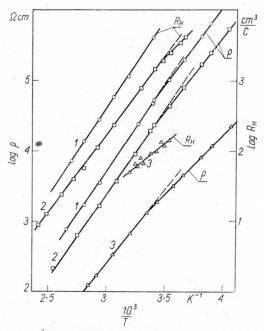

FIG. 11.2. The temperature dependence of the Hall coefficient and resistivity of CoO for three samples containing different concentrations of lithium:[179] 1—0·04 at. %, 2—0·043 at. %, 3—0·46 at. %.

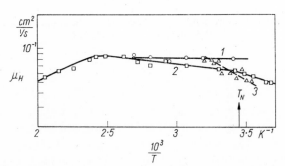

FIG. 11.3. The Hall mobility in CoO as a function of reciprocal temperature for three samples of different lithium content:[179] 1—0·04 at. % Li, 2—0·043 at. % Li, 3—0·46 at. % Li.

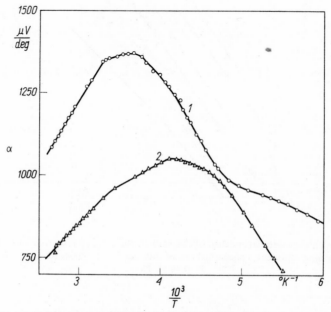

FIG. 11.4. The temperature dependence of Seebeck coefficient in Li-doped CoO:[179]
1—0·04 at. % Li, 2—0·46 at. % Li.

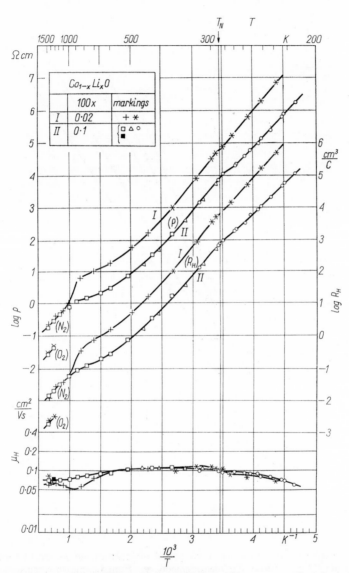

FIG. 11.5. Resistivity ρ, Hall coefficient R_H, and Hall mobility μ_H, as a function of reciprocal temperature for p-type, Li-doped ceramic CoO.[181] The measurements were made in technical N_2 (10^{-4} atm of O_2). Some data obtained at high temperatures in 1 atm of O_2 are also presented. The Néel temperature T_N is indicated.

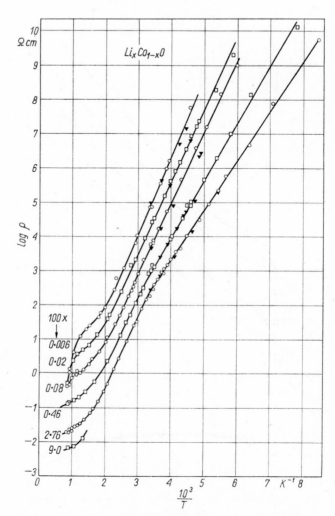

FIG. 11.6. Resistivity ρ as a function of reciprocal temperature for p-type Li-doped ceramic
CoO.[235] O, □—from d.c. measurements, ▼—from a.c. measurements.

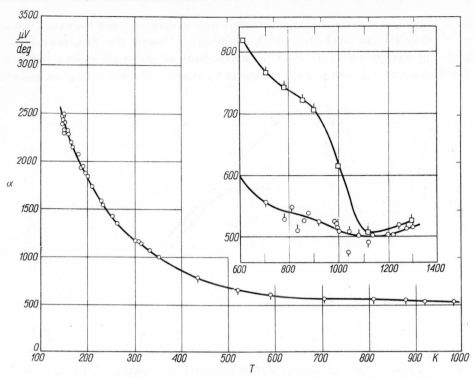

FIG. 11.7. Seebeck coefficient α as a function of temperature for CoO containing 0·08 at. % Li[235] (O, Q, Ò). The inset shows the high temperature measurements on a larger scale. The measurements on CoO containing 0·006 at. % Li (□) are presented.

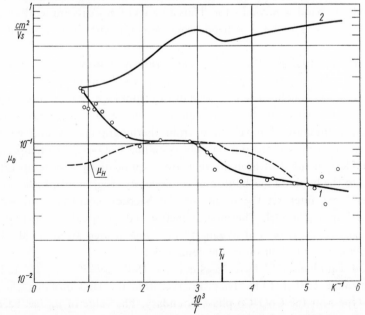

FIG. 11.8. Drift mobility μ_D and Hall mobility μ_H of CoO containing 0·08 at. % Li as a function of reciprocal temperature.[235] Curves 1 and 2 are calculated from conductivity and Seebeck effect measurements using N_v = constant and $N_v \sim T^{3/2}$, respectively.

that N_v is given by formula (9.13) (band model), then μ_D decreases with increasing temperature showing band conduction in this compound. Despite this fact, Bosman and Crevecoeur have called in question the applicability of the small-polaron theory to CoO. This doubt has been recently dissipated by extensive studies of Bosman and van

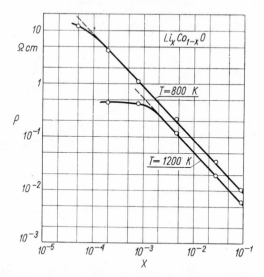

FIG. 11.9. Resistivity ρ of Li-doped CoO at 800 and 1200 K as a function of the Li concentration.[235] At low lithium concentrations the conduction due to cobalt vacancies predominates.

Daal,[236] who have shown that below about 1200 K CoO can be consistently conceived as a large-polaron band semiconductor. Thus authors of more recent works on cobaltous oxide believe that this oxide is a band semiconductor with large polarons as charge carriers.

A number of authors[18, 19, 233, 238] have shown, however, that evidence exists supporting the small-polaron hopping conduction in CoO at temperatures higher than about 1200 K. These conclusions have been drawn from high temperature measurements of electrical conductivity, the Seebeck coefficient and from thermogravimetry.

Fisher and Tannhauser[18] have found from thermogravimetric and electrical conductivity measurements carried out on polycrystalline CoO over the temperature range of 1200–1600 K that the drift mobility increased exponentially with temperature which would point to the hopping mechanism of conductivity (Fig. 11.10). Fisher, Tannhauser and Wagner[18, 233] interpret the results of the Seebeck coefficient measurements in terms of the hopping model. Thermogravimetric and electrical conductivity measurements carried out by Eror and Wagner[19] at temperatures from 1170–1470 K also point to the hopping mechanism of the conductivity.

Gvishi and Tannhauser[568] have measured the Hall mobility in pure and Ti-doped CoO in the range 1271–1413 K. They observed that the Hall mobility changes from p-type to n-type near the CoO/Co phase boundary. The value of μ_H has been found to be at least six times larger for electrons as compared with holes, the latter amounting to 0·06 cm^2/Vs. Thus the Hall mobility of the holes is too low for wide band conduction and is also much lower than the drift mobility (0·3 cm^2/Vs) obtained by Fisher and Tannhauser.[18] Hence, the problem of small or large polaron conduction in CoO is still a matter for discussion. As can be seen from the above considerations many experimental data concerning transport phenomena in this oxide have been obtained, but their interpretations, especially at high temperatures, differ largely.

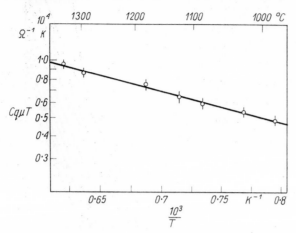

Fig. 11.10. The product of hole mobility and temperature in CoO as a function of reciprocal temperature.[18] C is a constant depending on geometry of the sample, q is an elementary charge.

The structure of point defects in CoO is not well understood as yet. The extensive studies on this problem were performed by Fisher and Tannhauser[18] on the basis of electrical conductivity, Seebeck coefficient and thermoelectric measurements as a function of oxygen pressure and temperature. The results obtained by them are shown in Figs. 11.11–11.13. Figure 11.11 shows the dependence of the electrical CoO conductance G on the oxygen pressure for different temperatures. As is seen from this figure, at higher oxygen pressures the slope of the plot $\partial \log G/\partial \log P_{O_2} = 3·8$–$4·3$ which indicates that the defects are singly ionized, whereas at lower pressures this slope is $5·7$–$6·1$, implying double ionization of the defects. According to Fisher and Tannhauser these defects are due to cobalt vacancies. The two regions, A and B, of oxygen pressure in which a different slope of the log G vs. log P_{O_2} plot is observed are separated in Fig. 11.11 by a broken line. In Fig. 11.12 the electrical conductance of CoO is plotted as a function of the deviation from stoichiometry. This deviation was determined by the thermogravimetric method. The broken line separated the two regions of oxygen pressure. In region A the relation $G \sim P_{O_2}^{1/4}$ is valid. Figure 11.13 demonstrates the results of the Seebeck effect measurements as a function of the oxygen pressure, as obtained by Fisher and Tannhauser. It seems, however, that these results do not support the interpretation of thermogravimetric and electrical conductance measurements forwarded by the quoted authors.[18]

Eror and Wagner[19] carried out electrical conductivity and thermogravimetric measurements of CoO within the pressure range from 10^{-4} to 1 atm and the temperature range 1170–1470 K (Figs. 11.14–11.17). They observed that in this range electrical conductivity is proportional to the fourth root of the oxygen pressure, which implies that the

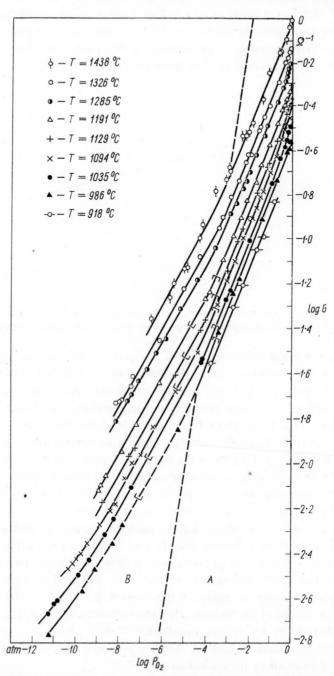

FIG. 11.11. Electrical conductance of CoO as a function of partial pressure of oxygen for different temperatures;[18] brackets show the range of oxygen pressure in which the measurements may be burdened with larger errors.

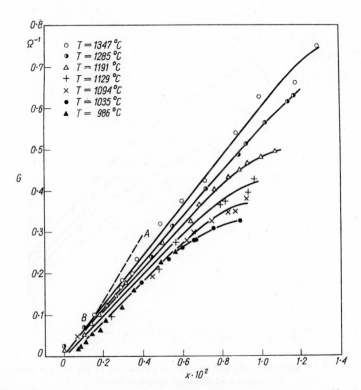

FIG. 11.12. Electrical conductance of CoO as a function of the excess oxygen:[18] x is defined by the formula: CoO_{1+x}, the dashed line separates two regions, A and B (cf. Fig. 11.11).

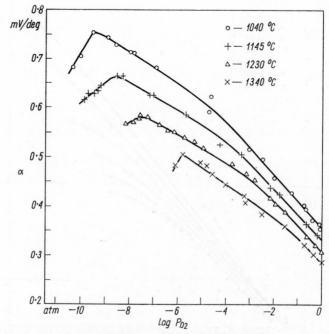

FIG. 11.13. Seebeck coefficient in CoO as a function of the oxygen partial
pressure at different temperatures.[18]

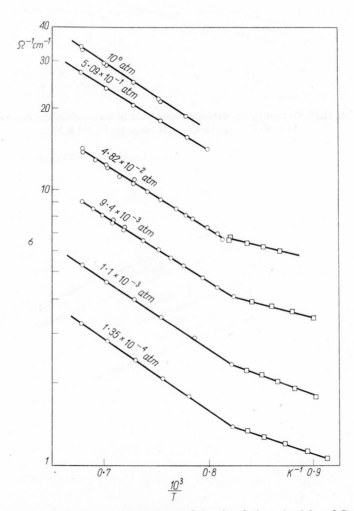

FIG. 11.14. Temperature dependence of the electrical conductivity of CoO for various oxygen partial pressures.[19]

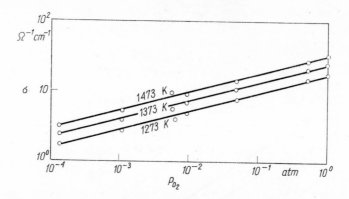

FIG. 11.15. Oxygen partial pressure dependence of the electrical conductivity of CoO over the temperature range 1273–1473 K.[19]

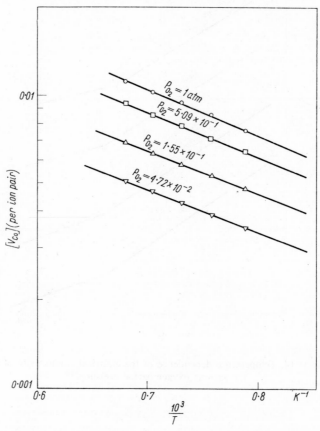

FIG. 11.16. Temperature dependence of the cobalt vacancy concentration in CoO.[19]

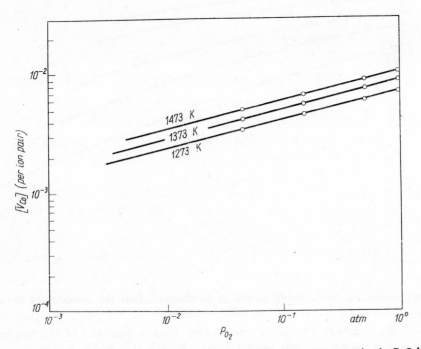

FIG. 11.17. Oxygen partial pressure dependence of the cobalt vacancy concentration in CoO.[19]

defects (cobalt vacancies according to these authors) are singly ionized. Similar data on electrical conductivity of CoO (prepared by oxidation of cobalt) were reported by Duquesnoy and Marion.[237]

Recently Hed[238] put forward a controversial hypothesis assuming the existence in CoO of the singly ionized complex defects, e.g. of the $(V_{Co}Co_iV_{Co})$ type. He examined electrical conductance in CoO over the temperature range 1120–1470 K and the pressure range from $10^{-0.88}$ to $10^{-2.88}$. From the results obtained (shown in Fig. 11.18) Hed

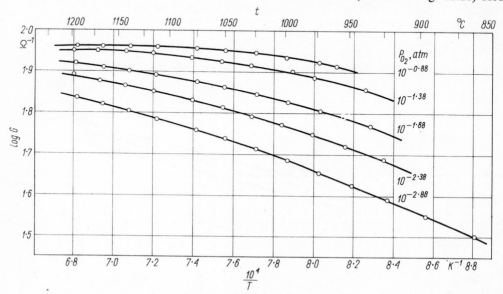

FIG. 11.18. The electrical conductance of CoO at various constant pressures as a function of temperature.[238]

deduced, assuming the hopping model of conduction, that the enthalpy of the defect formation in CoO is negative as the slope of the log σ vs. $1/T$ plot at constant oxygen pressure decreases with increasing temperature. Such a character of the temperature dependence of the conductivity implies the occurrence of complex defects.

Data on self-diffusion and chemical diffusion in CoO are summarized in Table 10.

TABLE 10. SELF-DIFFUSION AND CHEMICAL

Year	Authors	Diffusing element	Material
1954	Carter and Richardson[239]	Co	polycrystalline
1962	Thompson[240]	O	polycrystalline single crystal
1967	Holt[241]	O	polycrystalline single crystal
1969	Chen and Jackson[242]	O	single crystal
1969	Chen, Peterson and Reeves[243]	Co	single crystal
1966	Price and Wagner[212]	chemical	single crystal

11.2. Wüstite, FeO

At temperatures above 203 K FeO has a structure of the NaCl type, with the lattice constant of 4·31 Å.[244] Below 180 K there is a rhombohedral distortion which is negative with regard to those of NiO since the (111) axis is elongated by about 0·8%. FeO is an antiferromagnetic with the Néel temperature of 198 K,[245] density 5·7 g/cm³, and m.p. 1690 K.

Wüstite shows an exceptionally wide range of the nonstoichiometric phase which is terminated at the oxygen-rich composition. The stability limits of wüstite have been studied in many works, but despite this the strict ranges of existence of the various phases have not been as yet satisfactorily determined.[16, 246–253] The phase diagram of FeO is shown in Fig. 11.19.

Tannhauser[254] has measured the conductivity and Seebeck effect in FeO as a function of the O/Fe ratio at temperatures higher than 1270 K. He found that the conductivity, showing only a very small temperature dependence, changes slightly on crossing the FeO/Fe_3O_4 phase boundary, but decreases rapidly in both phases as the composition approaches stoichiometry for FeO and Fe_2O_3, respectively. The Seebeck coefficient is p-type in FeO of low oxygen content and change to n-type at high oxygen content. The activation energy of high-temperature conductivity of wüstite was found to be about 0·067 eV. Electrical conductivity of FeO is relatively high and amounts at room temperature to about 20 ohm⁻¹cm⁻¹.

Tannhauser interpreted his results in terms of an electron transfer model which predicts a jump rate proportional to the pairing probability of a trivalent cation and a divalent cation in the neighbouring octahedral sites, and thus to the product of the concentration of the two types of cations.

Ariya and Brach[255] studied the conductivity of wüstite as dependent on the deviation from stoichiometry over the temperature range of 900–1100 K. They found that the activation energy of conductivity of 0·07 eV is in good agreement with the Tannhauser's results, irrespective of the composition of the samples.

Bransky and Tannhauser[256] examined the electrical conductivity, Seebeck coefficient and deviation from stoichiometry in single crystals and polycrystalline FeO over the temperature range of 1170–1600 K. They report the proportionality of electrical

FFUSION COEFFICIENTS IN CoO

Method	Temperature range K	D_0 cm²/s	ΔH eV
o⁶⁰ radiotracer	1070–1620	$2·15 \times 10^{-3}$	$1·55 \pm 0·02$
¹⁸ mass spec.	1270	—	—
¹⁸ reaction (p, n) F¹⁸	1170–1670	—	—
¹⁸ mass spec.	1450–1830	50	$4·12 \pm 0·22$
ɔ⁶⁰ radiotracer	1240–1810	$(5·0 \pm 0·4) \times 10^{-3}$	1·67
ectrical conductivity	1070–1370	$4·33 \times 10^{-3}$	1·04
			1·3 given by Kofstad[490]

conductivity to the sixth root of the oxygen pressure in the composition range $1.05 <$ O/Fe < 1.10. Analogous results were obtained by Geiger *et al.*[257] On the basis of their results the quoted authors[256] speculate that doubly ionized iron vacancies are the dominating defects.

A detailed analysis of the electrical properties of FeO at high temperatures was recently made by Seltzer and Hed[262] on the assumption of the hopping mechanism of

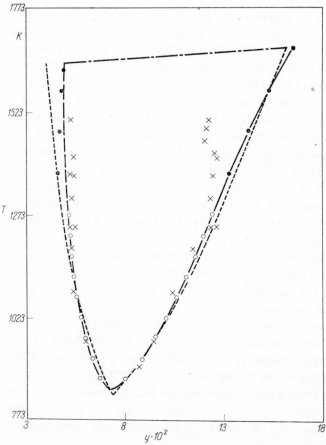

FIG. 11.19. Phase diagram of Fe$_{1-y}$O:[253] ●—according to Darken and Gurry,[246] ×—according to Marion,[247] ○—according to Engell.[249]

TABLE 11. SELF-DIFFUSION AND CHEMIC

Year	Authors	Diffusing element	Material
1953	Himmel, Mehl and Birchenall[263]	Fe	polycrystalline
1954	Carter and Richardson[239]	Fe	polycrystalline
1965	Desmarescaux, Bocquet and Lacombe[264]	Fe	polycrystalline
1965	Levin and Wagner[265]	Fe	polycrystalline
1970	Childs and Wagner[266]	chemical	polycrystalline

the conductance in this oxide. According to these authors the mobility of the charge carriers is proportional to the jump probability which is assumed to be influenced by two factors, namely a blocking factor which renders a fraction of the sites neighbouring a charge carrier unavailable for occupancy and a self-screening parameter which partially opposes the blocking. They used the following expression for the mobility in FeO:

$$\mu = \mu_0 z^{1/2}(1-4z)\exp\left[-\frac{E_u}{kT}\right] \qquad (11.1)$$

where μ_0 is a constant, z a concentration of ionized defects, and E_u the activation energy of motion for the charge carriers, which has been assumed to be 0·01 eV.

The defect structure in FeO is still a problem for discussion. As it was already stated, doubly ionized iron vacancies were suggested in this oxide.

Roth[258] found in the course of neutronographic studies carried out on FeO cooled to room temperature that the defect structure of this oxide is more complicated and involves the defect complexes composed of two octahedral iron vacancies and an interstitial cation in tetrahedral position. This hypothesis was later confirmed by X-ray studies carried out by Smuts[259] also on the cooled samples.

Such a system may be thus regarded as a solution of Fe_3O_4 in FeO.

Salmon[260] employed this model of defect structure in his calculations of the activity of Fe_3O_4 in wüstite at high temperatures obtaining a good agreement with the experimental data of Darken and Gurry.[246]

On the basis of Roth's hypothesis Kofstad and Hed[261] proposed a new model of the defect structure in FeO assuming the presence of singly ionized complexes of the $(V_{Fe}Fe_i V_{Fe})$ type. They suggested the following reactions of formation of this complex:

$$Fe_{Fe}^x + V_i + 1/2O_2^{(g)} \rightleftarrows (V_{Fe}Fe_i V_{Fe})^x + O_O^x \qquad (11.2)$$
$$Fe_{Fe}^x + (V_{Fe}Fe_i V_{Fe})^x \rightleftarrows (V_{Fe}Fe_i V_{Fe})' + Fe_{Fe}^{\cdot} h^{\cdot} \qquad (11.3)$$

Such a complex was also accepted by Seltzer and Hed.[262]

Recently Cheetham et al.[569] have carried out accurate high-temperature neutron diffraction experiments in the range of 1070 to 1470 K on polycrystalline FeO of composition between $Fe_{0.947}O$ and $Fe_{0.906}O$. These authors found that the ratio of octahedral iron vacancies to tetrahedral iron interstitials is close to the value of 3·25. These results are in reasonable agreement with the Koch and Cohen's model[570] rather than with the Roth's model.

The data on self-diffusion and chemical diffusion in FeO are summarized in Table 11.

USION COEFFICIENTS IN FeO

Method	Temperature range K	D_0 cm²/s	ΔH eV
[55] radiotracer	970–1270	0·118	1·29
[55] tracer	970–1270	0·014	1·34
[59] tracer	1130–1530	—	1·08–1·43
weight change	1170–1370	—	1·08–1·62
traphase kinetics	1070–1570	—	—

11.3. Manganese Oxide, MnO

At temperatures above 120 K MnO possesses a crystal structure of NaCl-type with a lattice constant of 4·44 Å.[267] Below 120 K this oxide undergoes a 0·8% rhombohedral distortion similar to that of NiO, but much larger.[154] Manganese oxide is an anti-ferromagnetic, with the Néel temperature of 122 K,[245] density of 5·18 g/cm³, and m.p. of 2058 K; the forbidden energy gap has the value of 2·7 eV.[268] Pure MnO is an insulator at low temperatures, its room temperature conductivity is 10^9–10^{15} ohm cm.[269]

Manganese oxide, MnO, is unique among simple transition metal oxides because it shows a minimum in the conductivity plotted as a function of oxygen pressure. This fact has led to speculation about a possible p–n transition in manganese monoxide. Several models have been proposed to account for this behaviour. Thus Nagels, Denayer et al.[270-272] concluded that the increase of conductivity with temperature in the oxide considered here is almost fully determined by the increase of the charge carrier concentration. On the other hand, Heikes and Johnston[141], who first measured the electrical conductivity in Li-doped MnO, assumed the thermally activated mechanism of the conduction in this oxide. Finally it was ascertained that MnO may be either a p- or n-type semiconductor depending on its preparation.[274, 275]

In contradistinction from NiO and CoO the holes in p-type MnO seem to have small-polaron character.[236, 273, 277]

Hed and Tannhauser[277] have measured the deviation from stoichiometry, electrical conduction and Seebeck effect in MnO as a function of temperature in the range of 1370–1830 K and oxygen partial pressures of 10^{-8} to 10^{-1} atm. Over the whole range of these measurements the mobility of the holes has been found to rise exponentially with temperature, the activation energy of motion being $(0·37 \pm 0·07)$ eV. The values of α obtained by these authors support the hopping model of conduction in this oxide.

Crevecoeur and de Wit[273] investigated the electrical conductivity, Seebeck effect and dielectric losses in Li-doped MnO as a function of temperature. It has been found that the depth of the Li acceptors is 0·4 eV, and the activation energy of the mobility of holes is about 0·3 eV. The latter value is much lower than the one obtained by Hed and Tannhauser[277] (0·57 eV when corrected for $1/T^{3/2}$, predicted by Holstein's theory). Crevecoeur and de Wit[273] have obtained the value 3×10^{-5} cm²/Vs for the mobility at room temperature. Between 200 and 1000 K the mobility changes by a factor of 10^5. They suggest that the difference between NiO and CoO on the one hand and MnO on the other is caused by Jahn–Teller deformations brought about by holes in manganese oxide.

An energy level diagram for MnO has been proposed by McKinzie.[571] (see also the paper by O'Keeffe and Valigi[572]). This model is based on the work of van Houten.[166] The conduction levels in this model are assumed to be associated with Mn^+ and the valency levels with Mn^{2+} with an energy gap of 1·8–2·2 eV.

Gvishi, Tallan and Tannhauser[276] estimated the Hall electron mobility in MnO at high temperatures to be about 10 cm²/Vs. The same value of the Hall mobility at high temperatures was obtained also in n-type manganese oxide preparated by doping with titanium.[236] It was also observed that the electron Hall mobility increased with the decreasing temperature attaining the value of 20–40 cm^2/Vs at room temperature.[236] Thus the n-type MnO may be regarded as a large band semiconductor.

The defect structure of MnO has been investigated by Hed and Tannhauser,[277, 573] and O'Keeffe and Valigi.[572] All these authors agree that MnO always contains an excess of oxygen, the predominate defects being the doubly ionized manganese vacancies at lower oxygen pressure, which are produced according to the reaction:

$$2\,MnO + 1/2\,O_2 \rightleftarrows 2\,Mn_{Mn}^{\cdot} + V_{Mn}'' + 3\,O_O^{\times} \tag{11.4}$$

It may be also expected that other defects such as manganese interstitials or oxygen vacancies are present in smaller quantities.

O'Keeffe and Valigi[572] assumed also that chromium is incorporated into the manganese sublattice according to following reaction:

$$Cr_2O_3 \rightarrow 2\,Cr_{Mn}^{\cdot} + V_{Mn}'' + 3\,O_O^{\times} \tag{11.5}$$

The data concerning diffusion in MnO are given by Childs and Wagner.[266]

CHAPTER 12

RUTILE, TiO$_2$

12.1. Electronic Transport Phenomena in TiO$_2$ at Low and Intermediate Temperatures

Titanium dioxide occurs in three polymorphic forms: anatase, brukite and rutile. The most stable of them is rutile which crystallizes in tetragonal symmetry with lattice parameters: $a = 4\cdot59$ Å, $c = 2\cdot96$ Å. Its density is $4\cdot26$ g/cm^3, and the m.p. 2120 K.

Electrical properties of titanium dioxide have been in recent years extensively studied. The review of these studies is given by Grant,[278] Hurlen,[279] Frederikse,[280] van Hippel and co-workers,[281] and by Bogomolov, Kudinov and Firsov.[282] The experiments were carried out on single crystals of good quality and the results obtained by different authors are virtually in accord. Theoretical interpretation of the results presents, however, great difficulties. Detailed analysis of this problem is beyond the scope of this book. However, the literature quoted in this chapter will enable the reader to learn the whole of the results of studies on transport of current carriers in TiO$_2$.

Becker and Hosler[283, 284] studied the temperature dependence of Hall effect and of electrical conductivity in rutile over the temperature range 20–600 K. After annealing at various temperatures and at various oxygen pressures their samples displayed the room temperature conductivity of about 10^{-6} to 10^2 ohm^{-1}cm^{-1}. The greatest electrical conductivity was shown by the samples annealed at 1273 K under the hydrogen pressure of 1 atm. The Hall coefficient values were similarly contained in the wide range depending on the conditions of the thermal treatment. The Hall mobility was practically independent of the concentration of the current carriers, amounting to $0\cdot2$ cm^2/Vs at room temperature.

The temperature dependence of the Hall coefficient R_a for the case when magnetic induction is parallel to axis a is shown in Fig. 12.1 for three samples of TiO$_2$ subjected to different thermal treatment. Sample 1 was annealed at 1070 K under the air pressure of 150 Tr. Sample 2 was annealed at the same temperature under the pressure of 30 Tr. Sample 3 was annealed at 1270 K at the pressure of 2×10^{-7} Tr. Since the thermal treatment was carried out under different partial pressures of oxygen, the concentration of native defects (interstitial titanium ions) in the samples was different.

The dependence of resistivity ρ_c in the direction of axis c on the reciprocal temperature for the same samples of TiO$_2$ is shown in Fig. 12.2. Figure 12.3 illustrates the temperature dependence of the ratio R_c/R_a where R_c is the Hall coefficient for the case when the magnetic induction vector is parallel to axis c. At temperatures lower than 40 K the ratio R_c/R_a is independent of temperature. With the increase in temperature this ratio is increased reaching a maximal value of 2·5 at 110 K. With the further increase in temperature R_c/R_a decreases to 0·2 at 625 K. The ratio ρ_a/ρ_c where ρ_a and ρ_c are resistivities in direction of axes a and c, respectively, has at low temperatures approx-

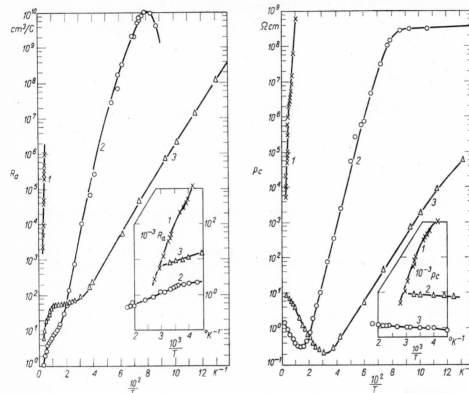

FIG. 12.1. Hall coefficient in rutile as a function of temperature for three samples subjected to different thermal treatment:[284] magnetic induction was parallel to axis a; the temperature dependence of the Hall coefficient in the vicinity of room temperature is given in the inset on the larger scale.

FIG. 12.2. Resistivity of rutile in direction of axis c as a function of temperature:[284] The inset shows this dependence magnified in the vicinity of room temperature; 1, 2, 3, numbers of samples (the same as in Fig. 12.1).

imately a constant value of 2, whereas at higher temperatures it increases similarly like the ratio R_c/R_a reaching a maximum at 100 K. At still higher temperatures it decreases slowly with the increasing temperature attaining at 625 K the value of about 2. Anisotropy of electrical properties of TiO_2 was also observed by Bogomolov, Shavkunov and Zhuze,[285, 286] and Cronemeyer.[287]

Figure 12.4 shows the temperature dependence of anisotropy of the conductivity $k_\sigma = \sigma_c/\sigma_a$ (curve 1), the Hall coefficient $k_H = R_c/R_a$ (curve 2) and of the ratio of these two parameters $y = k_H/k_\sigma$ (curve 3) presented by Bogomolov and Zhuze[288] on the basis of data reported by different authors. The continuous line corresponds to the data obtained by Bogomolov, Shavkunov and Zhuze,[285, 286] the dashed line to those by Becker and Hosler,[284] and the dotted line to the values reported by Cronemeyer.[287]

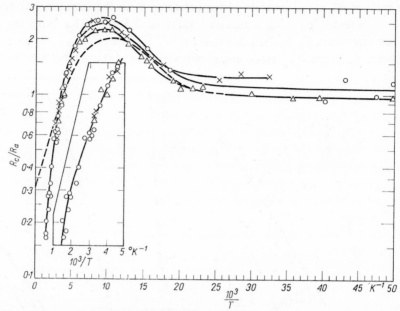

FIG. 12.3. Anisotropy of Hall coefficient R_c/R_a in rutile as a function of temperature for three samples subjected to different thermal treatment:[284] R_c—Hall coefficient measured at magnetic induction $B\|c$, R_a—at induction $B\|a$.

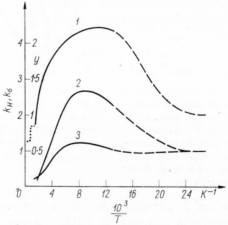

FIG. 12.4. Anisotropy of electrical conductivity and Hall coefficient in rutile as a function of temperature:[288] 1—anisotropy of electrical conductivity k_σ, 2—anisotropy of Hall coefficient k_H, 3—ratio $y = k_H/k_\sigma$.

As seen from the above considerations the experimental data on the temperature dependence of electrical conductivity and Hall coefficient in rutile obtained by different authors are in good agreement. The theoretical interpretation of the mechanism of the conductivity in this oxide given by various workers is, however, different. Becker and Hosler[284] try to explain the complex character of the temperature dependence of the electrical conductivity and the Hall coefficient in terms of the multi-band model. Bogomolov and co-workers[282, 288] consider, however, this model inconsistent with the experimental data. They examined the effect of hydrostatic pressure on electrical conductivity and Hall constant of rutile[289] and on its optical absorption.[290] The results obtained cannot be readily accounted for in terms of the band theory.

The current interpretation of the conductivity mechanism in TiO_2 has been recently criticized by Bogomolov and co-workers.[282, 288] They have shown that concentration of the current carriers in rutile cannot be calculated in the usual way from the Hall coefficient, since the Hall mobility in this oxide is essentially different from the drift mobility. They claim that all the electrical properties of rutile observed can be explained in terms of the small polaron theory, if one assumes that the concentration of the current carriers is constant at temperatures higher than 100 K. If this assumption were correct, then the exponential increase of the electrical conductivity in rutile with the increasing temperature observed experimentally would indicate the exponential increase of the current carrier mobility on temperature, which is just the dependence resulting from the small polaron theory.

The results of studies on optical absorption of rutile, which show anisotropy and resonance character of the absorption with a maximum of the photon energy of about 0·82 eV, are also in agreement with the small polaron theory. It has been shown,[290] namely, that such the character of the absorption can be explained by interaction of photons with small polarons. Bogomolov and co-workers[282] proposed even to regard titanium dioxide as a model semiconductor for this mechanism of electrical conductivity.

It should be noted, however, that the small polaron conductivity model in TiO_2 has not been as yet adequately verified and may be questioned.[137]

Bransky and Tannhauser[291] measured the Hall mobility in TiO_2 in the wide temperature range from 300 to 1250 K in the atmosphere of pure CO_2 and in the mixture CO_2–CO, the ratio CO_2/CO being equal to 49. They found that the Hall mobility in rutile does not depend on the type of the surrounding atmosphere and rapidly decreases with the increasing temperature as shown in Fig. 12.5.

The temperature dependence of the Hall mobility in TiO_2 obtained by Bransky and Tannhauser is difficult to explain in terms of the small polaron theory suggested by some authors for TiO_2. As seen from the above review, the mechanism of transport of current carriers in TiO_2 is far from being well understood.

Jakubowski[296] investigated the temperature dependence of the electrical conductivity in sintered TiO_2 over the temperature range 290–1270 K. He observed maxima on the log σ vs. $1/T$ plot, the position and magnitude of which depended on the extent of reduction of rutile in the CO–CO_2 atmosphere.

Thurber and Mante[297] studied the temperature dependence of the Seebeck coefficient over the temperature range 5–300 K. Their results obtained on four samples prepared in different conditions are shown in Fig. 12.6. Sample 1 contained $1·6 \times 10^{19}$ cm^{-3} atoms of niobium and its resistivity at room temperature was 0·31 ohm cm. Samples 2 and 3 had 10^{19} excess titanium atoms and their resistivities were 3·5 and 1·05 ohm cm, respectively. Sample 4 contained 10^{20} excess titanium atoms and its resistivity was

0·35 ohm cm. The high value of the Seebeck coefficient observed for rutile is most probably due to the appreciable contribution of the phonon drag.

Itakura et al.[298] studied electrical properties of TiO_2 both of ceramic material and single crystals doped with Nb_2O_5 and Ta_2O_5. The content of impurities was from 0·02

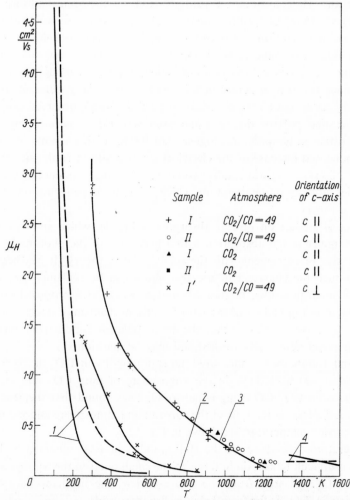

Sample	Atmosphere	Orientation of c-axis
+	I	$CO_2/CO = 49$	c ‖
o	II	$CO_2/CO = 49$	c ‖
▲	I	CO_2	c ‖
■	II	CO_2	c ‖
×	I'	$CO_2/CO = 49$	c ⊥

Fig. 12.5. Hall mobility of rutile as a function of temperature:[291] 1—measured by Bogomolov and Zhuze:[286] ——— samples with $c_\perp$, — — — samples with $c_\|$. 2—measured by Bransky and Tannhauser,[291] samples with $c_\perp$. 3—measured by Bransky and Tannhauser,[291] samples with $c_\|$, 4—drift mobility of single crystal with $c_\|$, calculated by Blumenthal et al.,[292] from combined electrical conductivity and thermogravimetric measurements.[293-295]

to 10 mole %, the X-ray studies showed, however, that for concentration of impurities higher than 1 mole % the formed material was heterophasic, consisting of two phases, e.g. $TiO_2 \cdot Nb_2O_5$.

The electrical properties of TiO_2 were strongly dependent on the impurity concentrations up to the content of 4 mole %. The material under study displayed the properties of non-degenerate n-type semiconductor. From the Hall and Seebeck effects data the effective mass of electrons in TiO_2 was estimated to be 20 m_0, where m_0 is the mass of an electron. This value is comparable with the value of the effective mass of current carriers in TiO_2 obtained earlier by Breckenridge and Hosler[299] and Frederikse.[280]

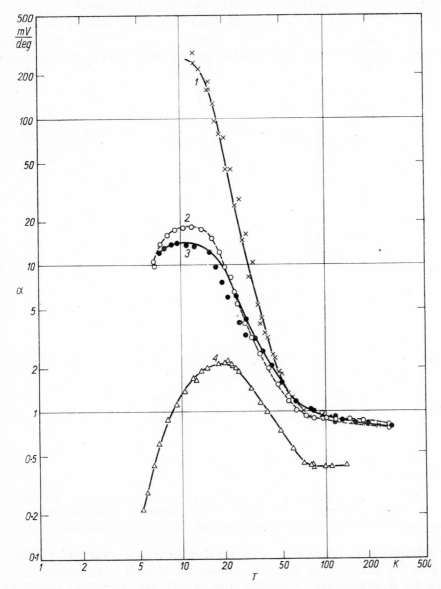

FIG. 12.6. The temperature dependence of Seebeck coefficient in rutile:[297] 1—for the niobium-doped sample, 2, 3, 4—for three samples containing different amounts of excess titanium atoms.

The activation energy of donors was 0·02 eV. For the reduced samples without the introduced impurities this energy was 0·01 eV. The Hall mobility at room temperature decreased with the increasing impurity concentration amounting to 0·4 cm^2/Vs for the lowest content of the impurities and 10^{-2} cm^2/Vs for their highest content.

Bogomolov and co-workers[300] have shown that in TiO_2 doped with Nb_2O_5 the niobium addition fills the lattice sites in the cationic sublattice in the form of Nb^{+5} ions, whereas the chromium addition is incorporated in the form of Cr^{3+} ions. In this latter case the electrical conductivity of titanium dioxide is very low.

We shall describe now an interesting property of rutile consisting in the changes of its electrical conductivity with time. This phenomenon was recently studied by White-hurst and co-workers[301] on single crystals and on polycrystalline sintered material.

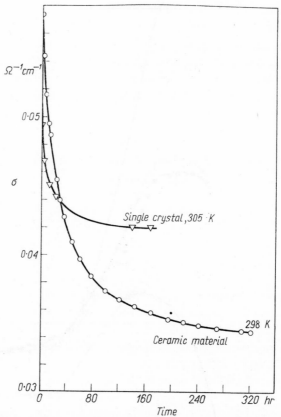

FIG. 12.7. The change of conductivity with time in single crystals and ceramic material of rutile.[301] The measurement temperature is given at the side of the curves; the samples were cooled from 673 K to this temperature.

The single crystals were heated for 1 hr at 853 K at the pressure of the order of 10^{-5} Tr. Owing to this treatment the electrical conductivity of rutile in the direction of axis c reached at room temperature the value of about 0·03 ohm^{-1}cm^{-1}. The polycrystalline samples displayed the conductivity from 0·005 to 1 ohm^{-1}cm^{-1}. The materials prepared in this way were then heated in air at temperatures from 373 to 673 K. The heating time was several minutes. The rutile samples were then cooled for 1 minute to the temperature of the measurement which varied within the range 273–373 K. The changes of the electrical conductivity with time are shown in Fig. 12.7 for the TiO_2 samples cooled from the temperature of 673 K. The measurement temperature for single crystals and polycrystalline specimens was 305 and 298 K, respectively. The time change of the conductivity was influenced neither by the composition of the surrounding atmosphere nor by the oxygen pressure.

Whitehurst has found that the time dependence of the conductivity can be expressed by the following formula:

$$\sigma = \sigma_\infty + B\left(\frac{\sigma_0 - \sigma}{t}\right) \tag{12.1}$$

where σ is the electrical conductivity at time t, σ_0 is the conductivity in the initial period just after the cooling, σ_∞ is the electrical conductivity value, constant after appropriately long time, B is a parameter constant for given isothermal conditions. The authors reason that the phenomenon observed is inherent for the bulk of rutile. It was believed earlier that it involved rather the capturing of electrons by traps at the metal-oxide phase boundary.[302, 303] The nature of this phenomenon has not been as yet adequately explained.

12.2. Defect Structure and Transport Phenomena in TiO$_2$ at High Temperatures

The results of the Hall and Seebeck effects measurements[278, 280] indicate that non-stoichiometric rutile contains an excess of metal which leads to the n-type of the electrical conductivity. As known the electronic conductivity in non-stoichiometric compounds may be due to the presence in the crystal lattice of either oxygen vacancies or interstitial metal atoms. Cronemeyer,[287, 304] Kofstad[293] and others assume the existence of anionic vacancies in the crystal lattice of titanium dioxide. The results of the recent works, however, seem to indicate that non-stoichiometry in rutile is due rather to the presence of interstitial atoms of titanium.[279, 305-310] The detailed studies on defect structure in TiO$_2$ have been recently performed by Blumenthal and co-workers.[294, 308] They measured the electrical conductivity of single crystals of TiO$_2$ as a function of partial oxygen pressure in its wide range from 1 to 10^{-15} atm and as a function of temperature from 1273 to 1773 K. Since rutile shows anisotropy, the electrical conductivity was measured for two directions, namely along axes c and a. Figures 12.8 and 12.9 illustrate the temperature dependence of the electrical conductivity of rutile at different partial pressures of oxygen. In Figs. 12.10 and 12.11 the dependence of the electrical conductivity of rutile on the oxygen pressure is shown.

Blumenthal and co-workers[294, 308] have proved that the results of these studies may be interpreted in terms of the defect structure model which assumes the existence of triply and quadruply ionized interstitial titanium atoms. According to this model the processes of formation of atomic and electronic defects in titanium dioxide can be represented by the following reactions:

$$\text{Ti}_{\text{Ti}}^x + 2\text{O}_\text{O}^x \rightleftarrows \text{Ti}_i^{3+} + 3e' + \text{O}_2^{(g)}; \qquad \Delta H_a^\circ = (9\cdot6 \pm 0\cdot2)\ \text{eV} \tag{12.2}$$

$$\text{Ti}_{\text{Ti}}^x + 2\text{O}_\text{O}^x \rightleftarrows \text{Ti}_i^{4+} + 4e' + \text{O}_2^{(g)}; \qquad \Delta H_b^\circ = (10\cdot8 \pm 0\cdot2)\ \text{eV} \tag{12.3}$$

$$\text{Ti}_i^{3+} \rightleftarrows \text{Ti}_i^{4+} + e'; \qquad \Delta H_c^\circ = (1\cdot2 \pm 0\cdot4)\ \text{eV} \tag{12.4}$$

$$\text{I}^x \rightleftarrows \text{I}^+ + e'; \qquad \Delta H_d^\circ = (3\cdot7 \pm 0\cdot2)\ \text{eV} \tag{12.5}$$

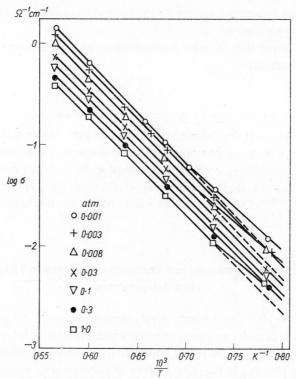

FIG. 12.8. Log electrical conductivity of single crystals of TiO_2 in direction of axis c as a function of reciprocal temperature for different oxygen pressures.[294]

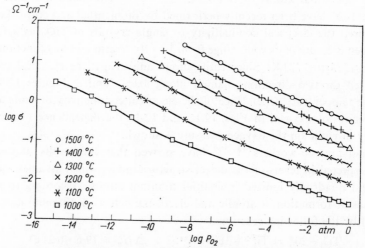

FIG. 12.10. Log electrical conductivity in single crystals of TiO_2 in direction of axis a as a function of log oxygen pressure for different temperatures.[294]

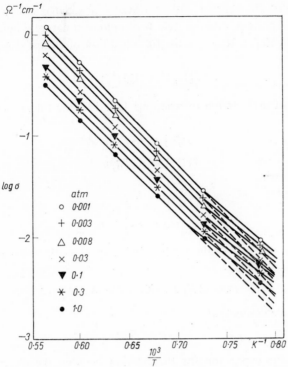

FIG. 12.9. Log electrical conductivity of single crystals of TiO$_2$ in direction of axis a as a function
of reciprocal temperature for different oxygen pressures.[294]

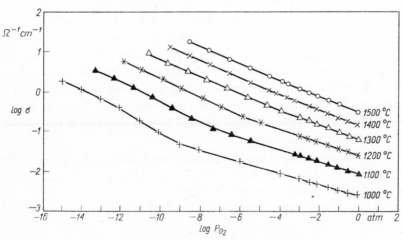

FIG. 12.11. Log electrical conductivity in single crystals of TiO$_2$ in direction of axis c as a function
of log oxygen pressure for different temperatures.[294]

To obtain the full agreement of the above model of defect structure in rutile with the experimental results, Blumenthal and co-workers postulated a hypothetical reaction (12.5) describing ionization of lattice defects of unknown nature (impurities). According to the model of the defect structure the full condition of electroneutrality assumes the form:

$$n = 3[\text{Ti}_i^{3+}] + 4[\text{Ti}_i^{4+}] + [\text{I}^+] \tag{12.6}$$

Applying the law of mass action to reactions 12.2–12.5 the following relationships are obtained:

$$[\text{Ti}_i^{3+}] = K_1 P_{\text{O}_2}^{-1} n^{-3} \tag{12.7}$$

$$[\text{Ti}_i^{4+}] = K_2 P_{\text{O}_2}^{-1} n^{-4} \tag{12.8}$$

$$\frac{[\text{Ti}_i^{4+}]}{[\text{Ti}_i^{3+}]} = K_3 \tag{12.9}$$

$$[\text{I}^+] = K_4 [\text{I}^\times] n^{-1} \tag{12.10}$$

where K_1, K_2, K_3 and K_4 are the equilibrium constants. By substituting eqs. (12.7)–(12.10) into eq. (12.6) we get:

$$n^5 = (3K_1 n + 4K_2) P_{\text{O}_2}^{-1} + K_4 [\text{I}^\times] n^3 \tag{12.11}$$

Making then use of the relation:

$$\sigma = n e \mu \tag{12.12}$$

we obtain finally the expression for the relation between the electrical conductivity of rutile and the equilibrium pressure of oxygen:

$$\sigma^5 = (A\sigma + B) P_{\text{O}_2}^{-1} + C\sigma^2 \tag{12.13}$$

where $A = 3K_1 e^4 \mu^4$, $B = 4K_2 e^5 \mu^5$, $C = [\text{I}^\times] K_4 e^2 \mu^2$. The authors computed parameters A, B and C for temperatures from 1273–1773 K. From the temperature dependence of these parameters they determined the activation energies for the reactions (12.2)–(12.5), assuming after Frederikse[280] that the mobility μ is the exponential function of temperature: $\mu \sim \exp{(0 \cdot 1 \text{ eV}/kT)}$. The values of the activation energies derived in this way are given at the sides of the corresponding reactions (12.2)–(12.5).

It follows from the above considerations that the model proposed by Blumenthal and co-workers for the defect structure of the crystal lattice of rutile assuming the existence of the interstitial metal ions remains in agreement with the results of the electrical conductivity measurements.

Kofstad[311] considers another model assuming the existence of triply and quadruply ionized interstitial titanium atoms and doubly ionized oxygen vacancies. He assumes the following reactions of defect formation in TiO_2:

$$\text{Ti}_{\text{Ti}}^\times + 2\text{O}_\text{O}^\times \rightleftarrows \text{Ti}_i^{3+} + 3\text{e}' + \text{O}_2^{(\text{g})} \tag{12.14}$$

$$\text{Ti}_i^{3+} \rightleftarrows \text{Ti}_i^{4+} + \text{e}' \tag{12.15}$$

$$\text{O}_\text{O}^\times \rightleftarrows \text{V}_\text{O}^{\cdot\cdot} + 2\text{e}' + 1/2\text{O}_2^{(\text{g})} \tag{12.16}$$

This concept was confirmed in papers[312, 313] which have shown on the basis of precise measurements of density of TiO_2 annealed in vacuum that the type of defect situations in this oxide depends on the temperature of thermal treatment. At temperatures lower than 870 K oxygen vacancies are formed, above 1070 K interstitial titanium atoms play the dominant role.

The analogous measurements on the TiO_2 samples annealed in the hydrogen atmosphere showed that in this case the temperature at which the oxygen vacancies are observed is considerably lower.

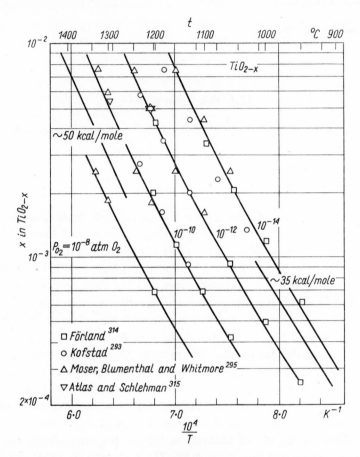

FIG. 12.12. The value of x in TiO_{2-x} as a function of the reciprocal absolute temperature and oxygen pressure.[311]

In Fig. 12.12 is given a summary of the published data on the deviation from stoichiometric composition, where x (in TiO_{2-x}) is plotted as a function of the reciprocal absolute temperature at different oxygen pressures (after Kofstad[311]).

Little is known about the self-diffusion in rutile. The available data on this problem are collected in Table 12.

Barbanel and Bogomolov[313] determined the defect diffusion coefficient in TiO_2 over the temperature range from 370 to 1070 K. The activation energy was calculated as 0·84 eV.

TABLE 12. SELF-DIFFUSION

Year	Authors	Diffusing element	Material
1960	Haul, Just and Dümbgen[316]	O	single crystal
1962	Haul and Dümbgen[317]	O	single crystal
1965	Haul and Dümbgen[318]	O	single crystal
1965	Carnahan and Brittain[319]	Ti	single crystal

12.3. Thin Films of TiO_2

Thin films of titanium dioxide can be prepared by the following methods:
(a) reaction in the gas phase,
(b) cathode sputtering,
(c) vacuum evaporation,
(d) anodic oxidation.

Preparation of thin films of rutile by the first of these methods described by Feuersanger[91] and Yokozawa et al.[98] has been already reviewed in Chapter 3. Below, we shall discuss some properties of thin films of TiO_2 obtained by this method. Refraction index and density of the films obtained at temperatures from 590–810 K in the presence of air were: $n = 2.00–2.5$, $d = 2.40–2.49$ g/cm. For the films prepared in the oxygen-free atmosphere and at temperatures from 380–1020 K $n = 2.08–2.13$, $d = 2.50–2.60$ g/cm^3. For comparison, the refraction index and density of single crystals of anatase are $n = 2.565$, $d = 3.82–3.95$ g/cm^3, and those of rutile are $n = 2.75$, $d = 4.26$ g/cm^3.

The gas-reaction method of the thin film preparation and the properties of the films grown by this method have been also described by Tamiguchi and Honda.[320]

Prokhorov[321] and van den Berghe and Perny[322] have obtained thin films of TiO_2 by cathodic sputtering technique. Thin films of TiO_2 can be obtained in this method either by high-frequency sputtering of titanium dioxide in the atmosphere of an inert gas, or by reactive sputtering of titanium in the oxygen atmosphere. Each of these methods has its advantages and drawbacks. The first method yields the TiO_2 films of the a priori determined composition but the rate of the film growth is small. In the second method the rate of the sputtering is considerably higher, but at the same time the reaction parameters such as the composition of the surrounding atmosphere, ionic current density, voltage, etc. which determine the properties of the films, should be carefully adjusted.

Prokhorov[321] examined the effect of the sputtering parameters on the properties of a condenser made of titanium dioxide and gave the following conditions for preparation of thin films of TiO_2: The oxygen partial pressure 9×10^{-2} Tr, ionic current density 1.5 mA/cm^2, voltage 2 kV, the substrate temperature 470–520 K, sputtering time 35 min, the anode–cathode distance 2.5 cm. The capacity of the condenser of the surface area of 1 cm^2 prepared in these conditions was 2.15 μF and tangent of the loss

COEFFICIENTS IN TiO_2

Method	Temperature range K	D_0 cm²/s	ΔH eV
O^{18} mass spec.	1130–1300	1·1	3·17
O^{18} mass spec.	980–1220	2·3	3·25
	1220–1570	$1·4 \times 10^{-4}$	2·3
O^{18} mass spec.	980–1570	$2·0 \times 10^{-3}$	$2·65 \pm 0·07$
from changes in optical absorption	—	—	1·04

angle 6·5%. In the case of the aluminium substrate deposited on glass, a film of brukite with additions of higher valency oxides was formed. On the substrate made of mono-crystalline NaCl the film composition was more complex and depended markedly on the sputtering rate.

Van den Berghe and Perny[322] studied the composition of thin films of TiO_2 prepared by the cathodic sputtering method using the X-ray fluorescence technique.

Shiojiri[323] prepared thin films of TiO_2 by vacuum evaporation method. The anatase powder was evaporated from a tungsten boat. Sodium chloride was used as a substrate. No extra heating of the substrate was applied, its temperature could, however, raise to about 370 K owing to irradiation of the glowing tungsten boat. The crystalline structure of the TiO_2 films hence obtained was examined with aid of an electron micro-scope.

Preparation of thin films of TiO_2 by the vacuum evaporation method was described also by Travina and Mukkin.[324] They observed that the properties of thin films of TiO_2, in particular its resistivity, depended on the temperature of the film evaporation and that the evaporation of TiO_2 at temperatures 1520–1670 K yielded the thin films of resistivity of 10^{13} ohm cm. Application of this method to preparation of TiO_2 films can be also found in recent work by Dudenhausen and Mollenstedt.[325]

CHAPTER 13

OXIDES OF COPPER, ZINC AND CADMIUM

13.1. Cuprite, Cu_2O

Cuprous oxide has a cubic cell in which each oxygen atom is tetrahedrally bound to four copper atoms. The lattice constant is 4·28 Å. The density of Cu_2O is 6 g/cm^3, the m.p. about 1500 K. The forbidden energy gap assumes the value of 2·1 eV.

Cu_2O is stable only in the limited range of temperature and oxygen pressure. At low temperatures and at high oxygen pressures the stable oxide is CuO, whereas at high temperatures and at low oxygen pressures cuprite decomposes into copper and oxygen.[354]

Cuprite was one of the earliest studied semiconductors. The electrical conductivity of this oxide is p-type, and is due to the non-stoichiometry of Cu_2O consisting in the excess of oxygen.[326, 327] The conductivity, Hall effect and Seebeck effect in this oxide have been studied both at high temperatures, i.e. at thermodynamic equilibrium[328-338] and at low temperatures at which the point defects are frozen.[339-341]

For cuprous oxide the equilibrium values of electrical conductivity can be easily obtained at high temperatures. However, measurements made by different authors often led to inconsistent results.[328-336] It was shown that up to 1270 K the electrical conductivity of cuprite increases proportionally with the increasing oxygen pressure as $\sigma \sim P_{O_2}^n$, where n assumes values from 1/7 to 1/8.[332, 335, 336]

TABLE 13.   SELF-DIFFUSI

Year	Authors	Diffusing element	Material
1949	Castellan and Moore[348]	Cu	polycrystalline
1952	Moore and Selikson[349]	Cu	polycrystalline
1958	Moore, Ebisuzaki and Sluss[350]	O	polycrystalline
1959	Moore[351]	O	polycrystalline
		Cu	polycrystalline
1962	Sluss[352]	O	polycrystalline
1963	Ebisuzaki[353]	O	single crystal

Zuev[333] found that at high temperatures (1270–1470 K) the electrical conductivity of cuprous oxide persisted to be of the p-type but decreased with the increase in the oxygen pressure, the exponent n changing from 0 at about 1270 K to 1/3 at 1370 K. Some authors[330, 331] observed that at low oxygen pressures the conductivity of Cu_2O is independent of the pressure.

Zirin and Trivich[337] claim on the basis of the Seebeck coefficient measurements that Cu_2O is a p-type semiconductor at pressures higher than 2×10^{-6} Tr.

Bloem[327] proposed a model of the point defects structure in Cu_2O assuming the existence of the Schottky type defects, complexes $(V_{Cu} V_O)$ and the intrinisic electronic disorder. However, the structure of the point defects in Cu_2O is not well understood, and the model which could satisfactorily account for the results of all the experimental studies is lacking at present.

Vinetskii and Kholodar[339] estimated the energy of formation of the non-ionized point defects in Cu_2O to be 2·6 eV, and the ionization energy of these defects 0·64 eV.

Recently Zielinger et al.[340] examined the temperature dependence of the Cu_2O conductivity in vacuum over the temperature range 190–670 K. They report the existence of two acceptor and one donor levels in the forbidden energy band of cuprous oxide.

Zouaghi et al.[341] observed that in the temperature range 250–500 K the Hall mobility in the non-illuminated samples Cu_2O obeyed the relation $\mu_H \sim T^{-3\cdot6}$, whereas in samples illuminated with the light of 0·62–0·65 μm in the temperature range 400–500 K this relation had the form $\mu_H \sim T^{-6\cdot7}$ and at lower temperatures the relation has the same form as that for the non-illuminated samples. The values of the Hall mobility reported by these authors were contained in the range from 50 to 100 cm^2/Vs.

More recent results of research on conduction processes in Cu_2O have been published by Weichman, Kužel et al.,[362, 364, 464, 579, 580, 584, 586] McKinzie and O'Keeffe,[581] Fillard et al.,[582, 583] and Young and Schwartz.[585]

The photoelectric and optical properties of cuprous oxide have been described in refs. 342–344 and 500.

The band structure of Cu_2O has been extensively studied;[345–347] this problem is, however, far from being solved.

Self-diffusion data for Cu_2O are collected in Table 13.

FICIENTS IN Cu_2O

Method	Temperature range K	D_0 cm^2/s	ΔH eV
otracer during oxidation	1070–1270	$3\cdot58 \times 10^{-2}$	1·61
otracer	1070–1320	$4\cdot36 \times 10^{-2}$	$1\cdot57 \pm 0\cdot08$
mass spec.	1300–1390	$6\cdot5 \times 10^{-3}$	$1\cdot73 \pm 0\cdot18$
mass spec.	—	$6\cdot3 \times 10^{-3}$	$1\cdot73 \pm 0\cdot18$
		$1\cdot22 \times 10^{-1}$	$1\cdot57 \pm 0\cdot09$
mass spec.	1300–1370	—	$1\cdot88 \pm 0\cdot18$
mass spec.	1300–1390	$1\cdot5 \times 10^{-2}$	1·73

13.2. Zinc Oxide, ZnO

13.2.1. ELECTRICAL PROPERTIES OF ZnO AT LOW AND INTERMEDIATE TEMPERATURES

Zinc oxide crystallizes in the wurtzite structure with the lattice parameters $a = 3\cdot24$ Å and $c = 5\cdot19$ Å. The density of ZnO is $5\cdot6$ g/cm³. It decomposes at high temperatures. Under the pressure it melts at temperatures higher than 2070 K. The forbidden band width of this oxide is $3\cdot2$ eV at room temperature.

Zinc oxide is an n-type semiconductor. Its conductivity is due to the non-stoichiometry consisting in the excess of the metal.

A review of the earlier studies on the electrical properties and the structure of point defects in ZnO was given in the works of Heiland, Mollwo and Stockmann[355], Thomas,[356] Hutson[357] and Kröger.[358]

A thorough study on the temperature dependence of the Hall effect and electrical conductivity of single crystals of ZnO has been carried out by Hutson[357, 359] over the temperature range 55–300 K. His results of the Hall effect measurements obtained for single crystals of ZnO doped with hydrogen, lithium and zinc are shown in Fig. 13.1. Hutson analysed these results assuming that the electron gas in ZnO is non-degenerate and that ZnO has only one donor level.

The concentration of conduction electrons in this case can be described by the following formula (cf. Chapter 9):

$$n = N_c \left(\frac{m_e^*}{m_0}\right)^{3/2} \exp\left(\frac{E_F - E_c}{kT}\right) \qquad (13.1)$$

where

$$N_c = 2\left(\frac{2\pi m_0 kT}{h^2}\right)^{3/2}$$

m_0 is the electron mass, m_e^* denotes the effective mass of the density of states. According to Fermi–Dirac statistics the concentration of electrons at donor levels (concentration of non-ionized donors) n_D is given by:

$$n_D = \frac{[D]}{1 + g^{-1} \exp\left(\frac{E_D - E_F}{kT}\right)} \qquad (13.2)$$

where [D] is the donor concentration, g spin degeneracy of the donor states, E_D is the energy of the donor level, E_F is the Fermi level.

The electroneutrality condition in this case assumes the form:

$$[D] = n_D + n \qquad (13.3)$$

From eqs. (13.1)–(13.3) we obtain the following temperature dependence of the concentration of the conductivity electrons

$$\frac{n^2}{([D] - n)N_c} = \left(\frac{m_e^*}{m_0}\right)^{3/2} g^{-1} \exp\left(-\frac{E_d}{kT}\right) \qquad (13.4)$$

where E_d is the donor ionization energy: $E_d = E_c - E_D$. Hutson[359] compared his results with the relation described by eq. (13.4) by plotting $\log n^2 /([D]-n)N_c$ as a function of the reciprocal temperature (Fig. 13.2). The value of [D] was adjusted assuming that at the temperature of about 300 K almost all the donors are ionized. As seen from Fig. 13.1, this assumption seems to be plausible. The ionization energy of the donors

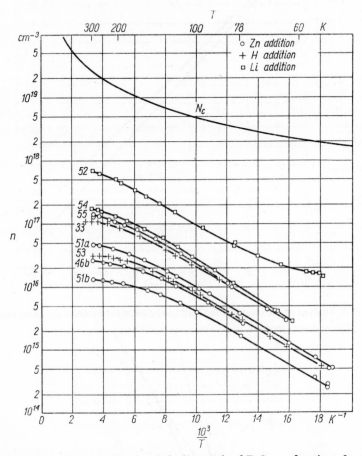

FIG. 13.1. Electron concentration in doped single crystals of ZnO as a function of temperature. For comparison the temperature dependence of the density of states in conductance band N_c is also given; figures at the side of the plots denote the numbers of samples.[359]

calculated by Hutson from the slope of the plot shown in Fig. 13.2 is approximately the same for hydrogen and for the excess zinc (0·05 eV), which may confirm the hydrogen model of the donors.

The electron mobility in ZnO at temperatures higher than 200 K is independent of the concentrations of the admixtures. Thus at not too low temperatures the current carriers are most probably scattered by acoustic and optical phonons only. As seen from Fig. 13.3, with this assumption the agreement between the experimental results and theoretical data for the scattering mechanisms under discussion is good. The contribution of the two terms in the expression for the mobility, i.e. μ_a (scattering on

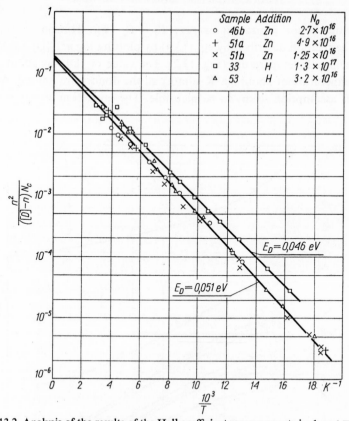

Sample	Addition	N_0
○ 46b	Zn	$2{\cdot}7 \times 10^{16}$
+ 51a	Zn	$4{\cdot}9 \times 10^{16}$
× 51b	Zn	$1{\cdot}25 \times 10^{16}$
□ 33	H	$1{\cdot}3 \times 10^{17}$
△ 53	H	$3{\cdot}2 \times 10^{16}$

$E_D = 0{,}046 \text{ eV}$

$E_D = 0{,}051 \text{ eV}$

FIG. 13.2. Analysis of the results of the Hall coefficient measurements in doped ZnO.[359]

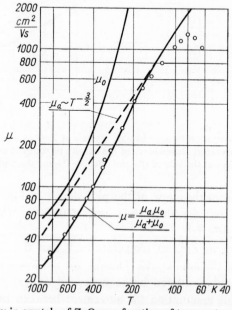

FIG. 13.3. Hall mobility in crystals of ZnO as a function of temperature and comparison of the experimental data with the theoretical dependence derived on the assumption that scattering on acoustical and optical phonons plays a main role in ZnO.[359]

the acoustic phonons) and μ_o (scattering on the optical phonons) was adjusted so as to obtain the agreement of the total mobility with the experimentally derived values. It should be, however, noted that the value of the ratio μ_a/μ_o may be obtained only with the accuracy of about 50% since the temperature dependences of μ_a and μ_o differ only slightly in the wide range of temperatures. The mobility values obtained in measurements on highly-doped ZnO are also consistent with the values calculated with the assumption that the main role in scattering of current carriers is played by ionized admixtures. The Seebeck effect studies have revealed a considerable contribution of phonon drag in ZnO.

Baer[369] determined in the measurements of the Faraday effect the effective mass in the single crystals of zinc oxide both pure and doped with indium. Taking into account the ionic character of the bonds in ZnO, Baer makes a distinction between the measurements at frequencies higher and lower than the frequency of longitudinal optical phonons. For high frequency Baer reports the value $m_e^* = 0.24 m_0$. At low

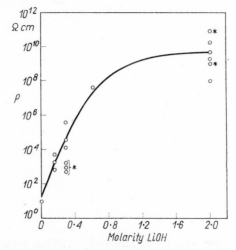

FIG. 13.4. Resistivity of single crystals of ZnO prepared by the hydrothermal method as a function of LiOH concentration in the solution. The points marked with a star are due probably to the non-homogeneity of the samples.[360]

frequencies the effective mass of the electron is replaced by the large polaron mass $m^{(P)}$ [140] which is related to the electron effective mass by the following equation:

$$m^{(P)} = m_e^*(1 + \alpha/6) \qquad (13.5)$$

where α is the coupling constant.

According to Baer the large polaron mass in ZnO amounts to $0.29 m_0$.

Recently, several works have been reported on the properties of the doped zinc oxide. Kolb and Laudise[360] examined the properties of ZnO single crystals doped with lithium. The single crystals were obtained by the hydrothermal method adding lithium hydroxide to the initial solution. Figure 13.4 shows the resistivity of the Li-doped oxide as a function of the concentration of LiOH in the solution. As seen, the logarithm of the resistivity is a linear function of the LiOH concentration up to the value of 0·6 mole. In Fig. 13.5 the logarithm of the ZnO resistivity is plotted as a function of Li concentration in the crystal. The linear relationship between these two parameters is observed. Kolb and Laudise obtained in this manner the ZnO crystals of the controlled resistivity changing from 10 to 10^{10} ohm cm. The increase of the resistivity with the increasing lithium concentration is due to the acceptor character of lithium atoms incorporated into the crystal lattice of ZnO.

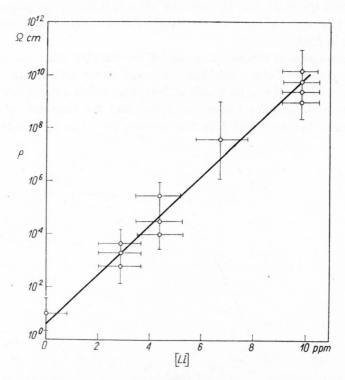

FIG. 13.5. The dependence of ZnO resistivity on lithium concentration.[360]

Sumita[361] studied the temperature dependence of the Hall coefficient and mobility in single crystals of ZnO doped with nickel and cobalt. The concentration of cobalt and nickel were respectively $1·7 \times 10^{18}$ cm^{-3} and $7·0 \times 10^{17}$ cm^{-3}. Ionization energies of the admixtures were determined in the manner analogous to that described above. Their values were 0·016 and 0·036 eV for cobalt and nickel, respectively. The temperature dependence of the electron concentration in these two cases is shown in Fig. 13.6 and the analogous dependence of the Hall mobility is given in Fig. 13.7. It follows from this latter plot that in both cases the current carriers are scattered at low temperatures mainly on the ionized admixtures, cobaltous ions having greater cross section than the nickel ions.

Savage and Dodson[59] obtained single crystals of zinc oxide doped with lithium and copper. They observed the increase of the ZnO resistivity with the increase in the addition concentration for both lithium and copper doped samples. The resistivity of the materials obtained by Savage and Dodson was from 50 to 100 ohm cm. The electron mobility was, however, low, assuming at room temperature the values: for Li-doped samples below 10 cm²/Vs, for Co-doped specimens—smaller than 20 cm²/Vs. The similar value of the mobility (2–8 cm²/Vs) at room temperature was also reported by Seitz and Whitmore[363] for samples of zinc oxide doped with lithium.

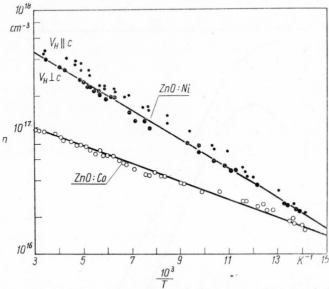

FIG. 13.6. The temperature dependence of electron concentration in ZnO doped with nickel and cobalt.[361] In the case of ZnO doped with nickel the Hall voltage data are given for directions parallel and perpendicular to axis c.

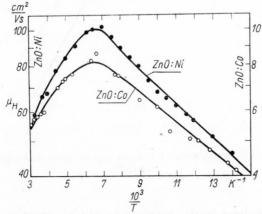

FIG. 13.7. The temperature dependence of Hall mobility in ZnO doped with nickel and cobalt.[361]

The resistivity of single crystals of ZnO without any addition was at room temperature 7–30 ohm cm, and the drift mobility was 125 cm²/Vs.[59] Figure 13.8 shows the temperature dependence of the current carriers concentration in single crystals of ZnO as given by Nielsen.[365] As seen from this figure in the vicinity of room temperature practically all donors are ionized. Nielsen estimated the value of the mobility in ZnO to be about 900 cm²/Vs at the temperature of about 80 K.

Krusemeyer and Thomas[366, 367] studied the effect of oxygen adsorption on semi-conducting properties of single crystals of ZnO doped with lithium. They found that the adsorption of oxygen may cause in the surface layers of the crystal the change from the *n*- to *p*-type of conductivity. Seitz and Whitmore[363] have measured electronic

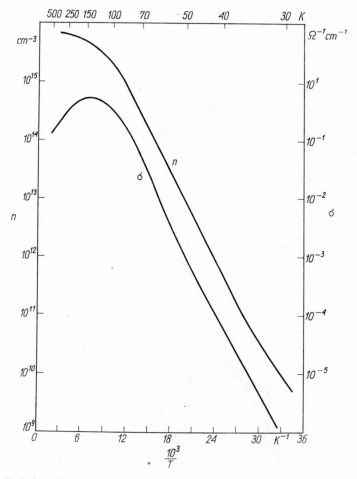

FIG. 13.8. Variation with temperature of electron concentration and conductivity for ZnO crystal.[365]

drift mobility and lifetimes in the range from 250 to 400 K in single crystals of Li-doped ZnO. The observed exponential temperature dependence of the mobility indicated that the electron drift mobility is primarily controlled by thermal release from trapping states, of density 10^{16} cm^{-3}, lying in a 0.29 eV region below the conduction band. The investigations carried out by these authors indicated also that discrete or narrow band traps existed in the 0.4 eV and in the 0.72–0.80 eV regions below the conduction band edge with densities of 4×10^{13} and 10^{17} cm^{-3}, respectively.

The properties of atoms or ions of lithium incorporated into the ZnO lattice have not been, however, adequately elucidated similarly like the nature of the copper species (atoms or ions) present in ZnO which also act as acceptors.[370,371]

13.2.2. DEFECT STRUCTURE AND ELECTRICAL PROPERTIES OF ZnO AT HIGH TEMPERATURES

On the basis of numerous studies on electrical and optical properties of zinc oxide and on diffusion processes occurring in this compound Kröger[358] was able to make some deductions as to the location of energy levels in the forbidden energy band. These energy levels are illustrated schematically in Fig. 13.9. Kröger assumed the pos-

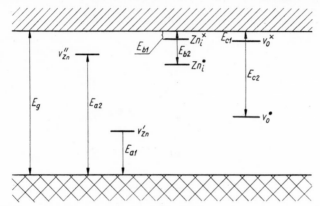

FIG. 13.9. Energy level scheme for native defects in ZnO:[358] $E_g = 3\cdot2$–$10^{-3}\,T$, eV; $E_{a_1} = 0\cdot7$–$2\times10^{-4}\,T$, eV; $E_{a_2} = 2\cdot8\times10^{-3}\,T$, eV; $E_{b_1} = 0\cdot05$ eV; $E_{b_2} = 0\cdot5$–$1\cdot5\times10^{-4}\,T$, eV; $E_{c_1} = 0\cdot05$ eV; $E_{c_2} = 2$–$6\times10^{-4}\,T$, eV.

sibility of the occurrence of vacancies in the both sublattices of ZnO and the presence of interstitial zinc atoms. Having estimated the position of the energy levels and making use of the experimental results in particular of the diffusion coefficient data, Kröger derived on the basis of thermodynamic theory of defects the parameters which determine equilibrium constants of possible reactions of the defect formation in ZnO. The results are collected in Table 14. To verify the Kröger model these parameters should be determined experimentally.

Garret[372] has shown that the results of the electrical measurements in ZnO can be most convincingly explained by assuming that the donor centres are supplied only by the interstitial zinc atoms. Assuming that $n = [\text{Zn}_i^{\cdot}]$, Kröger obtained the following expression:

$$n = 3\cdot8\times10^2 P_{\text{O}_2}^{-1/4} \exp\left(-2\cdot3\,e/kT\right) \quad \text{mole fraction/atm}^{1/4} \qquad (13.6)$$

where e is an elementary charge. Equation (13.6) is in good accord with the experimental results. It should be, however, noted that the equally good agreement with the experiment is obtained by assuming that oxygen vacancies are the donor species in ZnO, $n = [\text{V}_\text{O}^{\cdot}]$

$$n = 3\cdot3\times10^3 P_{\text{O}_2}^{-1/4} \exp\left(-2\cdot48\,e/kT\right) \quad \text{mole fraction/atm}^{1/4} \qquad (13.7)$$

The data on self-diffusion in ZnO are presented in Table 15.

TABLE 14. PARAMETERS DETERMINING THE EQUILIBRIUM CONSTANTS OF DISORDER REACTION IN ZnO AT ABOUT 1350 K[358]

Reaction	Equilibrium constant	K° (mol fraction atm)	E° (eV)
$ZnO \rightleftarrows Zn^{(g)} + \frac{1}{2} O_2^{(g)}$	K_{ZnO}	$1 \cdot 5 \times 10^{10}$	$4 \cdot 89$
$ZnO \rightleftarrows Zn^{(g)} + O^{(g)}$	K_{ZnO}	$7 \cdot 5 \times 10^{12}$	$7 \cdot 49$
$O_2^{(g)} \rightleftarrows 2O^{(g)}$	K_D	$2 \cdot 5 \times 10^5$	$5 \cdot 2$
$0 \rightleftarrows e' + h^\bullet$	K_i	$29 \cdot 4$	$3 \cdot 44$
$V_{Zn}^x \rightleftarrows V_{Zn}' + h^\bullet$	K_{a1}	$5 \cdot 25 \times 10^{-1}$	$0 \cdot 97$
$V_{Zn}' \rightleftarrows V_{Zn}^x + h^\bullet$	K_{a2}	$1 \cdot 44 \times 10^3$	$2 \cdot 97$
$V_O^x \rightleftarrows V_O^\bullet + e'$	K_{c1}	$2 \cdot 1 \times 10^{-2}$	$0 \cdot 22$
$V_O^\bullet \rightleftarrows V_O^{\bullet\bullet} + e'$	K_{c2}		$\cdot$
$Zn_i^x \rightleftarrows Zn_i^\bullet + e'$	K_{b1}	10^{-2}	$0 \cdot 22$
$0 \rightleftarrows V_{Zn}' + V_O^\bullet$	K_{S_1}	10^5	$4 \cdot 04$
$0 \rightleftarrows V_{Zn}^x + V_O^x$	K_S	$2 \cdot 8 \times 10^8$	$6 \cdot 29$
$Zn_{Zn}^x + V_i^x \rightleftarrows Zn_i^\bullet + V_{Zn}'$	K_{F_1}	$7 \cdot 9 \times 10^{-2}$	$4 \cdot 36$
$Zn_{Zn}^x + V_i^x \rightleftarrows Zn_i^x + V_{Zn}^x$	K_F	$8 \cdot 2 \times 10^2$	$6 \cdot 67$
$\frac{1}{2} O_2^{(g)} \rightleftarrows O_O^x + V_{Zn}^x$	$K_{O_2 V}$	$3 \cdot 06$	$2 \cdot 0$
$O^{(g)} \rightleftarrows O_O^x + V_{Zn}^x$	K_{OV}	$6 \cdot 1 \times 10^{-3}$	$-0 \cdot 6$
$Zn^{(g)} \rightleftarrows Zn_{Zn}^x + V_O^x$	K_{ZnV}	$6 \cdot 1 \times 10^{-3}$ (?)	$-0 \cdot 6$ (?)
$Zn_{Zn}^x \rightleftarrows Zn^{(g)} + V_{Zn}^x$	K_{Zn}	$4 \cdot 6 \times 10^{10}$	$6 \cdot 89$
$O_O^x \rightleftarrows O^{(g)} + V_O^x$	K_O	$4 \cdot 6 \times 10^{10}$ (?)	$6 \cdot 89$

TABLE 15. SELF-DIFFUSION COEFFICIENTS IN ZnO

Year	Authors	Diffusing element	Material	Method	Temperature range K	D_0 cm²/s	ΔH eV
1941	Miller[379]	Zn	polycrystalline	ionic conductivity	—	—	—
1952	Fritzsche[380]	Zn	polycrystalline	Zn^{65} radiotracer	—	—	—
1952	Lindner, Campbell and Åkerström[381, 397]	Zn	polycrystalline	Zn^{65} surface activity	1070–1640	1·3	73·7
1955	Munnich[382]	Zn	single crystal	Zn^{65} activity decrease	1120–1210	$3{\cdot}0\times10^{-9}$	20
					1210–1300	5·0	75
1955	Arneth[383]	Zn	single crystal	ionic conductivity	1100–1370	—	39
1955	Secco and Moore[384]	Zn	single crystal	Zn^{65} radiotracer	1170–1300	4·8	73±3
1956	Spicar[385]	Zn	polycrystalline	Zn^{65} radiotracer	1180–1430	—	—
1956	Spicar[386]	Zn	single crystal	Zn^{65} radiotracer	1180–1430	30	74
1956	Roberts[387]	Zn	polycrystalline	Zn^{65} radiotracer	1560	—	89
1957	Roberts and Wheeler[388]	Zn	polycrystalline	Zn^{65} radiotracer	1070–1570	0·1	89
1957	Thomas[389]	Zn	single crystal	ionic conductivity	450–620	$2{\cdot}7\times10^{-4}$	12·7
1958	Lamatsch[390]	Zn	single crystal	Zn^{65} radiotracer	1070–1460	170	—
1958	Moore[391]	Zn	polycrystalline	—	—	—	—
1959	Moore and Williams[392]	Zn	single crystal	Zn^{65} radiotracer	1270–1540	$1{\cdot}25\times10^{-5}$	43·5±10
		O	single crystal	O^{18} mass spec.	1370–1570	$6{\cdot}52\times10^{11}$	165±6
1959	Pohl[393]	Zn	single crystal	ionic conductivity	970–1500	$1{\cdot}6\times10^{-2}$	39
1960	Roberts and Wheeler[394]	Zn	polycrystalline	Zn^{65} radiotracer	1070–1670	100	73
1960	Secco[395]	Zn	polycrystalline	Zn^{65} radiotracer	990–1050	10	73
1961	Secco[396]	Zn	single crystal	Zn^{65} radiotracer	1070–1110 990–1050	$3{\cdot}0\times10^{-7}$	25
1970	Hoffman and Lauder[368]	O	single crystal	gaseous change	1423–1673	1·105	—

13.2.3. Thin Films of ZnO

Preparation of thin ZnO films has been in recent years described in many papers.[373-378] The most frequently employed method was reactive sputtering, described in more detail by Rozgonyi and Polito.[373] The sputtering was carried out in a chamber under the pressure of the order of 10^{-9}Tr (when the chamber was heated to 548 K) or at 10^{-7}Tr (without the heating). The crystals of pure ZnO were hot-pressed on a cylindrical cathode. Single crystals of sapphire or Pyrex glass were used as the substrates. The substrate temperature did not exceed 473 K. Before the sputtering the chamber was evacuated and then spectrally pure argon or argon–oxygen mixture was admitted. The pressure of the working gas was from 2×10^{-2} to 10^{-1}Tr. The negative potential applied to the cathode was usually 2 kV. In these conditions the cathode current density was 2 mA/cm^2 and the rate of the film deposition was contained from 50 to 130 Å/min. The thickness of the films obtained was from 0·1 to 10 µ. The electron diffraction studies showed that ZnO crystals in the film grown on the monocrystalline substrate had a hexagonal structure with axis perpendicular to the substrate. On an amorphous substrate the same orientation was observed, the grains being, however, smaller and axis c was deflected forming an angle with the normal to substrate plane.

Thin films of ZnO were colourless and transparent, displaying the properties of an n-type semiconductor. The resistivity of the films deposited in the atmosphere of pure argon was about 0·1 ohm cm and those obtained in pure oxygen about 10^4 ohm cm.

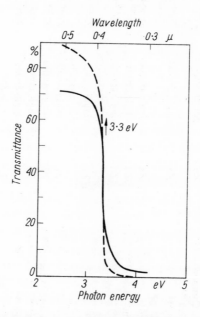

FIG. 13.10. Dependence of transmittance on photon energy.[373] ———— transmittance in films deposited in pure argon, — — — in pure oxygen: film thickness in both cases was 0·3 µ.

The resistivity of thin films grown in the mixture of these two gases assumed the intermediate values depending on the mixture composition. The Hall mobility was lower than 1 cm^2/Vs. The optical measurements showed that the energy gap in these films was 3·3 eV (Fig. 13.10).

13.3. Cadmium Oxide, CdO

Cadmium oxide has a cubic structure of the NaCl type and probably due to this fact exhibits different properties from those of ZnO which has a wurtzite-type structure. The lattice constant of this oxide is 4·69 Å, the density 8 g/cm^3. It decomposes at high temperatures. Cadmium oxide shows n-type conductivity of the order of 10^3–10^4 ohm^{-1}cm^{-1}, which results from the presence of interstitial cadmium atoms or oxygen vacancies acting as donors.

The results of the current studies on the defect structure and electrical properties of CdO have been reviewed by Jarzębski.[398, 399] As shown by many workers, cadmium oxide displays the deviation from stoichiometry consisting in excess of the metal, this excess attaining considerable values of the order of hundredths of atomic per cent. The present results do not permit, however, to decide whether the defect structure is limited to the cation sublattice involving interstitial cadmium atoms or to the anion sublattice in which case oxygen vacancies are the predominant defects. On the basis of studies on self-diffusion of oxygen Haul and Just[400] suppose that the defect structure is limited to the anion sublattice. The defect formation in cadmium oxide can be, according to these authors, described by the following reactions:

$$CdO \rightleftarrows V_O^{\cdot\cdot} + Cd_{Cd}'' + 1/2 O_2^{(g)} \tag{13.8}$$

$$2CdO \rightleftarrows V_O^{\cdot\cdot} + 2Cd_{Cd}' + O_O + 1/2 O_2^{(g)} \tag{13.9}$$

$$3CdO \rightleftarrows 2V_O^{\cdot\cdot} + 2Cd_{Cd}' + Cd_{Cd}'' + O_O + O_2^{(g)} \tag{13.10}$$

The above reactions lead to the following dependence of the concentration of oxygen vacancies on the oxygen pressure: $V_O \sim P_{O_2}^{1/5}$.

The above relation was confirmed by the studies on self-diffusion coefficient of oxygen in pure and doped with lithium and indium cadmium oxide.[400]

The measurements of the Hall coefficient, thermoelectric power and resistivity performed on annealed samples have shown that the thermodynamic equilibrium in this oxide can be attained at the temperatures higher than 900 K in the relatively short time of several hours.[401–403] It has been also observed that for CdO samples annealed for about 10 hr at temperatures higher than 1000 K, the scattering of current carriers on potential barriers at the grain boundaries is at room temperature negligible as compared with the scattering by ionized donors.[402–404,412]

Finkenrath and Ortenberg[405] and Jarzębski[403, 404] found the linear relation between the logarithm of the conductivity electrons concentration n at room temperature and the reciprocal of the absolute temperature of the previous thermal treatment at temperatures above 900 K. The experiments were done on sintered samples rapidly cooled to room temperature. The analogous dependence of log n on $1/T$ was recently obtained by Koffyberg[406] for single crystals of CdO subjected to thermal treatment under the oxygen pressure of 1 atm. The activation energy of the conductivity calculated from the

formula $\sigma \sim \exp(-E/kT)$ was according to Finkenrath and Ortenberg 0·6 eV, the
value reported by Jarzębski was 0·75 eV and that of Koffyberg 0·79 eV. This latter
author observed in the Hall effect measurements carried out on the rapidly cooled
samples that at lower electron concentration $n \sim P_{O_2}^{-1/6}$. This relation implies that the
defects in CdO are doubly ionized. However, at higher concentrations of electrons
the exponent $1/n$ decreases with the increase in the electron concentration. This is
undoubtedly due to the complete degeneracy of the electron gas in CdO. Koffyberg
estimated the enthalpy of formation of doubly ionized point defects in CdO (oxygen
vacancies or interstitial cadmium ions) to be 1·95 eV.

The electron mobility of CdO at room temperature varies from 100 to 300 cm²/Vs
depending on the conditions of the material preparation, distinctly decreasing with
the increase in the concentration of current carriers (Fig. 13.11), which indicates that

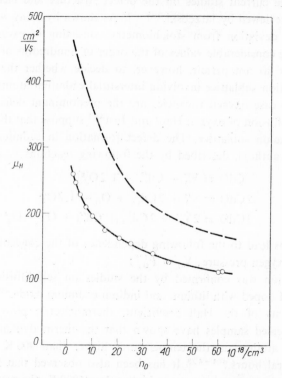

FIG. 13.11. The variation of the room temperature Hall mobility μ_H with carrier concentration n_0;
— o — o — o experimental data, — — — — calculated from ionized-donor scattering.[406]

at room temperature the conductivity electrons are scattered mainly by ionized
donors.[404-406] In the earlier works on CdO[407-409] the scattering by optical phonons
according to the Howarth and Sondheimer theory[410] was assumed. Cidilkovskii[411]
claims that at temperatures higher than the Debye temperature the temperature dependence of mobility in CdO is consistent with the theoretical dependence derived for
scattering by optical phonons: $\mu \sim T^{-1/2}$. Investigations of the electrical conduction
of CdO at high temperatures at the state of thermodynamic equilibrium have shown

that the conductivity is considerably lower and the current carriers are scattered mainly by optical phonons.[412] Similar conclusion has been drawn by Koffyberg.[574]

Thermoelectric properties of CdO depend on the conditions of thermal treatment and on the cooling conditions.[414, 415]

Höschl et al.[413] prepared the single crystals of CdO which displayed the following parameters at room temperature: $\sigma = 2500$ ohm^{-1}cm^{-1}, $n = 10^{20}$ cm^{-3}, $\mu_H = 250$ cm^2/Vs, $\alpha = 10$ μV/deg. The analysis of the band structure of CdO indicates that the conduction band in CdO is not parabolic.[416] The forbidden energy band is 2·3 eV, and the effective mass about $0·14m_0$.[417, 418]

More recent results are given in refs. 511, 543, 566, 575–578, 593.

Optical and electrical properties of thin films of CdO pure and doped with indium and copper were the subject of studies by Lakshmanan.[419] The films were grown by cathodic sputtering. For the preparation of the doped films the cathodes used were made of cadmium–indium or cadmium–copper alloys. The mixture of argon and oxygen of various ratio was used as a working gas. The total pressure in the chamber was 10^{-2}Tr. The measurements carried out at room temperature on the films thus obtained comprised the electrical conductivity and Hall coefficient. Their results are presented in Table 16. The gas composition is given by the volume ratio, and the

TABLE 16. ELECTRICAL PROPERTIES OF THIN FILMS OF CdO PURE AND DOPED WITH INDIUM AND COPPER, GROWN BY CATHODIC SPUTTERING (THE TOTAL PRESSURE IN THE CHAMBER WAS 10^{-2} Tr)[419]

Cathode	Argon/oxygen ratio	Thickness Å	Resistivity ohm/cm	Conductivity ohm^{-1} cm^{-1}	Hall coefficient cm^3/C	Hall mobility cm^2/Vs
Cd	98:2	2430	88	467	0·017	7·9
Cd	95:5	1850	490	110	0·045	5·0
Cd	90:10	2030	590	83	0·051	4·2
Cd	0:100	1390	22400	0·64	0·251	0·16
95 Cd-5 Cu	98:2	2430	390	106	0·030	3·2
95 Cd-5 Cu	95:5	2620	800	48	0·067	3·2
95 Cd-5 Cu	90:10	2810	1500	24	0·101	2·4
95 Cd-5 In	99:1	2810	188	189	0·012	2·3
95 Cd-5 In	98:2	2250	240	131	0·013	1·7
95 Cd-5 In	95:5	1690	466	127	0·017	2·2
95 Cd-5 In	90:10	1390	630	117	0·018	2·1

composition of the cathode alloys is expressed in the weight ratio. From the data collected in Table 16 it follows that the electron concentration in thin film of CdO, both pure and doped, decreases with the increase in the oxygen partial pressure. In the case of the indium doped samples the concentration of electrons is higher than that in pure CdO, whereas the copper admixture has the opposite effect. It follows from the above facts that indium atoms act as donors and copper atoms as acceptors. It should be, however, noted that the attempts at obtaining cadmium oxide of the p-type has not been as yet successful.

Lakshmanan measured also light permeability in his thin films of CdO pure and doped. The results obtained are shown in Fig. 13.12.

As seen from this figure the absorption edge is not sharp, however, the energy gap estimated from the adsorption threshold as 2·5 eV is in agreement with the earlier optical measurements.

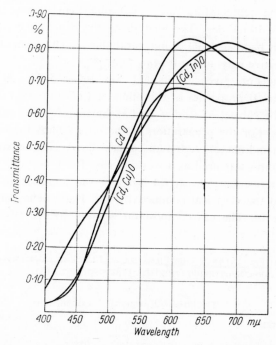

FIG. 13.12. Transmittance of thin films of CdO, pure and doped with indium and copper.[419]

The brief account of the studies on semiconducting properties of CdO given above indicates that the properties of this oxide are not satisfactorily known. This is due, as already mentioned, to large technological difficulties encountered in preparation of large and pure single crystals of thin oxide.

CHAPTER 14

ALUMINIUM OXIDE, Al₂O₃

ALUMINIUM oxide occurs in several modifications[420] the most stable of which is the α-modification of close packed hexagonal structure (cf. Chapter 4). The lattice parameters are 4·75 Å and 13 Å. Its density is 3·99 g/cm³, the m.p. is 2320 K.

The electrical conductivity of Al₂O₃, both of single crystals and of polycrystalline material, has been studied by many workers.[421-437] In all these studies the exponential dependence of the conductivity on temperature was observed, however, the values of the conductivity and activation energy obtained by various authors differed considerably; the conductivity values obtained in the earlier studies differed by about six orders of magnitude, and the activation energies ranged from 0·25 to 4 eV. These differences are undoubtedly due to the impurities present in Al₂O₃ and to the different conditions of the samples preparation and of the measurements. At room temperature Al₂O₃ is virtually an insulator. The semiconducting properties of Al₂O₃ appear only at relatively high temperatures. The review of the earlier works on the electrical conductivity of aluminium oxide has been presented by Cohen.[437]

In Figs. 14.1 and 14.2 the electrical conductivity data obtained by various authors are compared. Figure 14.1 is concerned with the polycrystalline material, Fig. 14.2 pertains to the conductivity of single crystals.

Pappis and Kingery[438] examined the electrical conductivity of Al₂O₃ as a function of the oxygen pressure at high temperatures up to 2000 K. Their results are presented in Fig. 14.3. As seen from this figure we can distinguish three regions of the oxygen pressures. At higher pressures, from 10^{-3}–1 atm $\sigma \sim P_{O_2}^{(0.20\pm0.03)}$, at low oxygen pressures (10^{-10}–10^{-7} atm) the relation $\sigma \sim P_{O_2}^{(-0.17+0.03)}$ is held, finally in the intermediate range of the oxygen pressures σ is independent of the pressure. The temperature dependence of the Al₂O₃ conductivity at the oxygen pressure of 1 atm obtained by Pappis and Kingery can be described by the following formula: $\sigma = 10^3 \exp(-2.97/kT)$ ohm⁻¹cm⁻¹. On the basis of the Seebeck coefficient measurements, Pappis and Kingery claim that at higher oxygen pressures the conductivity of aluminium oxide is of the p-type whereas at low oxygen pressures the n-type conductivity is observed.

Peters[439] studied the temperature dependence of the electrical conductivity and Seebeck coefficient of Al₂O₃ single crystals in air over the temperature range 673–1273 K. The results obtained are shown in Figs. 14.4 and 14.5. The electrical conductivity data reported by Peters are in agreement with the results of earlier studies carried out

243

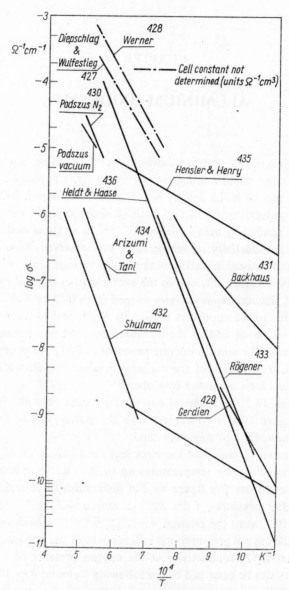

FIG. 14.1. The temperature dependence of electrical conductivity in polycrystalline Al_2O_3 according to various authors.[438]

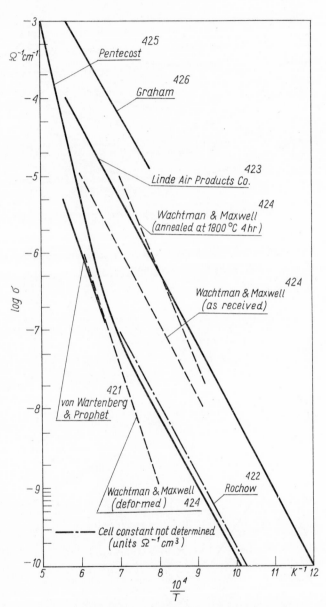

FIG. 14.2. The temperature dependence of electrical conductivity in single crystals of Al_2O_3 according to various authors.[438]

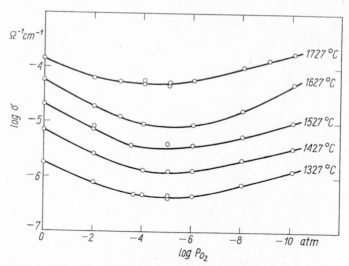

FIG. 14.3. Electrical conductivity of single crystals of Al_2O_3 as a function of oxygen pressure for different temperatures.[438]

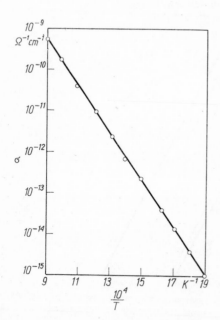

FIG. 14.4. The temperature dependence of electrical conductivity of Al_2O_3.[439]

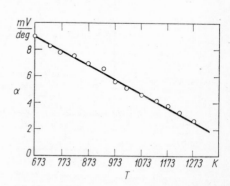

FIG. 14.5. Seebeck coefficient of Al_2O_3 as a function of temperature.[439]

by Champion.[440] The Seebeck coefficient has the positive sign which implies that the current carriers in Al_2O_3 are positive. Peters interpreted his results in terms of the band model of the current carriers transport, obtaining however improbably high value of the mobility. This fact may be explained by assuming the hopping model of the conductance in Al_2O_3. The high value of the mobility may also result from the too high value of the Seebeck coefficient due to ionic term of the Al_2O_3 conductance, which most probably does not play any essential role in the electrical conductivity measurements.

Dasgupta and Hart[441] measured the Seebeck coefficient in single crystals of sapphire over the temperature range 873–1373 K at various pressures of argon and air. Their

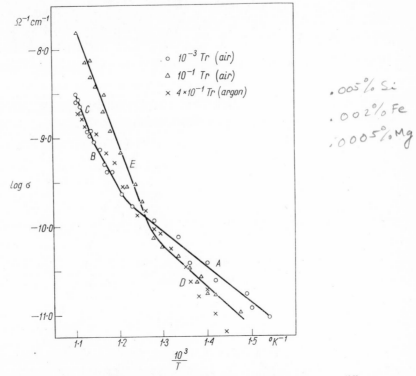

FIG. 14.6. Electrical conductivity of Al_2O_3 as a function of reciprocal temperature at different pressures of air and argon.[442]

results indicate that the value of the Seebeck coefficient in aluminium oxide changes with the change in the oxygen partial pressure. The temperature dependences of the Seebeck coefficient at various oxygen partial pressures observed by Dasgupta and Hart were however different.

Dasgupta[442] studied also the temperature dependence of the electrical conductivity measured at d.c. conditions and at various pressures of air and argon. The results obtained are presented in Figs. 14.6 and 14.7.

Figure 14.6 shows σ as a function of $1/T$ for a monocrystalline sample containing 0.01–0.001% Si, 0.001–0.0001% Mg and 0.005–0.0005% Fe. As seen from this figure at the air pressure of the order of 10^{-3} Tr the plot shows three different slopes at different temperature ranges. The segments of the plot of the different slopes are denoted by letters A, B and C. The values of the activation energies for segments A, B and C calculated by Dasgupta according to the formula $\sigma = \exp(-E/kT)$ are respectively 0·83, 1·90 and 2·50 eV. At higher oxygen pressures (0·2 Tr) only two slopes with slightly different values of the activation energies are observed (Fig. 14.6). In Fig. 14.7

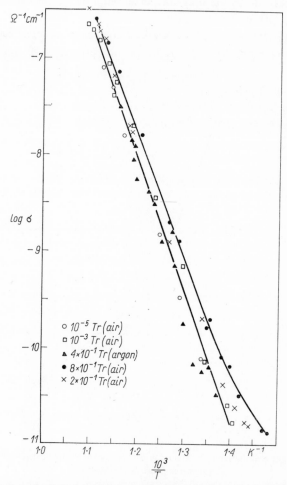

FIG. 14.7. Electrical conductivity of Al_2O_3 as a function of reciprocal temperature at different pressures of air and argon.[442]

the function $\log \sigma$ vs. $1/T$ is shown for the Al_2O_3 samples containing 0·001–0·0001% Si, 0·005–0·0005% Mg and 0·005–0·0005% B. In this case the slope of the plot was practically the same in the whole range of temperatures under study. The activation energies at various oxygen pressures were slightly different similarly like in the preceding case. The more detailed analysis of the data obtained is however difficult. It is necessary to study simultaneously several physical parameters and to reduce the content of impurities which presents considerable experimental difficulties.

Little is also known about the band structure of Al_2O_3. From the measurements of the reflection coefficient in ultraviolet region Loh[443] estimated the energy gap in Al_2O_3 at room temperature to be 10 eV. Pappis and Kingery[438] studied the electrical conductivity of aluminium oxide over the temperature range 1570–2020 K and found that at low oxygen pressures the activation energy above 1900 K amounted to about 5·5 eV. They suppose that at temperatures higher than 1900 K the intrinsic conduction prevails in Al_2O_3. If this assumption were true then the energy gap in Al_2O_3 should, at temperatures > 1900 K, have the value of 11 eV. Harrop[444] reports on the other hand the value of 6·0 eV at 1950 K. In this case the value of 5·5 eV obtained by Pappis and Kingery could be explained by assuming the occurrence of the hopping mechanism of conduction.

Vernetti and Cook[445] studied the effect of the additions of Co_2O_3, Cr_2O_3, CuO, Fe_2O_3, MnO_2, NiO and TiO_2 on the electrical conductivity of aluminium oxide over the temperature range 770–1670 K. They found that the addition of 0·5–2 mole % of CoO, 1 mole % of Fe_2O_3, 2 mole % of CuO, MnO_2 and NiO increases the conductivity of aluminium oxide whereas that of 4 mole % of Fe_2O_3 or Cr_2O_3 leads to the decrease of the conductivity. The addition of 2 mole % of TiO_2 leads to the increase of the conductivity of aluminium oxide at high temperatures and to its decrease at low temperatures.

The results of the electrical conductivity measurements obtained by Pappis and Kingery[438] (Fig. 14.3) indicate that at oxygen pressures higher than 10^{-4} atm triply ionized aluminium vacancies are the predominant defects. This hypothesis is in agreement with the data of Oishi and Kingery,[448] and Jones, Coble and Megab.[454] The structure of point defects in Al_2O_3 at low oxygen pressures remains however disputable.

The results presented in Fig. 14.3 for the oxygen pressures lower than 10^{-6} atm may be interpreted by assuming the presence in Al_2O_3 of either doubly ionized oxygen vacancies or triply ionized interstitial aluminium atoms. The first hypothesis is supported by Oishi and Kingery,[448] Dils, on the other hand, favours the second.[452]

At high pressures the self-diffusion coefficient of oxygen in Al_2O_3, determined by Oishi and Kingery, is at 2000 K smaller from the self-diffusion of aluminium only by 2 to 3 orders of magnitude. This indicates large disorder of the anionic sublattice in Al_2O_3 as compared with the disorder in the cationic sublattice. It seems hence plausible that at oxygen pressures lower than 10^{-6} atm, oxygen vacancies may be the predominant defects in Al_2O_3. Thus the self-diffusion data of Al_2O_3 imply the Schottky type disorder in this compound. In the intermediate range of the oxygen pressures the intrinsic electronic defects are suggested by the results of Pappis and Kingery. The analogous conclusion has been drawn by Harrop[444] who estimated the energy gap in Al_2O_3 at high temperatures to be 6 eV.

Dereń, Jarzębski and Kozłowska[455] proposed recently the following disorder reactions in Al_2O_3:

$$3/2 O_2^{(g)} \rightleftarrows 3 O_O^x + 2 V_{Al}''' + 6 h^\bullet \tag{14.1}$$

$$\text{zero} \rightleftarrows 2 V_{Al}''' + 3 V_O^{\bullet\bullet} \tag{14.2}$$

$$\text{zero} \rightleftarrows e' + h^\bullet \tag{14.3}$$

According to them the simplified electroneutrality condition in the range of high oxygen pressures assumes the form:

$$3[V'''_{Al}] = [h^\cdot] \qquad (14.4)$$

in the intermediate pressure range:

$$[e'] = [h^\cdot] \qquad (14.5)$$

and at low oxygen pressures:

$$2[V_O^{\cdot\cdot}] = [e'] \qquad (14.6)$$

This model of the defect structure in Al_2O_3 accounts for the current results, but it should be verified by further detailed studies on this oxide.

More recent results on conduction mechanism in Al_2O_3 are given in ref. 587.

Thin films of Al_2O_3 of good dielectric properties cannot be prepared by direct evaporation since this oxide partially decomposes on heating. They can be, however, obtained by so called *reactive evaporation*, described by Da Silva and White.[456] This method consists in evaporation of aluminium in the atmosphere of oxygen. The properties of the films hence obtained depend on the oxygen pressure and on the evaporation rate. At low oxygen pressures of the order of 10^{-5}Tr the films obtained display very low resistivity. At higher oxygen pressures the resistivity of thin films of Al_2O_3 depends on the rate of evaporation. The films of the resistivity of the order of 10^{14} ohm cm were obtained by evaporation of aluminium at the rate of 1–5 Å/s and at the oxygen pressure of 10^{-3} Tr.

Thin Al_2O_3 films can be also prepared by cathode reactive sputtering of pure aluminium in the oxygen-containing atmosphere, since, however, aluminium is one of the most difficult sputtered metals, the rate of growth of thin films of Al_2O_3 is very small. Frieser[457] found that the thickness of such films is a linear function of time and depends moreover on the potential applied, the total pressure in the discharge chamber and on the cathodic current density. By selecting the appropriate conditions Frieser prepared the films 7000 Å thick after the 6 hr sputtering. The structure of the film depends on the substrate temperature. Hiesenger and Koenig[458] report the formation of amorphous films on the cooled substrates and at the low current density. Crystalline films of the γ-Al_2O_3 structure were obtained on heated substrates at higher current densities and higher potentials.

Thin films of Al_2O_3 of uniform non-porous structure are usually prepared by anodic oxidation of thin aluminium films.[85] Solutions of phosphates, borates, citrates are used as electrolytes. To obtain a film of the thickness of the order of microns the voltage applied should be of the order of several hundreds volts (13 Å/V). According to Charlesby,[459] the voltage higher than 400–600 V is seldom successfully applied in this case. At high potentials the electrical break-up of the films is observed. The value of the critical voltage depends on the purity of aluminium, composition of the electrolyte and on other factors. Bernard and Cook[460] found that the thickness of thin Al_2O_3 films depends also on the current density. Such films are usually formed at constant current densities of the order of 1–2 mA/cm^2.

In recent years a new method of preparation of thin Al_2O_3 films have been worked out, consisting in plasma oxidation of thin aluminium films.[86, 461-463] The average rate of growth of oxide films on the aluminium substrate is in this method about 23 Å/V (cf. section 3.4).

The results of investigations of the self-diffusion coefficient of aluminium in Al_2O_3 were published in refs. 446, 447, 449, 450 and 453. The values of ΔH given in these works differed considerably, ranging from 114 to 230 kcal/mole.

The data on the oxygen self-diffusion coefficient in Al_2O_3 can be found in refs. 448 and 451.

CHAPTER 15

OXIDES OF TIN AND SILICON

15.1. Cassiterite, SnO_2

Cassiterite has a rutile type structure. Its lattice parameters are: $a = 4 \cdot 75$ Å, $c = = 3 \cdot 19$ Å. The density of this oxide is 6·95 g/cm^3, its m.p. is higher than 2170 K. It decomposes at very high temperatures.

The early studies on semiconducting properties of SnO_2 were carried out on sintered material and on thin polycrystalline films. The first investigations on single crystals of SnO_2 are due to Kohnke.[465] He measured optical absorption, electrical conductivity and the Hall coefficient in natural crystals of cassiterite. The energy gap determined by Kohnke from the optical measurements was 3·54 eV and the temperature coefficient of E_g, i.e. dE_g/dT in the temperature range 80–415 K had the value of 6×10^{-4} eV/K. The value of E_g extrapolated to the temperature of 0 K was 3·7 eV.

From the measurements of the temperature dependence of the SnO_2 conductivity carried out in the temperature range 100–500 K Kohnke determined the activation energy of this process, obtaining the value of 0·72 eV at temperatures higher than 300 K. At lower temperatures the activation energy was considerably smaller and the results were not reproducible. It was also found that the electrical conductivity is of the n-type and the Hall mobility at temperatures higher than 473 K obeys the relation $\mu_e \sim T.^{-1 \cdot 32}$

Nagasawa and co-workers[60] studied the electrical and optical properties of SnO_2 single crystals prepared by the method of gas phase reaction (cf. section 2.3). Figure 15.1 shows the results of the absorption studies obtained by these authors at the room temperature. The energy gap estimated from these measurements amounted to 3·5 eV being thus close to the value obtained by Kohnke.

On the basis of the electrical conductivity and Hall effect measurements it was found that SnO_2 is an n-type semiconductor like natural cassiterite. The concentration of the current carriers in SnO_2 is of the order of 10^{17} cm^{-3} and the room temperature mobility assumes the value of about 200 cm^2/Vs. The results obtained by Nagasawa and co-workers[466] on the temperature dependence of the current carrier concentration and the Hall mobility are shown in Fig. 15.2. At temperatures above 160 K the mobility followed the relation $\mu_e \sim T^{-2}$. The continuous line in Fig. 15.2 denotes the relation

$\mu_e = A T^{-2}$ where A is a constant. From the Hall effect and Seebeck effect data the effective mass of electrons in SnO_2 was estimated to be about 0·35 m_0.

Morgan and Wright[467] studied the electrical conductivity and Hall and Seebeck coefficients in single crystals of SnO_2 doped with antimony. The crystals were grown from the gas phase. The attempts at obtaining single crystals with the hole conductance by doping with indium and gallium were not successful.

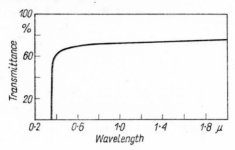

FIG. 15.1. Transmittance in single crystals SnO_2 at room temperature as a function of wavelength.[60]

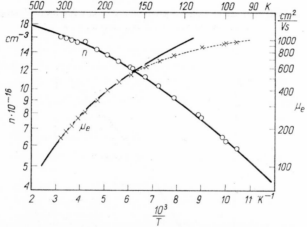

FIG. 15.2. The temperature dependence of Hall mobility μ_e and of electron concentration n in single crystals of SnO_2:[466] × —mobility. ○—electron concentration.

Figure 15.3 shows the temperature dependence of the Hall mobility taken from the data of Wright and Morgan.[467] At higher temperatures these authors observed the relation: $\mu_e \sim T^{-1/2}$. Figure 15.4 illustrates the temperature dependence of the Seebeck coefficient in SnO_2 doped with indium. They estimated the effective mass electrons in SnO_2 at high temperatures to be about 0·1m_0. At room temperature this value is somewhat higher. Summitt and Borelli[468] determined the electron effective mass in tin dioxide from the Faraday effect measurements. The value obtained was 0·14m_0.

Houston and Kohnke[469] analysed the scheme of the energy levels in SnO_2 single crystals with the photoelectric method.[470] The crystals were prepared by the molten salt method. Figure 15.5 is a schematic representation of the distribution of the trapping levels in SnO_2. The distance of the highest lying trapping level from the bottom of the

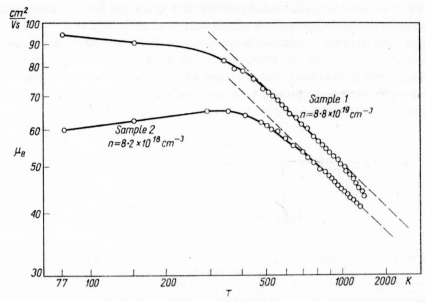

FIG. 15.3. Electron Hall mobility in single crystals of SnO_2 as a function of temperature;[467] the broken line represents the function $\mu_e \sim T^{-1/2}$.

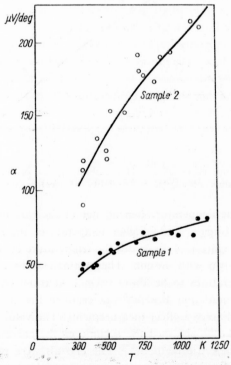

FIG. 15.4. Seebeck coefficient in single crystal of SnO_2 as a function of temperature;[467] the values of electron concentration for samples 1 and 2 are given in Fig. 15.3.

conduction band for the electrons is 0·21 eV. This level is stable and completely compensated. The two next trapping levels of the electrons are located at 0·52 and 0·60 eV from the bottom of the conduction band. The first of them is fully compensated, the second—only partially. In the upper part of the forbidden band there are presented three more levels at the distance of 1·0, 1·3 and 1·8 eV from the bottom of the conduction band. A stable trapping level for holes lies at 1·3 eV from the top of the valence band.[471] The forbidden energy gap determined by Houston and Kohnke is 4 eV.

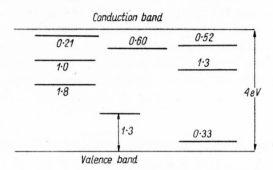

FIG. 15.5. Energy level scheme in SnO_2 as proposed by Houston and Kohnke.[469, 471] The energy values are given in eV.

Little is known about basic physical properties of SnO_2 and its band structure. The structure of native defects in SnO_2 is also unknown.

The electrical measurements imply that oxygen vacancies or interstitial tin atoms are the predominant defects. The mechanism of interaction of native defects and foreign atoms and the scattering mechanism in this oxide remain to be investigated. Nagasawa and co-workers suppose that at higher temperatures the scattering on acoustic phonons predominates, whereas Morgan and Wright assume that optical phonons act as the scattering species. One cannot obviously neglect the scattering by ionized donors, in particular at low temperatures.

More recent results concerning electrical and optical properties of SnO_2 have been published in the papers by Nagasawa and Shionoya[475, 588, 591, 592, 594, 595] and other authors. [589, 590, 596, 597]

Semiconducting and transparent films of SnO_2 are usually prepared by the three methods. The simplest of them consists in the chemical reaction of $SnCl_4$ with appropriately selected oxygen-containing compound (water, alcohol, etc.). The reaction may take place either in the gas phase or in the liquid state. The thin oxide film grows on the surface of the glass substrate heated to the appropriate temperature. The films grown by this method displayed large transparency up to 92%.[84] The electrical and optical properties of such films were studied by Koch.[472] He observed that in the range of the current carriers concentration from 10^{18} to 10^{20} cm^{-3}, i.e. in the region of the degeneracy, the relation $\sigma \sim n^{4/3}$ is held, in agreement with the theory of Howarth and Sondheimer,[410] which assumes the scattering of the current carriers by longitudinal optical phonons.

Highly-conductive films of SnO_2 of the carrier concentration of the order of 10^{19} cm^{-3} were prepared by the above method also by Arai.[473] He observed that antimony-doped thin films of SnO_2 are stable at higher temperatures (up to 1073 K), whereas the films of pure SnO_2 become unstable already at markedly lower temperatures. Ishiguro[474] found that the mobility of the current carriers in the films obtained by the chemical method was from 17 to 32 cm^2/Vs.

A convenient method for the preparation of the thin films of SnO_2 consists in the cathodic sputtering in the atmosphere of argon and oxygen of the appropriate composition.[84] With this method the transparent films of SnO_2 are obtained, of the electrical conductivity varying within the wide range, depending on the partial pressure of oxygen. It should be noted that with the cathodic sputtering method one may relatively easily obtain the doped films of SnO_2. The preparation with the above method of thin films of pure and doped SnO_2 and their properties were described recently by Vainshtein.[476] The electrical conductivity of these films is contained in the range from 10^{-8} to 10^2 ohm^{-1}cm^{-1}, depending on the preparation conditions and the addition concentration.

The third method of preparing thin films of SnO_2 is the vacuum evaporation method consisting in evaporation of powdered SnO_2.[477]

15.2. Silicon Oxides

Owing to the extensive applications of silicon oxides in electronics, the technology of their preparation and their electrical properties attract great attention. Most often these oxides are used in the form of films in integrated and hybrid microcircuits as capacitor dielectric, gate insulators for metal-insulator semiconductor field effect devices, insulators between layers of conductive films used for interconnections, for surface passivation, diffusion masks, etc.

Techniques developed for the preparation of such insulating films include r.f. reactive sputtering, vacuum evaporation, thermal and anodic oxidation, plasma anodization and chemical vapour deposition.

Two silicon oxides are usually distinguished, namely silicon monoxide SiO and silicon dioxide SiO_2, although some of the authors put in doubt the existence of the first of the oxides assuming that the stoichiometry corresponding to this oxide may be due to the mixture of silicon and silicon dioxide.[478, 479]

Since this problem has not been definitely solved as yet, in the further discussion we will distinguish both of the oxides. It should be, however, borne in mind that like other oxides, also silicon oxides exhibit deviations from stoichiometry and hence their chemical formula can be written as SiO_x where x may vary from 1 to 2.

The thin films of SiO can be relatively easily obtained by vacuum evaporation technique. Hill and Hoffman[480] showed that for preparation of the stable film of SiO the following conditions should be maintained:

(1) The partial pressures of oxygen and water vapour in the evaporation chamber should be very low, the rate of the film deposition being at the same time high. For

instance, at the rate of the film deposition of 10 Å/s the partial pressure of oxygen should be lower than 3.5×10^{-6} Tr, and the partial pressure of the water vapour lower than 2.5×10^{-6} Tr. To assure such the conditions silicon oxide has to be heated for about 2 hr at 1170 K prior to the evaporation.

(2) The angle of incidence of the SiO molecules on the substrate should be lower than 15°. If this condition is not fulfilled the films obtained are porous. Thus, to prepare a film of large surface area the appropriately large distance between the substrate and the source of the SiO vapour should be maintained.

(3) The temperature of the material under evaporation is not very important, however, it should not exceed 1670K since above this temperature SiO probably decomposes.

The films obtained under these conditions adhere well to the substrate and are stable at temperatures around room temperature. Volkenberg[481] reports also that the quality of the evaporated films of SiO depends on the rate of their deposition.

Hirose and Wada[482, 483] examined the current in a Al–SiO–Al capacitor as a function of potential and temperature. The surface area of the aluminium electrodes was 0.7 cm^2 and the thickness of the vacuum evaporated films of SiO was 2.3 μ. As seen from Fig. 15.6, the Ohm law is not obeyed with the exception of small potentials not exceeding 0.1 V. At low potential the resistivity of SiO was 1.5×10^{11} ohm cm.

Figure 15.7 is an illustration of the temperature dependence of the current I in this capacitor at different potentials. It follows from the plot that functions $\log I$ vs. $1/T$ are linear, with the slopes of the straight lines depending on the potential applied. Thus the activation energy is a function of the potential (Fig. 15.8).

It could be inferred that the non-ohmic behaviour of the $I = f(V)$ function at potentials higher than 0.1 V may be caused by the contact properties of the Al–SiO junctions. Hirose and Wada[482, 483] have shown, however, that the character of this function is the same also in the case of the gold electrodes. This implies that the deviation from the Ohm's law involves the bulk properties of SiO.

Hirose and Wada measured also the potentials at the capacitor plates as a function of the thickness of the SiO films at different values of the current. It has been found that the functions $V = f(d)$, where d is the thickness of the film, are linear, however the straight line do not pass through the origin of the coordinate system (Fig. 15.9). The linear character of the above function indicates that the electrical field in the film is uniform. The fact that the plots intersect the abscissa is ascribed to the presence of the Al_2O_3 film on the surface of an aluminium electrode before SiO is evaporated.

Hirose and Wada found that the current of the capacitor is at constant potential independent of time (up to 20 hr). This indicates that the conductance in SiO is electronic and not ionic.

Taking into account the shape of the $I = f(V)$ plot these authors distinguish three regions of the potential. In the first of them, up to 0.1 V, the Ohm's law is obeyed, the second region from 0.1 to 9 V is an intermediate region difficult to characterize, finally in the third region—above 9 V—the current is an exponential function of the square root of the potential.

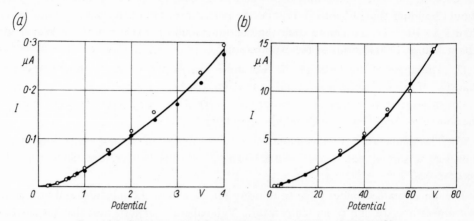

Fig. 15.6. Current–potential dependence in a SiO film at 291 K.[482]

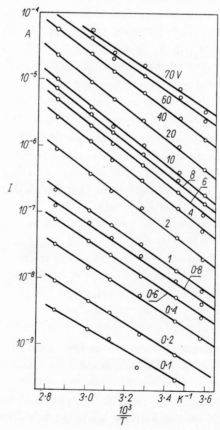

Fig. 15.7. Current in a SiO film as a function of reciprocal temperature at different potentials.[482]

Johansen[484] studied the electrical properties of the Al–SiO_x–Al system, where x was between 1 and 2. The preparations were obtained by vacuum evaporation method. The source of the vapours was provided by powdered SiO_x or the SiO_2 + Si mixture. The thickness of the SiO_x films under study was from 0·1 to 1 μ. The electrical conductivity of such films was measured as a function of the electric field and temperature.

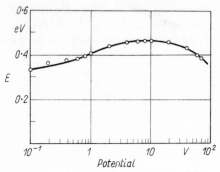

FIG. 15.8. Activation energy as a function of potential in a SiO film.[482]

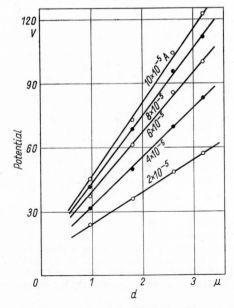

FIG. 15.9. Potential in a SiO film as a function of the film thickness for different currents at 303·5 K.[482]

Johansen found that the electrical conductivity of the SiO_x films increases with the increasing temperature of the substrate. He also observed that the electrical conductivity of the SiO_x depends on the thermal treatment of the thin films evaporated (Fig. 15.10) decreasing after such the treatment in air. The results obtained by Johansen on the dependence of the electrical conductivity on the electric field are in agreement with the earlier data of Hirose and Wada. Similar behaviour was also reported by Hartman, Blair and Bauer.[485]

Stuart[486] re-examined the dependence of the current on potential in SiO films of different thickness from 400 to 7000 Å. Aluminium electrodes were again used in these measurements. The pressure in the evaporation chamber was 10^{-6} Tr. Silicon oxide was evaporated from the silica crucible heated by the tungsten filament. The rate of the film growth was 20 Å/s.

The measurements were carried out at room temperature under the pressure of 5×10^{-3} Tr. Their results are shown in Fig. 15.11. From the temperature dependence of the current Stuart estimated the activation energy to be 0.4 eV.

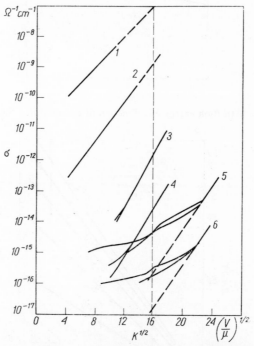

Fig. 15.10. Electrical conductivity in a SiO_2 film as a function of electric field for films prepared in different conditions:[484] 1—SiO_x films evaporated from SiO powder under the pressure of 10^{-6} Tr, 2—sample 1 heated for 2 hr at 473 K in air, 3—films evaporated from SiO powder under the oxygen pressure of 10^{-4} Tr, 4—films 3 heated for 2 hr at 473 K in air, 5 films of SiO_x obtained by evaporation of powder containing 68% SiO_2 and 32% Si under the oxygen pressure of 10^{-4} Tr, 6—sample 5 heated at 473 K for 2 hr in air.

Koide and Abe[487] investigated thin films of SiO obtained by the vacuum evaporation method. The rate of the film deposition was 30–50 Å/s. They found that the dielectric constant of SiO is independent of the film thickness up to 2000 Å.

The dielectric losses, on the other hand, increase with decreasing film thickness.

An important problem occurring in the technique of insulating films is the knowledge of their breakdown electrical properties. Extensive studies on this problem have been carried out by Budenstein et al.[544] who studied these properties in thin films capacitors with the dielectrics of SiO and with other materials. The capacitors were formed on glass substrates and had dielectric thickness from 900 to 16,000 Å. The cited authors

have shown that at temperature range 80–380 K breakdown characteristics are independent of pre-breakdown a.c. and d.c. condition. SiO show a threshold field for the onset
of breakdown of the order of 10^6 V/cm that is almost temperature independent and
varies with dielectric thickness d approximately as $d^{-1/2}$. This material have also
a threshold voltage for the cessation of breakdown which is typically between 10 and
20 V. The electrical resistance during breakdown remains nearly constant until the
voltage threshold for the cessation of breakdown is approached. The authors have
also observed that light is emitted during destructive breakdown. The spectral distribution of this light shows that it is produced by gaseous atoms and ions of the dielectric

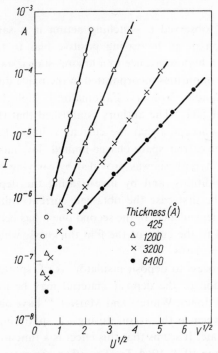

FIG. 15.11. Current in a SiO film as a function of potential for different film thickness.[486]

and of the materials of the two electrodes. Budenstein *et al.* have concluded that the
high conductance during breakdown is due to the gaseous arc, and this mechanism
accounts directly for the high current during breakdown, and the destruction of the
dielectric.

Silicon dioxide has the widest application as an insulating film, the most commonly
used processing method being thermal oxidation. Chou and Eldridge[545] have shown
that electrical breakdown characteristics of SiO_2 films thermally grown on silicon
depend strongly on oxide preparation and various subsequent treatments. According
to these authors a lowering of the concentration of mobile impurities reduces the
occurrence of defect-related breakdowns but it does not change the magnitude of the
intrinsic breakdown strength of this oxide. On the other hand, appropriate phospho-

silicate glassing—prepared by alloying the surface of SiO_2 with P_2O_5—not only effectively obliterates oxide defects but also raises the intrinsic strength of the films. Under identical silicon dioxide growth conditions, reduction of film thickness is accompanied by an increase in the density of oxide defects. High defect density in SiO_2 gives rise to a time dependence of the breakdown characteristics and can therefore lower the magnitude of the primary breakdown strength. The amount of glassing required for eliminating this effect is greater for SiO_2 films which have initially a higher defect density. The above observations are consistent with Fritzsche's breakdown model[546] which implies that processing steps promoting local crystallization of the oxide will result in an increase in defect-related breakdown, while glassing has an opposite and beneficial effect.

Lamb and Rundle[547] observed a switching action in a sandwich structure of Si–SiO_2–Al. The application of an increasing positive bias to the aluminium electrode results in a change from a high resistance to a low-resistance state. The authors assumed that it is associated with impurities incorporated in the oxide during device preparation.

Brander, Lamb and Rundle[548] observed anomalously high electrical currents through thermally grown films of SiO_2. The authors established that the current is not due to ionic transport and they accepted that the current–voltage characteristics can be best explained in terms of one carrier space charge-limited flow modified by traps. Further evidence to support this hypothesis was provided by carrying out conduction measurements under pulsed conditions, and by investigating the dependence of the current on films thickness. In the first case the obtained current–voltage characteristics have the expected square law dependence. In the second one it has been found that the current is inversely proportional to the cube of the film thickness, which is in agreement with the above-mentioned hypothesis.

Interesting vacuum process to deposit insulators is r.f. sputtering, wherein generally, stoichiometric composition of the deposit material may be maintained after transfer from source-to-substrate. Jones, Winters and Maissel[549] have observed that the addition of small amounts of oxygen to the argon during r.f. sputtering of SiO_2 leads to large decreases in deposition rate. It seems that this effect is a function of the partial pressure of the oxygen in the range 10^{-6}–10^{-4} Tr. The effect saturates at a partial pressure of about 5×10^{-4} Tr. The cited authors have explained these observations as owing to the replacement of oxygen atoms sputtered off the SiO_2 target electrode. Saturation occurs when the replacement rate is much faster than the removal rate. Thus the surface being sputtered is, effectively, always a monolayer of oxygen. Since the deposition rate at saturation is about 45% the rate in pure argon, it seems that about half the silicon atoms sputtered out of the SiO_2 target originate below the surface.

Pratt[550] found that silicon dioxide films obtained by r.f. sputtering technique indicate, generally, physical characteristics which are comparable to their counterparts formed by other methods. The deposited films were amorphous in structure. The breakdown strength were found to be thickness dependent. The sputtered SiO_2 films permit the fabrication of good capacitor structures with relatively large size electrodes.

Thin SiO_2 films can be also obtained by anodic oxidation. The dielectric breakdown of such films has been studied by Fritzsche.[551] The author has found that avalanche multiplication of electrons and ionic conductivity are closely related. This supports the impact ionization theory of anodization published in work.[552] Fritzsche[551] gives an improved theory which supplies equations for efficiency of anodization, growth at constant current, and current decay at constant voltage. This theory has been found to be in excellent agreement with experimental data.

The band structure of the MOS structures of the Si–SiO$_2$ type is not well understood as yet. Some data concerning this problem can be found in ref. 553.

The self-diffusion coefficient of oxygen in SiO$_2$ was investigated by many authors.[598-603] Like for other oxides, the values of ΔH found differed considerably, ranging from 29 to 71·2 kcal/mole.

An interesting technique of manufacturing semiconductor devices, e.g. discrete devices and integrated circuits, is the use of doped oxides as diffusion sources.[604-607] The principle underlying this method consists in that the oxide with a controlled concentration of dopant is deposited or grown directly on the substrate at a temperature well below that where any detectable diffusion takes place. The substrate is then heated to a higher diffusion temperature, normally in an inert ambient atmosphere, and the diffusion proceeds for a controlled length of time. After the diffusion process is terminated the doped oxide may either be removed or left on the substrate to act as a barrier to subsequent diffusion and as a passivating dielectric.

METHODS OF GROWING SINGLE CRYSTALS OF OXIDES

No.	Oxide	Method	References
1	Al_2O_3	Czochralsky technique	24, 37
2		Verneuil	24, 29, 491
		floating zone technique	24
		molten salt method	24, 492
		hydrothermal	493
		growth from the gas phase	494
	Al_2O_3 + Co, Mg	molten salt method	495
	BaO	Verneuil	31
		growth from the gas phase	496
3	BeO	molten salt method	497
		hydrothermal	498
4	CdO	growth from the gas phase	24, 413, 499
5	CeO_2	molten salt method	501, 502, 503
6	CoO	growth from the gas phase	504
7	Cr_2O_3	epitaxial growth	505
8	Cu_2O	hydrothermal	506
		from molten system Cu–O	507,612
		oxidation of copper	508
9	Er_2O_3	Verneuil	29, 509
10	EuO	from molten system EuO–Eu	510
11	FeO	growth from the gas phase	194
12	Fe_2O_3	molten salt method	512, 513
		chemical transport	514
13	Fe_3O_4	Czochralsky technique	36
		Horn technique	40
		growth from the gas phase	515
14	Ga_2O_3	molten salt method	516, 517
15	HfO_2	molten salt method	518
16	HgO	from solution	519
17	MgO	growth from the gas phase	520
18	MnO	Verneuil	521
19	Mn_3O_4	Verneuil	522
20	Nd_2O_3	Verneuil	29
21	MoO_2	oxidation of molybdenum	523
22	MoO_3	growth from the gas phase	524
23	NiO	Verneuil	525
24	SiO_2	hydrothermal	50
25	SnO_2	growth from the gas phase	60, 526
		hydrothermal	24
		molten salt method	527
26	SrO	Verneuil	31
27	TeO_2		528
28	TiO_2	floating zone technique	45
		Verneuil	24, 29
		hydrothermal	24
		molten salt method	529, 530

No.	Oxide	Method	References
29	ThO_2	molten salt method	502
30	UO_2	floating zone technique	44
31	U_4O_9		531
32	V_2O_5	growth from the gas phase	532, 533
33	VO_2	growth from the gas phase	532, 534, 535
		from solution	536
		chemical transport	537
		epitaxial growth	538
34	VO_3	growth from the gas phase	524
35	V_3O_5	growth from the gas phase	532
36	V_2O_3	growth from the gas phase	532
		Verneuil	536
37	WO_2	growth from the gas phase	539
38	Y_2O_3	Verneuil	509
39	Yb_2O_3	Verneuil	509
40	ZnO	growth from the gas phase	540, 541, 608-611
		hydrothermal	360, 542
41	ZrO_3	Verneuil	29

REFERENCES

1. P. CHARPENTIER, P. DESCHAMPS and J. MANENC, *C. R. Acad. Sci. (France)* **265 C**, 69 (1967).
2. J. A. BURTON, R. C. PRIM and W. P. SLICHTER, *J. Chem. Phys.* **21**, 1987 (1953).
3. W. G. PFANN, *Zone Melting*, J. Wiley, New York; Chapman & Hall, London, 1958.
4. W. D. LAWSON and S. NIELSEN, *Preparation of Single Crystals*, Butterworths, London, 1958.
5. W. PARRISH, *Philips Tech. Rev.* **17**, 269 (1956).
6. M. G. INGHRAM, *J. Phys. Chem.* **57**, 809 (1953).
7. A. J. SOCHA, *J. Vacuum Sci. Technol.* **7**, 310 (1970).
8. G. W. C. MILNER and L. J. SLEE, *Ind. Chemist*, **33**, 494 (1957).
9. J. B. MULLIN, *J. Electronics Control*, **4**, 358 (1958).
10. B. A. THOMPSON, B. M. STRAUSS and M. B. LEBOEUF, *Analyt. Chem.* **30**, 1023 (1958).
11. G. LIBOWITZ, *J. Amer. Chem. Soc.* **75**, 1501 (1953).
12. H. J. ALSOPP, *Analyst*, **82**, 474 (1957).
13. J. DEREŃ, J. HABER and J. SŁOCZYŃSKI, *Chem. Anal.* **6**, 659 (1961).
14. I. M. KOLTHOFF and J. E. BELCHER, *Volumetric Analysis*, Vol. 3, p. 53, Interscience, New York, 1957.
15. H. J. ENGELL, *Z. Elektrochem.* **60**, 905 (1956).
16. H. G. SOCKEL and H. SCHMALZRIED, *Ber. Bunsengesell. Phys. Chem.* **72**, 745 (1968).
17. Y. D. TRETYAKOV and R. A. RAPP, *AIME Trans.* **245**, 1235 (1969).
18. B. FISHER and D. S. TANNHAUSER, *J. Chem. Phys.* **44**, 1663 (1966).
19. N. G. EROR and J. B. WAGNER, JR., *J. Phys. Chem. Solids*, **29**, 1597 (1968).
20. W. B. A. SHARP and D. MORTIMER, *J. Phys. E*, **1**, 843 (1968).
21. F. A. KRÖGER, *J. Phys. Chem. Solids*, **7**, 277 (1958).
22. R. A. LAUDISE, *Bell. Lab. Record*, **40**, 244 (1962).
23. E. A. D. WHITE, *J. Appl. Phys.* **16**, 1415 (1965).
24. H. S. PEISER, ed., *Proc. Intern. Conf. on Crystal Growth*, Boston, 1966, Pergamon Press, Oxford, 1967; *J. Phys. Chem. Solids*, Sup. No. 1 (1967).
    A. C. PASTOR, *Materials Res. Bull.* **1**, 205 (1966).
    R. C. PASTOR and A. C. PASTOR, *Materials Res. Bull.* **1**, 275 (1966).
25. KEN-ICHI SHIROKI, *Rev. Sci. Instrum.* **38**, 1541 (1967).
26. P. H. KECK, *Rev. Sci. Instrum.* **25**, 298 (1959).
27. W. H. BAUER and W. G. FIELD, *The Art and Science of Growing Crystals*, J. J. GILMAN, ed., p. 398, J. Wiley, New York, 1963.
28. R. E. DE LA RUE and F. A. HALDEN, *Rev. Sci. Instrum.* **31**, 35 (1960).
29. F. A. HALDEN and R. SEDLACEK, *Rev. Sci. Instrum.* **34**, 622 (1963).
30. T. B. REED, *J. Appl. Phys.* **32**, 821, 2534 (1961).
31. R. J. GAMBINO, *J. Appl. Phys.* **36**, 656 (1965).
32. D. I. WILLIAMS and W. A. SMITH, *J. Amer. Ceram. Soc.* **51**, 32 (1968).
33. T. B. REED and W. J. LA FLEUR, *Appl. Phys. Letters*, **5**, 191 (1964).
34. F. ORDWAY and P. R. MILLER, *Bull. Amer. Ceram. Soc.* **43**, 253 (1964).
35. M. TANENBAUM, in *Semiconductors*, N. B. HANNAY, ed., Reinhold Publ. Corp., New York; Chapman & Hall, London, 1959.
36. F. H. HORN, *J. Appl. Phys.* **32**, 900 (1961).
37. A. E. PALADINO and B. D. ROITER, *J. Amer. Ceram. Soc.* **47**, 465 (1964).
38. F. H. HORN, *J. Electrochem. Soc.*, **105**, 393 (1958).

39. R. P. POPLAWSKY and J. E. THOMAS, Jr., *Rev. Sci. Instrum.* **31**, 1303 (1960).
40. R. P. POPLAWSKY, *J. Appl. Phys.* **33**, 1616 (1962).
41. D. TRIVICH and G. P. POLLACK, *J. Electrochem. Soc.* **117**, 345 (1970).
42. J. J. BARLIC, *J. Sci. Instrum.* **42**, 361 (1965).
43. D. B. GASSON, *J. Sci. Instrum.* **42**, 114 (1965).
44. A. T. CHAPMAN and G. W. CLARK, *J. Amer. Ceram. Soc.* **48**, 494 (1965).
45. J. HOLT, *Brit. J. Appl. Phys.* **16**, 639 (1965).
46. D. G. GASSON and B. COCKAYNE, *J. Materials Sci.* **117**, 345 (1970).
47. G. CRONIN, M. JONES and O. WILSON, *J. Electrochem. Soc.*, **110**, 582 (1963).
48. H. A. C. HEDZEY and D. T. J. HURLE, *Brit. J. Appl. Phys.* **17**, 699 (1966).
49. S. V. AIRAPETYANTS and G. J. SHMELEV, *Soviet Phys. Solid State*, **2**, 689 (1960).
50. A. A. BALLMAN and R. A. LAUDISE, *The Art and Science of Growing Crystals*, J. J. GILMAN, ed., p. 231, J. Wiley, New York, 1963.
51. A. KREMHELLER and A. K. LEVINE, *J. Appl. Phys.* **28**, 746 (1957).
52. R. A. LAUDISE, *The Art and Science of Growing Crystals*, J. J. GILMAN, ed., p. 252, J. Wiley, New York, 1963.
53. R. A. LAUDISE, R. C. LINARES and E. F. DEARBORN, *J. Appl. Phys.* **33**, 1362 (1962).
54. T. TSUSHIMA, *J. Appl. Phys.* **37**, 443 (1966).
55. W. H. GRODKIEWICZ and D. J. NITTI, *J. Amer. Ceram. Soc.* **49**, 576 (1966).
56. G. A. WOLFF and H. E. LaBELLE, Jr., *J. Amer. Ceram. Soc.* **48**, 441 (1965).
57. F. A. KRÖGER, *The Chemistry of Imperfect Crystals*, p. 37, North-Holland Publ. Co., Amsterdam, 1964.
58. R. L. SPROULL, W. C. DASH, W. W. TYLER and A. R. MOOSE, *Rev. Sci. Instrum.* **22**, 410 (1951).
59. E. M. DODSON and J. A. SAVAGE, *J. Materials Sci.* **3**, 19 (1968); **4**, 809 (1969).
60. NAGASAWA *et. al.*, *Japan. J. Appl. Phys.* **4**, 195 (1965).
61. H. SCHÄFFER, *Chemical Transport Reactions*, Academic Press, New York, 1964.
62. A. RABENAU and H. RAU, *Z. Phys. Chem. (Frankfurt)*, **1**, 155 (1967).
63. C. VAN DE STOLPE, *J. Phys. Chem. Solids*, **27**, 1952 (1966).
64. P. B. CLAPHAM, *Brit. J. Appl. Phys.* **18**, 363 (1967).
65. L. I. MAISSEL, in *Physics of Thin Films*, G. HASS and R. E. THUN, eds., vol. 3, p. 61, Pergamon Press, New York and London, 1966.
66. N. W. PLESHIVTSEV, *Katodnye raspyleniye (Cathodic Sputtering)*, Atomizdat, Moscow, 1968.
67. M. L. LIEBERMAN and R. C. MEDRUD, *J. Electrochem. Soc.* **116**, 242 (1969).
68. W. A. GRANT and G. CARTER, *Vacuum*, **15**, 477 (1965).
69. J. M. SEEMAN, *Vacuum*, **17**, 129 (1967).
70. J. M. SEEMAN, *Trans. 8th AVS, Nat. Vac. Symp. on Metallurgy*, New York, 1965.
71. N. SCHWARTZ, *Trans. 10th AVS, Nat. Vac. Symp.* Macmillan, New York, 1963, p. 324.
72. D. GERSTENBERG, *Bell Lab. Record*, 365 (1964).
73. G. K. WEHNER, *Advances in Electronics and Electron Physics*, **7**, 239 (1955).
74. G. S. ANDERSON, W. N. MAYER and G. K. WEHNER, *J. Appl. Phys.* **33**, 2991 (1962).
75. R. V. STUART and G. K. WEHNER, *J. Appl. Phys.* **33**, 2345 (1962).
76. P. D. DAVIDSE and L. I. MAISSEL, *J. Appl. Phys.* **37**, 574 (1966).
77. H. S. BUTLER and G. S. KINO, *Phys. of Fluids*, **6**, 1346 (1963)
78. P. D. DAVIDSE, *Vacuum*, **17**, 139 (1967).
79. I. H. PRATT, *AIME Trans.* **242**, 526 (1968).
80. L. HOLLAND, T. PUTNER and G. N. JACKSON, *J. Sci. Instrum.* Ser. 2, **1**, 32 (1968).
81. H. C. COOK, C. W. COVINGTON and J. F. LIBSCH, *AIME Trans.* **236**, 314 (1966).
82. C. E. ROSSI and W. PAUL, *J. Phys. Chem. Solids*, **30**, 2295 (1969).
83. N. MANDANI and K. G. NICHOLS, *J. Phys. D*, **3**, L 7 (1970).
84. L. HOLLAND, *Vacuum Deposition of Thin Films*, Chapman & Hall, London, 1958.
85. L. YOUNG, *Anodic Oxide Films*, Academic Press, London–New York, 1961.
86. J. L. MILES and P. H. SMITH, *J. Electrochem. Soc.* **110**, 1240 (1963).
87. J. F. O'HANLON, *J. Vacuum Sci. Technol.* **7**, 330 (1970).
88. T. A. JENNINGS and W. MCNEILL, *J. Electrochem. Soc.* **114**, 1134 (1967).
89. T. A. JENNINGS and W. MCNEILL, *Appl. Phys. Letters*, **12**, 25 (1968).
90. L. D. LOCKER and L. P. SKOLNICK, *Appl. Phys. Letters*, **12**, 396 (1968).
91. A. E. FEUERSANGER, *Proc. IEEE*, **52**, 1463 (1964).
92. N. GOLDSMITH and W. KERN, *RCA Rev.* **28**, 153 (1967).
93. M. L. HAMMOND and G. M. BOWERS, *AIME Trans.* **242**, 546 (1968).

94. T. L. CHU, J. R. SZEDON and G. A. GRUBER, *AIME Trans.* **242**, 532 (1968).
95. C. G. FONSTAD, A. LINZ and R. H. REDIKER, *J. Electrochem. Soc.*, **116**, 1269 (1969).
96. R. G. LIVESEY, E. LYFORD and H. MOORE, *J. Phys. E*, **1**, 947 (1968).
97. L. V. GREGOR, in *Physics of Thin Films*, G. HASS and R. E. THUN, eds., vol. 3, p. 131, Pergamon Press, New York–London, 1966.
98. M. YOKOZAWA, H. IWASA and I. TERAMOTO, *Japan. J. Appl. Phys.* **7**, 96 (1968).
99. M. OHNISHI, M. YOSHIZAWA and S. IBUKI, *Japan. J. Appl. Phys.* **9**, 412 (1970).
100. G. A. BASSETT,, J. W. MENTER and D. W. PASHLEY, *Structure and Properties of Thin Films*, C. NEUGEBAUER *et al.*, eds., p. 11, J. Wiley, New York, 1959.
101. M. H. FRANCOMBE and H. SATO, eds., *Single-crystal Films*, Proc. of an Intern. Conf. held at Philco Scientific Laboratory, Blue Bell, Pensylvania, May 1963. Symposium Publications Division, Pergamon Press, Oxford, 1964.
102. D. W. PASHLEY, *Advances in Phys. (GB)*, **14**, 327 (1965).
103. O. A. WEINREICH, *J. Appl. Phys.* **37**, 2924 (1966).
104. D. L. DEXTER and R. S. KNOX, *Excitons*, J. Wiley, New York, 1965.
105. J. M. BURGERS, *Proc. K. Ned. Acad. Wetensch.* **42**, 293, 378, Amsterdam, 1939.
106. F. C. FRANK, *Phil. Mag.* **42, 809** (1951).
107. F. C. FRANK and W. T. READ, *Phys. Rev.* **79**, 722 (1950).
108. J. M. BURGERS, *Proc. Phys. Soc.* **52**, 23 (1940).
109. W. L. BRAGG, *Proc. Phys. Soc.* **52**, 54 (1940).
110. W. SHOCKLEY and W. T. READ, *Phys. Rev.* **75**, 692 (1949); **78**, 275 (1950).
111. R. G. RHODES, *Imperfections and Active Centers in Semiconductors*, Pergamon Press, Oxford, 1964.
112. H. G. VAN BUEREN, *Imperfections in Crystals*, North-Holland Publ., Co., Amsterdam, 1961.
113. W. SHOCKLEY *et al.* eds., *Imperfections in Nearly Perfect Crystals*, J. Wiley, New York; Chapman & Hall, London, 1952.
114. W. T. READ, JR., *Dislocations in Crystals*, McGraw-Hill, New York, 1953.
115. G. G. LIBOWITZ, *Energetics in Metallurgical Phenomena*, W. M. MUELLER, ed., Gordon & Breach, New York, 1968.
116. C. WAGNER and W. SCHOTTKY, *Z. Phys. Chem. B*, **11**, 163 (1930).
117. C. WAGNER, *Z. Phys. Chem. Bodenstein-Festband*, p. 177 (1931); *Z. Phys. Chem. B*, **22**, 181 (1933)
118. R. A. SMITH, *Semiconductors*, Cambridge University Press, 1961.
119. F. A. KRÖGER, H. J. VINK and J. VAN DEN BOOMGAARD, *Z. Phys. Chem. B*, **203**, 1 (1954).
120. F. A. KRÖGER and H. J. VINK, in *Solid State Physics*, F. SEITZ and D. TURNBULL, eds., vol. 3, p. 307, Academic Press, New York, 1956.
121. G. BROUWER, *Philips Res. Rep.* **9**, 366 (1954).
122. R. F. BREBRICK, in *Progress in Solid State Chemistry*, H. REISS, ed., vol. 3, p. 213, Pergamon Press, Oxford, 1966.
123. J. TELTOW, *Ann. Physik*, **5**, 63, 71 (1949).
124. I. EBERT and J. TELTOW, *Ann. Physik*, **15**, 268 (1955).
125. A. B. LILIARD, *Phys. Rev.* **94**, 29 (1954); *Repts. Conf. on Defects in Crystalline Solids*, Univ. Bristol, 1954, p. 283 (1955).
126. G. G. LIBOWITZ, *J. Phys. Chem. Solids*, **28**, 1145 (1967).
127. G. G. LIBOWITZ, *J. Solid State Chem.* **1**, 50 (1969).
128. J. G. KIRKWOOD and I. OPPENHEIM, *Chemical Thermodynamics*, McGraw-Hill, New York, 1961.
129. R. H. BUBE, *Photoconductivity of Solids*, J. Wiley, New York, 1960.
130. W. ALBERS, C. HAAS and H. J. VINK, *Philips Res. Rep.* **18**, 372 (1963).
131. J. W. MITCHELL, *J. Appl. Phys.* **33**, Suppl., 406 (1962).
132. A. F. IOFFE, *Physics of Semiconductors*, Onfosearch Limited, London, 1960.
133. T. HOLSTEIN, *Ann. Phys. (USA)*, **8**, 343 (1959).
134. G. L. SEWELL, *Proc. Phys. Soc.* **76**, 987 (1960).
135. G. L. SEWELL, *Phys. Rev.* **129**, 597 (1963).
136. L. FRIEDMAN, *Phys. Rev. A*, **133**, 1668; **135**, A 233 (1964).
137. M. I. KLINGER, *Phys. Status Solidi*, **27**, 479 (1968).
138. I. G. LANG, *Fiz. Tverdogo Tela*, **10**, 2381 (1968).
139. J. SCHNAKENBERG, *Phys. Status Solidi*, **28**, 623 (1968).
140. J. APPEL, Polarons, in *Solid State Physics*, vol. 21, p. 193, F. SEITZ, D. TURNBULL and H. EHRENREICH, eds., Academic Press, New York and London, 1968.
141. R. R. HEIKES and W. D. JOHNSTON, *J. Chem. Phys.* **26**, 582 (1957).
142. J. R. MANNING, *Diffusion Kinetics for Atoms in Crystals*, D. van Nostrand, London, 1968.

143. B. I. BOLTAKS, *Diffusiya w poluprovodnikach* (*Diffusion in Semiconductors*), Gos. Izd. Fiz.-Mat. Literatury, Moscow, 1961.
144. L. A. GIRIFALCO, *Atomic Migration in Crystals*, Blaisdell Publ. Co., New York, Toronto, London, 1964.
145. N. F. MOTT and R. W. GURNEY, *Electronic Processes in Ionic Crystals*, p. 34, Oxford University Press, 1953.
146. M. O'KEEFFE, Intern. Conf., *Sintering and Related Phenomena*, G. C. KUCZYŃSKI, ed., Gordon & Breach, New York, 57 (1967).
147. C. WAGNER, *Z. Phys. Chem.* **B 21**, 25 (1933); **B 32**, 447 (1936).
148. C. WAGNER, *A.S.M. Symposium, Atom Movements*, Cleveland, p. 153 (1951).
149. C. WAGNER, *J. Phys. Chem. Solids*, **29**, 1925 (1968).
150. R. F. BREBRICK, *J. Appl. Phys.* **30**, 911 (1959).
151. L. S. DARKEN, *Trans. AIME*, **175**, 184 (1948).
152. J. R. MANNING, *Phys. Rev.* **139 A**, 126 (1965); *Acta Met.* **15**, 817 (1967).
153. J. B. PRICE, Ph. D. Thesis, Nothwestern University (1968).
154. G. SLACK, *J. Appl. Phys.* **31**, 1571 (1960).
155. M. W. VERNON and M. C. LOVELL, *J. Phys. Chem. Solids*, **27**, 1125 (1966).
156. F. J. MORIN, *Phys. Rev.* **93**, 1199 (1954).
157. E. J. W. VERWEY, *Chem. Weekblad*, **44**, 705 (1948).
158. J. H. DE BOER and E. J. W. VERWEY, *Proc. Phys. Soc.* **49**, 59 (1937).
159. E. J. W. VERWEY, *Semiconducting Materials*, pp. 151–161, Butterworths, London, 1951.
160. F. J. MORIN, *Phys, Rev.* **83**, 1005 (1951).
161. F. J. MORIN, *Phys. Rev.* **93**, 1195, 1199 (1954).
162. F. J. MORIN, *Bell Syst. Tech. J.* **37**, 1047 (1958).
163. F. J. MORIN, in *Semiconductors*, N. M. HANNAY, ed., Reinhold Publ. Co., New York, 1959.
164. G. PARRAVANO, *J. Chem. Phys.* **23**, 5 (1954).
165. R. R. HEIKES, A. A. MARADUDIN and R. C. MILLER, *Ann. Phys.* (*France*), **8**, 733 (1963).
166. S. VAN HOUTEN, *J. Chem. Phys. Solids*, **17**, 7 (1960).
167. S. FUJIME, M. MURAKAMI and E. HIRAHARA, *J. Phys. Soc. Japan*, **16**, 183 (1961).
168. S. KOIDE, *J. Phys. Soc. Japan*, **20**, 123 (1965).
169. M. NACHMAN, L. N. COJOCARU and L. V. RIBCO, *Phys. Status Solidi*, **8**, 773 (1965).
170. YA. M. KSENDZOV, L. N. ANSELM, L. L. VASIL'EVA and V. M. LATYSHEVA, *Soviet Phys. Solid State*, **5**, 1116 (1963).
171. V. P. ZHUZE and A. I. SHELYKH, *Soviet Phys. Solid State*, **5**, 1278 (1963).
172. M. ROILOS and P. NAGELS, *Solid State Commun.* **2**, 285 (1964).
173. J. ZIÓŁKOWSKI, *Bull. Acad. Polon. Sci.*, *Sér. Sci. Chim.* **16**, 195, 203 (1968).
174. A. J. BOSMAN, H. J. VAN DAAL and G. F. KNUVERS, *Phys. Letters*, **19**, 372 (1965).
175. A. J. SPRINGTHORPE, I. G. AUSTIN and B. A. SMITH, *Solid State Commun.* **3**, 143 (1965); *Phys. Letters*, **21**, 20 (1966).
176. A. J. BOSMAN and C. CREVECOEUR, *Phys. Rev.* **144**, 763 (1966).
177. S. P. MITOFF, *J. Chem. Phys.* **35**, 882 (1961).
178. YA. M. KSENDZOV, B. K. AVDEENKO and V. V. MAKAROV, *Soviet Phys. Solid State*, **9**, 828 (1967).
179. I. G. AUSTIN, A. J. SPRINGTHORPE, B. A. SMITH and C. E. TURNER, *Proc. Phys. Soc.* **90**, 157 (1967).
180. V. V. MAKAROV, YA. M. KSENDZOV, and V. I. KRUGLOV, *Soviet Phys. Solid State*, **9**, 512 (1967).
181. H. J. VAN DAAL and A. J. BOSMAN, *Phys. Rev.* **158**, 736 (1967).
182. J. G. AIKEN and A. G. JORDAN, *J. Phys. Chem. Solids*, **29**, 2153 (1968).
183. S. KABASHIMA and T. KAWAKUBO, *J. Phys. Soc. Japan*, **24**, 493 (1968).
184. D. ADLER, in *Solid State Physics*, F. SEITZ, D. TURNBULL and H. EHRENREICH, eds., vol. 21, p. 1 (1968).
185. I. G. AUSTIN, B. D. CLAY and C. E. TURNER, *J. Phys. C* (*Proc. Phys. Soc.*), Ser. 2, **1**, 1418 (1968).
186. I. G. AUSTIN and N. F. MOTT, *Advances in Phys.* **18**, 41 (1969).
187. J. FEINLEIB and D. ADLER, *Phys. Rev. Letters*, **21**, 1010 (1968).
188. R. NEWMAN and R. M. CHRENKO, *Phys. Rev.* **114**, 1507 (1959).
189. YA. M. KSENDZOV and I. A. DRABKIN, *Soviet Phys. Solid State*, **7**, 1519 (1965).
190. H. H. V. BAUMBACH and C. WAGNER, *Z. Phys. Chem.* **B 24**, 59 (1934).
191. S. PIZZINI and R. MORLOTTI, *J. Electrochem. Soc.* **114**, 1179 (1967).
192. R. UNO, *J. Phys. Soc. Japan*, **22**, 1502 (1967).
193. I. BRANSKY and N. M. TALLAN, *J. Chem. Phys.* **49**, 1243 (1968).
194. R. E. CECH and E. I. ALESSANDRINI, *Trans. Amer. Soc. Metals*, **51**, 150 (1959).

195. N. G. EROR and J. B. WAGNER JR., *Phys. Status Solidi*, **35**, 641 (1969).

196. J. T. COX and C. M. QUINN, *J. Materials Sci.* **4**, 33 (1969).

197. J. DEREŃ, Z. M. JARZĘBSKI, S. MROWEC and T. WALEC, *Bull. Acad. Polon. Sci., Sér. Sci. Chim.* **19**, 147 (1971).

198. M. L. VOLPE and J. REDDY, *J. Chem. Phys.* **53**, 1117 (1970).

199. T. B. REED and E. R. POLLARD, *J. Cryst. Growth*, **2**, 243 (1968).

200. J. C. BRICE, G. W. LELIEVRE and P. A. C. WHIFFIN, *J. Phys.* E, **2**, 1063 (1969).

201. Z. M. JARZĘBSKI and S. MROWEC, *Oxidation of Metals*, **1**, 267 (1969).

202. N. M. TALLAN and D. S. TANNHAUSER, *Phys. Letters*, **26** A, 131 (1968).

203. J. DEREŃ, Z. M. JARZĘBSKI and S. RUSIECKI, *Zeszyty Naukowe AGH*, Ceramika **18**, 57 (1971).

204. Z. M. JARZĘBSKI, *Acta Phys. Polon.* A**42**, 371 (1972).

205. M. T. SHIM and W. J. MOORE, *J. Chem. Phys.* **26**, 802 (1957).

206. R. LINDNER and A. ÅKERSTRÖM, *Disc. Faraday Soc.* **23**, 133 (1957).

207. J. S. CHOI and W. J. MOORE, *J. Phys. Chem.* **66**, 1308 (1962).

208. S. M. KLOTSMANN, A. N. TIMOFEYEV and I. SH. TRAKTENBERG, *Phys. Metals Metallography*, **14**, 91 (1962).

209. F. Y. WANG, *J. Appl. Phys.* **37**, 929 (1966).

210. M. O'KEEFFE and W. J. MOORE, *J. Phys. Chem.* **65**, 1438 (1961).

211. K. FUEKI and J. B. WAGNER, *J. Electrochem. Soc.* **112**, 384 (1965).

212. J. B. PRICE and J. B. WAGNER, *Z. Phys. Chem.* (*Frankfurt*) **49** S, 257 (1966).

213. J. DEREŃ, Z. M. JARZĘBSKI, S. MROWEC and T. WALEC, *Bull. Acad. Polon. Sci., Sér. Sci. Chim.* **19**, 153 (1971).

214. R. FRERICHS, *J. Appl. Phys.* **33**, 1898 (1962).

215. A. BIELAŃSKI, K. DYREK and Z. KLUZ, *Bull. Acad. Polon. Sci. Sér. Sci. Chim.* **14**, 795 (1966).

216. A. BIELAŃSKI, K. DYREK, Z. KLUZ, J. SŁOCZYŃSKI and T. TOBIASZ, *Bull. Acad. Polon. Sci. Sér. Sci. Chim.* **12**, 657 (1964).

217. A. BIELAŃSKI, K. DYREK and Z. KLUZ, *Bull. Acad. Polon. Sci. Sér. Sci. Chim.* **13**, 285 (1965).

218. J. DEREŃ and J. ZIÓŁKOWSKI, *Bull. Acad. Polon. Sci. Sér. Sci. Chim.* **14**, 443 (1966).

219. J. DEREŃ, J. NOWOTNY and J. ZIÓŁKOWSKI, *Bull. Acad. Polon. Sci. Sér. Sci Chim.* **15**, 109 (1967).

220. J. DEREŃ, and J. NOWOTNY, *Bull. Acad. Polon. Sci. Sér. Sci. Chim.* **15**, 115 (1967).

221. J. DEREŃ, J. NOWOTNY and J. ZIÓŁKOWSKI, *Bull. Acad. Polon. Sci. Sér. Sci. Chim.* **16**, 45 (1968).

222. A. BIELAŃSKI and J. DEREŃ, *Symposium on Electronic Phenomena in Chemisorption and Catalysis on Semiconductors*, Moscow, July 2–4, 1968. K. HAUFFE and TH. WOLKENSTEIN, eds., Walter de Gruyter, Berlin, 1969, p. 149.

223. N. KEIER, *Kinetika i Kataliz*, **1**, 221 (1960).

224. G. PARRAVANO and M. BOUDART, *Adv. Catalysis*, **7**, 67 (1955).

225. F. A. KRÖGER, *The Chemistry of Imperfect Crystals*, North-Holland Publ. Co., Amsterdam, 1964, p. 493.

226. N. C. TOMBS and H. P. ROOKSBY, *Nature*, **165**, 442 (1950).

227. S. GREENWALD and J. S. SMART, *Nature*, **166**, 523 (1950).

228. S. SAITO, K. NAKAHIGASHI and Y. SHIMOMURA, *J. Phys. Soc. Japan*, **21**, 850 (1966).

229. F. A. KRÖGER, *The Chemistry of Imperfect Crystals*, North-Holland Publ. Co., Amsterdam, 1964, p. 192.

230. W. D. JOHNSTON, R. R. HEIKES and D. SESTRICK, *J. Phys. Chem. Solids*, **7**, 1 (1958).

231. V. P. ZHUZE and A. I. SHELYKH, *Fiz. Tverdogo Tela*, **8**, 629 (1966); *Soviet Phys. Solid State*, **8**, 509 (1966).

232. A. I. SHELYKH, K. S. ARTEMOV and V. E. SHVAIKO-SHVAIKOVSKII, *Fiz. Tverdogo Tela*, **8**, 883 (1966); *Soviet Phys. Solid State*, **8**, 706 (1966).

233. B. FISHER and J. B. WAGNER, *J. Appl. Phys.* **38**, 3838 (1967).

234. A. MÜNSTER, *Chemische Thermodynamik*, Akademie-Verlag, Berlin 1969.

235. A. J. BOSMAN and C. CREVECOEUR, *J. Phys. Chem. Solids*, **30**, 1151 (1969).

236. A. J. BOSMAN and H. J. VAN DAAL, *Advances in Phys.* **19**, 1 (1970).

237. A. DUQUESNOY and F. MARION, *C. R. Acad. Sci.* (*France*), **256**, 2862 (1963).

238. A. Z. HED, *J. Chem. Phys.* **50**, 2935 (1969).

239. R. E. CARTER and F. D. RICHARDSON, *Trans. AIME*, **200**, 1244, (1954).

240. B. A. THOMPSON, Ph. D. Thesis, Rensselaer Polytechnique Institute, 1962.

241. J. B. HOLT, *Proc. Brit. Ceram. Soc.* **9**, 157 (1967).

242. W. K. CHEN and R. A. JACKSON, *J. Phys. Chem. Solids*, **30**, 1309 (1969).

243. W. K. CHEN, N. L. PETERSON and W. T. REEVES, *Phys. Rev.* **186**, 887 (1969).

244. J. S. SMART, *Phys. Rev.* **82**, 113 (1951).
245. H. BIZETTE, *Ann. Phys. (France)*, **1**, 306 (1946).
246. D. S. DARKEN and R. W. GURRY, *J. Amer. Chem. Soc.* **67**, 1398 (1945).
247. F. MARION, *Doc. métallurg.* **24**, 87 (1955).
248. K. HEDDEN and G. LEHMAN, *Arch. Eisenhüttenwes.* **B 35**, 839 (1964).
249. H. J. ENGELL, *Arch. Eisenhüttenwes.* **E 28**, 109 (1957).
250. B. E. F. FENDER and F. D. RILEY, *J. Phys. Chem. Solids*, **30**, 793 (1969).
251. P. VALLET and P. RACCAH, *Mem. Sci. Rev. Met.* **62**, 1 (1965).
252. H. F. RIZZO, R. S. GORDON, and I. B. CATLER, *J. Electrochem. Soc.* **116**, 266 (1969).
253. G. LEHMANN, *Ber. Bunsengesell. Phys. Chem.* **73**, 349 (1969).
254. D. S. TANNHAUSER, *J. Phys. Chem. Solids*, **23**, 25 (1962).
255. S. M. ARIYA and B. YA. BRACH, *Soviet Phys. Solid State*, **5**, 2565 (1964).
256. I. BRANSKY and D. S. TANNHAUSER, *Trans. AIME*, **239**, 75 (1967).
257. G. H. GEIGER, R. L. LEVIN and J. B. WAGNER, *J. Phys. Chem. Solids*, **27**, 947 (1966).
258. W. L. ROTH, *Acta Cryst.* **13**, 140 (1960).
259. J. SMUTS, *J. Iron Steel Inst.* **204**, 237 (1966).
260. O. N. SALMON, *J. Phys. Chem.* **65**, 550 (1961)
261. P. KOFSTAD and A. Z. HED, *J. Electrochem. Soc.* **115**, 102 (1968).
262. M. S. SELTZER and A. Z. HED, *J. Electrochem. Soc.* **117**, 815 (1970).
263. L. HIMMEL, N. F. MEHL and C. E. BIRCHENALL, *Trans. AIME*, **197**, 827 (1953).
264. PH. DESMARESCAUX, J. P. BOCQUET, and P. LACOMBE, *Bull. Soc. Chim. France*, **15**, 1106 (1965).
265. R. L. LEVIN and J. B. WAGNER, *Trans. AIME*, **233**, 159 (1965).
266. P. E. CHILDS and J. B. WAGNER, *Heterogeneous Kinetics at Elevated Temperature*, Plenum Press, New York, 1970, p. 269.
267. B. RUHEMAN, *Physik. Z. (Sowjetunion)*, **7**, 590 (1935).
268. T. M. WILSON, *J. Appl. Phys.* **40**, 1588 (1969).
269. V. G. BHIDE and R. H. DANI, *Physica*, **27**, 821 (1961).
270. P. NAGELS and M. DENAYER, *Solid State Commun.* **5**, 193 (1967).
271. P. NAGELS, M. DENAYER, H. J. DE WIT and C. CREVECOEUR, *Solid State Commun.* **6**, 695 (1968).
272. M. ALI, M. FRIDMAN, M. DENAYER and P. NAGELS, *Phys. Status Solidi*, **28**, 193 (1968).
273. C. CREVECOEUR and H. J. DE WIT, *J. Phys. Chem. Solids*, **31**, 783 (1970).
274. H. J. DE WIT and C. CREVECOEUR, *Phys. Letters A*, **25**, 393 (1967).
275. C. CREVECOEUR and H. J. DE WIT, *Solid State Commun.* **6**, 843 (1968).
276. M. GVISHI, N. M. TALLAN and D. S. TANNHAUSER, *Solid State Commun.* **6**, 135 (1968).
277. A. Z. HED and D. S. TANNHAUSER, *J. Chem. Phys.* **47**, 2090 (1967).
278. F. A. GRANT, *Rev. Mod. Phys.* **31**, 646 (1959).
279. T. HURLEN, *Acta Chem. Scand.* **13**, 365 (1959).
280. H. P. R. FREDERIKSE, *J. Appl. Phys.*, Suppl. **32**, 2211 (1961).
281. A. VAN HIPPEL et al., *J. Phys. Chem. Solids*, **23**, 779 (1962).
282. V. N. BOGOMOLOV, E. K. KUDINOV and YU. A. FIRSOV, *Fiz. Tverdogo Tela*, **9**, 3175 (1967).
283. J. H. BECKER and J. HOSLER, *J. Phys. Soc. Japan*, **18**, Suppl. II, 152 (1963).
284. J. H. BECKER and J. HOSLER, *Phys. Rev.* **137**, A 1872 (1965).
285. V. N. BOGOMOLOV and P. M. SZAVKUNOV, *Fiz. Tverdogo Tela*, **5**, 2027 (1963).
286. V. N. BOGOMOLOV and V. P. ZHUZE, *Fiz. Tverdogo Tela*, **5**, 3285 (1963).
287. D. C. CRONEMEYER, *Phys. Rev.* **87**, 876 (1952).
288. V. N. BOGOMOLOV and V. P. ZHUZE, *Fiz. Tverdogo Tela*, **8**, 2390 (1966).
289. V. N. BOGOMOLOV, *Fiz. Tverdogo Tela*, **8**, 3659 (1966).
290. V. N. BOGOMOLOV et al., *Fiz. Tverdogo Tela*, **9**, 2077 (1967).
291. I. BRANSKY and D. S. TANNHAUSER, *Solid State Commun.* **7**, 245 (1969).
292. R. N. BLUMENTHAL, J. C. KIRK and W. M. HIRTHE, *J. Phys. Chem. Solids*, **28**, 1077 (1967).
293. P. KOFSTAD, *J. Phys. Chem. Solids*, **23**, 1579 (1962).
294. R. N. BLUMENTHAL et al., *J. Electrochem. Soc.* **114**, 172 (1967).
295. J. B. MOSER, R. N. BLUMENTHAL and D. M. WHITMORE, *J. Amer. Ceram. Soc.* **48**, 384 (1965).
296. W. JAKUBOWSKI, *Acta Phys. Polon.* **33**, 465 (1968).
297. W. R. THURBER and J. H. MANTE, *Phys. Rev.* **139**, A 1655 (1965).
298. M. ITAKURA, N. NÜZEKI, H. TOYODA and H. IWASAKI, *Japan. J. Appl. Phys.* **6**, 311 (1967).
299. R. G. BRECKENRIDGE and W. R. HOSLER, *Phys. Rev.* **91**, 793 (1953).
300. N. BOGOMOLOV, I. A. SMIRNOV and E. W. SHADRICHEV, *Fiz. Tverdogo Tela*, **11**, 3214 (1969).
301. H. B. WHITEHURST et al., *J. Phys. Chem. Solids*, **28**, 861 (1967).

302. M. G. Harwood, *Brit. J. Appl. Phys.* **16**, 1493 (1965).

303. J. A. van Raalte, *J. Appl. Phys.* **36**, 3365 (1965).

304. D. C. Cronemeyer, *Phys. Rev.* **113**, 1222 (1959).

305. D. S. Tannhauser, *Solid State Commun.* **1**, 223 (1963).

306. J. Yahia, *Phys. Rev.* **130**, 1711 (1963).

307. E. H. Greener et al., *J. Amer. Ceram. Soc.* **48**, 623 (1965).

308. R. N. Blumenthal et al., *J. Phys. Chem. Solids*, **27**, 643 (1966).

309. P. Kofstad, *J. Phys. Chem. Solids.* **28**, 1842 (1967).

310. W. M. Hirthe, Rep. ARL 68–0065 (1968).

311. P. Kofstad, *J. Less-Common Metals*, **13**, 635 (1967).

312. V. I. Barbanel, V. N. Bogomolov, S. A. Borodin and S. I. Budarina, *Fiz. Tverdogo Tela*, **11**, 534 (1969).

313. V. I. Barbanel and V. N. Bogomolov, *Fiz. Tverdogo Tela*, **11**, 2671 (1969).

314. K. S. Förland, *Acta Chem. Scand.* **18**, 1267 (1964).

315. L. M. Atlas and G. J. Schlehman, Rep. ANP 6960; reported by Moser et al. (295).

316. R. Haul, D. Just and G. Dümbgen, *Reactivity of Solids*, International Conference (Amsterdam, May, 1960). J. H. de Boer, ed., Elsevier, Amsterdam, 1961, p. 65.

317. R. Haul and G. Dümbgen, *Z. Elektrochem.* **66**, 636 (1962).

318. R. Haul and G. Dümbgen, *J. Phys. Chem. Solids*, **26**, 1 (1965).

319. R. D. Carnahan and J. D. Brittain, *J. Amer. Ceram. Soc.* **48**, 365 (1965).

320. I. Tamiguchi and M. Honda, *Sci. Engng. Rev. Doshida Univ.* (Japan), **10**, 92 (1969).

321. Ju. A. Prokhorov et al., *Fiz. Tverdogo Tela*, **9**, 1398 (1967).

322. P. van den Berghe and G. Perny, *J. Phys.* (*France*), **27**, 748 (1966).

323. M. Shiojiri, *J. Phys. Soc. Japan*, **21**, 335 (1966).

324. T. S. Travina and Ju. A. Mukkin, *Izv. WUZ, Fiz.* **9**, 74 (1966).

325. B. Dudenhausen and G. Mollenstedt, *Z. Angew. Phys.* **27**, 191 (1969).

326. C. Wagner and H. Hammen, *Z. Phys. Chem.* B **40**, 197 (1938).

327. J. Bloem, *Philips Res. Rep.* **13**, 167 (1958).

328. V. P. Zhuze and B. V. Kurchatov, *Zh. Eksper. Teor. Fiz.* **2**, 309 (1932).

329. J. S. Anderson and N. N. Greenwood, *Proc. Roy. Soc.* **215 A**, 353 (1952).

330. O. Böttger, *Ann. Phys.* (6) **10**, 232 (1952).

331. J. Gundermann, K. Hauffe and C. Wagner, *Z. Phys. Chem.* B **37**, 148 (1957).

332. K. Stecker, *Ann. Phys.* (7), **3**, 55 (1959).

333. K. P. Zuev, *Soviet Phys. Solid State*, **1**, 703, 1007 (1959).

334. F. L. Weichman, *Phys. Rev.* **117**, 998 (1960).

335. R. S. Toth, R. Kilkson and D. Trivich, *Phys. Rev.* **122**, 482 (1961).

336. M. O'Keeffe and W. J. Moore, *J. Chem. Phys.* **35**, 1324 (1961).

337. M. H. Zirin and D. Trivich, *J. Chem. Phys.* **39**, 870 (1963).

338. V. L. Vinetskii and G. A. Kholodar, *Fiz. Tverdogo Tela*, **6**, 3452 (1964).

339. V. L. Vinetskii and G. A. Kholodar, *Phys. Status Solidi*, **19**, 41 (1967).

340. J. P. Zielinger, M. Tapiero, C. Roubaud and M. Zouaghi, *Solid State Commun.* **8**, 1299 (1970).

341. M. Zouaghi, M. Tapiero, J. P. Zielinger and R. Burgraf, *Solid State Commun.* **8**, 1823 (1970).

342. J. Spyridelis, J. Stoimenos and N. Economou, *Phys. Status Solidi*, **20**, 623 (1967).

343. M. Zouaghi, A. Coret and J. O. Eymann, *Solid State Commun.* **7**, 311 (1969).

344. M. Zouaghi and A. Coret, *Phys. Letters*, **28** A, 513 (1969).

345. S. Brahms, J. P. Dahl and S. Nikitine, *J. Phys.* **28**, Suppl. to No. 5–6, C 3–32 (1967).

346. S. Nikitine, S. Brahms, J. Ringeissen, J. P. Dahl and K. S. Song, *Proc. Int. Conf. on Luminescence*, 1966.

347. S. Brahms, S. Nikitine and J. P. Dahl, *Phys. Letters*, **22**, 31 (1966).

348. G. W. Castellan and W. J. Moore, *J. Chem. Phys.* **17**, 41 (1949).

349. W. J. Moore and B. Selikson, *J. Chem. Phys.* **19**, 1539 (1951), **20**, 927 (1952).

350. W. J. Moore, Y. Ebisuzaki and J. A. Sluss, *J. Phys. Chem.* **62**, 1438 (1958).

351. W. J. Moore, *Z. Elektrochem.* **63**, 794 (1959).

352. J. A. Sluss, *Diss. Abs.* **23**, 1947 (1962).

353. Y. Ebisuzaki, *Diss. Abs.* **23**, 2712 (1963).

354. R. H. Campbell and M. O'Keeffe, *Kinetics of Reactions in Ionic Systems*, T. J. Gray and V. D. Fréchette, eds., Plenum Press, New York, 1969, p. 413.

355. G. Heiland, E. Mollwo and Z. Stockmann, *Solid State Phys.* **8**, 191 (1959).

356. D. G. Thomas, *Semiconductors*, N. B. Hannay, ed., Reinhold Publ. Corp., New York, 1959.

357. A. R. HUTSON, *Semiconductors*, N. B. HANNAY, ed., Reinhold Publ. Corp., New York, 1959.
358. F. A. KRÖGER, *The Chemistry of Imperfect Crystals*, North-Holland Publ. Co., Amsterdam, 1964, p. 691.
359. A. R. HUTSON, *Phys. Rev.* **108**, 222 (1957).
360. E. D. KOLB and R. A. LAUDISE. *J. Amer. Ceram. Soc.* **49**, 302 (1966).
361. M. SUMITA, Japan, *J. Appl. Phys.* **6**, 1469 (1967).
362. R. KUŽEL and F. L. WEICHMAN, *Can. J. Phys.* **48**, 2463 (1970).
363. M. A. SEITZ and D. M. WHITMORE, *J. Phys. Chem. Solids*, **29**, 1033 (1968).
364. F. L. WEICHMAN *et al. Can. J. Phys.* **48**, 2657 (1970).
365. K. F. NIELSEN, *J. Cryst. Growth*, 3, **4**, 141 (1968).
366. H. J. KRUSEMEYER and D. G. THOMAS, *J. Phys. Chem. Solids*, **16**, 78 (1958).
367. H. J. KRUSEMEYER, *Phys. Rev.* **114**, 655 (1959).
368. J. W. HOFFMAN and I. LANDER, *Trans. Faraday Soc.* **66**, 2346 (1970).
369. W. S. BAER, *Phys. Rev.* **154**, 785 (1967).
370. G. BOGNER, *J. Phys. Chem. Solids*, **19**, 235 (1961).
371. M. SUMITA, *Japan. J. Appl. Phys.* **6**, 418 (1967).
372. C. G. B. GARRETT, *Adv. Electronics and Electron Physics*, **14**, 1 (1961).
373. G. A. ROZGONYI and W. J. POLITO, *Appl. Phys. Letters*, **8**, 220 (1966).
374. N. L. KENIGSBERG and A. N. CHERNETS, *Fiz. Tverdogo Tela*, **10**, 2834 (1968).
375. K. V. SHALIMOVA *et al.*, *Kristallografiya*, **13**, 679 (1968).
376. N. F. FOSTER, *J. Vacuum Sci. Technol.* **6**, 111 (1969).
377. R. A. RABADANOV *et al.*, *Fiz. Tverdogo Tela*, **12**, 1431 (1970).
378. D. L. RAIMONDI and E. KAY, *J. Vacuum Sci. Technol.* **7**, 96 (1970).
379. P. H. MILLER, *Phys. Rev.* **60**, 890 (1941).
380. H. FRITZSCHE, *Z. Phys.* **133**, 422 (1952).
381. E. LINDNER, D. CAMPBELL and A. ÅKERSTRÖM, *Acta Chem. Scand.* **6**, 457 (1952).
382. F. MUNNICH, *Naturwissenschaften*, **42**, 340 (1955).
383. R. ARNETH, Diploma project, Univ. of Erlangen, Germany, 1955.
384. W. A. SECCO and W. J. MOORE, *J. Chem. Phys.* **23**, 1170 (1955); **26**, 942 (1957).
385. E. SPICAR, *Reactivity of Solids*, 1st International Conference, Madrid, 1956, Proceedings, Elsevier, Amsterdam, 1957, p. 637.
386. E. SPICAR, Thesis, Stuttgard, 1956.
387. J. P. ROBERTS, J. HUTCHINGS and C. WHEELER, *Trans. Brit. Ceram. Soc.* **55**, 75 (1956).
388. J. P. ROBERTS and C. WHEELER, *Phil. Mag.* **2**, 708 (1957).
389. D. G. THOMAS, *J. Phys. Chem. Solids*, **3**, 229 (1957).
390. H. LAMATSCH, Diploma project, Univ. of Erlangen, Germany, 1958.
391. W. J. MOORE, *Z. Elektrochem.* **63**, 794 (1958).
392. W. J. MOORE and E. L. WILLIAMS, *Disc. Faraday Soc.* **28**, 86 (1959).
393. R. POHL, *Z. Phys.* **155**, 120 (1959).
394. J. P. ROBERTS and C. WHEELER, *Trans. Faraday Soc.* **56**, 570 (1960).
395. E. A. SECCO, *Reactivity of Solids*, International Conference, Amsterdam, May, 1960; Proceedings, J. H. DE BOER, ed., Elsevier, Amsterdam, 1961, p. 188. Preliminary work in *Disc. Faraday Soc.* **28**, 94 (1959).
396. E. A. SECCO, *Can. J. Chem.* **39**, 1544 (1961).
397. R. LINDNER, *Z. Naturforsch.* **10 A** 1027 (1955).
398. Z. M. JARZĘBSKI, *Wiadomości Chem.* **22**, 45 (1968).
399. Z. M. JARZĘBSKI, *Wiadomości Chem.* **21**, 581 (1967).
400. R. HAUL and D. JUST, *J. Appl. Phys.* **335**, 487 (1962).
401. Z. M. JARZĘBSKI, *Acta Phys. Polon.* **29**, 37 (1966).
402. Z. M. JARZĘBSKI, *Bull. Acad. Polon. Sci. Sér. Sci. Chim.* **17**, 215 (1969).
403. Z. M. JARZĘBSKI, Ph. D. Thesis, School of Mining and Metallurgy, Cracow, 1966.
404. Z. M. JARZĘBSKI, *Bull. Acad. Polon. Sci. Sér. Sci. Chim.* **17**, 221 (1969).
405. H. FINKENRATH and M. VON ORTENBERG, *Z. Angew. Phys.* **22**, 279 (1967).
406. F. P. KOFFYBERG, *J. Solid State Chem.* **2**, 176 (1970).
407. J. A. BASTIN and R. W. WRIGHT, *Proc. Phys. Soc.* A **68**, 312 (1955).
408. R. W. WRIGHT and J. A. BASTIN, *Proc. Phys. Soc.* **71**, 109 (1958).
409. J. A. BASTIN and R. W. WRIGHT, *Proc. Phys. Soc.* **72**, 65 (1958).
410. D. J. HOWARTH and E. H. SONDHEIMER, *Proc. Roy. Soc.* A **219**, 53 (1953).
411. I. M. CIDILKOVSKII, *Termomagnitnye yavleniya v poluprovodnikach*, Fizmatgiz, Moscow, 1960.

412. Z. M. JARZĘBSKI, B. MUSZYŃSKA and J. OBŁĄKOWSKI, *Acta Phys. Polon.* **A42**, 383 (1972).

413. P. HÖSCHL, Č. KOŇÁK and V. PROSSER, *Materials Res. Bull.* **4**, 87 (1969).

414. R. TRYKOZKO, *Przegląd Elektron.* (Poland) **5**, 62 (1964).

415. R. TRYKOZKO, Zeszyty Naukowe P. W., *Elektronika*, **30**, 87 (1964).

416. F. P. KOFFYBERG, *Phys. Letters*, **30 A**, 37 (1969).

417. K. MASCHKE and U. RÖSSLER, *Phys. Status Solidi*, **28**, 577 (1968).

418. M. ALTWEIN *et al.*, *Phys. Status Solidi*, **29**, 203 (1968).

419. T. K. LAKSHMANAN, *J. Electrochem. Soc.* **110**, 548 (1963).

420. A. S. RUSSEL *et al.*, *Aluminium Research Lab. Tech. Paper* No. 10 (1956).

421. H. VON WARTENBERG and E. PROPHET, *Z. Elektrochem.* **38**, 849 (1932).

422. E. G. ROCHOW, *J. Appl. Phys.* **9**, 664 (1938).

423. Linde Air Products Company, *Product Eng.* **14**, 668 (1943).

424. J. B. WACHTMAN, JR. and L. H. MAXWELL, *J. Amer. Ceram. Soc.* **37**, 291 (1954), **40**, 377 (1957).

425. J. L. PENTECOST, J. G. DAVIES and P. E. RITT, Sixtieth Annual Meeting, The American Ceramic Society, Pittsburgh, April 29, 1958 (Electronics Division No. 17-L-58).

426. H. C. GRAHAM, N. M. TALLAN and D. P. DETWILER, Sixtieth Annual Meeting, The American Ceramic Society, Pittsburgh, April 29, 1958 (Electronics Division No. 12-L-58).

427. E. DIEPSCHLAG and F. WULFESTIEG, *J. Iron Steel Inst.* **120**, 297 (1929).

428. K. WERNER, *Sprechsaal*, **63**, 537, 557, 581, 599, 619 (1930).

429. H. GERDIEN, *Z. Elektrochem.* **39**, 13 (1933).

430. E. PODSZUS, *Z. Elektrochem.* **39**, 75 (1933).

431. K. BACKHAUS, *Ber. deut. keram. Gessell.*, **19**, 461 (1938).

432. A. R. SHULMAN, *Zh. Tekh. Fiz.* **9**, 389 (1939).

433. H. RÖGENER, *Z. Elektrochem.* **46**, 25 (1940).

434. T. ARIZUMI and S. TANI, *J. Phys. Soc. Japan*, **5**, 442 (1950).

435. J. R. HENSLER and E. C. HENRY, *J. Amer. Ceram. Soc.* **36**, 76 (1953).

436. A. HELDT and G. HAASE, *Z. Angew. Phys.* **6**, 157 (1954).

437. J. COHEN, *Bull. Amer. Ceram. Soc.* **38**, 441 (1959).

438. J. PAPPIS and W. D. KINGERY, *J. Amer. Ceram. Soc.* **44**, 459 (1961).

439. D. W. PETERS, *J. Phys. Chem. Solids*, **27**, 1560 (1966).

440. J. A. CHAMPION, *Brit. J. Appl. Phys.* **15**, 633 (1964).

441. S. DASGUPTA and J. HART, *Brit. J. Appl. Phys.* **16**, 725 (1965).

442. S. DASGUPTA, *Brit. J. Appl. Phys.* **17**, 267 (1966).

443. E. LOH, *Solid State Commun.* **2**, 269 (1964).

444. P. J. HARROP, *Brit. J. Appl. Phys.* **16**, 729 (1965).

445. R. A. VERNETTI and R. L. COOK, *J. Amer. Ceram. Soc.* **49**, 194 (1966).

446. R. L. COBLE, *J. Amer. Ceram. Soc.* **41**, 55 (1958).

447. G. C. KUCZYNSKI, L. ABERNETHY and J. ALLAN, *Kinetics of High Temperature Processes*, Conference, W. D. KINGERY, ed. Dedham, Mass., 1958; Proceedings, J. Wiley, New York, 1959.

448. Y. OISHI and W. D. KINGERY, *J. Chem. Phys.* **33**, 480 (1950).

449. S. I. WARSHAW, Thesis, Massachusetts Inst. Tech. June, 1961, quoted by A. E. PALADINO and R. L. COBLE, *J. Amer. Ceram. Soc.* **46**, 133 (1963), and P. J. HARROP, *J. Materials Sci.* **3**, 206 (1968).

450. A. E. PALADINO and W. D. KINGERY, *J. Chem. Phys.* **37**, 957 (1962).

451. D. HAYES, D. W. BUDWORTH and J. P. ROBERTS, *Trans. Brit. Ceram. Soc.* **62**, 507 (1963).

452. R. R. DILS, Ph.D. Thesis, Stanford University, 1965, quoted in reference 454.

453. R. P. NELSON, *Acta Polytech. Scand. Chem. Ser.* No. 60 (1967).

454. T. P. JONES, R. L. COBLE and C. J. MOGAB, *J. Amer. Ceram. Soc.* **52**, 331 (1969).

455. J. DEREŃ, Z. M. JARZĘBSKI and A. KOZŁOWSKA, *Zeszyty Naukowe AGH, Ceramika*, **22**, 17 (1972).

456. E. M. DA SILVA and P. WHITE, *J. Electrochem. Soc.* **109**, 12 (1962).

457. R. G. FRIESER, *J. Electrochem. Soc.* **113**, 357 (1966).

458. L. HIESINGER and H. KOENIG, *Festschrift 100 Jahre Heraeus Platinschmelze*, Hanau, 1951, p. 376.

459. A. CHARLESBY, *Proc. Phys. Soc.* **66**, 317, 533 (1953).

460. W. J. BERNARD and J. W. COOK, *J. Electrochem. Soc.* **106**, 643 (1959).

461. G. J. TIBOL and R. W. HULL, *J. Electrochem. Soc.* **111**, 1368 (1964).

462. G. J. TIBOL and W. M. KAUFMAN, *Proc. IEEE*, **52**, 1465 (1964).

463. D. WHITE, *Vacuum*, **15**, 317 (1965).

464. R. KUŽEL and F. L. WEICHMAN, *Can. J. Phys.* 1585 (1970).

465. E. E. KOHNKE, *J. Phys. Chem. Solids*, **23**, 1557 (1962).

466. M. NAGASAWA *et al.*, *J. Phys. Soc. Japan*, **20**, 1093 (1965).

467. D. F. Morgan and D. A. Wright, *Brit. J. Appl. Phys.* **17**, 337 (1966).
468. R. Summitt and N. F. Borelli, *J. Phys. Chem. Solids*, **26**, 921 (1965).
469. J. E. Houston and E. E. Kohnke, *J. Appl. Phys.* **36**, 3931 (1965).
470. R. H. Bube, *Photoconductivity of Solids*. J. Wiley, New York, 1960.
471. J. E. Houston and E. E. Kohnke, *J. Appl. Phys.* **37**, 3083 (1966).
472. E. E. Koch, *Phys. Status Solidi*, **3**, 1059, 1619 (1963).
473. T. Arai, *J. Phys. Soc. Japan*, **15**, 916 (1960).
474. K. Ishiguro *et al.*, *J. Phys. Soc. Japan*, **13**, 296, 755 (1958).
475. M. Nagasawa and S. Shionoya, *Japan. J. Appl. Phys.* **10**, 472 (1971).
476. F. N. Vainshtein, *Optiko-Mekhan. Prom.* No 1, 46 (1967).
477. Y. Katsube and S. Katsube, *J. Vacuum. Soc. Japan*, **9**, 443 (1966); *Vacuum*, **17**, 193 (1967), Abstr. 603.
478. M. V. Coleman and D. J. D. Thomas, *Phys. Status Solidi*, **22**, 593 (1967).
479. J. Benyon, *Vacuum*, **20**, 293 (1970).
480. A. E. Hill and G. R. Hoffman, *Brit. J. Appl. Phys.* **18**, 13 (1967).
481. A. Volkenberg, *Vacuum*, **17**, 559 (1967).
482. H. Hirose and Y. Wada, *Japan. J. Appl. Phys.* **4**, 639 (1965).
483. H. Hirose and Y. Wada, *Japan. J. Appl. Phys.* **3**, 179 (1964).
484. I. T. Johansen, *J. Appl. Phys.* **37**, 499 (1966).
485. T. E. Hartman, J. C. Blair and R. Bauer, *J. Appl. Phys.* **37**, 2468 (1966).
486. M. Stuart, *Brit. J. Appl. Phys.*, **18**, 1637 (1967).
487. N. Koide and R. Abe, *Japan. J. Appl. Phys.* **5**, 346 (1966).
488. W. C. Tripp and N. M. Tallan, *J. Amer. Ceram. Soc.* **53**, 531 (1970).
489. R. Morlotti, *Z. Naturforsch.* **24** a, 441 (1969).
490. P. Kofstad, *High Temperature Oxidation of Metals*, J. Wiley, New York, 1966, p. 93.
491. N. I. Ikornikova and A. A. Popova, *Dokl. Akad. Nauk SSSR*, **106**, 460 (1956).
492. R. C. Linares, *J. Appl. Phys.* **33**, 1747 (1962).
493. R. A. Laudise and A. A. Ballman, *J. Amer. Chem. Soc.* **80**, 2655 (1958).
494. P. S. Schaffer, *J. Amer. Ceram. Soc.* **48**, 508 (1965).
495. M. G. Townsed and O. F. Hill, *Trans. Faraday Soc.* **61**, 2597 (1965).
496. R. L. Sproull *et al.*, *Rev. Sci. Instrum.* **22**, 410 (1951).
497. S. B. Austerman, *J. Nuclear Materials*, **14**, 225 (1964).
498. V. G. Hill and R. I. Harker, *J. Electrochem. Soc.* **115**, 294 (1968).
499. S. van Houten, *Nature*, **195**, 484 (1962).
500. M. Hayashi and M. Ogawa, *J. Phys. Soc. Japan*, **26**, 121 (1969).
501. C. B. Finch and G. W. Clarc, *J. Appl. Phys.* **37**, 3910 (1966).
502. R. C. Linares, *J. Phys. Chem. Solids*, **28**, 1285 (1967).
503. B. M. Wanklyn, *J. Cryst. Growth*, **5**, 219 (1969).
504. A. Kremheller *et al.*, *J. Electrochem. Soc.* **107**, 12 (1960).
505. R. H. Sailors, G. L. Liedl and R. E. Grace, *J. Appl. Phys.* **38**, 4928 (1967).
506. A. Kinoshita and T. Nakano, *Japan. J. Appl. Phys.* **6**, 656 (1967).
507. A. Kinoshita and T. Nakano, *Japan. J. Appl. Phys.* **5**, 1121 (1966).
508. M. Grosmann, *J. Chim. Phys.* **62**, 1129 (1965).
509. R. A. Lefever, *Rev. Sci. Instrum.* **33**, 1470 (1962).
510. C. F. Guerci and M. W. Shafer, *J. Appl. Phys.* **37**, 1406 (1966).
511. Č. Koňák *et al.*, *Crystal Growth*, Pergamon Press, 1967, p. C 23 (cf. ref. 24).
512. M. Schieber, *J. Appl. Phys.* **37**, 4588 (1966).
513. R. A. Voskanyan and I. S. Zheludey, *Kristallografiya*, **12**, 539 (1967).
514. H. Scholz, *Philips Tech. Rev.* **28**, 316 (1967).
515. Z. Hauptmann, *Czech. J. Phys.* **12**, 148 (1962).
516. J. P. Remeika and M. Marezio, *Appl. Phys. Letters*, **8**, 87 (1966).
517. G. Katz and R. Roy, *J. Amer. Ceram. Soc.* **49**, 168 (1966).
518. V. Loc, A. M. Anthony and R. Bouaziz, *C. R. Acad. Sci.* B **268**, 1715 (1966).
519. K. Aurivilius and I. B. Carlson, *Acta Chem. Scand.* **11**, 1070 (1959).
520. P. P. Budnikov, D. B. Sandulov and N. M. Popov, *Dokl. Akad. Nauk SSSR*, **170**, 1310 (1966).
521. E. Loh and R. Newman, *J. Appl. Phys.* **32**, 470 (1961).
522. M. V. Rozhdestvenskaya *et al.*, *Kristallografiya*, **11**, 903 (1966).
523. R. C. Vickery and J. C. Hipp, *J. Appl. Phys.* **37**, 2926 (1966).
524. B. M. Wanklyn, *J. Cryst. Growth*, **2**, 4, 251–3 (1968).

525. H. KONDOH et al., J. Phys. Soc. Japan, **13**, 579 (1958).
526. T. B. REED et al., J. Appl. Phys. **33**, 1014 (1962).
527. H. F. KUNKLE and E. E. KOHNKE, J. Appl. Phys. **36**, 1489 (1965).
528. J. LIEBERTZ, Kristall. Tech. (Germany), **4**, 2, 221–6 (1969).
529. T. SUGAI et al., Japan. J. Appl. Phys. **6**, 901 (1967).
530. J. S. BERKES, W. B. WHITE and R. ROY, J. Appl. Phys. **36**, 3276 (1965).
531. N. MASAKI, J. Cryst. Growth, **6**, 207 (1970).
532. H. TAKEI and S. KOIDE, J. Phys. Soc. Japan, **21**, 1010 (1966).
533. A. A. ABDULLAEV et al., Kristallografiya, **14**, 1095 (1969).
534. I. KITAHIRO et al., J. Phys. Soc. Japan, **21**, 196 (1966).
535. N. KIMIZUKA et al., Materials Res. Bull. **5**, 403 (1970).
536. L. E. SOBON and P. E. GREENE, J. Amer. Ceram. Soc. **49**, 106 (1966).
537. Y. BANDO et al., Japan. J. Appl. Phys. **8**, 633 (1969).
538. S. KOIDE and H. TAKEI, J. Phys. Soc. Japan, **22**, 946 (1967).
539. A. ADDAMIANO and M. AVEN, J. Appl. Phys. **31**, 36 (1960).
540. T. TAKAHASHI et al., Japan. J. Appl. Phys. **5**, 560 (1966).
541. Y. S. PARK and D. C. REYNOLDS, J. Appl. Phys. **38**, 756 (1967).
542. R. A. LAUDISE, A. A. BALLMAN, J. Phys. Chem. **64**, 688 (1960).
543. M. ZVÁRA et al., Phys. Stat. Solidi, **42**, K5 (1970).
544. P. P. BUDENSTEIN et al., J. Vacuum Sci. Technol. **6**, 289 (1969).
545. N. J. CHOU and J. M. ELDRIDGE, J. Electrochem. Soc. **117**, 1287 (1970).
546. C. FRITZSCHE, Z. Angew. Phys. **24**, 48 (1967).
547. D. R. LAMB and P. C. RUNDLE, Brit. J. Appl. Phys. **18**, 29 (1967).
548. R. W. BRANDER, D. R. LAMB and P. C. RUNDLE, Brit. J. Appl. Phys. **18**, 23 (1967).
549. R. E. JONES, H. F. WINTERS and L. I. MAISSEL, J. Vacuum Sci. Technol. **5**, 84 (1968).
550. I. H. PRATT, Solid State Technol. **49**, Dec. 1969.
551. C. R. FRITZSCHE, J. Phys. Chem. Solids, **30**, 1885 (1969).
552. C. R. FRITZSCHE, Solid State Commun. **6**, 341 (1968).
553. B. F. KORZO, P. S. KIREEV and G. A. LIASHCHENKO, Fiz. Techn. Poluprovod. **2**, 1852 (1968).
554. C. M. OSBURN and R. VEST, J. Phys. Chem. Solids, **32**, 1343 (1971).
555. F. A. KRÖGER, J. Phys. Chem. Solids, **29**, 1889 (1968).
556. I. G. AUSTIN and N. F. MOTT, Science, **168**, 78 (1970).
557. B. FISHER and D. S. TANNHAUSER, J. Electrochem. Soc., **111**, 1194 (1969).
558. E. J. W. VERWEY et al. Philips Res. Rep. **5**, 173 (1950).
559. I. G. AUSTIN, J. Non-cryst. Solids, **2**, 474 (1970).
560. I. G. AUSTIN et al. Phys. Letters, **21**, 20 (1966).
561. A. ADLER and J. FEINLEIB, Phys. Rev. B, **2**, 3112 (1970).
562. R. A. BARI, D. ADLER and R. V. LANGE, Phys. Rev. B, **2**, 2898 (1970).
563. C. M. OSBURN and R. W. VEST, J. Phys. Chem. Solids, **32**, 1331 (1971).
564. M. L. VOLPE, N. L. PETERSON and J. REDDY, Phys. Rev. B, **3**, 1417 (1971).
565. M. HOCH and R. SZWARC, Technical Report AFML-TR-67-331, Nov., 1967.
566. J. KOČKA and C. KOŇÁK, Phys. Stat. Solidi, **43**, 731 (1971).
567. K. KATADA et al., Japan. J. Appl. Phys., **9**, 1019 (1970).
568. M. GVISHI and D. S. TANNHAUSER, Solid State Commun. **8**, 485 (1970).
569. A. K. CHEETHAM, B. E. F. FENDER and R. I. TAYLOR, J. Phys. C: Solid State Phys. **4**, 2160 (1971).
570. F. KOCH and J. B. COHEN, Acta Crystallogr. **B 25**, 275 (1969).
571. H. L. MCKINZIE, Ph.D. Thesis, Arizona State University, 1967.
572. M. O'KEEFFE and M. VALIGI, J. Phys. Chem. Solids, **31**, 947 (1970).
573. A. Z. HED and D. S. TANNHAUSER, J. Electrochem. Soc. **114**, 314 (1967).
574. F. P. KOFFYBERG, Can. J. Phys. **49**, 435 (1971).
575. N. F. MOTT and W. D. TWOSE, Advances in Phys. **10**, 107 (1961).
576. N. F. MOTT, Advances in Phys. **16**, 59 (1967).
577. R. P. BENEDICT and D. C. LOCK, Phys. Rev. **B 2**, 4949 (1970).
578. D. C. LOOK, Phys. Rev. **184**, 705 (1969).
579. F. L. WEICHMAN and R. KUŽEL, Can. J. Phys. **48**, 63 (1970).
580. R. KUŽEL, Czech. J. Phys. **B 11**, 133 (1961).
581. H. L. MCKINZIE and M. O'KEEFFE, Phys. Letters, **24** A, 137 (1967).
582. J. P. CHARLES and J. P. FILLARD, J. Phys. Chem. Solids, **31**, 2141 (1970).
583. J. P. FILLARD and J. GASIOT, J. Phys. Chem. Solids, **31**, 2139 (1970).

584. F. L. WEICHMAN and R. KUŽEL, *J. Appl. Phys.* **41**, 3491 (1970).
585. A. P. YOUNG and C. M. SCHWARTZ, *J. Phys. Chem. Solids*, **30**, 249 (1969).
586. R. KUŽEL and F. L. WEICHMAN, *J. Appl. Phys.* **41**, 271 (1970).
587. J. J. MILLS, *J. Phys. Chem. Solids*, **31**, 2577 (1970).
588. M. NAGASAWA and S. SHIONOYA, *J. Phys. Soc. Japan*, **30**, 1213 (1971).
589. R. D. CUNNINGHAM and J. P. MARTON, *J. Appl. Phys.* **40**, 4664 (1969).
590. H. E. MATTHEWS and E. E. KOHNKE, *J. Phys. Chem. Solids*, **29**, 653 (1968).
591. M. NAGASAWA and S. SHIONYA, *Japan. J. Appl. Phys.* **10**, 727 (1971).
592. M. NAGASAWA and S. SHIONOYA, *J. Phys. Soc. Japan*, **30**, 1118 (1971).
593. M. SCHLAAK and A. WEISS, *Solid State Commun.* **8**, 1241 (1970).
594. M. NAGASAWA and S. SHIONOYA, *Phys. Rev. Letters*, **21**, 1070 (1968).
595. M. NAGASAWA and S. SHIONOYA, *J. Phys. Soc. Japan*, **30**, 158 (1971).
596. J. A. TUNHEIM, *J. Phys. Chem. Solids*, **31**, 1991 (1970).
597. D. F. CRABTREE *et al.*, *Brit. J. Appl. Phys.* (*J. Phys.* D), Ser. 2, **2**, 1503 (1969).
598. S. W. ING, R. E. MORRISON and J. E. SANDOR, *J. Electrochem. Soc.* **109**, 221 (1962).
599. E. W. SUCOV, *J. Amer. Ceram. Soc.* 46, **14** (1963).
600. E. L. WILLIAMS, *J. Amer. Ceram. Soc.* **46**, 190 (1963).
601. A. CHOUDHURY *et al.*, *Solid State Commun.* **3**, 119 (1965).
602. D. W. PALMER, *Nucl. Instr. Methods*, **38**, 187 (1965).
603. G. H. FRISCHAT and H. J. OEL, *Z. Angew. Phys.* **20**, 195 (1966).
604. M. L. BARRY and P. OLOFSEN, *Solid State Technology*, **2**, 39 (1968).
605. M. L. BARRY and P. OLOFSEN, *J. Electrochem. Soc.* **116**, 854 (1969).
606. M. L. BARRY, *J. Electrochem. Soc.* **117**, 1405 (1970).
607. M. L. BARRY and J. MANOLIU, *J. Electrochem. Soc.* **117**, 258 (1970).
608. M. HIROSE and I. KUBO, *Japan, J. Appl. Phys.* **8**, 402 (1969).
609. M. HIROSE *et al.*, *Japan. J. Appl. Phys.* **9**, 726 (1970).
610. M. HIROSE, *Japan. J. Appl. Phys.* **10**, 401 (1971).
611. M. HIROSE and Y. FURUYA, *Japan. J. Appl. Phys.* **9**, 423 (1970).
612. D. TRIVICH *et al.*, *J. Electrochem. Soc.* **117**, 334 (1970).

AUTHOR INDEX

Abe, R.   260
Adler, D.   163
Aiken, J. G.   161
Åkerström, A.   178, 182, 237
Alessandrini, E. I.   166, 188, 189
Arai, T.   256
Ariya, S. M.   207
Arneth, R.   237
Austin, I. G.   158, 161, 191–192
Avdeenko, B. K.   154

Ballman, A. A.   27
Barbanel, W. I.   223
Barlic, J. J.   20
Bauer, R.   259
Baumbach, A. A.   164, 174
Becker, J. H.   212, 214
Bernard, W. J.   250
Bielański, A.   181, 183–184
Blair, J. C.   259
Bloem, J.   227
Blumenthal, R. N.   216, 219, 222
Bogomolov, V. N.   212–217, 218–219, 223
Borelli, N. F.   253
Bosman, A. J.   152–154, 158, 161, 163, 170, 175, 192, 198
Boudart, M.   184
Bowers, G. M.   49
Brach, B. Ya.   207
Bragg, W. L.   64
Brander, R. W.   262
Bransky, I.   166–170, 174, 176–177, 207, 215–216
Brebrick, R. F.   67, 147
Breckenridge, R. G.   217
Brittain, J. D.   224
Brouwer, G.   67
Budenstein, P. P.   260–261
Burgers, J. M.   64
Butler, H. S.   41

Campbell, D.   237
Carnahan, R. D.   224

Carter, R. E.   206
Castellan, G. W.   226
Cech, R. E.   166, 188–189
Champion, J. A.   243
Chapman, A. T.   21
Charlesby, A.   250
Cheetham, A. K.   209
Chen, W. K.   206
Childs, P. E.   211
Choi, J. S.   178, 182
Chou, N. J.   261
Chrenko, R. M.   163
Chu, T. L.   49
Cidilkovsky, I. M.   240
Clark, G. W.   21
Coble, R. L.   249
Cockayne, B.   22
Cohen, J. B.   209, 243
Cook, R. L.   249, 250
Cox, J. T.   170, 173, 174
Crevecœur, C.   152, 153, 154, 158, 192, 198
Cronemeyer, D. C.   213–214, 219

Darken, D. S.   209
Dasgupta, S.   247
Da Silva, E. M.   250
Davidse, P. D.   41
Dearborn, E. F.   28
De La Rue, R. E.   15
Denayer, M.   210
Dereń, J.   175, 177, 181, 184, 186, 234, 249
Dils, R. R.   249
Dodson E. M.   31, 232
Drabkin, I. A.   163
Dudenhausen, B.   225
Dümbgen, G.   224
Duquesnoy, A.   206

Ebisuzaki, Y.   226
Eldridge, J. M.   261
Engell, H. J.   11
Eror, N. G.   170, 174, 176–177, 198–199

279

SUBJECT INDEX